Christianity 101

Christianity 101

A Textbook of Catholic Theology

Gregory C. Higgins

Paulist Press
New York/Mahwah, NJ

The Scripture quotations contained herein are from the New Revised Standard Version: Catholic Edition Copyright © 1989 and 1993, by the Division of Christian Education of the National Council of the Churches of Christ in the United States of America. Used by permission. All rights reserved.

Cover design by Joy Taylor
Book design by Lynn Else

Copyright © 2007 by Gregory C. Higgins

Library of Congress Cataloging-in-Publication Data

Higgins, Gregory C., 1960–
    Christianity 101 : a textbook of Catholic theology / Gregory C. Higgins.
        p.   cm.
    Includes bibliographical references and index.
    ISBN 0-8091-4208-2 (alk. paper)
    1. Catholic Church—Doctrines. I. Title. II. Title: Christianity one hundred one. III. Title: Christianity one hundred and one.
BX1751.3.H54 2007
230′.2—dc22

                                                                        2006029220

Published by Paulist Press
997 Macarthur Boulevard
Mahwah, New Jersey 07430

www.paulistpress.com

Printed and bound in the
United States of America

CONTENTS

Contents

For Emily and James

INTRODUCTION

Teaching introductory courses and taking introductory courses each has its own set of challenges. From a teacher's point of view, the question is always, "Which topics do I cover and in how much depth?" There are a limited number of class hours, so what are the essential issues or thinkers that must be covered? From a student's point of view, especially those who have no background in the area, the question is always, "Does this course really *introduce* me to the subject?" So those teaching the course should not presume the students have an extensive background in that particular academic discipline. The search for a "good introductory text," then, is driven by these legitimate concerns on both sides. This present work will be judged by teachers on how well it *informs* students, and by students on how well it *introduces* issues.

In terms of the approach employed, I have divided the text along traditional lines in systematic theology (God, Jesus, church, etc.). In each area I have taken a historical approach. Beginning with the scriptural data, I trace the development of thought in the ancient church, the Middle Ages, the Reformations, and the modern era. It is my hope that the questions at the end of each chapter will spark a good deal of profitable class discussion. The list of "suggested readings" is not only for those who wish to pursue a topic in greater depth, but a reminder that it is always good to get another person's perspective on these vital issues of the Christian faith. Two helpful works that students may wish to consult are Richard P. McBrien's *Catholicism*, New Edition (San Francisco: Harper Collins, 1994), and Francis Schüssler Fiorenza and John P. Galvin, eds., *Systematic Theology*, Volumes One and Two (Minneapolis: Fortress Press, 1991).

The internet also provides students with a number of valuable resources. For introductions to the various areas of systematic theology, the four following Web sites are good places to start.

1. Spring Hill College provides a nice overview at "The Theology Library" at www.shc.edu/theolibrary/.
2. The Wabash Center at Wabash College provides a very good "Guide to Internet Resources" at www.wabashcenter.wabash.edu/Internet/front.htm.
3. The Irish Theological Association site contains a number of valuable resources, including historical background on various theologians at www.theology.ie/.
4. The Woodstock Theological Center at Georgetown University offers "Theological Resources on the Web" at www.georgetown.edu/centers/woodstock/web-theo.htm.

For primary sources in theology, see the Web site sponsored by both the College of St. Benedict and St. John's University, "Internet Theology Resources" at www.csbsju.edu/library/internet/theosyst.html.

For moral theology, see the Web site for the course "Catholic Social Thought" taught by Professor Joseph Incandela of St. Mary's College in Indiana at www.saintmarys.edu/~incandel/cst.html. See also Joseph M. Incandela, "In Cyberspace, All Things Catholic," *Commonweal*, CXXIV, 15 (December 5, 1997), 31.

For official church documents, see the Vatican home page at www.vatican.va and the United States Conference of Catholic Bishops homepage at www.nccbuscc.org/.

For a more complete list of online resources, see Thomas C. Fox, *Catholicism on the Web* (New York: Henry Holt and Co., 1997).

In closing, I need to thank a number of people. First of all, I must thank the students of Christian Brothers Academy in Lincroft, New Jersey, and Georgian Court University in Lakewood, New Jersey, without whom this book simply could not have been written. I would also like to thank Dr. Christopher Bellitto of Paulist Press for his loyal support of this project and his careful editing of the text. Special thanks to Kevin Coyne, Eileen Higgins, Joseph Incandela, and Fr. James Massa for their very helpful comments and suggestions.

1

WHAT IS THEOLOGY?

It seems that every academic discipline has its own catch-phrase that professors like to impart to their students on the first day of class. In history, it's George Santayana's observation: "Those who ignore history are doomed to repeat it." In philosophy, it's the saying attributed to Socrates: "The unexamined life is not worth living." In theology, it's St. Anselm's description of theology as "faith seeking understanding." While these expressions could easily deteriorate into platitudes, each of them contains just enough wisdom to prevent that from happening. For students taking only one or two courses in history, philosophy, or theology for their degree, these are often the ideas that are most readily recalled years later.

It seems wise, then, that we begin with the idea that theology is "faith seeking understanding" and that we look back through history to see how that search has been conducted by Christians. Like those studying history, we will attempt to learn from the past, and like those studying philosophy, we will bring our critical skills to bear on the questions that are vitally important to our lives. In the process, we hope to gain some of the understanding Anselm prayed to receive.

An Overview of Christian History

Christians doing theology endeavor to examine more critically, to understand more fully, and to live more faithfully what they believe to be true on the basis of faith. However, in various times and places, this process has taken very distinctive forms. For convenience, we will divide Christian history into five eras: the ancient church, the medieval period, the Reformation, the modern age, and

1

the postmodern age. Throughout the text we will discuss the major controversies and thinkers in each of these time periods; but for now, a brief overview of the tradition will reveal the diversity in Christian theology that has existed over the past two millennia.

THE ANCIENT OR PATRISTIC PERIOD

The era of the ancient church, commonly called the patristic era because the "fathers" of Christian theology lived during that time, spans approximately the first six centuries of Christian history. Gregory the Great (d. 604) is generally regarded as the last "father" of Western theology. As one might expect, the early Christian thinkers had many theological tasks to perform. There was, first of all, the need to establish correct (that is, "orthodox") Christian belief or doctrine. Christians engaged in often acrimonious debates about the sacraments and the church, but the greatest amount of energy went into debates about the identity of Christ and the doctrine of the Trinity. The beginnings of doctrinal dispute can be detected on the pages of the Pastoral Epistles (1 Tim, 2 Tim, and Titus) in the New Testament. Here we find warnings against teaching a "different doctrine" (1 Tim 1:3) and instructions to "(h)old to the standard of sound teaching that you have heard from me" (2 Tim 1:13), and after "a first and second admonition, have nothing more to do with anyone who causes divisions" (Titus 3:10). The second job of Christian thinkers was to respond to their critics from the wider Roman society who regarded Christianity as illogical, immoral, or socially irresponsible. Those who offered rebuttals to these critics are known as apologists. An "apology" is not a request for a pardon, but rather a defense for one's beliefs or actions. The third demand placed on early Christian thinkers was to address the spiritual and moral lives of Christians. The rapid expansion of the church in the early centuries of its existence presented its own set of practical challenges: converts needed to be instructed, liturgies needed to be celebrated, and homilies needed to be preached. Manuals of instruction were composed, liturgical texts were collected, and sermons were recorded in order to aid present and future generations of Christians. The missionary efforts of the church continually pushed the geographical boundaries of Christianity.

Consequently, local churches developed their own particular religious customs, church organization, and theological styles. This diversity would prove to be both a source of renewal for the church throughout its history, and a cause of many bitter, divisive theological disputes.

THE MEDIEVAL PERIOD

Historians differ on when the era of the ancient church ended and the medieval period of Western history began. The official designation of a "Western Roman Empire" begins with the Emperor Diocletian (reigned 285–305). In order to provide greater internal political cohesion and a stronger military defense for the vast Roman Empire, he divided it into two halves: the Western Empire and the Eastern Empire. Diocletian ruled in the East and appointed the general Maximian as emperor of the West. Despite Diocletian's attempt to arrange an orderly line of succession, the various armies throughout the West acclaimed different generals to be emperor after Maximian's retirement in 305. The troops in York hailed the general Constantine as Emperor, and by 312 Constantine had vanquished his rivals and consolidated his control of the West. Constantine would exert a tremendous influence in the life of the church, and we will refer to him at various points later in this book. One of his actions that would profoundly impact both the course of church history and the fate of the Western Roman Empire was his decision to relocate the capital city of the Empire from Rome to the city of Byzantium, which he renamed Constantinople. During the reign of the emperor Constantine (306–37), the balance of power shifted markedly toward the East. In the years that followed, the military, political, and economic power of the West gradually declined. Barbarian tribes advanced easily on the borders of the Western Empire, and the last emperor in Rome was deposed in 476. Some scholars date the fall of Rome as the beginning of the medieval period.

Other historians see intermittent revivals of the Western Empire, the most impressive of which being the reign of Charlemagne, who was crowned Holy Roman Emperor by Pope Leo III on Christmas Day in the year 800. Hopes for a restored empire on the grand scale of the former Western Roman Empire were soon dashed, as infighting among Charlemagne's grandsons began a process of division of territory that would weaken Charlemagne's domain. In time, invasions by the Vikings from the north, and the Slavs and Magyars from the East, shattered whatever unity was left, and Western Europe slipped into what is commonly called the Dark Ages. During this time, the Christian tradition was preserved in the West by monks, such as the Benedictines, whose monasteries were enclaves of scholarship, stability, and spirituality centered on prayer and work. Gradually the population of the West increased, trade routes developed, and cities began to dot the European landscape. Some scholars prefer to date the beginning of the Middle Ages during this period of revival in Western Europe.

One of the most enduring institutions to emerge during the twelfth century—the university—appeared first in Bologna and then spread throughout the Western world. In the university setting, theology was described as a science; that is, an orderly inquiry into a subject. In this "scholastic" approach, a theologian divides the field of theology into different areas, methodically working through the relevant questions in each of those areas, resulting in a grand summary, or summa, of the essential Christian beliefs. The towering figure in Scholastic theology was St. Thomas Aquinas, a member of the Order of Preachers (better known as the Dominicans), who produced the highly influential *Summa Theologiae*. The scholastic theologians compiled quotations from scripture, from revered teachers of Christian tradition, and from official church pronouncements to argue their positions. Aquinas and other like-minded theologians also drew upon the growing number of works by Aristotle that were being reintroduced into Western thought at the time. While some of Aristotle's works had been preserved in the West, Muslim scholars had preserved a far greater number in Arabic. During Aquinas's life those Arabic texts were rapidly being translated into Latin. Aquinas's theological work synthesized the diverse sources into a systematic whole that provided readers with a coherent, integrated account of the Christian life. In the centuries following Aquinas, scholars often rigidified his work, focusing on the distinctions he drew rather than on the wisdom he conveyed. The theological reaction against scholastic thought was unleashed during the Protestant Reformation in the sixteenth century.

THE PROTESTANT REFORMATION

Martin Luther posted his Ninety-Five Theses on the church door at Wittenberg in 1517, protesting the church's sale of indulgences. Subsequent Protestant thinkers developed theologies that challenged or repudiated Catholic claims regarding the authority of the pope or bishops, the sacraments, and the proper role of tradition, among other things. New Christian churches were established outside the control of Catholic authorities. The Roman Catholic Church was forced, therefore, to declare officially those beliefs that are to be held by Catholics. The church made those pronouncements at the Council of Trent (1545–63), after the Protestant Reformation. The decisions of Trent exercised tremendous influence on the style and substance of Catholic theology well into the twentieth century.

THE MODERN AGE

The rise of modern science in the seventeenth century ushered in the next era of Christian history. Discoveries in astronomy by Galileo Galilei (1564–1642), in chemistry by Robert Boyle (1627–91), and in physics by Sir Isaac Newton (1642–1727) engendered an entirely new way to understand the world. This increase in knowledge in turn made possible countless inventions that affected every aspect of life in the later Western world, from the light bulb, to the X-ray, to the computer chip. As scientists unlocked the mysteries of physical, biological, and chemical processes, confidence grew that many of the ills that beset humanity in prior centuries would now be eradicated. Some thinkers, known as deists, called for a reinterpretation of the Christian understanding of God to bring it into conformity with known scientific laws. Likened to a watchmaker, the God of deism created the universe, set in place certain unalterable laws by which the universe would be governed, and then let the universe go. Of course, not all thinkers shared this deistic outlook or the general cultural exaltation of reason. For example, Blaise Pascal (1623–62), the French mathematician and religious thinker, emphasized the role of the heart in dealing with questions of God and the meaning of life.

Reflecting this widespread confidence in human reason, philosophers in the eighteenth century such as Immanuel Kant (1724–1803) designated their age as the Enlightenment, believing that former superstitions and childish ideas would be surrendered. Religious beliefs were scrutinized according to the scientific standards of the day. Many of the leading thinkers questioned the veracity of the biblical accounts of such miracles as the parting of the Red Sea. In general, Christian theologians in the Enlightenment emphasized the reasonableness of Christianity or the moral code that it promoted.

In the nineteenth century, atheistic thinkers such as Friedrich Nietzsche (1844–1900) and Karl Marx (1818–83) argued that belief in God is detrimental to personal fulfillment and social progress. Political upheavals in the century (e.g., the French Revolution) overturned governments that had previously secured a privileged position for the church. Theologians struggled with the question of how to present the gospel in a technological, industrial age far-removed culturally from first-century Palestine. In his 1864 "Syllabus of Errors," Pope Pius IX condemned many modern ideas. Later some Catholic thinkers, labeled Modernists, were censured (and some excommunicated) by the Vatican for what church officials believed to be a capitulation to modernity and a surrender of the central tenets of Catholic belief. The most influential thinker in Catholic thought during this time was Cardinal John Henry Newman (1801–90), whose interests spanned a wide range of theological issues, including the development of doctrine, patristic studies, and educational theory. In other quarters, theological manuals composed for use in seminaries, and catechisms for lay religious education, provided a clear, orderly exposition of Catholic belief. However, many twentieth-century theologians would reject this "manualist tradition" and approach the central questions of the faith in a manner that was arguably far more responsive to the faith-questions of modern Christians.

A defining moment in the Catholic Church's response to the modern world came in 1962 when all the bishops gathered in Rome for the Second Vatican Council. The documents of Vatican II produced dramatic changes in Catholic life throughout the world. Those most obvious changes in the local parishes were liturgical:

the priest now faced the congregation, the Mass was celebrated in vernacular language rather than Latin, and lay people began to distribute the Eucharist.

THE POSTMODERN AGE

Many of the assumptions of the modern age were called into question in the latter decades of the twentieth century. The earlier confidence in reason, and the belief in the inherent goodness of scientific advancement exhibited by Enlightenment thinkers, began to waver. Many modern thinkers had assumed that if all persons would follow the dictates of reason, humans would establish "rational" political, economic, and religious systems. With the passage of time, thinkers began to see that such a mentality often justified force against "unenlightened" cultures. Along with this came the recognition of modern technology's vast potential for harm to human life and the environment, signaled most clearly by the mushroom cloud rising from Hiroshima. Two world wars and repeated state-sanctioned acts of genocide created an ambivalent attitude toward the ideas of the leading modern thinkers. For this reason, theologians speak of us living in a "postmodern" world whose course has not yet been clearly charted.[1] The early voices of this postmodernism can, however, be detected in the twentieth century: in physics, Max Planck (1858–1947) and quantum physics; in literary theory, Jacques Derrida (1930–2004) and his project of deconstruction; and in philosophy, the pragmatism of Richard Rorty (b. 1931).

Elements of a Christian Theology

This brief survey of the Christian tradition has indicated that Christian theologians have addressed different audiences, lived in a wide range of cultures, and allowed a number of issues to dominate their thinking. Theological works have been devoted to clarifying doctrine, defending belief, offering spiritual guidance, explaining scriptural passages, and describing the ethical beliefs of Christians. Theological reflection has been carried on in cloistered monasteries, university lecture halls, and adult education centers. Theological ideas have been expressed in textbooks, pamphlets, and church pronouncements. Theology, in other words, does not appear in exactly the same form in every time or every place, or from one theologian to the next. It is a creative enterprise that bears the personal imprint of the one doing theology. This, however, is only half the story.

Theology is also an act of obedience. Theologians must be faithful to the gospel message. We are not free to construct any position whatsoever and label it as Christian. The two sources to which Christians have historically appealed to address issues of belief and practice are scripture and tradition. To borrow an architectural image from 1 Peter, the Bible is the indispensable foundation for Christian belief and practice. Christ is the cornerstone. Likewise, tradition is the edifice that has been built century by century on that foundation. "Come to him, a living stone, though rejected by mortals yet chosen and precious in God's sight, and like living stones, let yourselves be built into a spiritual house, to be a holy priesthood, to offer spiritual sacrifices acceptable to God through Jesus Christ" (1 Pet 2:4–5).

While few would dispute that theology is an act of obedience, many people would argue about what that obedience entails. How is scripture properly interpreted? Who makes the decision as to which interpretation is correct? What authority does tradition have? Are the creeds that were composed hundreds of years after Christ's death and resurrection binding on Christians living today? Are there elements of scripture or tradition that are simply wrong and should not be obeyed?

We can begin to sketch the following schematic diagram of various elements that are involved in the process of theological reflection.

THE PROCESS OF THEOLOGICAL REFLECTION

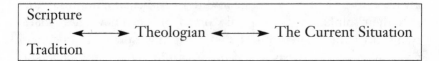

Scripture
Tradition ⟷ Theologian ⟷ The Current Situation

At the center stands the theologian, who draws upon scripture and tradition, and who speaks to the current situation. To one side, we have scripture and tradition. To the other side, we have the current situation in which the theologian is working. A few introductory comments need to be made regarding each side of the diagram.

Scripture and Tradition: One of the very first questions theologians must address is the issue of authoritative sources: On what should we rely when constructing a theological position? Roman Catholic theologians identify scripture and tradition as the two authoritative sources for their work. When doing Catholic theology, the theologian selects various scriptural passages, themes, or images and draws upon the wisdom preserved in the tradition to craft a particular theological position. Much will be said about both scripture and tradition throughout this book, but for now, a few introductory comments are required. First, Christian theologians as a whole accept the scriptures as a source for theology. They believe in some sense that the scriptures reveal God's intentions for humanity. This certainly raises a host of thorny problems about how to interpret scripture. In fact, many of the theological debates that we will discuss will have compelling scriptural arguments on both sides. Despite this, scripture is an indispensable element of any theology that identifies itself as Christian. Second, tradition is the living heritage of the church that has been handed down (*traditio* means "handing on") from earlier generations. Different Christian denominations will give different weight to tradition. For Roman Catholics, the creeds of the church (e.g., the Nicene Creed) function as the standard of orthodox belief for Catholic thinkers. In the Catholic tradition, the bishops and the pope are regarded as the authoritative teachers. However, just as there are debates over scriptural interpretation, there are controversies over the role of the Catholic theologian in the church, the authority of the pope, and the relationship between bishops and universities; these are ongoing matters of dispute within the theological community.

The Current Situation: Not only do theologians make choices regarding the use of scripture and tradition, they gear their writing to a particular audience, such as adults being initiated into the church, graduate students studying theology, Christians struggling with their faith. These audiences have their own questions and concerns: Does the Bible endorse sexism? What must I do to inherit eternal life? Does God control the course of human history? They also live in a particular time and place (a collapsing empire, a tranquil monastic community, or an ever-increasing secularized society), and in a culture in which certain schools of thought dominate (Platonism, Romanticism, Postmodernism). All of these factors comprise "the current situation" out of which theological perspectives emerge.

Every theologian keeps both sides in view when doing theology. The great twentieth-century Protestant theologian Paul Tillich nicely summarizes this dynamic in theology when he writes, "A theological system is supposed to satisfy two basic needs: the statement of the truth of the Christian message and the interpretation of this truth for every new generation."[2] It is this very dynamic that produces the rich diversity of Christian theologies. Theologians in this way are similar to painters. Two painters may work with the same palette of colors and try to depict the same object, but produce radically different works. Each theologian advocates particular interpretations of key passages from scripture, or highlights various elements in the Christian tradition and downplays others. Each reads the current situation in his or her own way. Whereas one theologian may see the wider culture as filled with spiritual seekers, another may see a society overtaken by consumerism. For example, during the Protestant Reformation, Luther attacked any practice that suggested we can earn our way into heaven by doing "work." Luther believed Paul's letters as containing the heart of the gospel message, but referred to the Letter of James as "an epistle of straw." Luther's opponents, in return, highlighted passages that they believed established certain practices or beliefs (e.g., penance in John 20:22–23; papal authority in Matt 16:18–19).

The position of the theologian is not much different from that of a college student who plans on returning to the family business after graduation. Suppose this family enterprise (imagine it to be whichever occupation you know best) was begun two generations ago and has provided for the student and her family, and afforded her the opportunity to attend college with a minimal number of loans. In her business management and marketing classes, she learns the latest approaches to financing, advertising, and product distribution. After graduation, she joins the family business. Which ways of doing business does she suggest the company abandon? Which should be updated? Which new ideas should be implemented? What is the best approach when suggesting changes if her fellow family members in the business are not convinced that her proposals are sound? In both theology and business, there exists a creative tension between tradition and innovation, and decisions in both fields call for a careful reading of the situation, and require a method of assessing the consequences of our choices.

Three Schools of Thought in Contemporary Theology

While no two theologians will produce the exact same theology, certain common features or "family resemblances" among theologians can be discerned. There are schools of thought in contemporary theology just as there are in politics, economics, and psychology. We will identify three theological models without suggesting that these represent the sum total of theological options being explored today. Then we will picture these three approaches in terms of how each relates scripture and tradition to the current situation.

The first school of thought, which will be labeled *traditionalist,* locates truth in scripture and tradition. The cultural situation in which that truth is received varies over time; consequently, different methods may be employed for *conveying* the truth found in scripture and tradition, but little emphasis is placed on the situation *affecting* the truth. The relationship can be pictured as follows:

TRADITIONALIST SCHOOL OF THOUGHT: TRANSMISSION

Scripture and Tradition
↓
The Current Situation

Not only are the chief Christian resources of scripture and tradition believed true, the transmitter of those truths (i.e., in Roman Catholic theology, the church under the leadership of the pope and other bishops) has faithfully preserved the central truths of the Christian faith over time. While some disciplines and devotional practices may change over time (e.g., abstaining from eating meat on Fridays throughout the year), there can be no alteration in the foundational beliefs of the faith, such as those found in the Nicene Creed, that are binding on all who profess to be Christian. Theology in this view consists in the *transmission* of the truths of Christianity from one generation to the next.

The second school of thought, which will be labeled *liberal*, affirms that truth resides in scripture and tradition, but believes that truths discovered in other areas of human inquiry can be brought to bear on Christian beliefs. This exchange may confirm Christian belief or alter it in some way. The liberal theologian will not exclude in advance either possibility. The theologian S. W. Sykes offers the following helpful description of this approach:

> Liberalism in theology is that mood or cast of mind which is prepared to accept that some discovery of reason may count *against* the authority of a traditional affirmation in the body of Christian theology. One is a theological liberal if one allows autonomously functioning reason to supply arguments against traditional belief and if one's reformulation of Christian belief provides evidence that one has ceased to believe what has been traditionally believed by Christians.[3]

The job of the liberal theologian is to assess the truth of traditional beliefs and, when necessary, revise Christian theology in light of an ever-expanding body of knowledge. For example, the acceptance of the theory of evolution would lead one to interpret the seven-day creation story as a religious myth rather than a scientific account of the appearance of the human species. The results of carbon dating would determine what credence one gives the story of the taking of the city of Jericho in the book of Joshua. Liberal theology is essentially an exercise in *dialogue* between theologians who present

Christian truth-claims, and thinkers from other disciplines who present the findings of their investigations. Here scripture and tradition, and the current situation are balanced:

LIBERAL SCHOOL OF THOUGHT: DIALOGUE

Scripture and Tradition ←——————→ The Current Situation

The third school of thought, which will be labeled *radical*, sees scripture and tradition as contaminated because they reflect the interests of the powerful parties who codified them rather than the original liberating message of the movement's founder. The designation *radical* often carries strong connotations, either positive or negative, but here it refers only to the willingness of those theologians to alter substantially the claims found in scripture and tradition. The radical theologian measures the truth of both the Bible and the tradition by an idea promoted in the current situation (e.g., social equality of women and men). For some radical thinkers, the idea may be an entirely new one in the evolution of human thought. For others it may be buried underneath centuries of rubble or tucked in between stories in the gospels. Thomas J. J. Altizer, one of the leading representatives of the radical theology of the 1960s, remarks, "It can be said, however, that the radical Christian invariably attempts by one means or another to return to the original message and person of Jesus with the conviction that such a return demands both an assault upon the established Church and a quest for a total or apocalyptic redemption."[4] Radical theology is apocalyptic in that it is willing to shatter the world of traditional Christian belief. In this approach, the current situation holds the superior position.

RADICAL SCHOOL OF THOUGHT: RECONSTRUCTION

The Current Situation ↓ Scripture and Tradition

Radical theologians are willing, and perhaps even inclined, to demolish ancient structures of thought and to fashion from the remaining fragments a vision that is able to inspire Christians to make the world a better place in which to live. Theology in this view is an effort at fundamental *reconstruction*.

The Status of Scripture and Tradition in Traditionalist, Liberal, and Radical Theology

Another way to think of the three theological methods we have outlined—theology as *transmission, dialogue,* and *reconstruction*—is to look only at the status each accords scripture and tradition.

The traditionalist regards scripture and tradition as reliable sources of divine revelation. The doctrines that have been drawn from these sources are true and need to be faithfully passed down from one generation to the next. The carefully crafted classic formulations of Christian doctrine (often arrived at after intense debates within the church) express Christian belief as precisely as possible, and any attempt to "improve" upon them runs the serious risk of falling back into the very heresies that prompted the need to declare them in the first place.

The liberal believes that scripture and tradition are critically important for Christian theology, but that they are also human compositions that reflect the thoughts of past thinkers or cultures. The liberal believes that the essential message (defined in various ways) of Christianity is truthful, but also insists that Christians must enter into profitable, mutually enriching dialogue with the leading currents of thought in the wider culture. Both sides in that dialogue possess elements of truth, and through the exchange of ideas, each moves the other to a more complete understanding of the truth.

The radical casts a suspicious eye toward the ideas contained in scripture and tradition, believing that texts held to be authoritative by leading officials of any religious or political body reflect their own interests in maintaining power. Biblical stories legitimate oppressive social conditions for women, slaves, and minorities by saying that this is the way God intended the world to be. A Christian radical may identify a particular theme in scripture by which to judge the acceptability of all other biblical teachings or later teachings in the church tradition. Other radical thinkers will relativize scripture and tradition by granting equal (or perhaps greater) status to writings that were excluded from the final collection of scripture or to later writings in the tradition that were suppressed or condemned by church officials.

Three Theological Essays

Our consideration of these three theological methods so far has been theoretical. It might be helpful, therefore, to see how these approaches actually manifest themselves in theological writings. The first piece that we will examine is by Henri de Lubac, one of the most influential Roman Catholic theologians of the twentieth century. The second work was written by one of the most important biblical theologians of the past century, Rudolf Bultmann. The third essay was penned by a leading contemporary feminist biblical scholar and theologian, Elisabeth Schüssler Fiorenza.

Henri de Lubac's
"The Council and the Para-Council"

Vatican II was the most significant event in twentieth-century Catholicism. Henri de Lubac's pioneering work, especially in the fields of patristics and medieval theology, laid the groundwork for many of the new ideas found in the decrees and declarations of Vatican II. During the 1960s, de Lubac became increasingly troubled by many of the developments within the church. He was especially concerned with the general misunderstanding of Vatican II that some of his fellow theologians were promoting in the media. In 1968 he delivered a speech at St. Louis University expressing his concerns; this speech, "The Council and the Para-Council," was published in his work *A Brief Catechesis on Nature and Grace*. Because of de Lubac's stature in the church and his vital role in paving the way for the Council, these observations drew the attention of many theologians. De Lubac's position and the reaction to

15

it illustrate how different theologians read and react to the current situation in significantly different ways.

De Lubac attacks the promotion of what he calls the "para-Council"; that is, the interpretation of the Second Vatican Council promoted by liberal theologians and embraced by the mass media. Quoting an unidentified pamphlet that was circulating at the time, de Lubac cites the litany of ideas promoted by supporters of the para-Council.

> So what we need is "a Church undergoing rapid muta-tions," a Church whose "entire content of faith" must be "reinterpreted in terms of the new problems which the world faces..." She will no longer have to transmit a her-itage, for henceforth she will "be based less on fidelity to tradition than on a future that must be invented." She will no longer be "a Church laying down eternal verities" but "a locus for creativity, invention, newness." She will no longer need to "defend the deposit of faith" but must adapt herself humbly to "the new art of living" which the world is in the process of beginning.[5]

De Lubac regards this reading of the Vatican II documents as a serious distortion of the teachings promulgated by the bishops.

According to de Lubac, the supporters of this para-Council employ two different strategies in their arguments. First, they selectively read the Council's documents, highlighting those pas-sages that promote their own theological agenda, while seeing other passages as political compromises intended to placate a small group of conservative bishops. Second, they argue that the docu-ments themselves fail to capture the true intentions of the bishops. For example, para-Council proponents contend, "Old habits of thought could not be dropped overnight, and these 'did not allow the intuitions of Vatican II to produce their effects.' So the new doctrine, which was supposedly that which in the depths of their hearts the Fathers really wanted to promote, 'did not succeed in finding expression in the official documents.'"[6] De Lubac lambastes such suggestions.

For the para-Council, on the contrary, the Church, which has finally attained adulthood after an infancy that had lasted for twenty centuries, is bringing about a "radical revolution" within herself. She must no longer pretend to interpret the world to us in terms of the Christian faith; she must cease considering herself "as the depository of the truth"! She must accept generalized "pluralism"; she must proceed to "secularize" herself; she must give herself a "democratic" structure, imitating that of modern states; she must cast aside those old wives tales about "interior life," and so on.[7]

On a cautionary note, de Lubac warns that

this famous "spirit of the Council," which those who invoke it most have nourished with their own ideologies, is so seductive and so powerful that it soon obliges its adorers to accept a whole "new theology," the foundation of a "new Church"; and if later on it happens that an unfortunate pope tries to show himself faithful to the truth the Church has always believed in and that the Council itself once again stated, he finds himself accused by overbearing critics of making himself the "trimphalistic herald" and the "super-annuated champion" of "old-time theology."[8]

In response to what he regards as a dangerous drift in church thought and discipline, de Lubac emphasizes the need to uphold essential doctrine, and reasserts the binding authority of scripture and tradition as interpreted by the legitimate shepherds of the church. Here we see the critical role the reading of the contemporary situation plays in theology. De Lubac's supporters would insist that he is sounding a corrective warning to a church mired in confusion about what Vatican II really taught. De Lubac's critics would regard his argument as a call to return to a bygone era in church history that is simply unresponsive to the real needs of today's church.

17

RUDOLF BULTMANN'S
"NEW TESTAMENT AND MYTHOLOGY"

In Rudolf Bultmann's 1941 essay "New Testament and Mythology," we find a different reading of the situation, and a different set of concerns occupying our attention than we did in de Lubac's essay from the 1960s. No doubt the historical and denominational differences of the two theologians play a significant role here: de Lubac was addressing pressing issues that concerned his fellow Roman Catholics during the 1960s; Bultmann was writing in Germany during World War II, out of the Lutheran tradition with its strong emphasis on biblical interpretation and the task of preaching. We will break down Bultmann's essay into two components: first, the problem he describes, and second, the solution he offers.

Bultmann contends that the fundamental problem is that modern, scientifically minded Christians simply can no longer accept the "mythological" elements of the New Testament stories. Our view of the universe (i.e., our cosmology) has been shaped by modern physics and astronomy. By contrast,

> The cosmology of the New Testament is essentially mythical in character. The world is viewed as a three-storied structure, with the earth in the centre, the heaven above, and the underworld beneath. Heaven is the abode of God of the celestial beings—angels. The underworld is hell, the place of torment. Even the earth is more than the scene of natural, everyday events, or the trivial round and common task. It is the scene of supernatural activity of God and his angels on one hand, and of Satan and his daemons on the other. These supernatural forces intervene in the course of nature and in all that men think and will and do.[9]

Modern people can not disregard what they accept as true about the world when they pick up the gospels. Bultmann continues,

> It is impossible to use electric light and the wireless and to avail ourselves of modern medical and surgical discoveries,

and at the same time to believe in the New Testament world of spirits and miracles. We may think we can manage it in our lives, but to expect others to do so is to make the Christian faith unintelligible and unacceptable to the modern world.[10]

Are we to conclude, then, that the Bible is simply a glorified version of *Grimm's Fairy Tales?* No, says Bultmann. First, the gospel is based on the historical fact of Christ's life, death, and resurrection. Second, there is a way to bridge the vast cultural chasm that exists between the modern scientific worldview and the worldview assumed by the gospel writers. In Bultmann's language, we accomplish this task when we "demythologize" the biblical writings.

Demythologizing involves stripping away the mythological elements from the biblical stories and extracting the *kerygma*—the proclamation of the early church—and then translating that kerygma in ways that will both preserve the original meaning and present a relevant and meaningful version to modern Christians. The ancient mythological worldview may be obsolete, but the message is not. Bultmann continues,

> We are therefore bound to ask whether, when we preach the Gospel message to-day, we expect our converts to accept not only the Gospel message, but also the mythical view of the world in which it is set. If not, does the New Testament embody a truth which is quite independent of its mythical setting? If it does, theology must undertake the task of stripping the Kerygma from its mythical framework, of "demythologizing" it.[11]

In his own theology, Bultmann prefers to translate the kerygma into the language of "authentic existence" that he borrows from the philosopher Martin Heidegger. "The authentic life," argues Bultmann, "means the abandonment of all self-contrived security. This is what the New Testament means by 'life after the Spirit' or 'life in faith.'"[12] Bultmann sees the Christian life as the placing of our very lives in the hands of a transcendent power, an act that is nothing less than crucifixion of the self and a resurrection to a life of faith.

Bultmann's essay sparked a storm of controversy on both sides of the Atlantic. The theologian Roger Johnson reports,

> Bultmann first proposed his project for demythologizing the New Testament in a 1941 lecture (published that same year as an essay), "New Testament and Mythology." While the essay provoked an immediate controversy within Germany, even during some of the most devastating conditions of World War II, it was not generally known in the wider world until its 1948 publication in *Kerygma und Mythos*. For the next fifteen years the subject of demythologizing stirred up a continuing controversy in the theological literature of several languages as well as in the life of the church in both Germany and the United States. In both countries, "heresy trials" and other church disciplinary actions were initiated by ecclesiastical authorities against clergy who were using Bultmann's theology in their preaching. Demythologizing was one theological proposal which did not pass unnoticed.[13]

One of the most frequently voiced criticisms of Bultmann charges that he fails to take his theology to its logical conclusion; namely, the consigning of Christ to mythological status and subsequently eliminating him, or demythologizing him, which reduces the gospel to a general admonition to live courageously in the face of life's adversities. In other words, once the process of demythologizing has begun, where does it end? Bultmann repeatedly insists that the kerygma is based in the historical fact of Christ's life, death, and resurrection (though he was often skeptical about how many actual details of Jesus' life could be uncovered, and cautioned that faith should not be tied to the results of historical research). Bultmann also chastises his liberal forebears who often reduced the Gospel to one cultural embodiment of a universal message found in countless other cultures around the globe. Despite Bultmann's objections, we are left to determine whether the liberal approach rescues the essential biblical message from obscurity, or compromises the uniqueness of the gospel message.

ELISABETH SCHÜSSLER FIORENZA'S "THE WILL TO CHOOSE OR TO REJECT: CONTINUING OUR CRITICAL WORK"

Bultmann's theology addresses the problem of how to communicate the biblical message to Christians living in a modern scientific age. In his view, the kerygma remains true and relevant. The difficulty lies in the medium, not the message. For our next author, the problem runs much deeper than finding a suitable vehicle for expressing the biblical message. For Elisabeth Schüssler Fiorenza, the New Testament writings themselves are often part of the problem. Some of the passages promote ancient patriarchal views that contemporary feminists are committed to overturning. In theological language, as the gap between ancient beliefs and contemporary feminist ideals widens, the problem of hermeneutics—the area of theology concerned with the proper interpretation of texts—becomes more acute. Fiorenza begins her article by identifying "the central challenge of a feminist biblical hermeneutics."[14]

> Feminist consciousness radically throws into question all traditional religious names, texts, rituals, laws, and interpretative metaphors because they all bear "our Father's names." With [feminist scholar] Carol Christ I would insist that the central spiritual and religious feminist quest is the quest for women's self-affirmation, survival, power, and self-determination.[15]

The feminist quest seeks "liberation from all patriarchal alienation, marginalization, and oppression."[16] From this vantage point, several hermeneutical questions naturally arise. How should those committed to feminist ideals view the Bible and the Christian tradition? Should biblical religion be abandoned, or is it possible to salvage a message from the Bible or the tradition that speaks to the concerns of feminists and their ethical commitments? Are there elements within the Bible itself that challenge patriarchal attitudes and practices, or should we look outside the Bible for a standard by which to judge the truthfulness of biblical claims?

21

In the hands of Christians, argues Schüssler Fiorenza, the Bible has been used both to liberate victims of horrible social injustice and to legitimate brutally oppressive social systems. On the one hand, "the Bible was used to halt the emancipation of women and slaves. Not only in the last century but also today, the political Right laces its attacks against the feminist struggle for women's rights and freedoms in the political, economic, reproductive, intellectual, and religious spheres with biblical quotations and appeals to scriptural authority."[17] On the other hand, the Bible has also "provided authorization for women who rejected slavery, colonial exploitation, anti-Semitism, and misogynism as unbiblical and against God's will. It has inspired countless women to speak out against injustice, exploitation, and stereotyping and energized them to struggle against poverty, unfreedom, and denigration."[18] Given this checkered past, does the Bible have a positive role to play in the lives of Christian feminists? Schüssler Fiorenza believes it does, but again the matter of hermeneutics is crucial. Feminist scholars insist that the Bible can play a positive role in the life of the church if we preserve those elements of the biblical message that contribute to the liberation of women, and eliminate those elements that oppress them.

Schüssler Fiorenza proposes a "multidimensional model of biblical interpretation" consisting of five elements. First, she calls for a "hermeneutics of suspicion." She notes that "a feminist critical hermeneutics of suspicion places a warning label on all biblical texts: *Caution! Could be dangerous to your health and survival...*The first and never-ending task of a hermeneutics of suspicion, therefore, is to elaborate as much as possible the patriarchal, destructive aspects and oppressive elements in the Bible."[19] Second, Schüssler Fiorenza's proposal requires that critical decisions be made regarding the biblical texts. Who is qualified to make such determinations? Schüssler Fiorenza places this task of "critical evaluation" in the hands of "the women-church"—that assembly (or church, in Greek *ekklesia*) of women and men who have joined together for the cause of women's self-affirmation, power, and liberation. This critical evaluation "must sort through particular biblical texts and test out in a process of critical analysis and evaluation how much their content and function perpetrates and legitimates patriarchal structures, not only in their original historical contexts but also in our contemporary situation."[20] Third, certain biblical texts should no longer be proclaimed from pulpits. "A careful feminist assessment of the selection and reception of biblical texts for proclamation in the liturgy must therefore precede an inclusive translation of them. Patriarchal texts should not be allowed to remain in the lectionary but should be replaced by texts affirming the discipleship of equals."[21] Fourth, Schüssler Fiorenza calls for "a hermeneutics of remembrance" that compels us to dig underneath the biblical text and historically reconstruct the actual nonpatriarchal way of life practiced by the early Christians. Fifth, the women-church should create alternative rituals, songs, and liturgical celebrations to create and sustain the experience of liberation from patriarchy.

Scripture and Tradition: A Concluding Thought

We can now see more clearly the distance we have traveled since discussing the traditionalist approaches to theology. For de Lubac, scripture and tradition are authoritative because they contain God's revelation. For Schüssler Fiorenza, "The locus or place of divine revelation and grace is therefore not the Bible or the tradition of a patriarchal church but the *ekklesia* of women and the lives of women who live the 'option for our women selves.'"[22] Pamela Dickey Young, a theologian sympathetic to Schüssler Fiorenza's feminist concerns, nevertheless has reservations about her method.

> Indeed, much in Scripture and tradition is patriarchal. We have to be open to the possibility that it is wholly and unrelentingly patriarchal. And if it is wholly and unrelentingly patriarchal, why would a feminist still want to see herself within this tradition? One danger of ignoring the normativeness of the Christian tradition for Christian theology is that we continue to remain in an irreformable tradition. The greater danger of ignoring the normativeness of Christian tradition is that we lose sight of what might be said to constitute the Christian tradition as *Christian*. We need, of course, to take the

contemporary situation into consideration. If the core of any religious tradition is its capacity to meet the needs of its adherents, the needs of present adherents must be met or the religion loses its relevance. But if that same religious tradition is to maintain any of its identity as a tradition, its theology must be in touch with what makes that particular religious tradition unique.[23]

Whenever one advances or attacks a theological position, one has made prior decisions regarding the status of scripture and tradition, decrees of church councils, papal pronouncements, contemporary experience, and all other elements that one factors into his or her theological position. It might prove a helpful exercise as we work through the various issues that will be discussed throughout this text to circle back to the question of sources and the weight that should be given scripture, tradition, current systems of thought, and so on, when doing theology.

Divisions within Christian Theology

We began our inquiry with Anselm's definition of theology as "faith seeking understanding." This one simple, central impulse has produced a wide range of disciplines within the field of Christian theology. Without suggesting that this is an exhaustive list, some of the most important areas of theological study include the following. These terms, as well as others, are repeated in the glossary.

Biblical Theology: deals with the proper interpretation and use of biblical writings in contemporary theology.

Christology: literally, "the study of Christ"; investigates the question of Jesus' identity.

Ecclesiology: literally, "the study of the church"; deals with questions of the nature and purpose of the church; includes questions of church authority and the relationship between the church and the world.

Eschatology: literally, "the study of the 'last things'"; deals with the "end" either in a personal sense of afterlife or in the end of human history.

Moral Theology: deals with the proper conduct for Christians in personal and social matters; synonymous with "Christian ethics."

Philosophical Theology: is concerned with the overlapping areas of inquiry in both philosophy and theology (questions of ultimate reality, the relationship between time and eternity, etc.).

Sacramental Theology: discusses the theory and practice of what Catholics hold to be the seven central celebrations in the life of the church.

Soteriology: literally, "the study of salvation"; studies the "work" of Christ as the one who brings about salvation.

Spiritual Theology: explores the various ways in which we come to a greater knowledge and love of God.

Systematic Theology: provides an orderly investigation of the entire body of Christian beliefs, and studies the interrelation of the various areas of beliefs.

Theological Anthropology: constructs a Christian understanding of the human person.

Theology: literally, "the study of God" ; evaluates Christian beliefs and practices; when used in the most restricted sense, deals with questions related to God (God's nature, God's activity, the Trinity, etc.).

In the following chapters, we will investigate different ways of reading the Bible (chapter two), trace the history of the church (chapter three), discuss the meaning of faith and revelation (chapter four), explore traditional and modern understandings of God (chapters five and six), examine ancient and modern Christologies (chapters seven and eight), review different models of the church (chapter nine), situate the sacraments in the life of the church (chapters ten and eleven), delve into the moral theology of the church (chapter twelve), compare the spiritual traditions within Christianity (chapter thirteen), assess different views of the end of history and the afterlife (chapter fourteen), and conclude with a summary of our findings (chapter fifteen).

Discussion Questions

Below are a few of the areas of theological reflection. Read the two statements under each heading. Do you accept or reject the statement? Why? Why not? Identify as best you can the sources you used to arrive at your conclusion.

- GOD
  God works miracles in the world today.
  An all-loving God would never condemn someone to hell for eternity.

- THE BIBLE
  Adam and Eve existed.
  Moses' parting of the Red Sea probably resulted from a quick change in the tides.

- JESUS CHRIST
  Jesus knew that he was the Second Person of the Trinity when he began his public ministry.
  Jesus walked on water.

- PHILOSOPHICAL THEOLOGY
  God doesn't know the future because the future does not yet exist.
  God controls the events of our lives; therefore, we do not have free will.

- ECCLESIOLOGY
  The pope has the authority to speak infallibly on matters of faith and morals.
  We should ordain women to the priesthood.

- SACRAMENTAL THEOLOGY
  We should not baptize infants.
  You don't need to go to a priest for confession; asking for forgiveness from the one you offended is enough.

- MORAL THEOLOGY
  Homosexuals should be allowed to enter into marriages recognized by the church.
  Wealthier nations have an obligation to help the poorest countries in the world.

Suggested Readings

For a short, yet solid introduction to the nature of theology, see the entry "Theology," by William J. Hill, in *The New Dictionary of Theology*, edited by Joseph A. Komonchak, Mary Collins, and Dermot A. Lane (Wilmington, DE: Michael Glazier, 1987). For overviews of the history of theology, see "Theology, History of," by Wayne L. Fehr, in *The New Dictionary of Theology*, and "Theology, History of," by P. De Letter, in volume XIV of *The New Catholic Encyclopedia* (New York: McGraw-Hill Book Co., 1967). See also Robert H. King, "The Task of Systematic Theology," chapter one in *Christian Theology*, edited by Peter C. Hogson and Robert H. King (Philadelphia: Fortress Press, 1982), and Daniel L. Migliore, "The Task of Theology," chapter one of *Faith Seeking Understanding: An Introduction to Christian Theology* (Grand Rapids: William B. Eerdmans Publishing Co, 1991).

For a longer, more technical introduction, see Francis Schüssler Fiorenza, "Systematic Theology: Task and Methods," in *Systematic Theology: Roman Catholic Perspectives*, volume one, edited by Francis Schüssler Fiorenza and John P. Galvin (Minneapolis: Fortress Press, 1991).

For examples of the three theological approaches, see Edward D. O'Connor, *The Catholic Vision* (Huntington, IN: Our Sunday Visitor, 1992) for a very readable, traditionalist approach. For an able defense of the liberal approach, see Langdon Gilkey, "Theology: Interpretation of Faith for Church and World," chapter three of *Through the Tempest: Theological Voyages in a Pluralistic*

Culture (Minneapolis; Fortress Press, 1991). For a radical approach, see Rosemary Radford Reuther, "Feminist Theology: Methodology, Sources, and Norms," chapter one in *Sexism and God-Talk: Toward a Feminist Theology* (Boston: Beacon Press, 1993).

For helpful anthologies of both the traditionalist and liberal approaches in contemporary Roman Catholic thought, see *Being Right: Conservative Catholics in America*, edited by Mary Jo Weaver and R. Scott Appleby (Bloomington: Indiana University Press, 1995), and *What's Left?: Liberal American Catholics*, edited by Mary Jo Weaver (Bloomington: Indiana University Press, 1999).

Notes

1. For an overview of the issues, see the Introduction to Diogenes Allen, *Christian Belief in a Postmodern World* (Louisville, KY: Westminster / John Knox Press, 1989).

2. Paul Tillich, *Systematic Theology* (Chicago: University of Chicago Press, 1951), 1:3.

3. S. W. Sykes, *Christian Theology Today* (London: Mowbrays, 1971), 12.

4. Thomas J. J. Altizer, "William Blake and the Role of Myth in the Radical Christian Vision," in *Radical Theology and the Death of God* by Thomas J. J. Altizer and William Hamilton (Indianapolis: The Bobbs-Merrill Co., 1966), 185.

5. Henri de Lubac, *A Brief Catechesis on Nature and Grace* (San Francisco: Ignatius Press, 1984), 239.

6. Ibid., 246.

7. Ibid., 257.

8. Ibid., 251–52.

9. Rudolf Bultmann, "New Testament and Mythology," in *Kerygma and Myth*, Hans Werner Bartsch, ed. (New York: Harper and Row, 1961), 1.

10. Ibid., 5.

11. Ibid., 3.

12. Ibid., 19.

13. Roger Johnson, *Rudolf Bultmann: Interpreting the Faith for the Modern Era* (London: Collins, 1987), 39–40.

14. Elisabeth Schüssler Fiorenza, "The Will to Choose or to Reject: Continuing Our Critical Work," in *Feminist Interpretation of the Bible*, Letty Russell, ed. (Philadelphia: Westminster Press, 1985), 125–26.

15. Ibid., 126.

16. Ibid.

17. Ibid., 129.

18. Ibid.

19. Ibid., 130.

20. Ibid., 131.

21. Ibid.

22. Ibid., 128.

23. Pamela Dickey Young, *Feminist Theology / Christian Theology: In Search of Method* (Minneapolis: Fortress Press, 1990), 75–76.

2

THE BIBLE

The Catholic canon, or list of accepted books in the Bible, includes forty-six books in the Old Testament and twenty-seven books in the New Testament. We begin with an overview of the biblical writings. In order to deal with this library of texts, we will divide the Bible into ten sections. After we have completed this survey of the Bible, we will turn our attention to the formation of the canon and the history of biblical interpretation.

Overview of the Biblical Writings

1. TORAH (OR PENTATEUCH, OR LAW)

The first section comprises the first five books of the Bible: Genesis, Exodus, Leviticus, Numbers, and Deuteronomy. In Genesis 1–11, we find some of the most familiar biblical stories of all: the stories of creation, Cain and Abel, Noah's ark, and the tower of Babel. The bulk of Genesis tells the stories of the biblical patriarchs, or "founding fathers," of Judaism and Christianity: Abraham, Isaac, and Jacob. The critically important biblical notion of covenant (i.e., an agreement or pact between God and Israel) underlies much of Genesis's drama: God promises the land of Canaan, numerous descendants, and a son to Abraham. At various times in the story of Abraham, each of these promises becomes endangered. Abraham almost gives the land to his nephew Lot, trades away his wife Sarah to the pharaoh of Egypt, and nearly sacrifices his son. Only God's intervention can save Abraham and keep the promise alive. Beginning in Genesis 37, we follow the twists and turns in the story of Joseph: his brothers' plot to sell him into slavery, his appointment to head the pharaoh's grain-distribution program during the time of severe famine, and his eventual reunion with his family in Egypt.

The situation changes rapidly in Exodus. The Israelites are enslaved, and God calls Moses to lead the Israelites back to the land of Canaan. In Exodus we find the memorable stories of the burning bush, the ten plagues, the parting of the Red Sea, the Ten Commandments, and the golden calf. The second half of Exodus deals mostly with the divine instructions regarding, and the human construction of, the "tent of meeting" that serves as a portable place of worship, the ark that carries the tablets of the Ten Commandments, and other items needed for worship during the Israelites' sojourn in the desert.

Leviticus deals with the establishment of Israel's priesthood, the various responsibilities the priests assume in terms of offering sacrifice, and the enforcement of various purity regulations (e.g., the readmission of cured lepers into the community; the avoidance of eating meat that contains blood). Leviticus contains the holiness code that proscribes certain forms of sexual behavior, unjust business practices, and idolatry. Key holy days in the Jewish calendar are established (see Lev 23), most importantly the Day of Atonement—the high holy day in the annual cycle.

Numbers takes its name from the opening chapter's census of the people. The Israelites wander in the desert for forty years for their unfaithfulness, journeying from Sinai to the land of Moab, which is located to the east of the Dead Sea. Even Moses himself disobeys God's command in Numbers 20, and is told by God that he will not live to lead the people into the promised land. In Numbers 22–24, as the Israelites enter the land of Moab, we find the delightful tale of Balaam and his talking donkey. Numbers concludes with the Israelites poised to enter the promised land, but before they do, Moses offers one final summary of the law in Deuteronomy.

In Deuteronomy Moses bids farewell to his people and repeats the law to them (Deuteronomy means "second law"). Moses sets before the people the choice of spiritual life or death: follow the Lord's ways and live, or ignore the Lord's ways and perish (Deut 30:15–20). Moses commissions Joshua to lead the people into the promised land. The Torah ends with the death and burial of Moses, a biblical character of monumental importance, yet one who does not live to see his dream of entering the land of Canaan realized.

2. THE HISTORICAL BOOKS

The series of historical books includes Joshua, Judges, Ruth, 1 and 2 Samuel, 1 and 2 Kings, 1 and 2 Chronicles, Ezra, Nehemiah, Tobit, Judith, Esther, and 1 and 2 Maccabees. The historical books encompass a wide span of history: the entrance into Canaan; the period of the judges who first led Israel; the kingships of Saul, David, and Solomon; the division of the twelve tribes into the nations of Israel and Judah; the fall of Israel at the hands of the Assyrians; the exile of Judah to Babylon; and the Persian and Greek domination of the Jews. In this section of the canon we read of the walls of Jericho tumbling down to the ground, Samson getting his hair cut, David slaying Goliath, Solomon drawing his sword to divide a child in two, the Temple being constructed and later reconstructed. There is also the stark loneliness of the Babylonian Exile, and the institution of the feast of Hannukah, which is celebrated about the same time as the Christians' Christmas each year.

3. THE WISDOM BOOKS

Included in this category are the books Job, Psalms, Proverbs, Ecclesiastes, Song of Songs, Wisdom, and Sirach. The psalms are liturgical poetry. They evoke a variety of moods and express an equally wide range of emotions. The proverbs are pithy one-line sayings that capture an element of a life well lived. In the Book of Proverbs, the wise person heeds the call of Sophia, the personification of wisdom (*sophia* means "wisdom"), as she invites all people to feast at her banquet table, to learn from her, and to love her. The works of Sirach and Wisdom offer more-extended reflections on the common themes of the pursuit of wisdom and the avoidance of folly. Ecclesiastes and Job confront head-on the most profound questions of human existence. Ecclesiastes ponders the possibility of the utter futility and meaninglessness of all human effort. The character Job, while pious and innocent, bears the full weight of human suffering: the loss of family and fortune, severe illness, and emotional collapse. Song of Songs celebrates the power of erotic love shared by the bride and her bridegroom.

On an emotional level, the wisdom literature strikes a number of chords within the reader, from the sublime to the horrifying. On a scholarly level, the absence of the traditional themes of covenant, law, and Temple worship sets the wisdom literature apart from the majority of biblical writings.

4. THE PROPHETS

The prophetic literature includes the work of four "major" prophets (Isaiah, Jeremiah, Ezekiel, and Daniel), twelve "minor" prophets, and other works that are associated with the prophets, such as Lamentations and Baruch. The designation *major* or *minor* does not refer to importance of the work as much as to its length, though it is fair to say that the four major prophets have exercised more influence on Jewish and Christian thought than the shorter prophetic works. Scholars regard the Book of Daniel as a work of "apocalyptic literature" rather than a prophetic work, and we will discuss that particular genre of biblical writing later when we discuss the Book of Revelation. The prophetic writings are often designated as *classical prophecy* to differentiate these biblical figures from earlier ones who are called prophets, such as Samuel, Nathan, and Elijah.

The classical prophets are divinely commissioned messengers, called by God to deliver a message to the people. The typical prophetic utterance, therefore, begins, "Thus says the Lord..." The prophets remind Israel in blunt and often uncouth language that the blessing of the covenant relationship they enjoy with God carries a heavy burden of responsibility "to do justice, and to love kindness, and to walk humbly with your God" (Mic 6:8). Whether in the royal court, the marketplace, or the Temple, the prophets proclaim a message that the people usually do not wish to hear. Kings and paupers alike frequently ridicule the prophets, who often dramatize their predictions about Israel's fate in bizarre ways: Hosea marries a prostitute to illustrate Israel's unfaithfulness, Jeremiah dons a yoke as a sign of the future domination of Judah by the Babylonians, and

Ezekiel "attacks" a clay tablet with the city of Jerusalem drawn upon it. The prophets hand down the Lord's indictment of the people who have failed to uphold the covenant by worshipping other gods, neglecting the poor, and relying on foreign nations' military might rather than the Lord to protect them. As a consequence, the prophet warns, the Lord will soon punish the nation.

For Christians, the prophetic literature also foretells the life, death, and resurrection of Jesus of Nazareth. While this foretelling appears in numerous Christian writings, the Gospel of Matthew represents one of the most deliberate efforts to highlight the theme of Jesus as the fulfillment of Old Testament prophecy. For example, Matthew's account of Jesus' birth and early years is replete with allusions to the Old Testament in general, and direct quotations from the prophets in particular. For example, Matthew recounts Jesus' birth in light of the prophecy of Isaiah, "All this took place to fulfill what was spoken by the Lord through the prophet: 'Look, the virgin shall conceive and bear a son, and they shall name him Emmanuel,' which means, 'God is with us'" (Matt 1:22–23). Matthew carries that theme throughout his Gospel; even Judas' betrayal of Jesus for thirty pieces of silver fulfills an earlier prophecy by Jeremiah (Matt 27:9–10).

Malachi, the final prophetic work in the Christian arrangement of Old Testament texts, speaks of the return of the prophet Elijah, who did not die but was taken to heaven in a chariot of fire (2 Kgs 2:11). In the opening book of the New Testament, we encounter John the Baptist, a figure who resembles Elijah in attire, appearing in the wilderness proclaiming that a figure more powerful than himself was about to appear.

5. THE GOSPELS

The New Testament begins with the four gospel accounts (*gospel* means "good news") of the life, death, and resurrection of Jesus of Nazareth. The identities of the actual gospel writers are not known, but tradition attributes them to Matthew, Mark, Luke, and John. Scripture scholars Norman Perrin and Dennis Duling offer the following helpful summary:

The gospels were not written by eyewitnesses of the ministry of Jesus. They were written in the period between A.D. 70 and 100, forty years or more after the crucifixion, and originally they circulated anonymously. It has to be understood that in the ancient world it was quite common to attach important names to anonymous works, or to write in the name of some teacher or famous person from the past....Many modern scholars believe that authoritative "apostolic" names were attached to the gospels in the second century A.D. We simply do not know who wrote them...and when we speak of "Matthew," "Mark," Luke," or "John" we do so only for convenience; the actual names of the evangelists are forever lost to us.[1]

Scholars believe that Mark was the first Gospel written, and that Matthew and Luke use Mark as one of their sources when composing their own Gospels. Because of their overarching similarity, the Gospels of Matthew, Mark, and Luke are called *Synoptic Gospels*. Perrin and Duling note, "The gospels of Matthew, Mark, and Luke are usually called the synoptic gospels (from the Greek *synoptikos*, 'seeing the whole together') because they tell much the same story in much the same way. They can be set side by side and read together."[2] John's Gospel presents a markedly different account of Jesus and his teachings—a point that will be highlighted later in our discussion of the church's understanding of Jesus.

Each of the four Gospels emphasizes a particular feature of the early Christian proclamation about Jesus. The evangelists, or gospel writers, tailored their message to their audiences, highlighting those features that responded to the questions and concerns of their particular communities. Mark highlights the suffering that Christ endured; Matthew situates Jesus in the context of Jewish history; Luke prefers to stress Jesus' outreach to Gentiles—that is, adherents of religions other than Judaism; and John accents the divinity of Christ.

6. ACTS OF THE APOSTLES

This work is actually the second part of Luke's Gospel—it even begins, "In the first book..." In Acts, the author chronicles the spread of Christianity through the Mediterranean world, beginning in Jerusalem and concluding with the "apostle" Paul under house arrest in Rome (Paul was not one of the original twelve apostles). In this work, we find the memorable scenes of the ascension of Jesus, Pentecost, the martyrdom of Stephen, and the conversion of Paul on the road to Damascus. Responding to a crisis in the young Christian movement, the church leaders meet at Jerusalem (Acts 15) and determine that circumcision would not be required of the Gentile converts to Christianity. This both greatly expands the scope of early Christian missionary activity, and contributes to the increasing friction between the Christian movement and mainline Judaism.

7. PAUL'S LETTERS

In Acts 9, Saul of Tarsus (later known as Paul) is traveling to Damascus to arrest Christians, when he is struck to the ground by a blinding light. After his baptism, this zealous persecutor of the church becomes a tireless advocate of the Gospel. Paul undertakes three missionary journeys in Acts, covering lands from modern-day Turkey to Italy. In his travels, he experiences both success and failure. In Acts, for example, Paul is hailed as a god by the crowds in the city of Lystra (14:11–12), only to be later stoned and left for dead on the edge of town (14:19). Paul himself reports:

> Five times I have received from the Jews the forty lashes
> minus one. Three times I was beaten with rods. Once I
> received a stoning. Three times I was shipwrecked; for a
> night and a day I was adrift at sea; on frequent journeys,
> in danger from rivers, danger from bandits, danger from
> my own people, danger from Gentiles, danger in the city,
> danger in the wilderness, danger at sea, danger from false
> brothers and sisters; in toil and hardship, through many
> a sleepless night, hungry and thirsty, often without food,
> cold, and naked. (2 Cor 11:24–27)

As he travels from city to city, he is met by messengers with news of how the young churches in other regions are faring. Unable to revisit these churches personally, Paul sends letters. In many of them, Paul responds to the questions raised by the particular church, or outlines the doctrinal and ethical principles that stem from faith in Christ. In a few letters, he fiercely denounces his critics, or chastises a church for having departed from the Gospel. The one critical exception to this pattern is Paul's Letter to the Romans, which serves not as a response to problems at a church he earlier founded, but as a letter of introduction to an established church he is yet to meet. Paul's letters were preserved by the churches and eventually collected and deemed authoritative scripture. The letters appear in the Christian canon after Acts and are arranged in order of length, beginning with Romans and concluding with Philemon.

Modern scholarly opinion holds that not all of the letters attributed to Paul were in fact written by him. The concept of authorship was far more fluid in the ancient world: disciples writing in the spirit of their former mentors would attribute their literary works to them. The undisputed letters of Paul are Romans, 1 and 2 Corinthians, Galatians, Philippians, 1 Thessalonians, and Philemon. The remaining letters—Colossians, Ephesians, 1 and 2 Timothy, Titus, and 2 Thessalonians—are often regarded as "deutero-Pauline"; literally, "second Paul," meaning that they are attributed to Paul, but probably were not written by him. These determinations are based on differences in writing style and word usage, and scholars often disagree on questions of authorship. 1 and 2 Timothy and Titus are known collectively as the Pastoral Epistles and we will refer to them when we discuss the development of leadership positions in the early church.

8. HEBREWS

The Letter to the Hebrews defies easy categorization. It might be best described as a homily or theological meditation on the priesthood of Christ. Using intricate scriptural argumentation and philosophical speculation, Hebrews paints a unique christological portrait. Its apparent rejection of the possibility of postbaptismal repentance (see Heb 6:4–6) would stand in tension with the church's practice of readmitting to the community those who committed murder, adultery, or apostasy (i.e., denial of the faith) after the time of their baptism. The identity of the author is unknown. Scripture scholar Stephen L. Harris reports, "Although some early Christians attributed the work to Paul, many others recognized that the theology, language, and style of Hebrews were distinctly un-Pauline....Most scholars agree with Origen, a church scholar prominent during the early third century, who remarked that the writer's identity is known only to God."[3]

9. THE CATHOLIC (OR GENERAL) EPISTLES

In addition to the Pauline and deutero-Pauline letters, there are seven "catholic," or general, epistles: James; 1 and 2 Peter; 1, 2, and 3 John; and Jude. The Letters of John are believed to have come from the same community that produced John's Gospel. Although we do not know who wrote the Letter of James, it is traditionally attributed to James, "the Lord's brother" (Gal 1:19) and one of the "acknowledged pillars" (Gal 2:9) of the church in Jerusalem. Jude is traditionally believed to be the "brother of James" (Jude 1:1; see Matt 13:55). The authorship of the two letters credited to the apostle Peter is also a matter of scholarly debate. However, the scripture scholar Luke Timothy Johnson, offers the sound reminder: "In any case, the authority of New Testament writings does not derive from their authorship but from their inclusion in the canon. Attention is therefore better paid to the situation of Peter's first readers, and how the message shaped for them retains enduring value for readers in every age."[4] One theme of enduring value in James is the author's insistence on the connection of faith and good works in the lives of Christians. There are intriguing christological passages in 1 and 2 Peter, a reflection on the meaning of Christian baptism, and words of assurance to Christians concerned about the delay in Christ's second coming.

10. REVELATION

The final book of the Christian canon is an apocalyptic work that has captured the imagination of theologians, as well as poets and novelists, throughout Christian history. Earlier we have seen apocalyptic sections in the book of Daniel and in the Gospels (e.g., Mark 13), but this is the first time an entire book fits the category. The fundamental concern of apocalyptic literature centers on the present state of history and the power of God: Why has God allowed the corrupt rulers of this age to persecute the holy ones of God? Apocalyptic writers do not attempt to answer that problem in detached, philosophical terms. Rather, they record the terrifying visions that God has granted an individual; for example, Daniel, and John in Revelation. In these visions God reveals (*apocalyptic* means "unveiling") the timetable of human history in coded form, using frightening beasts, mysterious telltale signs, and symbolic numbers. The author informs the reader that if properly interpreted, these visions will disclose the events that will occur before the end of the world.

In an apocalyptic drama, human history is divided into two ages. In the old age, God (for reasons unknown to us) has allowed evil to run rampant, but in the new age that is soon to erupt, God will reward those who have remained faithful and punish the wicked. The short time that separates the two ages is the time of tribulation—the last stand of evil before its final destruction by God. This time is often portrayed as the worst time of persecution of God's holy ones. The time of tribulation is an experience of the birth pangs (see Mark 13:8) of the new age. The pains of a woman's labor are great, but they signal that soon a child will be born. Apocalyptic writing, therefore, speaks to the oppressed and assures them that God's judgment on the wicked rulers of this age will soon take place. It says, in effect, "Keep the faith; your reward is near."

From the beast bearing the number 666, to the war in heaven in which Satan is cast down to earth, to the final bloody battle of Armageddon, the fiery images of Revelation have ignited frenzied speculation about the end of the world. Throughout history, numerous Christian groups ardently believed that the Book of Revelation was being fulfilled in the events of their time. Scripture scholar Raymond E. Brown, SS, notes that "preachers have identified the Beast from the Earth whose number is 666 as Hitler, Stalin, the Pope, and Saddam Hussein, and have related events from [Revelation] to predict the exact date of the end of the world."[5] On the other hand, the Book of Revelation has also comforted countless Christians with its vision of a new Jerusalem where God will wipe every tear from our eyes and death will be no more (see Rev 21:3–4). By ending as it does with Revelation, the biblical narrative stretches from the beginning of time to the final defeat of evil at the end of time. The biblical epic provides the indispensable framework for understanding Christian belief, worship, and morality. It is the substance of what Christians profess in faith, anticipate in hope, and live in love.

The Development of the Hebrew Canon

Jews refer to their canonical scriptures—the same body of writings that Christians call the Old Testament—as the Tanak. The word *TaNaK* is an acronym for Torah, Prophets (in Hebrew, *Nebiim*), and the Writings, or the Wisdom books (in Hebrew, *Ketubim*).[6] As is true of the New Testament canon, the Tanak was finalized after centuries of debate regarding those texts that are authoritative for Jewish belief and practice. For example, some rabbis argued against the inclusion of Ecclesiastes (sometimes called Qoheleth) in the canon on the basis of its skeptical and pessimistic tone. The Torah reached canonical status by the fifth or fourth century BC, and the Prophets in approximately the third century BC. In the Gospels, Jesus refers to the scriptures as "the law and the prophets" (see Matt 7:12), indicating that the first two divisions of the Hebrew canon were fixed by that time. Not until the late first century AD did there emerge a general consensus regarding the Wisdom books[7] (Psalms, Job, Proverbs, Ruth, Song of Songs, Ecclesiastes, Lamentations, Esther, Daniel, Ezra, Nehemiah, and 1 and 2 Chronicles).

The inclusion of a text into the canon is the end result of a long process. First, the event occurs. Second, the story of the event is passed down in the oral tradition. Third, at some later date, the stories in the oral tradition are put into writing. Fourth, these writings may be joined with other accounts. For example, the present book of Isaiah is believed to be comprised of three separate works ranging from the eighth century BC (chapters 1–39), the time of the Babylonian Exile (40–55), and the time following the return of the exiles to the promised land (56–66). Finally, religious leaders include or exclude writings from the canon.

THE COMPOSITION OF THE TORAH

Modern theories about the composition of the Torah illustrate this four-stage process. Biblical scholars believe that the Torah reached its present form after the Babylonian Exile in the sixth century BC. At that time, editors united four sources, which were written at different times and in different places, into one unified narrative. Scholars identify these four sources as Yahwist, Elohist, Priestly, and Deuteronomic. Sometime around the reign of Solomon (ca. 950 BC), an author put into writing the previously oral history of the Hebrew people from the creation to the entrance into Canaan. Because the name *Yahweh* was consistently used for God throughout this work, modern German biblical scholars referred to this source as "J" (the word *Yahweh* in German is *Jahve*). After the twelve tribes divided, scribes in the northern kingdom of Israel composed a history that emphasized the events and persons associated with the northern cities. The situation resembled what occurred in our own American history during the Civil War; so imagine, the radically different histories of the United States that might have been produced by partisan thinkers in the North and the South.

In the history written in the northern tribes of Israel, the name *Yahweh* is not used of God until that divine name is revealed to Moses. Until then, God is called *Elohim*, hence this source was called "E." After the fall of the northern kingdom in 722–21 BC, these two sources were joined. A reform movement spearheaded by King Josiah gained momentum when a book of the law was "discovered" while renovations were being made in the Temple (see 2 Kgs 22). This book was believed to be Deuteronomy, or the "D" source. Finally, priests during the Babylonian Exile assembled material (called the Priestly or "P" source) that emphasized Jewish practices that could be continued despite the loss of the land, the Temple, and the kingship. These priestly editors wove the four traditions into one continuous narrative.

This editorial work in the Bible can be detected by comparing the two creation stories in Genesis (1:1–2:4a and 2:4b–25). There is a noticeable difference in language, writing style, and theology. In the first story (the P source), God creates by commanding, "Let there be light," and so on. In the second story (the J source), God plants a garden, creates the man by blowing the breath of life into a ball of clay, and builds up the woman from one of the ribs taken from the man while he slept.

The Development of the Christian Canon

The present-day New Testament canon of twenty-seven books gradually took shape over the course of the first few centuries of Christian history. Some writings were almost unanimously accepted at a very early date (e.g., Paul's Letters to the Corinthians), while others were a source of contention well into the fourth century (e.g., Revelation, Hebrews). The church did, however, eventually reach a consensus. We're familiar with the books that were included (numbers 5 through 10 in the overview that began this chapter). Many others were excluded (e.g., works such as the *Apocalypse of Peter* and *The Shepherd of Hermas*, which were highly, regarded by many early Christians, but ultimately excluded from the canon). While it is impossible to specify the exact moment certain books were included or excluded, a general history of the selection process can be sketched. This history of the formation of the canon extends from the time when the earliest New Testament writings were composed, to the close of the formation of the Christian canon, including Old Testament books, in the sixteenth century. We will divide this history into three phases: the composition of the New Testament texts, the internal church struggles over the number of acceptable texts and their proper interpretation, and the eventual resolution of the question of the canon.[8]

THE DATE OF COMPOSITION
OF THE NEW TESTAMENT WRITINGS

Biblical scholars debate the date of composition of the various New Testament writings. To complicate matters, some works were most likely not written by a single author at a specific time. For example, 2 Corinthians may contain fragments of other letters written by Paul to the Corinthian church, and John's Gospel may well have been edited on various occasions before reaching its present form. A rough chronology of the writings, however, can be drawn. The oldest work in the New Testament is most likely 1 Thessalonians, written approximately AD 50. The remaining undisputed Pauline letters were written in the 50s. Paul was executed in Rome approximately AD 62. In 66 the Jewish revolt against Rome erupted, and the Romans retaliated by burning down the Temple in Jerusalem in AD 70. Around this time, Mark wrote the first Gospel. Matthew and Luke used Mark as a source as they composed their Gospels about a decade later. By the end of the first century, John's Gospel probably had reached its present form; Hebrews and Revelation were also being committed to writing. Chronologically, the latest writing in the New Testament is probably 2 Peter, which was composed during the first few decades of the second century. Again, it is important to remember that, while these writings bear the names of gospel characters, they frequently were not written by them.

THE IMPACT OF MARCION, GNOSTICISM, AND MONTANISM

The second phase in the history of the formation of the Christian canon centers on the question of which books should be included and which should be excluded as authoritative for Christian belief and practice. The issue was forcefully raised by Marcion (ca. 85–ca. 160) who appeared in Rome around the year 140 preaching and establishing communities who accepted his version of the gospel message. Marcion contrasted the God of the Old Testament with the God found in the New, seeing the former as a God of Law, a God described by one commentator as "fickle, capricious, ignorant, despotic, and cruel,"[9] while the God of the New Testament was seen as a benevolent God of love and grace. Marcion's proposal for the canon followed from this perception. He included only an edited version of Luke's Gospel and ten of Paul's letters, and he rejected the Old Testament in its entirety.

Gnosticism (*gnosis* means "knowledge") was a widespread movement that promoted beliefs that were often a threat to orthodox

Christian belief. Gnosticism took various forms, but certain general characteristics united them. First, the basic framework of Gnostic systems was dualistic in that it divided all reality into two categories: matter vs. spirit, light vs. darkness, good vs. evil, and so on. Like Marcion, Gnostic Christians contrasted the God of the Old Testament who created the material world, with the God of the New Testament who sent the Holy Spirit. Second, Gnostics understood the moral struggles within the human person in terms of the fundamental struggle between flesh and spirit. In Paul's Letter to the Galatians, Marcion found a text that he regarded as the key to Christian theology: "Live by the Spirit, I say, and do not gratify the desires of the flesh. For what the flesh desires is opposed to the Spirit, and what the Spirit desires is opposed to the flesh; for these are opposed to each other, to prevent you from doing what you want" (Gal 5:16–17). Third, Gnostics insisted that true knowledge of spiritual realities could be gained by those who properly understood the hidden (or secret) meaning of Christ's teachings. Not all people can grasp these truths; hence, there was an element of elitism in many Gnostic teachings. Gnostics, however, insisted that Jesus himself taught these to the apostles: "To you has been given the secret of the kingdom of God, but for those outside, everything comes in parables, in order that 'they may indeed look, but not perceive, and may indeed listen, but not understand; so that they may not turn again and be forgiven'" (Mark 4:11–12). John's Gospel was particularly appealing to the Gnostics because John describes Jesus as the Light in a world of darkness (see John 1:5), whose words are "spirit and life" (John 6:63), and whose kingdom is not of this world (John 18:36).

Another movement that gained popularity in the church in the mid-second century centered around a charismatic preacher named Montanus who claimed that he was a prophet of God, and that two of his women disciples, Maximilla and Priscilla, were prophetesses. The content of their apocalyptic teaching was that the church had entered the age of the Holy Spirit at Pentecost, but that this age was soon to come to an abrupt close. The Montanists combined this belief with a rigorous moral code and an encouragement to seek martyrdom for the faith. One of the most famous converts to Montanism was Tertullian, whom we will discuss later. Historians differ on the impact of this movement on the formation of the canon. Some believe that the Montanists, while not rejecting the Gospels and Paul's letters, accorded equal authority to their own writings. Consequently, the church began to identify and limit the number of works that should be regarded as canonical. Others argue that Montanism, with its appeal to the direct inspiration of the Holy Spirit, threatened the authority of the bishops, but exerted little influence on the decision to create a canon.[10]

THE RESPONSES OF JUSTIN MARTYR, IRENAEUS, AND EUSEBIUS

Marcion's call for a total rejection of the Old Testament forced the church to explicitly address the question of the canon, especially the status of the Old Testament in Christian theology. The response came from a philosopher and theologian named Justin, better known in Christian history by the title accorded him by his death around the year 165, Justin Martyr. Justin Martyr's work proved significant in the formation of the canon in two ways. First, he accorded the Gospels, or "memoirs of the apostles" as he referred to them, scriptural status. A contributor to *The Oxford Companion to the Bible*, Andrie B. du Toit, noted in his article on the New Testament canon: "Justin (*Apology* I.67.3–4) reports that the memoirs of the apostles (i.e., the Gospels) are not only read but also commented upon in public worship, which put them on a par with the Old Testament books."[11] Second, Justin defended the inclusion of the Old Testament in the canonical body of texts for Christians. He contended that the Old Testament contained crucial foreshadowings of events in the New Testament and prophecies that were fulfilled in Christ. This approach to reading the Old Testament will occupy our attention when we turn our focus to the topic of biblical interpretation.

The most significant church official involved in the second-century controversies over the canon was Irenaeus, who served as bishop of Lyons from around 178 to around 200. In his *Against Heresies*, Irenaeus refuted the claims of the Gnostics. This work was important not only for its theological content, but also for the manner in which it dealt with the problems. Beliefs had to agree with the teachings of the apostles, as transmitted to subsequent generations in the "rule of faith," or body of essential teaching, by the bishops of the church. Irenaeus's methodology was a three-pronged approach based on the canon of scripture, on the rule of faith, and on the authority of church leaders. As a consequence, in order to meet the standard of orthodoxy, doctrines needed to be apostolic in origin. Apostolicity eventually became a standard in all areas of early Christian theology. As the patristics scholar Rowan Greer explains,

> In thinking through the vexed question of which Christian writings were to be authorities for Christians, the Great Church [i.e., the entire Christian community, along with the bishops, and leading theologians] concluded that "apostolicity" should be the criterion for the inclusion of books in the New Testament canon. No novel writings were to be admitted, and only those which could claim to preserve the apostles' witness to Christ could claim authority. This decision avoided the danger of Montanism, that is, the implication that the revelation in Christ was not final and could be superseded.[12]

By the end of the second century, the move toward a canon was well under way, but the final resolution of that question would elude the church for centuries to come.

In his *Church History*, Eusebius of Caesarea (ca. 260–339), the great church historian of the fourth century, recorded the earliest catalogue or list of canonical texts. Lee M. McDonald offers the following summary of Eusebius's account:

> Eusebius (ca. 325) established three categories for Christian books: those that were "accepted" as scripture, those that were "questionable" or "disputed," and those that were "spurious." He included in the first group twenty of the current New Testament books (the four Gospels, Acts, thirteen epistles of Paul, 1 John, and 1 Peter). The "questionable" group—James, 2 Peter, Jude, 2 and 3 John, and possibly Hebrews and Revelation—was probably not a part of Eusebius's own biblical canon. The "spurious" group was rejected outright and included such

works as the Gospels of *Peter, Thomas,* and *Matthias;* the *Acts of Andrew, Paul,* and *John;* the *Didache;* and the *Apocalypse of Peter.* In time, the middle group ("the questionable" books) was accepted by most churches, but the latter group failed to find acceptance.[13]

Also in the fourth century, Athanasius, bishop of Alexandria and a figure we will discuss at greater length when dealing with the council of Nicaea, included in his Thirty-ninth Easter Letter a list of accepted books in the New Testament. His list was the first to correspond exactly to the present twenty-seven books of the New Testament. Yet is was not until the sixteenth century, during the fourth session of the Council of Trent, that the Roman Catholic Church *officially* recognized the present canon.[14]

The bishops at Trent also accepted forty-six books in the Old Testament canon. This was in contrast to the Protestant churches that recognized only thirty-nine books. This difference goes back to the presence of two canons of scripture in the Jewish tradition. Beginning in the third century BC, Jews living in Greek-speaking regions needed a Greek translation of their scriptures. Known as the Septuagint, this Greek translation of the Old Testament contained seven books (Tobit, Judith, 1 Maccabees, 2 Maccabees, Sirach or Ecclesiasticus, Wisdom, and Baruch) that were not found in the Hebrew canon as defined by Jewish leaders in the first century AD. In the late fourth century, at the request of Pope Damasus, St. Jerome produced a Latin translation of the Bible called the Vulgate that became the standard text for scholars until the Renaissance. The canon of the Vulgate—forty-six books in the Old Testament and twenty-seven books in the New Testament—was officially adopted at Trent. The Protestant Reformers, by contrast, accepted the shorter canon, and labeled the seven additional books as "apocryphal" or "deuterocanonical." In 1646, the "Westminster Confession of Faith," an important statement of Presbyterian theology, gave classic expression to the Protestant position: "The books commonly called Apocrypha, not being of divine inspiration, are no part of the Canon of Scripture; and therefore are of no authority in the Church of God, nor to be any otherwise approved, or made use of, than other human writings."[15]

Determining the exact number of books in the New Testament, however, was not the only issue the church needed to resolve. A second issue, equally important to the question of canon, was how to properly interpret the writings that were accepted. We turn our attention, therefore, to the question of biblical interpretation as it was practiced in the ancient, medieval, and Reformation eras, and then will conclude by comparing those early approaches to reading the Bible with the ones currently employed.

Biblical Interpretation in the Early Church

Early church thinkers engaged in theological battles on many fronts, including scriptural questions. Two of the most significant for the history of biblical interpretation were the arguments with mainline Judaism on the one hand, and with Gnostic Christians on the other. In their arguments with mainline Judaism, Christians argued that Christ fulfilled the prophecies of the Old Testament, and that the events of the Old Testament prefigured the events in the New Testament. In reply to the Gnostic interpreters of scripture who generally rejected the Old Testament, orthodox Christians insisted on keeping the Old Testament as part of the canon, and argued that the interpretation of scripture needed to be guided by the rule of faith.

These tense, early controversies in Christian theology continue down to our own day. Christians claim a rootedness in the Old Testament history, yet assert a new revelation has taken place in Christ; Christians reject wild speculative systems of thought common to Gnosticism, yet believe that scriptures contain meanings beyond what is conveyed by the literal wording. Out of these creative tensions, several methods of biblical interpretation developed within the early church. We will examine two of them: typological and allegorical.

TYPOLOGICAL INTERPRETATION OF THE BIBLE

St. Augustine, the most influential Latin-speaking theologian of the early church, succinctly captured the essence of the typological method of interpretation with the following axiom: "In the Old

Testament the New is concealed, in the New the Old is revealed."[16] In a typological interpretation, events in the Old Testament are seen as "types"; that is, foreshadowings or prefigurements of events in the New Testament. For example, in the following passage from 1 Peter, the author offers a typological interpretation of the Noah story:

> ...God patiently waited in the days of Noah, during the building of the ark, in which a few, that is, eight persons, were saved through water. And baptism, which this pre-figured, now saves you—not as a removal of dirt from the body, but as an appeal to God for a good conscience, through the resurrection of Jesus Christ...(3:20–21)

The waters of the flood that wiped evil from the earth provide the biblical reader with a glimpse of the future Christian practice of baptism (though the reader was certainly not aware of that larger meaning at the time). In his Letter to the Romans, Paul makes a typological comparison between Adam and Christ (5:14), except in this passage the element of contrast dominates: Just as through one man's disobedience, sin entered the world, and death came through sin, so too through one man's obedience, sin was conquered, and eternal life came through obedience.

This impulse to read the Old Testament typologically gained momentum throughout the patristic era. J. N. D. Kelly offers the following commonly held typological interpretations in the patristic era:

> There was general agreement about cardinal issues, such as that Adam, or again Moses the law-giver, in a real sense, foreshadowed Christ; the flood pointed to baptism, and also to judgment; all the sacrifices of the old Law, but in a pre-eminent way the sacrifice of Isaac, were anticipations of Calvary; the crossing of the Red Sea and the eating of manna looked forward to baptism and the eucharist; the fall of Jericho prefigured the end of the world.[17]

Patristic commentators found foreshadowings in the most seemingly insignificant details. For example, in the story of the fall of Jericho, the Israelite spies were protected by a woman in the town named

Rahab (Josh 2). Rahab asked the Israelites to spare both her and her family. The spies agreed, and she hung a scarlet cord (Josh 2:18) from her window to mark where she and her family were living. The invading Israelite forces destroyed Jericho, but spared Rahab's life (Josh 6:25). In the last decade of the first century AD, Clement of Rome, in a letter to the Corinthian church, typologically saw the scarlet cord hung out of the window by Rahab as a foreshadowing of Christ's blood being shed on the cross: "They went on to give her a sign, telling her she was to hang out a scarlet cord from her house— thereby typifying the redemption which all who put their trust and hope in God shall find, through the blood of the Lord."[18]

Modern readers certainly differ in their assessment of Clement's reading of the Rahab story. Some dismiss it as fanciful; others regard it as revelatory. Whatever its strengths or weaknesses, the typological approach treats the Bible as a continuous, unified narrative. The Old Testament sets the stage for the New Testament; the New Testament sheds light on the Old Testament. Marcion's position of rejecting the entire Old Testament is therefore overturned. However, typology often relegates Old Testament stories to a secondary status, seeing them merely as signs pointing to the New Testament. The larger question is whether Christian interpreters of the Bible are right to look for meanings in biblical texts beyond the obvious historical references or moral teachings. Early Christians obviously believed that such a search is legitimate, and in some cases, necessary. This leads us to the second popular method of biblical interpretation: the allegorical method of interpretation.

ALLEGORICAL INTERPRETATION OF THE BIBLE

Paul summarizes the underlying principle of the allegorical method when he writes: "The letter kills, but the Spirit gives life" (2 Cor 3:6). Paul's maxim presupposes that in addition to the literal meaning of a biblical passage, there are deeper, more profound spiritual truths hidden in the text. The Bible, as a divinely inspired work, contains several layers of meanings. The reader of the Bible, therefore, needs to reflect prayerfully and seek the Lord's guidance in uncovering the spiritual treasures buried beneath the surface of the text.

The ancient city of Alexandria in Egypt served as the intellectual center of allegorical interpretation. Philo of Alexandria (ca. 20 BC–ca. 50 AD), the great Jewish biblical scholar, popularized the allegorical interpretation of the Torah. In Christian circles, Origen (ca. 185–ca. 254), the head of the catechetical school in Alexandria, produced countless allegorical interpretations of biblical passages. For example, in one of his homilies on the Gospel of Luke, Origen cited an allegorical interpretation of the parable of the Good Samaritan (Luke 10:30–37) that he received from an elder:

> One of the elders wanted to interpret the parable as follows. The man who was going down is Adam. Jerusalem is paradise, and Jericho is the world. The robbers are the hostile powers. The priest is the Law, the Levite is the prophets, and the Samaritan is Christ. The wounds are disobedience, the beast is the Lord's body, the *pandochium* (that is, the stable), which accepts all who wish to enter, is the Church. And further, the two *denarii* mean the Father and the Son. The manager of the stable is the head of the Church, to whom its care has been entrusted. And the fact that the Samaritan promises he will return represents the Savior's second coming.[19]

Although Origen differs with the elder's interpretation on some points (e.g., "'*Two denarii*' appear to me to be knowledgeable of the Father and the Son..."),[20] he generally accepts the elder's allegorical interpretation that sees in the parable the entire biblical narrative in miniature.

The allegorical method had its supporters and detractors in the ancient world. Even Origen, in his work *On First Principles*, asked rhetorically about the first creation story: "Now what man of intelligence will believe that the first and the second and the third day, and the evening and the morning existed without the sun and moon and stars?"[21] Yet other passages, such as when Moses sees God's back (Exod 33:18–23), cried out for a spiritual rather than a literal interpretation. Critics, however, charged that the allegorical method did not sufficiently safeguard against fantastic readings of biblical passages. In addition, the allegorical method of interpretation seemed to

play right into the hands of the Gnostics, who formed grand speculative systems from the most innocuous verses. For these reasons, the
thinkers in the Syrian city of Antioch, the other great intellectual
center of the early church, gave the allegorical method a much cooler
reception than it found in Alexandria. While not dismissing it completely, they placed greater emphasis on the historical or literal
meaning of the text.

Biblical Interpretation in the Middle Ages

In medieval times it was common to speak of "four senses of
scripture." As scripture scholar Raymond E. Brown explains,

> The guiding theoretical principle of medieval exegesis
> may be said to stem from John Cassian's (d. ca. 435) dis-
> tinction of the four senses of Scripture: (1) the historical
> or literal, (2) the allegorical or Christological, (3) the
> tropological or moral or anthropological, (4) the ana-
> gogical or eschatological....
>   The four senses of Jerusalem, an example supplied
> by Cassian, illustrates the theory. When Jerusalem is
> mentioned in the Bible, in its literal sense it is a Jewish
> city; allegorically, however, it refers to the Church of
> Christ; tropologically Jerusalem stands for the soul of
> man; anagogically it stands for the heavenly city.[22]

The four senses of scripture were nicely summarized by thirteenth-
century thinker Augustine of Denmark: "The literal teaches facts,
the allegorical what you are to be believe, the moral what you are
to do, the anagogical what you are to hope for."[23] Thomas Aquinas,
the great medieval Scholastic theologian, was quick to insist that
the four meanings do not contradict themselves. It was not a case
of arguing that if the allegorical sense was right, then the moral
sense must be wrong. Rather, "in Holy Writ [i.e., the Bible] no
confusion results, for all senses are founded on one—the literal—
from which alone can any argument be drawn." Aquinas furthermore, displaying his emphasis on the literal sense, stated that

"nothing necessary to faith is contained under the spiritual sense [i.e., the allegorical, moral, or eschatological meanings] which is not elsewhere put forward by the Scripture in its literal sense."[24]

Luther and Biblical Interpretation

Martin Luther and the other Protestant Reformers sought to reconstruct Christian beliefs and practices according to what they believed to be sound biblical teachings. While the Roman Catholic Church claimed to be the guardian of the scriptures and the arbiter of conflicts regarding their proper interpretation, Luther placed all church teachings (e.g., the primacy of the pope) and practices (e.g., the sacrament of penance) under the judgment of scripture. This principle became known as *sola scriptura;* that is, scripture alone. Traditions or institutions that were not explicitly endorsed in scripture were to be rejected. As a practical consequence of the principle of *sola scriptura*, the need for the papacy, creeds, and ecumenical councils was eliminated.

For Luther, scripture—and scripture alone—played the central and defining role in the Christian life. The Bible is able to play this pivotal role because, for Luther, its meaning is clear. Gerhard Ebeling, one of the leading authorities on Luther's theology, notes that Luther came to reject the medieval belief in the fourfold meaning of scripture. Commenting on Luther's work on the psalms in 1519, Ebeling writes, "It is now clear that he considers that there is only one genuine meaning of scripture, and that is the literal sense, which as such is spiritual because of the content of the scripture."[25] Thus the individual replaces the church as the final authority in scriptural interpretation. The certainty of one's interpretation comes not from conformity to the norms of the church, but from the interior illumination of the Holy Spirit. Finally, all scripture points to Christ. As Luther says, "Christ is the point in the circle from which the whole circle is drawn."[26] Not all of scripture does an equally satisfactory job of "showing Christ" to the reader. Luther preferred John's Gospel, the First Letter of John, Romans, Galatians, Ephesians, and 1 Peter, but famously believed the Letter of James to be worthless. We will discuss the reasons for Luther's harsh assessment of the Letter of James when we evaluate his theology in the church history chapter.

Biblical Interpretation in the Modern Age

With the rise of modern science, confidence grew that we could discover the laws that govern all physical processes, from bacterial infection in the human body to the motion of the planets. Underlying these different investigations in chemistry, biology, physics, and astronomy is the common assumption that unalterable laws control these observable phenomena. If scientists could determine the precise nature of these laws, then outcomes could be reliably predicted in advance. The scientific method—investigating and collecting data, developing hypotheses, and testing those hypotheses through experimentation—became the standard of rationality in the western world.

In the field of theology, the scientific approach to the Bible investigated the biblical text with the same critical spirit that researchers in other areas brought to their studies. This resulted in three important shifts in biblical scholarship. First, scholars compared the biblical texts to other writings of equal antiquity from cultures with which the Israelites and early Christians would have had contact. The biblical creation story, for example, was compared with the Babylonian creation story that the Israelites would have heard during the time of the Babylonian exile. Second, just as Newton's physics replaced Aristotle's, new theories of biblical authorship supplanted traditional views. For example, scholars rejected traditional claims about Moses' authorship of the Torah, and began to assign different portions of the Torah to one of four sources (J, E, P, and D, discussed earlier). The Torah was viewed, therefore, not as a continuous narrative written by an individual author, but a composite work that resulted from the editing of several different sources of material. Unlike the earlier typological and allegorical approaches, this new scientific approach emphasized to a far greater degree the human involvement in the composition of the biblical texts. Third, the truth of the Bible became increasingly joined with the historical factuality of the stories. If evolution were true, many reasoned, then the Bible must be wrong. Along with this, the historicity of the miracle stories was openly questioned by those both favoring and attacking the Gospel. The biblical texts seemed to suffer a crisis of credibility in the eyes of many scientifically minded modern readers.

Christian thinkers responded to this new scientific approach in one of three ways. The first was a complete rejection of the critical study of biblical works and vigorously reasserted divine authorship of biblical texts. This trend develops into modern fundamentalism, a movement committed to the historical inerrancy of the Bible. The second approach that emerged subjected all Christian teachings to the prevailing standards of rationality and rejected, or at the very least reinterpreted, any doctrine that seemed unscientific. This was the route pursued by the deists who believed that God created the world and then left it to run according to preestablished laws. In this view, the biblical moral code was commendable, but its miracle accounts were dubious. The third route, developed by eighteenth- and nineteenth-century Protestant biblical scholars and eventually officially endorsed in Pope Pius XII's 1943 encyclical letter *Divino Afflante Spiritu*, has become known as the historical-critical approach to the Bible. This method first situates biblical texts in their original historical context, and then makes a determination as to their proper categorization as, for example, an historical account, a satire, or a symbolic story meant to convey spiritual truths.

The Critical Tools of the Historical-Critical Method

The historical-critical approach to biblical interpretation employs a number of critical tools to examine the scriptures. We will focus on three: textual criticism, form criticism, and redaction criticism.

Textual Criticism

Textual criticism determines the original wording of a text. In the case of the New Testament, for example, we have no original copies of the manuscripts. The earliest fragment of a New Testament writing is a small piece of papyrus called Rylands Greek Papyrus 457, containing verses from John 18, dated to about 125 to 135. The biblical scholar Raymond E. Brown estimates the number of manuscripts (whole or in part) of the Greek New Testament at approximately three thousand. In addition to that, Brown notes, there are approximately twenty-two hundred manuscripts containing sections of the New Testament for use in liturgy. These various manuscripts and fragments do not agree on the exact wording of the Gospels, or other biblical writings. Consequently, biblical scholars must reconstruct what they believe to be the original wording of the text. Lively scholarly debate, of course, exists over such matters.

Often such discussions can be discovered in the footnotes of Bibles. The most obvious example is probably the ending of Mark's Gospel. The earliest manuscripts we have end at Mark 16:8. That makes for an inconclusive ending in the minds of many readers: There is no appearance of the Risen Lord; the angel at the tomb speaks of Jesus meeting the disciples in Galilee, but no such event is described; and the final verse has the women fleeing the tomb, "saying nothing to anyone, for they were afraid" (Mark 16:8). The majority of scholars believe that Mark intended to end his Gospel at 16:8; others are unconvinced, arguing instead that the original ending has most likely been lost. Most modern editions of the Bible discuss the textual issues in the footnotes to chapter sixteen. Contemporary commentaries on Mark's Gospel discuss the issue in even greater detail. A similar discussion can be found regarding the story of the woman being taken off to be stoned for adultery in John 7:53—8:11. In many ancient manuscripts of John, this famous story is not included; and in some manuscripts the story appears in Luke, not John. A close reading of John 7—8 will reveal that the story interrupts the flow of the narrative, and that the text flows more smoothly if the reader skips immediately from John 7:52 to John 8:12.

FORM CRITICISM

Once scholars agreed that the gospel writers incorporated pre-existing material into their Gospels, then the challenge became how to identify these sources that the gospel writers had at their disposal and how they used them. In a popular introductory text on form criticism, Edgar V. McKnight explains, "The 'fundamental assumption,' and in some sense the assumption which makes form criticism both necessary and possible, is that tradition consists basically of individual sayings and narratives joined together in the Gospels by the work of the editors."[28] This approach can be illustrated by the modern treatment of Jesus' parables. In Mark 4:1–9 Jesus tells the parable of the sower, and in 4:13–20 he gives an allegorical interpretation in which the seeds represent various people's response to the gospel message. Joachim Jeremias, in one of the groundbreaking works in twentieth-century scholarship on the study of parables, writes, "Even in the very earliest period, during the first few decades after the death of Jesus, the parables underwent a certain amount of reinterpretation. At a very early stage the process had begun treating them as allegories—of attributing some special significance to every detail...and for centuries that kind of allegorical interpretation obscured their real meaning like a thick veil."[29]

This thick veil found its way into the final edition of Mark's Gospel in which Jesus utters both the parable and its allegorical interpretation. Form critics, however, differentiate between the original parable that reflects the Palestinian farming practices common in Jesus' day, and the allegorical interpretation that reflects the successes and failures experienced by early Christian missionaries. Jeremias writes,

> As they come down to us, Jesus' parables have a double historical setting. (1) The original setting of the parables, as of all his utterances, is some specific situation in the course of his activity. Many of the parables are so vividly told that it is natural to assume that they arise out of some occurrence. (2) But subsequently, before they assumed a written form, they "lived" in the primitive Church, which proclaimed, preached, and taught the words of Jesus in its missionary activities, its assemblies, and in its catechetical instruction. It collected and arranged his sayings under specific headings, and created settings for them, sometimes modifying their form, expanding here, allegorizing

there, always in relation to its own situation between the cross and the second coming of Christ.[30]

The task assumed by the form critic, therefore, is to identify the original "setting in life" in which the parable was first uttered, and then speculate how the church may have adapted the parable to speak to its own situation. By extension, the gospel writers were not simply compiling information, but in fact editing the received material and shaping their Gospels in ways that would be responsive to the questions and concerns of their communities. This leads us into a discussion of redaction criticism.

REDACTION CRITICISM

Redaction criticism investigates the changes the gospel writers made to the received material. Most scholars maintain that Mark was the first Gospel written, and that Matthew and Luke used Mark as one of their sources. If this is accurate, we can compare the stories in Mark with their parallel accounts in Matthew and Luke, and note the changes made by Matthew and Luke. The easiest way to do this is by consulting *Gospel Parallels*, a standard reference text that presents the stories of Mark alongside their parallel accounts in Matthew and Luke.[31]

The account of Jesus' baptism serves as a helpful illustration. In Mark 1:9–11, John baptizes Jesus. Two questions arise in the minds of many readers. First, if John's baptism is "a baptism for the forgiveness of sins" (1:4), then is Mark suggesting that Jesus had sinned? Second, does the fact that Jesus submits to John's baptism in any way suggest that John had a superior role? Matthew and Luke offer their own distinctive editorial touches to address these issues. In Matthew, we find a dialogue inserted between John and Jesus (Matt 3:13–15), with John expressing astonishment that Jesus should come to him for baptism. In Luke, John the Baptist is imprisoned in the verses preceding the baptism story (Luke 3:19–20). As the scripture scholar Luke Timothy Johnson notes,

Luke's version of the baptism deviates from the other Synoptists in several respects. We can note first his distinctive way of dealing with the possible misunderstanding that could be caused by having Jesus baptized by John. Mark appears unaware of the problem. But Matthew's dialogue between Jesus and John concerning who is greater and the need for righteousness (Matt 3:13–15) tells us the two possible implications to be drawn from Jesus being baptized by John: that John was greater than Jesus, and that Jesus was a sinner who required repentance. Luke has no dialogue of this sort. Instead, he virtually removes John from the scene. He notes his imprisonment in 3:19, and then extends the distance between him and Jesus by means of a series of adverbial clauses. As a result, the reader does not see Jesus acted on by John, but John in prison and Jesus baptized amid a crowd of people.[32]

Within each Gospel are similar instances of redaction—of individual sayings of Jesus, the content of miracle stories, and Jesus' last words on the cross. The textual, formal, and redactional analysis of the Gospel, however, is only the first step in the process of biblical interpretation.

Hermeneutics

The task of biblical interpretation involves two sets of questions. The first set of questions examines what the text meant to those who first heard it; historical setting, literary devices, and cultural assumptions are identified in order to shed light on the original meaning of the text. In formal theological language, this is the task of *exegesis*. The second set of questions focuses on the meaning of the text for contemporary readers and the application of those biblical teachings to the lives of ordinary Christians. In formal theological language, this is the task of *hermeneutics* that we discussed in the previous chapter.

This two-step process of biblical interpretation would most likely be the route we would take if we were called upon to offer a scriptural reflection in a liturgical setting, something like a priest's homily. We would need to gather historical information about the text, but we would also want to connect that passage with the lives of those present at the liturgy. For example, Peter's walking on water may be a lesson in faith for us today. The demons expelled by Jesus might be understood as the destructive forces at work in our lives. The miracle of the loaves and fishes may be a mandate to feed the hungry of our own day.

The following historical piece serves as a useful illustration of the need for both steps in the process of interpretation.

> Four score and seven years ago our fathers brought forth, upon this continent, a new nation, conceived in Liberty and dedicated to the proposition that all men are created equal.
>
> Now we are engaged in a great civil war, testing whether that nation, or any nation, so conceived, and so dedicated, can long endure. We are met here on a great battlefield of that war. We have come to dedicate a portion of that field, as a final resting place for those who here gave their lives that that nation might live. It is altogether fitting and proper that we should do this.
>
> But in a larger sense we can not dedicate—we can not consecrate—we can not hallow—this ground. The brave men, living and dead, who struggled here, have consecrated it far above our poor power to add or detract. The world will little note, nor long remember what we say here, but it can never forget what they did here. It is for us, the living, rather, to be dedicated here to the unfinished work which they who fought here have thus far so nobly advanced. It is rather for us to be here dedicated to the great task remaining before us—that from these honored dead we take increased devotion to that cause for which they gave the last full measure of devotion—that we here highly resolve that these dead shall not have died in vain—that this nation, under God, shall have a new birth of freedom—and that government

of the people, by the people, for the people, shall not perish from the earth.[33]

The Gettysburg Address does not mention the name of the person delivering the address, the location at which the address is given, or the date. There is also an interesting textual question—there are different versions of the Address in existence, and there is some debate over which version Lincoln actually delivered at Gettysburg. In order to understand the content of the Address, the reader needs to know the meaning of a "score," and what occurred "four score and seven years ago" in American history, and why 1776 is significant to Americans. Allusions are made to foundational texts, such as the Declaration of Independence. As Americans we understand the Gettysburg Address because we know the history that is needed in order for the text to make sense. Without that knowledge, the address would be virtually unintelligible to the reader. Its power, however, is not confined to its status as an important historical work in American history. On the one-year anniversary of the attack on the World Trade Center in New York City, several dignitaries joined the families who lost loved ones for a memorial service at Ground Zero. Included in that memorial was a reading of the Gettysburg Address by Governor George Pataki of New York. Lincoln's speech, originally delivered on November 19, 1863, which the president himself believed "the world will little note, nor long remember," was reinterpreted in light of the tragic events of September 11, 2001. Texts take on a life of their own; they are preserved in the life of a community who treasures them. Likewise, scriptural texts are remembered and reinterpreted by a living body of believers whose very lives are shaped by its teachings, images, and dreams.

Discussion Questions

1. Why would the church want a canon of scripture? What criteria should be applied when making that selection?
2. How would you respond to Marcion? What role should the Old Testament play in Christian belief and practice?

3. Why might Gnosticism be appealing to Christians? What beliefs do Gnostics and Christians share? Where do they disagree?
4. Does the Bible contain layers of meaning that can be discovered through prayer and study? What implications follow from your answer for how we should read the Bible?
5. Is reading the story of Noah and the flood as a foreshadowing of Christian baptism a legitimate interpretation?
6. Would it bother you if the allegorical interpretation of the parable of the sower (Mark 4:13–20) came from the early church and not Jesus?
7. What is your reaction to the findings of redaction critics? Are later writers simply changing the received material to suit their own needs?

Suggested Readings

For a helpful overview of biblical writings, see the Reading Guides that are included in *The Catholic Study Bible*, edited by Donald Senior (New York: Oxford University Press, 1990). For an introduction to the Old Testament, see Lawrence Boadt, *Reading the Old Testament* (Mahwah, NJ: Paulist Press, 1985). For an introduction to the New Testament, see Raymond E. Brown, *An Introduction to the New Testament* (New York: Doubleday, 1997). Also, *The New Jerome Biblical Commentary*, edited by Raymond Brown et al. (Englewood Cliffs, NJ: Prentice Hall, 1990) provides a helpful single-volume commentary on the Bible.

For a discussion of early Christian biblical interpretation, see the "Introduction" to *Biblical Interpretation in the Early Church*, edited by Karlfried Froehlich (Philadelphia: Fortress Press, 1984). For typology, see John E. Alsup's entry "Typology" in *The Anchor Bible Dictionary*, edited by David Noel Freedman (New York: Doubleday, 1992).

For a personal reflection on the acceptance of the historical-critical method in Roman Catholic circles, see John R. Donahue, "A Journey Remembered: Catholic Biblical Scholarship 50 Years after *Divino Afflante Spiritu*" in *America* 169 (7), 1993, 6–11.

Notes

1. Norman Perrin and Dennis C. Duling, *The New Testament: An Introduction*, 2nd ed. (New York: Harcourt Brace Jovanovich, 1982), 42.

2. Ibid., 66.

3. Stephen L. Harris, *The New Testament: A Student's Introduction*, 2nd ed. (Mountain View, CA: Mayfield Publishing Co., 1995), 301.

4. Luke Timothy Johnson, "The General Letters and Revelation," in *The Catholic Study Bible* (New York: Oxford University Press, 1990), 553–54.

5. Raymond Brown, *An Introduction to the New Testament* (New York: Doubleday, 1997), 773.

6. Lawrence Boadt, *Reading the Old Testament* (Mahwah, NJ: Paulist Press, 1984), 15.

7. Werner H. Schmidt, *Old Testament Introduction* (New York: Crossroad, 1984), 6–8.

8. Here I have benefited from the work of John Barton, *Making the Christian Bible* (London: Darton, Longman, and Todd, 1997).

9. *The Oxford Dictionary of the Christian Church*, 3rd ed., E. A. Livingstone, ed. (New York: Oxford University Press, 1997), 1034.

10. See Lee M. McDonald, *The Formation of the Christian Biblical Canon*, rev. ed. (Peabody, MA: Hendrickson Publishers, 1995), 172–76 for a helpful summary of the debate.

11. Andrie B. du Toit, "Canon, New Testament," in *The Oxford Companion to the Bible*, Bruce M. Metzger and Michael D. Coogan, eds. (Oxford: Oxford University Press, 1993), 103.

12. Rowan Greer, "The Christian Bible and Its Interpretation," in *Early Biblical Interpretation* by James L. Kugel and Rowan A. Greer (Philadelphia: Westminster Press, 1986), 110.

13. Lee M. McDonald, "Canon" [of Scripture], in *Encyclopedia of Early Christianity*, 2nd ed., ed. Everett Ferguson (New York: Garland Publishing, 1997), 208.

14. See Norman P. Tanner, ed., *Decrees of the Ecumenical Councils*, vol. 2 (London: Sheed and Ward / Washington, DC: Georgetown University Press, 1990), 663–64.

15. "The Westminster Confession of Faith," I, III, in John H. Leith, ed., *Creeds of the Churches*, 3rd. ed. (Atlanta: John Knox Press, 1982), 195.

16. Quoted in J. N. D. Kelly, *Early Christian Doctrines*, rev. ed. (San Francisco: Harper and Row, 1978), 69.

17. Ibid., 72.

18. Clement of Rome, "The First Epistle of Clement," #12, in *Early Christian Writings*, Maxwell Staniforth, trans. (New York: Penguin Books, 1968), 29.

19. Origen, "Homily on Luke," 34.3, in *Homilies on Luke*, Joseph T. Lienhard, trans. (Washington, DC: The Catholic University of America Press, 1996), 138.

20. Ibid., 140.

21. Origen, *On First Principles*, IV.3.1, trans. G. W. Butterworth (Glouster, MA: Peter Smith, 1973), 188.

22. Raymond E. Brown, "Hermeneutics," in *The Jerome Biblical Commentary* (Englewood Cliffs, NJ: Prentice-Hall, 1968), 612.

23. This translation is offered by Joseph A. Fitzmyer in "The Senses of Scripture Today," in *Irish Theological Quarterly* 62 (2–3), 1996–97, 110.

24. Thomas Aquinas, *Summa Theologica*, I. QI, 9 in James J. Megivern, *Bible Interpretation* in the Official Catholic Teachings series (Wilmington, NC: Consortium Books, 1978), 170.

25. Gerhard Ebeling, *Luther: An Introduction to His Thought* (Philadelphia: Fortress Press, 1970), 107.

26. Quoted in Robert M. Grant with David Tracy, *A Short History of the Interpretation of the Bible*, 2nd ed. (Philadelphia: Fortress Press, 1984), 94.

27. Brown, *An Introduction to the New Testament*, 48.

28. Edgar V. McKnight, *What Is Form Criticism?* (Philadelphia: Fortress Press, 1969), 18.

29. Joachim Jeremias, *Rediscovering the Parables* (New York: Charles Scribner's Sons, 1966), 10.

30. Ibid., 16.

31. *Gospel Parallels*, 4th ed., Burton H. Throckmorton, Jr, ed. (Nashville: Thomas Nelson, 1979).

32. Luke Timothy Johnson, *The Gospel of Luke*, vol. 3 in the Sacra Pagina series, ed. Daniel J. Harrington (Collegeville, MN: Liturgical Press, 1991), p. 71.

33. I am using the version of the Gettysburg Address found on the Library of Congress website at http://www.loc.gov/exhibits/gadd/4403.html.

3

THE CHRISTIAN TRADITION

In the opening chapter, we identified two essential elements in Christian theology: scripture and tradition. In the previous chapter we examined the various writings in the Old and New Testaments, the historical development of the canon, and the various approaches to interpreting the Bible in both the premodern and modern eras. In this chapter we turn our attention to an overview of the Christian tradition. Obviously there is an enormous body of information that could be discussed, but the two goals in this chapter are very modest.

First, we will acquaint ourselves with some of the leading thinkers and significant events in the ancient or patristic period (AD 50–800), the medieval period (800–1500), the Protestant and Catholic Reformations (1500–1700), and the modern age (1700 to the twentieth century).

Second, we will develop a general historical framework for understanding contemporary theological debates. For example, we cannot understand contemporary discussions regarding the Roman Catholic understanding of the Eucharist without knowing about the Council of Trent in the sixteenth century, the Bread of Life discourse in John's Gospel, and the philosophical terminology employed by Aristotle.

With these two goals in mind, we begin our survey of the Christian tradition.

The Ancient Church

Early Christianity began as a movement within Judaism in the eastern portion of the Roman Empire. It was in relation to these two realities—Judaism and the Roman Empire—that early Christianity forged its own identity, advancing claims that put it at odds with both parties. The friction between Christianity and Judaism can be detected in some of the earliest canonical writings in the New Testament. (For example, Paul's Letter to the Galatians says: "And we have come to believe in Christ Jesus, so that we might be justified by faith in Christ, and not by doing works of the law, because no one will be justified by the works of the law" (2:16). The fact that Nero used the Christians as a scapegoat for the fire in Rome in AD 64 indicates that Christians were both sufficiently well-known and despised in the capital city by that time. Out of this uneasy relationship with mainline Judaism on the one hand, and with the wider Roman Empire on the other, the early Christian movement formulated its distinctive beliefs, moral codes, and liturgical celebrations.

JUDAISM AND EARLY CHRISTIANITY

The Judaism of first century Palestine was filled with diverse groups committed to ways of life that they believed best fulfilled the covenant relationship they enjoyed with God. Although these groups differed in significant ways, they shared a deep unifying sense of being members of a covenant with God. Covenants were agreements, or pacts, that bound two parties in a mutual relationship of fidelity. Israel's covenant relationship with Yahweh—"I will take you as my people, and I will be your God" (Exod 6:7a)—lay at the heart of Jewish thought and practice. The Old Testament covenants differed in form and content. For example, at various times God promised Abraham land, a son, and numerous descendants. On some occasions, God merely stated the promise; at other times, God instructed Abraham to perform some ritual (e.g., Gen 15 reflects the ancient covenant practice of splitting animals in two and having each party walk between the pieces to ratify the pact). The most famous covenant took place at Mt. Sinai and included the giving of the Ten Commandments (Exod 20), as well as various dietary laws, feast days, and instructions regarding the construction of the "ark" in which the tablets of the Law were to be placed. Later in the history of Israel, the prophets would chastise the people for failing to abide by the covenant's demands by worshipping foreign gods and neglecting the poor. The prophet Jeremiah spoke of a future time when the Lord would make a "new covenant" that would be written on the hearts of all the people (Jer 31:31–34).

The covenant stories reflected the various situations in which Israelites lived: as migrating seminomads, as an independent nation with one central Temple, or as a people living in exile after their Temple had been destroyed. This notion of covenant, in whatever form it appears, conveyed a sense of both the unique relationship between Israel and God, and the corresponding demands that accompanied such a privileged position.

In first-century Palestine, various groups within the larger body of Judaism developed distinctive views of what a faithful response to the covenant required. Four groups were especially noteworthy for our understanding the rise of early Christianity: the Sadducees, the Pharisees, the Essenes, and the Zealots.

The Sadducees were an aristocratic group that controlled the Temple. They appear in the Gospels in a dispute with Jesus regarding the idea of the resurrection of the dead (see Mark 12:18–27). Accepting only what is explicitly stated in Torah as authoritative, the Sadducees rejected the belief that the dead would be raised. The base of the Sadducees' authority was the Temple—the magnificent structure in Jerusalem that was built by Solomon (ca. 950 BC), destroyed by the Babylonians (587 BC), rebuilt by the Jews during the era of Persian control of Palestine (ca. 520 BC), and later destroyed by the Romans (70 AD). The Temple was the very house of God on earth, the only true sanctuary in which observant Jews could present the prescribed offerings to a priest for sacrifice to God. It was at the Temple that once a year on the feast of Yom Kippur the high priest entered into the Holy of Holies, which was the inner most part of the Temple, to offer sacrifice for the sins of the people.

The Pharisees or rabbis figured prominently in the Gospels. They were often involved in disputes with Jesus over matters such as the payment of taxes to Caesar, or work on the Sabbath. The commandment to keep holy the Sabbath was central to covenant obedience. It left unanswered, however, which specific actions could be permitted and which couldn't. Was cooking a meal a violation of the command to rest on the Sabbath? Was purchasing a gift permissible? Was binding the wound of a neighbor acceptable? While many such debates may seem trivial, the Pharisees saw the

Law as a divine gift that should be faithfully observed. They also wanted to apply the Law to the changing social situations in which the Jews lived. The Pharisees especially sought to interpret biblical laws that were originally written for an agrarian society in ways that would be meaningful to urban Jews.

The Essenes were the only one of the four groups not mentioned in the New Testament. The Essenes were a desert community who regarded the line of Temple leaders presiding at the time as illegitimate. In response they established an ascetic community at Qumran on the shore of the Dead Sea. In 1947 a shepherd boy threw a rock into a cave and heard something break. Upon further investigation, he discovered that the noise came from the shattering of a clay vessel containing a scroll—one of many such works that we call the Dead Sea Scrolls. The boy had made one of the greatest biblical archaeological discoveries of all time. This Essene library has provided scholars with a treasure trove of ancient manuscripts: a scroll of Isaiah that predates any previously known copy by nine hundred years, an Essene commentary on the prophetic book of Habakkuk, and a "Manual of Discipline" that contains the rules and regulations of life at the Qumran community.[1]

The Zealots took their name from their "zeal" for the Law. They were revolutionaries who plotted the violent overthrow of the Romans who occupied Palestine in the first century AD. Inspired by their Maccabean ancestors who had successfully overthrown Greek domination of Jerusalem centuries earlier, the Zealots instigated the Jewish revolt against Rome in 66 AD that resulted in the Roman forces, led by Titus, burning down the Temple in 70 AD. The Western Wall in Jerusalem is the last remaining portion of the Temple complex standing today.

THE DEBATE OVER CIRCUMCISION

One of the earliest and most decisive points of contention between early Christianity and Judaism was the status of the Old Testament Law for those who believed that Jesus is the Messiah. Was the Law still in effect? Had Jesus established a new covenant that rendered earlier covenants obsolete? Were Christians obligated to keep the dietary laws in Torah, or celebrate Passover?

This raised the very practical question: Were male Gentile (i.e., non-Jewish) converts required to be circumcised? The issue centered on God's command to Abraham: "This is my covenant, which you shall keep, between me and you and your offspring after you: Every male among you shall be circumcised. You shall circumcise the flesh of your foreskins, and it shall be a sign of the covenant between me and you. Throughout your generations every male among you shall be circumcised when he is eight days old..." (Gen 17:10–12a). For mainline Jews, this passage clearly settled the issue. Since there was obviously only one God, the God speaking here was the same God whom Christians worship, and so the language of the covenant was clear: the command to circumcise was eternal ("throughout your generations"). To reject the practice of circumcision amounted to nothing less than a rejection of the fundamental covenant relationship between God and Israel.

On the other side of the debate were Christians (especially missionaries to Gentile communities) who believed that faith in Christ brought the Holy Spirit, the obvious sign of God's favor upon the people. Circumcision was, therefore, not required of Gentile converts. Although Paul was the leading advocate of this position in the New Testament, the author of Acts credited Peter with the breakthrough argument. In Acts 10 Peter had a vision in which a blanket descended from heaven and on it were all the creatures of the earth. God instructed Peter to eat all of them, and Peter adamantly refused because some animals were unclean and therefore not to be eaten according to Jewish law (see Lev 11). This bizarre vision confused Peter, but as he awoke he was greeted by men sent by Cornelius—a centurion stationed in the city of Caesarea who was a "God-fearer"; that is, a Gentile who was attracted to Jewish ethics and belief, but who did not wish to observe the dietary laws or undergo circumcision. Peter accompanied the men to Cornelius's house, where he announced, "I truly understand that God shows no partiality, but in every nation anyone who fears him and does what is right is acceptable to him" (10:34). Then the decisive moment came. "While Peter was still speaking, the Holy Spirit fell upon all who heard the word. The circumcised believers were astounded that the gift of the Holy

Spirit has been poured out even on the Gentiles..." (10:44–45a). Cornelius received baptism, setting the stage for the showdown that would occur at the council of Jerusalem.

The debate, between those who demanded circumcision of male Gentile converts and those who did not, needed to be resolved, so the leading representatives of the early Christian movement met in Jerusalem around the year 49 AD (see Acts 15). Peter delivered a message of support for the mission to the Gentiles without the requirement of circumcision; Paul and Barnabas then recounted their success in missionary efforts among the Gentiles; and finally, James, the leader of the church at Jerusalem, ruled that Gentiles are "to abstain only from things polluted by idols and from fornication and from whatever has been strangled and from blood" (15:20), but that circumcision would not be a condition for baptism. This decision encouraged Paul and other like-minded missionaries to bring the Gospel to the ends of the earth. This decision, however, increased the distance between the early Christian movement and Judaism.

THE JEWISH REVOLT AND THE COUNCIL OF JAMNIA

The unsuccessful Jewish revolt against the Romans in 66 AD changed not only the leadership structure of Judaism, but in the wake of the Temple's destruction, created an environment in which subversive ideas were not tolerated. With the destruction of the Temple, the Sadducees lost their power base. In the same campaign, the Romans leveled the Qumran community. Following the revolt, the Zealots lost much of their influence, but their numbers were not completely eliminated, and in 132 AD they attempted another unsuccessful rebellion against Rome. The Pharisees assumed leadership of post–70 AD Judaism, and gathered in the city of Jamnia (also called Javneh) to deliberate the future course of Judaism. They ruled on questions of canon and the interpretation of scripture, and eventually composed what is called the "Twelfth Benediction," to be read in synagogues. In his study on John's Gospel, the scripture scholar J. Louis Martyn recorded the following translation:

For the apostates let there be no hope
And let the arrogant government
be speedily uprooted in our days.
Let the Nazarenes [Christians] and the Minim
[heretics] be destroyed in a moment
And let them be blotted out of the Book of Life and not be
inscribed together with the righteous.
Blessed art thou, O Lord, who humblest the proud.[2]

Although the origin and implementation of this curse is a matter of scholarly debate, verses in John's Gospel (9:22, 16:2) and the entire twenty-third chapter of Matthew's Gospel seem to reflect Christian bitterness at being expelled from the synagogue.

CHRISTIANITY IN THE ROMAN EMPIRE

In addition to Judaism, the second essential element in the rise of the early church was the wider social and political world of the Roman Empire. Because of the unity and stability of the Roman Empire in the first and second centuries AD (traditionally called the *Pax Romana*), early Christian missionaries could travel freely from the deserts of Syria to the mountains of Spain. Along the network of Jewish synagogues that had been established throughout the Mediterranean world, the roadways of the Roman Empire provided the means for the convenient spread of the Gospel. These advantages, however, should not mask the fundamental opposition that existed between the Christian and Roman worldviews.

The Romans viewed the successes or failures of the Empire in terms of the pleasure or displeasure of the gods and goddesses who watched over them. Roman citizens had a civic duty to demonstrate the appropriate reverence to the gods and goddesses through sacrificial offerings and acts of piety. The appeasement of the heavenly overseers ensured military victory, economic prosperity, fertility of the soil, and avoidance of plagues. Disrespect to the gods and goddesses invited calamity. In other words, there was in the ancient world no separation of church and state: the affairs of state, the health of the economy, and the practice of religion were seamlessly joined.

The Roman authorities recognized that Jews could not participate in the worship of foreign gods, and soon after their conquest of Palestine, the Romans recognized Judaism as a licit religion *(religio licita)* within the Empire. This designation allowed the Jews within the Roman Empire to freely practice their religion, and exempted them from the duty to offer sacrifice to the Roman deities. As long as early Christians were seen as part of Judaism, they enjoyed this legal protection. Over time, however, as Christians began to separate from the main body of Judaism, they no longer were exempt from the obligation to offer sacrifice to the Roman gods and goddesses. It is for this reason that some scholars believe that one of the goals of Luke's Gospel is to make a case to the Roman authorities for the extension of the licit-religion status to Christianity. According to the scripture scholar Joseph Fitzmyer, SJ, in Luke and Acts we discover "Luke's concern to show that Christianity, rooted in Israel by the birth of its founder to Jewish parents and by the mark of the covenant (circumcision; cf. Gen. 17:11), has as much right to recognition as *religio licita*, a lawful religion, in the Roman Empire as Judaism itself."[3]

Without the legal protection accorded a licit religion, the early Christians were placed in a literal life-or-death struggle between the expectations of Roman authorities and adherence to the central tenets of their faith. Christians simply could not worship the Roman deities. Because of the inseparable joining of religion and politics, such religious defiance, if left unpunished, would have disastrous political, economic, and military effects. In the eyes of the Romans, the Christians were committing treason—they were undermining the welfare of the state. As both retribution for that crime and deterrent to others who might be contemplating joining their movement, Christians were dealt the worst kinds of punishment imaginable: they were covered in tar and set ablaze as outdoor lighting at Nero's banquets; they battled wild animals for the purpose of public amusement; and, like Jesus himself, they suffered the slow agonizing death of crucifixion. These martyrs who suffered unimaginable pain and gruesome deaths, who endured to the end without renouncing the faith, were praised by their contemporaries and hailed as the ideal Christians of their age. Other Christians would gather at the martyrs' graves on the anniversary of their death, and celebrate their birth into eternal life, a custom that will impact later beliefs on the afterlife and the practice of collecting relics.

The Roman persecutions were at first sporadic, but grew in scope and intensity as time went by. In the early second century (ca. 112), a Roman governor named Pliny wrote a letter to the Emperor Trajan in which he recounted his procedure for interrogating Christians and asked Trajan if his procedure was sound.[4] In their work on the social world of early Christianity, John E. Stambaugh and David L. Balch wrote,

> In his correspondence with the emperor Trajan (Letters 10.96) [Pliny] expresses a great deal of confusion as to what constitutes the crime: simply confessing the name of Christ, or the attendant subversive actions of refusing to offer incense to the emperor's image, or the various immoral actions that were being alleged against the Christian in his province of Bithynia. This shows that there was no specific legislation forbidding Christianity, but that judges all over the empire dealt with Christians on a largely individual basis. It also helps explain why the persecution of Christians was not continuous but happened only sporadically, at specific times and places.[5]

Then in AD 202, the Emperor Septimus Severus outlawed conversion to Christianity. Fifty years later, the Emperor Decius issued an edict around the year 250 that required all Roman citizens to offer sacrifice to the gods and to obtain a certificate attesting to that fact. The edicts of the Emperor Diocletian in 303–4, initiated what, in the opinion of many scholars, was the severest persecution Christians experienced under any emperor.[6]

Interestingly, this incremental rise in the Roman persecution of Christians had what statisticians call a counter-intuitive result. One might reasonably predict that the increased threat of harsh punishment and execution might reduce the number of Christians, and significantly lower the rate at which people converted to Christianity. However, the persecutions produced the opposite effect: the number of Christians continued to rise from one-half million in the first century, to two million in the second century, and five million, or twenty percent of the entire population of the Roman Empire, in the third century.[7] At the time of Diocletian's persecution, very few Roman citizens could have expected the complete reversal of the imperial policy toward Christians that would occur a decade later.

CONSTANTINE AND HIS IMPACT ON THE CHURCH

Christians living in Nicomedia, a city south of the Black Sea, who were born around 275, would have witnessed changes in the relationship of church and state that would have been simply unimaginable for any previous generation of Christians. In 303, they would have stood in horror as Diocletian's army leveled their cathedral. This catastrophe was followed the next day by an edict "declaring that all churches were to be destroyed, all Bibles and liturgical books surrendered, sacred vessels confiscated, and all meetings for worship forbidden."[8] Twenty years later, however, these same Christians from Nicomedia might have stood on the streets of the nearby city of Nicaea as the Roman Emperor entered the city to preside over a meeting of the bishops of the Christian church. That Emperor was Constantine, and it was he who was directly responsible for the one-hundred-and-eighty-degree turn in the imperial stance towards Christianity.

Constantine's gradual consolidation of power began in 306 when his troops acclaimed him emperor following the death of his father. Constantine secured political control of the Western Roman Empire in 312 when he led his troops into battle against his rival Maxentius at the Milvian Bridge just outside of Rome. According to Christian tradition, the night before this battle Constantine had a vision or dream in which he saw the cross, or the Chi-Rho, the ancient symbol of Christ that overlaps the first two letters of the word *Christ* in Greek (p and x). During this vision or dream, Constantine heard, "In this sign, you shall conquer." The next day Constantine commanded his soldiers to place that symbol on their shields and banners. His troops defeated Maxentius' forces, and Maxentius himself drowned in the Tiber River, sinking to the bottom under the weight of his armor. Constantine, who had formerly worshipped the sun god, now supported the movement that proclaimed Jesus to be the Son of God. In the following year, Constantine and Licinius, the Emperor of the Eastern Roman Empire, issued the Edict of Milan, which granted toleration toward all religions in the Roman Empire. In 324 Constantine defeated Licinius, and ruled as Emperor of both the Eastern and Western Roman Empire until his death in 337.

Constantine's influence on the church was immediate and profound, and the benefits numerous: churches were rebuilt, public buildings called basilicas were donated to Christians for use as churches, the construction of new pagan temples was halted, clergy were exempted from taxation, Sunday was recognized as a holy day, and the church was now able to legally own property.

In addition, three key shifts in the life of the church can be directly attributed to Constantine's actions as emperor. First, in 330 Constantine transferred his imperial court from Rome to Byzantium, which he renamed Constantinople. While the Eastern Roman Empire prospered economically and flourished culturally, the Western Empire languished. As the economic and military might of the West declined, the vulnerability to attack from neighboring territories increased. In 476 the last Roman Emperor in the West was deposed. The political void that was created needed to be filled, and the most obvious candidate in the West was the pope. The papacy became intimately involved in both religious and political governance, or in more traditional language, of both "spiritual and temporal affairs." Pope Gregory the Great (reigned from 590 to 604) was respected as much for the wisdom of his pastoral teachings as the diplomatic skill he displayed in his negotiations with the Lombards who threatened to attack Rome.

Second, Constantine learned, much to his dismay, that the Christian church of his time was divided on the question of Christ's divinity. He therefore ordered the bishops of the church to convene a council in the city of Nicaea for the purpose of settling the issue once and for all. This Council of Nicaea in 325, which we will discuss at greater length in the Christology chapter, marked the first time the bishops of the church had gathered as a single body. Local councils had been held before this time to discuss matters of local importance, but Nicaea was the first "ecumenical council." The question of what weight should be given the rulings of ecumenical councils would be a source of contention between Roman Catholics and the Orthodox, and later between Roman Catholics and Protestants.

Third, after Constantine the age of the martyrs in the Roman Empire had ceased. The martyrs had been revered by generations of Christians who believed that their willingness to die for Christ represented the embodiment of faithful Christian discipleship. After Constantine, a new model of the "ideal Christian" emerged: the monk. Beginning in Egypt, Christians began to live a solitary life in the desert. There they did battle with their own demons, and those who emerged victorious were hailed as triumphant spiritual warriors. Later, communities of men and woman dedicated to living "the common life" formed. In the Western tradition, this development reached its most enduring expression in the Rule, or regulations of a religious community, of St. Benedict (ca. 480–ca. 550). As the Western Roman Empire descended into what is commonly known as the Dark Ages, following the collapse of Charlemagne's empire, the Benedictine monasteries preserved the flickers of scholarship in Western world. We will return to Benedict and his vision of the Christian way of life in our discussion of Christian spirituality.

Constantine's legacy has been, and continues to be, a source of scholarly debate. Should he be praised as the one who ended the senseless persecution of Christians and allowed Christian ideals to influence all facets of life in the Western world, or should he be blamed for creating a highly politicized church? Each side could point to the certain features of the medieval church to support its contentions, and it is to that chapter in church history that we now turn.

The Medieval Church

In this section we will survey the vast changes in church life from the time of Charlemagne to the eve of the Protestant Reformation (800–1500). First, we will follow the tug-of-war between church leaders in Rome and Constantinople that erupted in mutual excommunication in 1054. Second, we examine the impact of Islam on the church in both the West and the East. Third, we will recount the papacy's engagement with the political leaders at various levels of western society, including the emperor, king, and local feudal lords. Finally, we will look at some of the reform movements in the medieval church. This will set the stage for our discussion of the Protestant Reformation.

ROME AND CONSTANTINOPLE

In the early medieval period, the fault line between Rome and Constantinople finally gave way, creating the first major breach within the Christian church. The beginnings of this division go back to the time of Constantine's move from Rome to Constantinople. The rise of Islam, which we will discuss shortly, exacerbated the situation by conquering three of the ancient world's five patriarchates. Patriarchates are the "autonomous, self-governing federation[s] of dioceses under the jurisdiction of a chief bishop, called 'patriarch,' and his synod."[9] The three that were conquered were Antioch, Alexandria, and Jerusalem, leaving only Constantinople and Rome. The final break came in 1054, when in an act of mutual excommunication, the Christian church was divided in two: the Orthodox, or Eastern, church centered around the patriarch of Constantinople, and the Roman Catholic, or Western, church under the authority of the patriarch of Rome. But let's back up to some of the key issues that led to the final break.

One of the first theological-political disputes to pit East against West occurred in the eighth century when the Emperor Leo III ordered the destruction of the huge icon (or image) above the gates of the imperial palace at Constantinople.[10] Leo thus initiated what has become known as the iconoclast controversy. Literally "image breakers," the iconoclasts rejected the use of images (i.e., icons, statues, and crucifixes) in Christian churches. For the iconoclasts, such artwork violated the First Commandment's prohibition against graven images and idolatry. Their opponents, the iconodules (those who defend the veneration of images) argued that such images were useful visual aids for the faithful and, in essence, were gateways to the divine, not divinity itself. Their use, therefore, was entirely appropriate. The political dimension of this seemingly purely theological debate occurred in 729, when, according to R. W. Southern, "the Greek emperor sent Pope Gregory II a mandate forbidding him to place pictures of martyrs and saints in the churches under his jurisdiction. It was an unwise move. The pope was already at loggerheads with the emperor over the payment of taxes, and the mandate raised the controversy from the sordid level of political disobedience, where the pope's legal position was weak, to the more elevated one of orthodoxy where he was strong."[11] The iconoclast position was officially denounced at the Second Council of Nicaea in 787—the last of the ecumenical councils to be recognized by both the Orthodox and the Roman Catholic churches.

The second great theological-political controversy involved the insertion of the *filioque* clause into the creed that was composed at the council of Nicaea (325) and the council of Constantinople (381). The creed stated that the Holy Spirit proceeds "from the Father." In time, however, a custom developed in the West that added to the creed the word *filioque*, meaning, "and the Son." Charlemagne pushed Pope Leo III to accept the additional word, but the pope found that to be unwise. Later popes, however, accepted the addition. The Eastern church resented the Western change. The original creed at Constantinople in 381 did not contain the expression, and officials in the East thought that it was presumptuous of the West to introduce such a change without the consent of all the church's bishops.

In many ways, the filioque debate brought to the fore the central complaint of the Eastern church; namely, the persistent claim by the patriarch of Rome to possess authority over all other bishops in the church. Constantinople believed that authority resided in ecumenical councils, not in the office of a single bishop, even the bishop of Rome. This clash of wills between leaders in the West and the East escalated, resulting in each church suppressing doctrines and practices supported by the opposite side. In 1054, Pope Leo IX dispatched a delegation to Michael Celarius, patriarch of Constantinople; the delegation was led by a strong-willed cardinal named Humbert. In his final act before leaving Constantinople, Humbert entered the grand cathedral known then as Sancta Sophia and placed a bull of excommunication on the altar. Despite attempts at reconciliation (most notably at the council of Florence in the mid-fifteenth century) and the mutual lifting of the bans of excommunication in 1965, this unfortunate division persists to the present day.

THE RISE OF ISLAM

Muhammad, the founder of Islam, died in 632. In the decades immediately following his death, Islam spread rapidly: Muslim forces took Damascus in 635, Jerusalem in 638, Alexandria in 642, and Carthage in 695.[12] In 711, after moving across the northern coast of Africa, Muslim armies landed in Spain, then drove into modern-day France where they were repelled by the forces of Charles Martel at the Battle of Tours in 732.

In the East, in 1071, Muslim forces had dealt the Byzantine forces a decisive blow, leaving Constantinople vulnerable to attack. In 1081 Alexius Comnenus took the throne in Constantinople. Relations with the pope in Rome soured, but in 1088, a new pope, Urban II, made a concerted effort to improve the relationship. In 1095, Alexius appealed to Urban for military assistance in battling the Turks. Alexius himself could not have predicted Urban's response.

In November of 1095, Pope Urban II addressed the council of Clermont and called for Christians to take up arms to aid the forces at Constantinople and to liberate the Holy Lands. The pope set August, 1096, as the date of departure. Some groups, most notably the one led by Peter the Hermit, set out before that date, averaging eighteen miles a day on their journey to Constantinople.[13] Other groups of crusaders followed—the total number of crusaders on the first campaign reached approximately 40,000[14]—arriving at Constantinople at various times. After setting out from Constantinople, the crusaders captured the city of Nicaea, and then after an arduous struggle took Antioch. By the summer of that year the crusaders reached the fortified city of Jerusalem. After constructing the necessary siege equipment, the crusaders launched their assault, and on July 15, 1099, took the city.

Over the next two hundred years, the political control of Jerusalem passed back and forth between Christians and Muslims. Crusades were intermittently launched until the thirteenth century.

In 1204 crusaders sacked the city of Constantinople, adding another bitter episode in the Western church's relationship with its Eastern counterpart.

CHURCH AND STATE

Perhaps the most dramatic transformation of the papacy between 800 and 1500 was the increased role it played in the affairs of state. While the beginnings of this trend date back to the time of Constantine, the events following the disintegration of the Western Roman Empire in the fifth century accelerated this process. Even before the last Western emperor was deposed in 476, the popes had begun to assume many of the duties traditionally assumed by political leaders. Pope Leo the Great (d. 461) had negotiated with Attila the Hun to spare Rome and, of greater lasting importance, had asserted, as no pontiff had done before, papal primacy among the bishops. Pope Gregory the Great (d. 604) financed the relief efforts that brought food to the starving citizens of Rome, and entered into a peace treaty on behalf of the city of Rome with the Lombards who had captured northern Italy. The fear of a Lombard invasion prompted Pope Stephen II (d. 757) to cross the Alps and declare Pepin king of the Franks in exchange for his commitment to defend Rome against Lombard invasion. The future of the Western church was placed in the hands of warrior-kings rather than emperors in the East. Pepin defeated the Lombards, and on the basis of a document known as "The Donation of Constantine" (purported to be from the Emperor Constantine, but later determined to be a forgery), Pepin granted the lands in central Italy called the Papal States to the pope. Pope Leo III crowned Pepin's son Charlemagne "Emperor of the Romans" on Christmas in the year 800. This scene captured the medieval belief in "Christendom"—a social arrangement in which the church and state were joined in partnership to achieve their political, social, and religious ends.[15]

After the death of Charlemagne, his kingdom quickly crumbled, and so did any realistic hope for Christendom. As Viking invaders swept into Western Europe, land and power were divided, reducing Charlemagne's vast unified empire to a set of much smaller independent regions controlled by local lords. In this fragmented world, life continued. The basic human needs still had to be met: crops had to be grown, homes had to be built, and loved ones had to be protected against attack. Feudalism provided a workable system for achieving these goals. Feudal life was based on mutual obligations of the lord and the vassals. The lord provided the land on which the vassals could grow crops, keep flocks and herds of animals, and raise their families; the vassal vowed allegiance to the lord, supplied the lord with a percentage of the produce of the land, and fought in the lord's army. This decentralization of political life undercut the ability of the papacy to craft or enforce policy governing the many churches throughout the Western world.

The social and economic situation of Western Europe began to change in the eleventh century. As the historian Carl A. Volz noted in his study of the medieval church, "The period from 1050 to 1130 has been called 'one of the great turning points in European history,' a period of enormous commercial expansion, the rise of urban communities, and the first expression of a truly middle class."[16] As larger cities began to dot the European landscape in the thirteenth century, a new form of religious order took shape. Francis of Assisi and Dominic of Guzman established two new mendicant orders, meaning that they relied upon begging for all or some of their income. While the Benedictine monasteries often stood on large tracts of lands and housed monks cloistered from the world, the Franciscans and Dominicans lived in urban areas where they preached and lived the gospel message of poverty and simplicity.

The twelfth and thirteenth centuries saw an increasing number of people of various social ranks appealing to the papal court for legal decisions. This participation in legal affairs increased the pope's control of affairs in the local churches. As the historian R. W. Southern observed, "There is one fact which more than any other sums up this period of papal history: every notable pope from 1159 to 1303 was a lawyer."[17]

The most politically astute of the popes of the era was Innocent III (1160–1216), who skillfully wielded the power of interdict, the halting of all sacraments in a given geographical region. When King Philip II of France persuaded a group of French bishops to annul his marriage so that he could marry the daughter of a Bavarian duke, the queen appealed his case to Innocent III, who ruled in her favor. Philip balked, and in 1199 Innocent III put France under interdict until Philip returned to his wife the following year. In 1208 England was placed under interdict when King John did not accept the election of Stephen Langton as archbishop of Canterbury. Once again, the pope emerged victorious when John acquiesced.

Boniface VIII (ca. 1235–1303), the last of the lawyer-popes, clashed with Philip IV of France, who was taxing the French clergy—an action Boniface insisted required his permission. This battle did not end favorably for the pope. After Philip outlawed the export of funds from France, thereby depriving the papacy of much-needed revenue from the French church, Boniface conceded. Philip and Boniface locked horns once more when Philip charged a papal representative with treason. Boniface responded in 1302 by issuing *Unam Sanctam*, which the church historian Williston Walker calls "the high-water mark of papal claims to supreme jurisdictional authority over civil powers."[18] Boniface was fighting not only Philip IV, but the rise of powerful nation-states that presented a far more powerful challenge to the papacy.

In the fourteenth, fifteenth, and sixteenth centuries, strong monarchies developed in France and England, a rivalry that ignited the Hundred Years' War. The marriage of Ferdinand and Isabella in 1469 solidified Spain's monarchy. In Italy, the situation was much different. There was no nation of Italy; rather, it was a conglomeration of city-states. The city-state of Florence, the center of international banking, was home to the powerful Medici family. The Medicis and other powerful families provided patronage to the Renaissance artists, but their deep influence also extended into papal elections. The result was some of the most worldly papacies in the history of the church (e.g., Innocent VIII, Alexander VI).

REFORM MOVEMENTS

The social structure of feudalism presented the church with a serious problem that threatened its independence from local lords throughout Europe. The practice that provoked this serious crisis was known as lay investiture, which referred to the practice of laypersons (lords, kings, dukes, etc.) selecting bishops, abbots, and high-ranking officers in the church; presiding at their installations; and conferring upon them the symbols (e.g., a bishop's crozier and ring) of their office. Regional authority resided solely with the feudal lords, and the local clergy were assumed to be under their jurisdiction. The lords often donated the land and funds for the construction of a church or monastery. It was therefore, in their eyes, fitting that they should choose the person charged with the care of that community.

The second problem that often accompanied the practice of lay investiture was simony: the buying and selling of church offices. Church lands were a source of income: tithes were paid to the church, fees were charged for religious services (e.g., baptisms, marriages), and endowments were created by wealthy patrons. High-ranking church offices provided a comfortable existence; consequently, members of the nobility bestowed them on their children. Like trust funds, these offices provided financial stability and an annual return that ensured that nobles' children would be kept in a lifestyle to which they had become accustomed.

As an early counteroffensive to the appointment of abbots by persons outside the monastery, a group of reform-minded Benedictine monks founded a new monastery at Cluny in Burgundy, France, in 910. Not only did they dedicate themselves to a strict observance of Benedict's Rule, they also insisted that the abbot be elected by the monks. No outside secular authority could choose the abbot, and the monastery was placed under the control of the pope to ensure its independence from local rulers. This model of organization quickly grew in popularity, from three hundred monasteries in 1100 to fifteen hundred in 1200.[19]

The problem of lay investiture was resolved in 1122 when Pope Callistus II and the Emperor Henry V signed the Concordat of Worms (Worms is a city in Germany). Emperors, it was decided, could be present at the election of bishops and abbots, but could not select the bishop or abbot themselves. In addition, only representatives of the church, could present the ring and crosier, the symbols of their spiritual authority, to newly elected bishops.

The fiercest combatant in the church's battle against lay investiture and simony was Pope Gregory VII (pope from

1073–85), and his actions had consequences that we feel today. Gregory's strategy was to shift the balance of power away from local and regional rulers, and toward Rome. Gregory VII believed that a strong centralized papacy would serve as a mechanism for church reform, freeing the church from interference. Later thinkers questioned the wisdom of this idea. Was it possible for the pope to have too much authority? Was it not theologically preferable and politically prudent to place authority in the hands of ecumenical councils rather than individual popes? This issue had earlier surfaced in the controversies between the Roman Catholics and the Orthodox; now it was an "in-house" debate among Catholic theologians regarding conciliarism, a movement that "held that a universal council, not the pope, was the church's highest authority and therefore could depose popes, proclaim doctrine, and legislate reforms."[20]

This issue took on great urgency when in 1309, under pressure from the French king, Pope Clement V moved the papal court to Avignon in southern France, where it remained until 1377. The situation turned utterly chaotic in 1378. Urban VI was declared pope, but four months later, twelve of the sixteen cardinals who elected him pope claimed that they had been threatened by the mobs in Rome. The cardinals announced that the election of Urban VI was invalid. In his place, they chose Clement VII, who promptly returned to Avignon. Thus began the Great Schism, that period in church history from 1348–1417 in which two rivals (and then three), one in Rome and one in Avignon, claimed to be the true pope. While the confusion was finally resolved at the Council of Constance (1414–18), the credibility of the papacy suffered.[21]

By the early sixteenth century, a general discontent with traditional theology pervaded. The great humanist Erasmus of Rotterdam (1466–1536) had contempt for the theologians of his day. He believed that they were concerned with abstract and insignificant details of theology rather than the formulation of creative expressions of the faith. He wanted Christians to live their faith authentically, not talk about it academically. Erasmus greatly admired the writings of the classical Greek and Latin writers, and he worked extensively on reconstructing the best possible Greek and Latin version of the New Testament. Erasmus believed the church of his day needed to be reformed, but he remained a member of the Catholic Church. Other contemporaries of Erasmus who shared his zeal for reform would pursue a different course of action.

Protestant and Catholic Reformations

In this section, we will deal with the Reformation, both Protestant and Catholic, that took place between 1500 and 1700. The Protestant Reformation consisted of four main branches: the Lutheran, the Calvinist or Reformed, the English Reformation, and the Radical Reformation. The Catholic, or Counter, Reformation saw the rise of new religious orders, and the convening of the council of Trent. The decrees of the Council of Trent delineated the doctrinal differences between the Catholic and Protestant churches.

LUTHER'S THEOLOGY

Luther's theological positions were shaped by three fundamental theological convictions. The first was "justification by faith alone." The apostle Paul dealt with the issue in his epistles, especially in the Letters to the Romans and the Galatians, two works on which Luther lectured at Wittenberg in 1515–17. Paul borrowed the term *justification* from the legal courts, where it meant a person was acquitted of the charge, and used it to describe the saving effect of Christ's death on the cross. Christ justified us by his death; we cannot become justified before God through any effort on our part. "For we hold that a person is justified by faith apart from works prescribed by the law" (Rom 3:28). This message was for Luther both personally meaningful and theologically decisive.

Luther's second theological principle was *sola scriptura* ("scripture alone"). Scripture alone possessed the authority to govern Christian belief and practice, not the pope, bishops, or ecumenical councils. Scripture judged us; we did not judge scripture. A corollary to this principle was that scripture's meaning was sufficiently plain for the average reader to comprehend. Individuals were therefore encouraged to read and study their Bibles.

The third tenet of Luther's theology was the "priesthood of all believers." Luther rejected the church or the priest as a *mediator* between God and humanity. All Christians shared in the priesthood of Christ and stood individually before God. Not only did this lead, as one would expect, to Luther's eventual rejection of penance as a sacrament, it also opened up the ministry to all members of the church, regardless of gender or marital status.

NINETY-FIVE THESES

Luther rose to prominence in 1517 when he posted his Ninety-Five Theses on the church door at Wittenberg. In the Theses, Luther attacked the sale of indulgences. An aggressive campaign to sell indulgences—spearheaded by a highly effective spokesman, Johann Tetzel—had recently begun in Germany. When Luther learned of Tetzel's preaching, he composed his Ninety-Five Theses, and invited any willing disputants to engage him in public debate on the subject of indulgences.

The practice of selling indulgences emerged out of a set of interrelated beliefs about the afterlife, the church, and the Christian life. The starting point was the urgent question of how to gain admittance to heaven after death. In the parable of the final judgement (Matt 25), Jesus taught that at the end of time all the nations of the world would be assembled before him and divided into two groups: those granted eternal life, and those condemned to eternal punishment. The former group received eternal life because they fed the hungry, gave drink to the thirsty, welcomed the stranger, clothed the naked, cared for the sick, and visited the imprisoned. Heavenly reward was granted to those who lived Christian lives on earth, and Christianity involved doing good deeds for one's neighbors.

If going to heaven required that Christ's disciples do works of charity, cultivate heroic virtue, and pray earnestly, then some exemplary Christians (e.g., the apostles, martyrs, and saints) must be enjoying that reward at the present moment. John's vision in Revelation seemed to confirm this, as he saw "a great multitude...robed in white." As the vision continued, an elder informed him that "These are they who have come out of the great ordeal; they have washed their robes and made them white in the blood of the Lamb" (Rev 7:9, 14). Most Christians interpreted this to mean that the martyrs were enjoying their heavenly reward for their faithfulness to God. The church, therefore, consisted not only of those on earth, but also those who were already with God in heaven.

Most Christians, however, did not attain the level of holiness of the martyrs and saints. However, their sinfulness was not severe enough to warrant hell. Therefore, at the death of these individuals, they entered neither heaven nor hell, but rather experienced a final cleansing of the soul in a state known as purgatory. The belief in purgatory fit with the practice of praying for the dead. If the dead were already in heaven, it was argued, there would be no reason to pray for them (see 2 Macc 12).

This brings us to the question of helping those in purgatory. Could the abundance of goodness (called the "Treasury of Merit") accumulated by the saints and martyrs be somehow applied to those in purgatory? If the church does indeed consist of those on earth and in heaven, it would seem that such an act of charity would be appropriate. The church, therefore, began to apply the merits of the saints to those on earth or in purgatory. A stipend was often attached to this practice, as Tetzel's memorable sales pitch attested: "As soon as the coin into the box rings, a soul from purgatory to heaven springs."[22] It was this belief that Luther attacked in his Ninety-Five Theses.

THE AFTERMATH OF THE NINETY-FIVE THESES

Events moved quickly after the Ninety-Five Theses. Luther was soon summoned to appear in Rome, but the local prince, Frederick of Saxony, insisted that he should remain in Germany. In 1518, Luther met with Cardinal Cajetan in the city of Augsburg, who demanded that Luther retract his statements. In 1519, Luther entered into public debate with a leading Catholic theologian of the day, Johann Eck. In the course of that debate, Luther affirmed the supreme authority of scripture, and rejected both papal authority and the binding force of decisions rendered by ecumenical councils. By the end of 1520 Luther was excommunicated. One last attempt at a resolution took place in 1521 when the emperor

Charles V presided at the Diet (i.e., a meeting) of Worms. In one of the most famous scenes in medieval Christian history, when Luther is asked to recant, he responded: "Unless I am proved wrong by Scriptures or by evident reason, then I am a prisoner in conscience to the Word of God. I cannot retract and I will not retract. To go against the conscience is neither safe nor right. God help me. Amen."[23] Tradition has added the memorable line: "Here I stand, I can do no other." The official statement of Lutheran theology appeared in 1530 when Charles V asked the Protestants to present a statement of their views. Philip Melanchthon, Luther's associate, authored the work, known as the Augsburg Confession. By his death in 1546, Luther had produced a massive body of writings, including translations of both the Old and New Testaments into German, volumes of theological treatises, biblical commentaries, sermons, and hymns.

JOHN CALVIN

In the Swiss cantons, or districts, a second wing of Protestantism known as Reformed Theology developed under the influence of Ulrich Zwingli (1484–1531) and John Calvin (1509–64). Calvin was to become the more famous of the two. Though he was born in France, Calvin gained international prominence through his work in Geneva where, after an earlier exile, he returned in 1541 to put into practice the ideas he presented in his magisterial work *Institutes of the Christian Religion* (first edition, 1536). In the *Institutes* Calvin spoke of "the order by which the Lord willed his church to be governed" (IV.3.1). Calvin believed that a specific church structure could be gleaned from the pages of the New Testament, and he sought to reinstitute this original system of church governance in Geneva. Calvin's church government consisted of four types of leaders: pastors, teachers, elders, and deacons.[24] Calvin also envisioned a Christian society in which a church body, known as the Consistory, would discipline erring Christians. The town council, if necessary, would enforce their rulings. The merits and drawbacks of Calvin's experiment in Geneva continue to be the source of much debate.

THE ENGLISH REFORMATION

The third branch of the Protestant Reformation began when King Henry VIII of England sought to have his marriage to Catherine of Aragon annulled to allow him to marry Anne Boleyn. Henry and Catherine's marriage created a political bond between England and Spain. It was Catherine's second such political-matrimonial bond. She had earlier been married to Henry's brother Arthur, who died within the first year of their marriage. Henry's own marriage to Catherine produced no male heir, as his two sons with her both died in early childhood. Desirous of a male heir to succeed him, Henry requested that Pope Clement VII annul his marriage to Catherine. Clement faced a difficult theological and political decision. The annulment would in effect declare that Pope Julius II's original dispensation, which allowed Henry to marry his brother's widow, was illegitimate and possibly infuriate Catherine's powerful family—her parents were Ferdinand and Isabella of Spain, and her uncle was Emperor Charles V. When the pope refused to grant the annulment, Henry declared himself head of the Church of England. Parliament approved the Supremacy Act in 1534, officially severing ties between England and the Roman Catholic Church.

There was political and religious turmoil in the decade following Henry VIII's death in 1547. Henry's only living son, Edward, born to Henry and Jane Seymour, succeeded his father, yet was only nine years old at the time. Thomas Cranmer, the Archbishop of Canterbury since 1532, directed church affairs. Edward's short reign ended with his death in 1553. He was succeeded by Mary Tudor, the daughter of Henry and Catherine of Aragon, who attempted to return the Church of England to Catholic control. Known as Bloody Mary, she persecuted religious dissidents, among them Thomas Cranmer, who was burned at the stake in 1556. At Mary's death, Elizabeth I, daughter of Henry VIII and Anne Boleyn, took the throne in 1558, and during her forty-five years, she steered a middle way between Calvinism and Catholicism. In 1563, the Thirty-nine Articles were published, listing the doctrine held by the Church of England. The Church of England retained the office of bishop, accepted the Nicene Creed, and in some quarters (the so-called "high church" Anglicanism) preserved a liturgy quite similar to the Catholic Mass, but the new church rejected the office of the papacy and the requirement of priestly celibacy.

Two subsequent developments in English history are significant for American religious history. First, many of those Protestants who fled England during the reign of Bloody Mary returned after Elizabeth's accession to the throne, only to be disappointed by the pace and degree of reform. Believing the church needed to be purified of many unscriptural features, a group known as the Puritans turned their eye toward the American colonies, where they hoped to create the type of church and state they longed for in England. Second, in the eighteenth century, a movement began to "revive"—that is, revitalize—the Church of England. Led by John and Charles Wesley, this revival movement relied upon passionate preaching and lively hymns—two enduring features of Methodism. The Methodists began in 1784 when they officially separated from the Church of England, and today it is one of the largest Protestant denominations in the United States, with over eight million members.[25]

THE RADICAL REFORMATION

The fourth branch of the Protestant Reformation consisted of a number of groups comprising the Radical Reformation. The leading group was the Anabaptists—those who rejected the practice of infant baptism on the basis that the person being baptized needed to make a conscious and informed profession of faith and commitment to living the Christian life. Those who were baptized as infants, therefore, needed to be rebaptized (Anabaptist means "re-baptizer"). The Baptist denomination today continues the practice of adult baptism, or "believer's baptism." The Radical Reformers generally preferred to create separate communities, with the goal of approximating the life of the early Christian community as closely as possible. They did not regard themselves bound by allegiance to secular leaders, so they were often persecuted by both Catholic and fellow Protestant authorities.

The movement suffered a serious credibility crisis when a series of apocalyptic leaders in the city of Münster, Germany, chief among them John of Leiden, believed that they had established the New Jerusalem mentioned in the Book of Revelation. The Catholic bishop was expelled, and he later recruited an army to recapture the city. While Münster was under siege, Leiden promoted polygamy, eliminated private property, and mandated that all inhabitants of Münster be baptized. The city fell in 1535 and the inhabitants were slaughtered. The bodies of three leaders, including that of Leiden, were placed in iron cages and hung in public display from St. Lambert's church.

Following the Münster disaster, the Anabaptist movement took a new direction under the leadership of Menno Simons. As the historian John Roth explained,

> Out of the ashes of Münster, a new Anabaptist group emerged, led by Menno Simons (1496–1565), a Catholic priest turned radical reformer. Menno restored stability to a group in which some had broken loose from their theological moorings. His leadership sought to balance the eschatological impulses of a persecuted sect with the model of a disciplined, visible church ruled by the authority of Scripture.[26]

Menno Simons' group became the Mennonites, one of the "peace churches" who have as a distinctive mark of their theology and way of life an absolute commitment to nonviolence. In America, Mennonite communities were first established in Pennsylvania, and a strong Mennonite and Amish presence remains to the present day in Lancaster County, Pennsylvania.

One of the most significant pacifist Christian bodies developed in England under the influence of George Fox (1624–91). Known officially as the Society of Friends, the early Quakers spoke of each person having an "Inner Light" or "Light of Christ." From this simple idea, a number of implications followed. First, the Quaker worship service, known as a meeting, consisted of an assembly of believers waiting in silence for the Inner Light to move someone to speak. If the Light prompted someone to stand and speak, the person simply stood and addressed the group. There was no need of any external actions; for example, sacraments, readings, hymns, or sermons. The convener would end the meeting when he or she sensed that everyone who was going to speak had done so. Second, because all humans have the Inner Light, violence against another human being—either by slavery or by participation in war—was condemned. Because they would not take up arms, the Quakers were widely persecuted by political authorities. In the United States, William Penn, himself a Quaker, provided safe haven for Friends in what is now Pennsylvania.

THE COUNTER REFORMATION

The cluster of Catholic activities aimed at countering the theological claims of the Protestant Reformers, and generating reform within the Roman Catholic Church, comprised what most people today refer to as the Counter Reformation, or the Catholic Reformation. The Council of Trent stood as the pivotal event within this larger reform movement. The Council of Trent stretched from 1545 to 1563, and consisted of three convocations that included twenty-five sessions.[27] In terms of theological opposition to the Protestant Reformation, the bishops reaffirmed the binding authority of both scripture and tradition (including the statements of ecumenical councils) over against Luther's principle of *sola scriptura*. The council fathers also insisted on the necessity of both faith and good works as integral to salvation. Salvation required faith, hope, and love, not just faith. The bishops asserted the authority of the Vulgate version of the Bible in terms of both content (i.e., canon) and translation. The bishops also rejected individual interpretation of scripture, insisting instead that the church was entrusted with the task of determining legitimate and illegitimate interpretations. Lastly, the number of true sacraments was fixed at seven.

In terms of internal reform, the bishops themselves assumed much of the responsibility. Bishops needed to live in their dioceses and hold only one ecclesiastical position. They also promised to establish seminaries so that candidates for the priesthood could be theologically prepared, pastorally effective, and spiritually grounded. New religious orders were founded. The Society of Jesus, or the Jesuits, was founded by Ignatius of Loyola (1491–1556). The Jesuits contributed enormously to the task of building and staffing large numbers of Catholic educational institutions. St. Philip Neri (1515–95) founded the Oratorians, whose mission was to improve the quality of seminary education and priestly spiritual formation. St. Vincent de Paul (1580–1660) founded the Vincentians, and cofounded the Daughters of Charity with Louise de Marillac, to feed and educate the poor, and improve the spiritual life of local parishes.

The decrees of Trent were in large part a response to the charges advanced by the Protestant Reformers. In the next phase of church history, the church would face a new set of challenges, yet ones equally important for understanding the shape of contemporary Roman Catholicism.

The Modern Age

When telling the story of the past, historians explain how to best understand a series of events. This typically involves making causal connections among various occurrences, and assigning greater significance to certain historical moments and figures than others from that time period. After all these are considered, historians, theologians, and thinkers across the humanities offer an evaluation of that history. Did a particular series of events generate positive or negative consequences? Did various world leaders make the right or wrong decisions? Were social movements that began centuries ago indications of social progress or symptoms of social decay? This dynamic of historical judgment and present evaluation is perhaps no more clearly displayed than in the contemporary perspectives on the church's engagement with "the modern world," or modernity. For example, in his survey of church history, Thomas Bokenkotter commented:

> The Catholic Church's reaction to the rise of modernity was largely defensive and negative. It was often unable to meet the free thinkers on their own grounds and frequently resorted simply to condemnation of their ideas and forceful repression. The result was a divorce of secular culture from the Church and the state of siege mentality that characterized modern Catholicism down to our day.[28]

By contrast, traditionalists would agree more with the assessment offered by Fr. Robert J. Fox:

> A spirit of liberalism with little respect for authority, which holds that man has no responsibility except to satisfy every human desire, continues to prevail in the world today. The Church continues to battle against these false theories which arose from the Renaissance and the Protestant Revolt. Liberalism holds that man's mind is greater than any other power. God himself is ignored.[29]

According to Bokenkotter, the history of the Catholic Church in the modern age is one marked by constant retreats from legitimate intellectual, theological, or ethical challenges. According to Fox, the church has wisely resisted the temptations and errors that have plagued Western thought for the past several centuries. We will keep open the question of whether the former or the latter perspective sheds the most light on our own current moment in the history of the church.

SCIENTIFIC DEVELOPMENTS

Advances in physics and higher mathematics in the seventeenth and eighteenth centuries shaped the modern worldview. Galileo Galilei (1564–1642), Johannes Kepler (1629–95), and Isaac Newton (1642–1727) unlocked the mysteries of planetary motion. Earth was no longer regarded as the center of the universe, and the ancient assumption that the planets followed a circular orbit was also disproved. Problems that had vexed physicists for centuries— for example, "Why do falling bodies accelerate as they moved toward Earth?"—were solved. More amazing still, physicists and astronomers discovered that bodies within the solar system operated according to certain principles that could be expressed in fairly short mathematical equations. The working model of the universe became that of a machine: God created the universe; put laws in place to regulate the smooth, orderly functioning of that universe, including moral laws for the conduct of humanity; and then stepped back and did not "interfere" with Creation. This understanding of

God, the world, and the relationship between the two constituted a system of belief known as deism.

The strongly rationalistic bent of deism prompted two contrasting responses. First, many thinkers followed the tenets of deism to what they regarded as their natural conclusions. In deism, God played no active role in the world. With the rise of modern atheism in the nineteenth century, thinkers such as Ludwig Feuerbach (1804–72), Karl Marx (1818–83), and Friedrich Nietzsche (1844–1900) dismissed altogether the need for God. Others thinkers took a different route. Friedrich Schleiermacher (1768–1834), the father of liberal Protestant theology, questioned the deistic emphasis on reason. Romanticism, in both its literary and philosophical forms, emphasized the emotional and spiritual depths of human experience. Theologians such as Schleiermacher who were influenced by Romanticism, exalted religious experience and placed it at the center of their theology. In Catholic theology, Blaise Pascal (1623–62) had earlier spoken of the essential role of the heart in life in general, and religion in particular. Pascal eloquently expressed that sentiment in his classic line, "The heart has its reasons, which reason does not know."[30]

POLITICAL DEVELOPMENTS

Developments in the political arena also challenged the church. In France, for example, a movement known as Gallicanism asserted the priority and independence of the French (i.e., Gallican) church from papal control. In 1682, during the reign of Louis XIV, the assembly of the French clergy issued the "Four Articles." The Articles prohibited the pope from interfering in affairs of state, asserted that ecumenical councils had greater authority than individual popes, insisted that the pope had to recognize the accepted laws of the French church, and required the pope to have his decisions ratified by an ecumenical council.[31] Not all French Catholics supported the Articles. Known as ultramontanes (literally meaning "over the mountains," i.e., over the Alps into Italy), these thinkers stressed the centrality and primacy of the pope as the head of the entire Catholic church. They also saw the wisdom in having a political counterbalance to edicts of local rulers.

France was also the site of the most significant political event in the life of the church in the eighteenth century. The French Revolution demolished not only the power of the French monarchy, but also the privileged status of Catholicism as the state religion. In France's prerevolutionary ancien régime (the old regime), society was comprised of three classes or Estates. The First Estate consisted of the clergy, the Second Estate was the nobility, and the Third Estate included citizens from a wide range of socioeconomic backgrounds. The Third Estate numbered about twenty-seven million people, or 98 percent of the entire population.[32] The church provided schools, orphanages, and hospitals, but it also owned 10 percent of the land and paid no taxes. Faced with an economic crisis, a severe shortage of food, and political unrest, Louis XVI convened a meeting of the Estates-General (the French equivalent of the Parliament), a move that had not been taken since 1614.[33] The Estates formed a National Assembly, members of which stormed the Bastille Prison, a symbol of the king's power, on July 14, 1789. In 1790 the Assembly confiscated church lands, issued the Civil Constitution of the Clergy, and required all clergy to take an oath of allegiance to the Constitution.

The final decade of eighteenth-century French history was a violent one: Louis XIV was beheaded on January 21, 1793, and during the Reign of Terror (September, 1793, to July, 1794), French leaders used repressive measures in their unsuccessful attempt to replace Catholicism with the "Cult of Reason." In 1799, a young, popular general named Napoleon Bonaparte became First consul of France. In 1802 he entered into a concordat, or treaty, with the pope, restoring some of the pope's authority in the French church, but in 1804 when Pope Pius VII came to Notre Dame Cathedral to crown him emperor, Napoleon took the crown from the pope's hands and placed it on his own head. This moment stood in sharp contrast to the coronation that occurred roughly a thousand years earlier when Pope Leo III crowned Charlemagne as king of the Franks. Napoleon expected political cooperation from the pope. When Pius VII would not agree to Napoleon's demands in 1808, the French general ordered his troops to arrest the pope. Pius VII remained a prisoner of Napoleon for the next six years. He was released only after Napoleon returned from his disastrous campaign in Russia.

The nineteenth century was not particularly kind to the papacy: political revolutions swept across Europe in 1848; Marx's atheistic philosophy gained popularity; Darwin published his work regarding the theory of evolution; and closer to home, the church lost the Papal States, the remaining lands controlled by the pope. Located in the central portion of modern-day Italy, the Papal States presented a geographical obstacle for unification of that country. In addition, the church faced rapid technological change, which produced profound social change, some of those changes for the better, some for the worse. Most had the potential to go in either direction. For example, the harnessing of electricity as a power source, the development of the steam engine, and the expansion of railroads altered life in the Western world in both positive and negative ways. Louis Pasteur (1822–1905) and other researchers improved our knowledge of bacterial infections and disease prevention. Breakthroughs were made in the field of communications: the telegraph, the telephone, and the radio all appeared in the the nineteenth century.

VATICAN I AND VATICAN II

The history of the nineteenth and twentieth centuries of church history can be drawn by comparing the last two ecumenical councils, Vatican I and Vatican II. Roughly one hundred years divided them, and two major world wars occurred in the span of time between them. The councils provided us with a cache of documents reflecting the issues and concerns of their respective eras. The items on the agenda, the deliberations that took place, and the resolution of those debates reflected the church's self-understanding and sense of its mission in the modern world.

Pope Pius IX convened the First Vatican Council in 1869, but it was interrupted by the outbreak of the Franco-Prussian War in 1870. By that time, the bishops had passed one significant item on the agenda: papal infallibility. Seen purely from a political perspective, it was an unabashed assertion of papal authority in a world that had challenged that authority in several ways. As the French troops who had been protecting Rome moved out of the city, Italian forces favoring national unification moved in. The final resolution of this crisis came in 1929 with the signing of the Lateran Treaty. The church was compensated for the lands it lost, in exchange for its recognition of the Italian State, and an independent Vatican City was established.

In the Second Vatican Council (1962–65), the bishops sounded a different note in their decrees and declarations regarding the church's role in the modern world. There was a greater openness to lay participation both in the life of the church and in causes of justice and peace in the secular arena. The ecumenical movement strove to unite separated Christian groups and to recognize the wisdom and truth of other world religions. Vatican II will be discussed as well in far greater depth in the chapter dealing with the church, but it was undoubtedly the most significant event in twentieth-century Roman Catholic history.

Vatican II was convened by Pope John XXIII, who died after the first session of the council in 1963. He was succeeded by Pope Paul VI, who reconvened that council and saw it to its conclusion in 1965. Pope Paul VI died in August 1978, and was succeeded by a man who made the novel gesture of taking the names of the two previous popes. John Paul I, however, died suddenly about a month into his reign. The dominant figure in post–Vatican II church history was then elected. Continuing his predecessor's act of paying homage to the two popes of Vatican II, Karol Wojtyla of Poland—the first pope from Poland and the first non-Italian pope since the sixteenth century—took the name John Paul II. His endearing personality and firm stands made him both a figure admired around the world, a powerful force in Eastern European politics, and an often controversial leader whose stances have been both vigorously defended and attacked by those within the church.

Discussion Questions

1. Should Christians still be obligated to celebrate Passover or obey Old Testament dietary law? What implications follow from your answer for the relationship between Judaism and Christianity?

2. Could the martyrs have accomplished more if they lied to the Romans and continued to spread Christianity?
3. Was the joining of religious and political power under Constantine a positive or a negative development for the church?
4. Is the use of icons a violation of scripture?
5. Was Luther right about the priority of the Bible over the pope?
6. Is the Quaker meeting the best form of Christian worship?
7. Who offered a better account of the Christian faith: the Reformers or the bishops at Trent? Why?
8. Is the understanding of God in deism acceptable or unacceptable? Why?
9. How did Vatican I and Vatican II differ in their stance toward "the modern world?" Which stance do you believe is better?

Suggested Readings

For a single volume introduction to church history, see Justo L. Gonzalez, *The Story of Christianity* (Peabody, MA: Prince Press, 1999), and Catherine A. Cory and David T. Landry, editors, *The Christian Theological Tradition* (Upper Saddle River, NJ: Prentice Hall, 2000). For a helpful multivolume series, see *The Pelican History of the Church*, edited by Owen Chadwick (New York: Penguin Books). Also helpful is the two-volume series *How to Read Church History* by Jean Comby (New York: Crossroad, 1985 and 1989). These two volumes by Comby also contain short excerpts from primary sources. Christopher M. Bellitto's *The General Councils* (Mahwah, NJ: Paulist Press, 2002) is a very helpful survey of the ecumenical councils. *Pilgrim Church* by William J. Bausch (Mystic, CT: Twenty-Third Publications, 1981) is a very readable introduction to church history.

Notes

1. See Stephen Harris, *The New Testament*, 2nd. ed. (Mountain View, CA: Mayfield Publishing Co.,1995), 52–56, and Bart D. Ehrman, *The New Testament*, 2nd ed. (New York: Oxford University Press, 2000), 218–21.

2. J. Louis Martyn, *History and Theology in the Fourth Gospel*, rev. ed. (Nashville: Abingdon, 1979), 58.

3. Joseph Fitzmyer, *The Gospel According to Luke I–IX* (Garden City, NY: Doubleday, 1981), 10.

4. Pliny's Letter to Trajan can be found in *Documents of the Christian Church*, 2nd ed., H. Bettenson, ed. (New York: Oxford University Press, 1963), 3–4.

5. John E. Stambaugh and David L. Balch, *The New Testament in Its Social Environment* (Philadelphia: Westminster Press, 1986), 33.

6. Robert Lee Williams, "Persecution," in *Encyclopedia of Early Christianity*, 2nd ed., Everett Ferguson, ed. (New York: Garland Publishing, 1997), 895–900.

7. Alfred Lapple, *The Catholic Church: A Brief History* (Mahwah, NJ: Paulist Press, 1982), 10; and J. Derek Holmes and Bernard E. Bickers, *A Short History of the Catholic Church* (Mahwah, NJ: Paulist Press, 1983), 31.

8. Henry Chadwick, *The Early Church* (New York: Dorset Press, 1967), 121.

9. "Patriarchate," in Richard P. McBrien, The *HarperCollins Encyclopedia of Catholicism* (San Francisco: HarperCollins, 1995), 966.

10. Holmes and Bickers, 53.

11. R. W. Southern, *Western Society and the Church in the Middle Ages* (New York: Penguin Books, 1970), 58–59.

12. See William A. Young, *The World's Religions* (Englewood Cliffs, NJ: Prentice-Hall, 1995), 357–58; and Justo Gonzalez, *The Story of Christianity*, vol. 1 (Peabody, MA: Hendrickson Publishers, 1999), 249 for key dates in Islamic history.

13. Tim Severin, "Retracing the First Crusade," in *National Geographic* 176, no. 3 (1989): 341.

14. See Thomas F. Madden, *A Concise History of the Crusades* (Lanham, MD: Rowman and Littlefield, 1999), 12.

15. For a very readable account of these developments, see Joseph H. Lynch, *The Medieval Church: A Brief History* (New York: Longman, 1992), esp. chapter ten.

16. Carl A. Volz, *The Medieval Church* (Nashville: Abingdon Press, 1997), 73.

17. Southern, 131–32.

18. Williston Walker et al., *A History of the Christian Church*, 4th ed. (New York: Charles Scribner's Sons, 1985), 371.

19. Christopher M. Bellitto, *Renewing Christianity* (Mahwah, NJ: Paulist Press, 2001), 72.

20. Ibid., 108–9.

21. Walker, 372–76.

22. Carter Lindberg, *European Reformations* (Cambridge, MA: Blackwell, 1996), 75.

23. Quoted in Owen Chadwick, *The Reformation* (New York: Penguin Books, 1972), 56.

24. Eric G. Jay, *The Church* (Atlanta: John Knox Press, 1978), 174.

25. *Yearbook of American and Canadian Churches 2002*, Eileen Lindner, ed. (Nashville: Abingdon Press, 2002), 359. This figure represents the entire membership of the United Methodist Church.

26. John D. Roth, "The Mennonites' Dirty Little Secret," in *Christianity Today* 40, no. 2 (October 7, 1996): 45.

27. R. Emmet McLaughlin, "Trent, Council of," in Richard P. McBrien, ed., *The HarperCollins Encyclopedia of Catholicism* (San Francisco: HarperCollins, 1995), 1267.

28. Thomas Bokenkotter, *A Concise History of the Catholic Church* (Garden City, NY: Doubleday, 1977), 239–40.

29. Robert J. Fox, *The Catholic Faith* (Huntington, IN: Our Sunday Visitor, 1983), 145.

30. Blaise Pascal, *Pensees* (New York: E. P. Dutton, 1958), 78.

31. Gerald R. Cragg, *The Church and the Age of Reason 1648–1789* (New York: Penguin Books, 1970), 24.

32. Elisabeth Gaynor Ellis and Anthony Esler, *World History* (Upper Saddle River, NJ: Prentice Hall, 2003), 469.

33. Ross J. S. Hoffman, Gaetano L. Vincitorio, and Morrison V. Swift, *Man and His History* (Garden City, NY: Doubleday, 1958), 447.

4

MYSTERY, FAITH, AND REVELATION

Before moving into our next topic, we need to pause and recap some of the main ideas we have explored up to this point. In the first chapter we outlined the general framework in which theologians approach their work. They draw upon scripture and tradition, yet relate those to the current situation. Because different weight is given to these elements, a number of approaches have developed in contemporary theology (e.g., traditionalist, liberal, and radical theology). In the second chapter, we devoted our attention to scripture. We reviewed the content of the canon, and the various methods of biblical interpretation. In the third chapter we focused on tradition and outlined some of the leading thinkers and events that impacted the history of the church. In this chapter, we will concentrate on the role that the current situation plays in theology. In the first section of this chapter we will deal with the perennial questions and concerns that figure prominently in theological debates (mystery, faith), as well as the issues that seem to occupy the thinking of contemporary theologians (pluralism). In the second section, we will apply some of the major themes in both scripture and tradition to the concepts of mystery, faith, and revelation.

Our Current Situation

While it is true that theologians of every era share a common set of concerns, there are particular issues, questions, or emphases that figure more prominently in one era than in others. For example, the proper interpretation of scripture, the question of Jesus' identity, and the nature of God are unavoidable questions for theologians of any era. However, after World War II and the horrors of the Holocaust, the Christian church honestly confronted the issue

103

of Christian anti-Semitism to a degree that it had not done at any prior time in its history. The current situation to which theologians address their work, therefore, includes some things old, some things new. We begin by looking at an example of each.

A continuous problem for theologians arises from the obvious fact that theology is unlike, for example, geology. In theology, the object of our investigation is immaterial, an eternal Being who "dwells in unapproachable light" (1 Tim 6:16). In geology, the object of our investigation is material, a created substance that can be collected, measured, and analyzed. Consequently, certain theological questions naturally present themselves, which have no counterpart in geology. How do we know which theological position is correct? What degree of truth can be accorded theological statements? How are disputes in theology to be resolved? While these questions certainly have taken different forms throughout the course of Christian thought, they are nonetheless present whenever two theological positions collide. The early church's battle with Gnosticism, the final eleventh-century rupture between the Orthodox and the Roman Catholics, the Protestant Reformation of the sixteenth century, and the rise of feminist theology in the twentieth century all in one way or another returned to the foundational questions regarding the discovery and demonstration of truthful statements in theology.

In addition to the perennial questions tackled by theologians, each time period has its own particular challenges. Peter L. Berger, a leading sociologist of religion, has offered the following thesis: "It is my position that modernity has plunged religion into a very specific crisis, characterized by secularity, to be sure, but characterized more importantly by pluralism."[1] Secularity refers to cultural ways of understanding the world without reference to God. Berger asserts that with the rise of modern science, large numbers of people began to interpret in a nonreligious fashion the events that took place in the world.

Berger, however, does not regard secularity as the leading challenge to religious belief in the modern age. Pluralism, which elsewhere Berger defined as "the coexistence and social interaction of people with very different beliefs, values and lifestyles,"[2] is a far more dangerous opponent. The existence of multiple and often conflicting systems of belief within a single culture poses a constant, often unspoken, challenge to theological, ethical, or philosophical truth-claims. How can we be sure that our deepest convictions about ourselves, humanity, and the world are true? More importantly, how can we be certain that those who reject our beliefs are wrong? Berger offered the following account of the current situation.

> Throughout most of history human beings have lived in situations in which there was general consensus on the nature of reality and on the norms by which one should lead one's life. This consensus was almost everywhere grounded in religion and it was taken for granted. The pluralistic situation necessarily changes this, for reasons that are not at all mysterious. They have to do with the basic fact that we are social beings and that our view of reality is shaped by socialization, first in childhood and later in the relationships of adult life. Where socialization processes are uniform, this view of reality is held with a high degree of taken-for-granted certainty. Pluralism ensures that socialization processes are *not* uniform and consequently, that the view of reality is much less firmly held.
>
> Put differently, certainty is now much harder to come by. People may still hold the same beliefs and values that were held by their predecessors in more uniform situations, but they will hold them in a different manner: what before was given through the accident of birth now becomes a matter of *choice*. Pluralism brings on an era of many choices and, by the same token, an era of uncertainty.[3]

Pluralism generates a nagging sense that in this life we will never know with any degree of certainty that our beliefs are true. If Berger's analysis is accurate, then the current situation that theologians address is an era of uncertainty.

The challenges of pluralism plague not only religious believers and theologians, but also literary critics, political theorists, and economists, to name but a few. For example, are there better and worse interpretations of Shakespeare? The literary critic Frederick Crews fears that the integrity of literary criticism is presently being undermined by his colleagues in the field who "argue that meaning is conferred not by authors but by readers, and that a work's meaning is therefore constantly subject to change. If that position is accepted, meaning ceases to be a stable object of inquiry and one interpretation is as lacking in persuasiveness as any other. The inevitable corollary is that debates among critics are entirely point-less."[4] How can disputes over the proper interpretation of Shakespeare's works be settled? Is there some kind of evidence that can be marshaled that would convince the participants in the debate that one interpretation is preferable to another?

Pluralism calls into question the reliability and truthfulness of our beliefs. When coupled with the absence of universally shared rules for resolving debates, this uncertainty erodes the belief that there is a right answer in matters of theology, ethics, or politics. The situation turns then from *pluralism* (a diversity of beliefs exists) to *relativism* (no belief is any truer than another). If there are no moral truths, then we cannot condemn state-sanctioned genocide, terrorism, or human-rights violations as immoral acts. While the implications of relativism are widely recognized to be horrifying, constructing a decisive rebuttal to the problem of relativism has proven challenging.

For example, consider the question of whether a law is just. At one time in the history of the United States, slavery was legal, and a significant proportion of the population did not regard the institution of slavery as unjust. This raises a number of fundamental questions about justice. Does justice exist as an eternally true concept, which some human laws more closely approximate than others, or is justice a culturally agreed-upon set of social conventions? If justice is a concept that exists apart from human manipulation, then it can function as a standard by which all legal systems are measured. Yet how do we gain accurate information about the concept of justice? If we, however, go the route of saying that justice means nothing more than what a given society accepts as permissible, then we cannot offer any substantive criticism of groups who torture political prisoners or target innocent populations.

Mystery

Given the nonphysical nature of the realities that theologians have sought to describe, and the ambiguities and uncertainties that arise in the course of theological debates, it is no wonder that the category of "mystery" has figured so prominently in the history of Christian thought. However, the meaning of mystery and the role it has played in theological works have varied, and continue to vary in contemporary theology. The very use of the word *mystery* illustrates the differences among the three theological approaches that were outlined in chapter one.

In the traditionalist school of thought, mystery or mysteries generally refer to aspects of Christian belief that are simply unknowable through the use of human reason. They are truths revealed by God (see Eph 1:9). In his *Fundamentals of Catholicism*, Kenneth Baker noted the following traditional distinction:

> Catholic theology distinguishes between relative and absolute mysteries of faith. A mystery is something "hidden" in the sense that we cannot understand it. A "relative" mystery is one that we human beings, in our present state, cannot understand but will be able to understand in our glorified state in heaven when we enjoy the face-to-face vision of God. An example of a relative mystery would be Jesus' raising Lazarus from the dead (John 11).
>
> An "absolute" mystery of faith is something the reality of which cannot be known before its revelation and the inner possibility of which cannot be positively be proved even after it has been revealed by God. There are three absolute mysteries of our Christian faith: the Holy Trinity, the Incarnation and divine grace.[5]

Traditionalist theologians, whether Catholic, Orthodox, or Protestant, continually emphasize the point that the mysteries of the faith are truths made known by divine revelation, not human investigation. Our awareness of the mysteries depends on God's initiative, not our own. Lesslie Newbigin, a Protestant scholar involved in missionary work, has offered a cautionary note that complements Baker's traditionalist Catholic approach.

> The liberal mind is at its best in challenging us to be open to new truth, to be fearless in exploring all reality, and to be humble in recognizing the vastness and mystery that we try to comprehend with our finite minds. But even the language about the greatness and the unfathomable depths of the mystery of God can be the cloak for a calamitous error. The error is the supposition that it is we who are the explorers, that the real questions are the ones we formulate and put to the universe, and that our minds have a sovereign freedom to explore a reality waiting to be discovered. Our peril is that, out of the vastness of the unplumbed mystery, we summon up images that are the creations of our own minds. The human heart, as Calvin said, is a factory of idols.[6]

In short, traditionalist theologians contend that Christianity is mysterious because God is mysterious. God's "secret and hidden" (1 Cor 2:7) wisdom, however, has been made known to us, and in faith we praise God for that revelation.

This traditionalist understanding of mystery has implications for how theology should be done. The general tenor of traditionalist theology is one of reverence and awe, as "faith adoring the mystery."[7] Theology calls for prayerful reflection more than critical analysis. Evagrius Ponticus (ca. 345–99), one of the early church's desert fathers, once wrote, "For knowledge of God, one needs not a debater's soul, but a seer's soul."[8] In the surrender of our intellect and will to these mysteries of the faith, we can enter into the mysteries and experience of their transformative power. Traditionalists, as we discussed in the first chapter, understand theology to consist of faithful transmission of revealed truths. "Hold to the standard of sound teaching that you have heard from me, in the faith and the love that are in Christ Jesus. Guard the good treasure entrusted to you, with the help of the Holy Spirit living in us" (2 Tim 1:13–14). Like deacons in the early church, theologians are charged to "hold fast to the mystery of the faith with a clear conscience" (1 Tim 3:9).

In liberal theology, mystery has a much broader meaning, encompassing a wide range of common human experience, and generally referring to those universal aspects of the human condition that demand our attention, yet have no definitive resolution. These include the deepest and most profound questions and concerns about human existence (e.g., the meaning of life, the problem of evil, the afterlife). The existentialist philosopher Gabriel Marcel distinguished between a "problem" and a "mystery." A problem is a question that I examine in a detached fashion. The resolution of the problem has little effect on my sense of purpose, or the meaning of my life. A mystery, by contrast, "is something in which I am myself involved, and which is therefore thinkable only as a sphere where the distinction between what is in me and what is before me loses its significance and its initial validity."[9] A medical researcher studying the progression of a cancer sees a problem; the person dying from the disease confronts a mystery.

Because mystery is a shared human experience, liberal theology understands theology as a conversation, a critical dialogue with other disciplines exploring the impenetrable mysteries of human life (e.g., psychology, philosophy, literature). The theologian Gordon Kaufman wrote,

> Since theology is principally concerned with what is ultimate mystery—mystery about which no one can be an *authority*, with true or certain answers to the major questions—I suggest the proper model for conceiving it is not a lecture (monologue); nor is it the text (for example, a book): it is, rather, *conversation*. We are all in this mystery together; and we need question one another, criticize one another, make suggestions to one another, help one another. Each of us is in a unique position within the mystery, a position occupied by no one else; and each of us, therefore, may have some special contribution to make to our common task of coming to terms with life's mysteries. It is imperative that the theological conversation be kept open to and inclusive of all human voices.[10]

This conversation, if it is to be a genuine give-and-take, requires that liberal theologians allow their sources (i.e., scripture and tradition) to be scrutinized and, in some cases, qualified or overridden by ideas emerging in other fields (e.g., evolution, the abolition of slavery). Liberal theologians would, however, see some "essence" or enduring message of Christianity as indispensable to the Christian proclamation of the gospel. For example, Bultmann's essay mentioned in the first chapter presented the case for demythologization, but without failing to see a core message that was timeless and relevant for Christians of every era in church history.

Radicals contend that the appeal to mystery is often a disguised attempt to legitimate the positions of those in power. Those seeking social change would regard the traditionalists' invocation of "the mysterious will of God" as nothing more than a power play. In her work *Beyond God the Father*, for example, Mary Daly wrote,

> The biblical and popular image of God as a great patriarch in heaven, rewarding and punishing according to his mysterious and seemingly arbitrary will, has dominated the imagination of millions over thousands of years. The symbol of the Father God, spawned in the human imagination and sustained as plausible by patriarchy, has in turn rendered service to this type of society by making its mechanisms for the oppression of women appear right and fitting. If God in "his" heaven is a father ruling "his" people, then it is in the "nature of things" and according to divine plan and the order of the universe that society be male-dominated.[11]

According to Daly, the mysterious and arbitrary will of God is nothing more than the cloak that covers the true intent of such claims: the continued oppression of women. The task of the radical theologian, therefore, is to tear away that cloak and expose the naked truth of patriarchy.

This brief review of three understandings of mystery in contemporary theology has brought us back full circle to a consideration of the current situation. Given the theological options before us, which approach should we take? The concept of mystery calls us, finally, to consider the question of faith. The Christian life calls for faith, but faith must be properly placed. This is why the question of faith is inextricably bound to the theological category of "revelation" (literally, "unveiling"), which can be broadly understood to refer to the ways in which God communicates with humans. The call for faith must be accompanied by a theological case for its acceptance. Faith always has an object. We have faith in someone or something.

If a theological proposal is to succeed, it must coordinate the call for faith with the case for faith. Take as an image in your mind the integrated movements of trapeze artists stationed high above a circus floor. They are able to cross sides by releasing the grip on one bar, tumbling through the air, and being caught by someone swinging from the opposite direction. A mistake on either artist's part sends someone plunging into the net below. In the Christian life, faith is the human outreach to God; revelation is God's outreach to humanity. It is a graceful and grace-filled movement that is thrilling to behold, and any theological account of that event needs to synchronize the movements of both parties.

In his work *Revelation and Its Interpretation*, Aylward Shorter discussed an episode in the life of the nineteenth-century Jesuit poet Gerard Manley Hopkins.

> Hopkins was trying to describe the notion of 'mystery of faith' to his friend Robert Bridges. Such a mystery, he said, was not mysterious because it was uncertain. A mystery of faith was not 'an interesting uncertainty' but 'an incomprehensible certainty.'…The question then to be asked is: How does one become certain (in faith) of things that one cannot satisfactorily comprehend or explain?[12]

In light of our discussion of mystery, we can appreciate Shorter's question: How can we become certain (or reasonably certain) about religious matters that we admittedly cannot fully understand? The traditional response is "by having faith in God," or more specifically, "by accepting on faith what God has made known to us." We will review some of the leading events and writings in both scripture and tradition that have tackled the question of faith and the ways in which God's will has been made known to us through revelation.

Mystery, Faith, and Revelation in Scripture

In the chapter dealing with scripture, we grouped the biblical writings into ten sections. The forty-six books of the Old Testament were divided into four groups: Torah, the historical books, the wisdom books, and the prophets. The twenty-seven books of the New Testament were categorized as the Gospels, Acts, Paul's letters, Hebrews, the Catholic or General Epistles, and Revelation. We will briefly survey some of the leading events and ideas contained within the books in these various sections of scripture that are relevant to our discussion of mystery, faith, and revelation.

THE OLD TESTAMENT

The overarching framework in which the stories of Torah are told is the deep, abiding covenant relationship between God and Israel. In the stories of the patriarchs, for example, God intervened at critical moments to ensure the continued survival of a people teetering on extinction. In the dramatic and abrupt beginning of the Abraham saga, the Lord called Abraham to leave his native land and travel to a land God would show him (Gen 12). Abraham obeyed. When promised offspring, though he was old and his wife barren (Gen 15), Abraham believed. When God informed Abraham of the plan to destroy Sodom (Gen 18), Abraham haggled. And when God commanded him to do the unthinkable (Gen 22), he complied. In the story of the near-sacrifice of Isaac, Abraham embodied unquestioning faithfulness to God. This has garnered the Abraham stories much admiration, as well as a fair amount of concern, down through the centuries. His willingness to sacrifice Isaac raised the issue of the relationship between faith and reason: Could faith in God require that we act in ways that would be regarded as patently immoral—even psychotic—by the overwhelming majority of people?

In Exodus through Deuteronomy, Moses occupied the role of chief mediator between Israel and God. Like the Abraham saga, the Moses stories have contributed a number of significant scriptural passages to the theological discussion of faith and revelation. The first significant passage is the exodus from Egypt, perhaps *the* greatest display of God's concern for Israel. It was a revelation of God's commitment to the covenant. Many Old Testament scholars see in the exodus the very origin of Israel's self-identity as a people. The Old Testament scholar Bernhard W. Anderson has argued that

> Israel's history had its true beginning in a crucial histor-
> ical experience that created a self-conscious historical
> community—an event so decisive that earlier happenings
> and subsequent experiences were seen in its light.
>
> This decisive event—the great watershed of Israel's
> history—was the Exodus from Egypt. Even today the
> Jewish people understand their vocation and destiny in
> light of this revealing event which made them a people
> and became their undying memory.[13]

The biblical interpretations given to the exodus contributed to the conviction in Israelite thought that God's actions are visible in the workings of history. Both the victories and defeats of Israel became understood as revelations of God's favor or disfavor with Israel. Later, in the book of Job, this straightforward equation of holiness and success would be called into question.

The second critically important passage that involved Moses centered on the covenant at Sinai, most especially the Ten Commandments, or Decalogue (Exod 20). Here God's revelation takes the form of ethical prohibitions. The first three commandments related to Israel's relationship with God: idolatry was forbidden, the proper use of the divine name was commanded, and sabbath observance was mandated. The fourth to the tenth dealt with relations among people, and prohibited murder, adultery, theft, and so on.

The third critical passage in the Moses material was the drama of Israel's unfaithfulness, which was clearly illustrated by the golden-calf story (Exod 32), and Israel's wandering in the desert for forty years (Num 14). In both cases, a large number of Israelites wavered in their trust in the Lord's promises. These stories served as powerful reminders that faith can be lost.

The historical books cover Israel's entrance into Canaan, the period of the judges, the rise and fall of both the northern and southern kingdoms, the eventual return to Israel, and the subsequent eras of Persian and Greek rule. As we might expect, these historical events are read within the context of God's involvement in history. The question then naturally arises: Is it possible to know the future course of history? Is there some human or earthly means available that could provide a glimpse of the future? In the early historical books, we are introduced to such means. There are individual seers, or prophets (1 Sam 9:9), and "companies of prophets" who fall into a "prophetic frenzy" (1 Sam 19:20); both relay God's future plans to the people.

In the prophetic writings, God calls and commissions certain individuals to be prophets. The first prophet in chronological order among the major and minor prophets was Amos, who explained that "the Lord took me from following the flock, and the Lord said to me, 'Go, prophesy to my people Israel'" (Amos 7:15). The calling of Isaiah took the form of an amazing vision of the heavenly court and six-winged angels (Isa 6). This sense of calling resulted in the prophets' insistence that the message they were preaching came from God, not themselves. Hence, the classic beginning of a prophetic utterance became "Thus says the Lord..." and added one more means of revelation in the biblical record.

Not all revelations of God in the Old Testament involved bizarre visions or certain individuals chosen by God. In the wisdom material, we find a completely different emphasis. A wise teaching—an adage, a parable, or a riddle—has the power to illuminate human experience. All humans possess the innate ability to recognize wisdom: those who live by such teachings are wise, and those who forsake such teaching are foolish. The scribes collected and included in the canon these proverbs and other forms of sage advice because they, too, shed light on living one's life in accordance with God's will. Wisdom material is not concerned necessarily with religious matters as much as it is with ethics, etiquette, and prudence. In the words of the scripture scholar R. B. Y. Scott, its object was "understanding about how life should be lived and what it means."[14] "Better to be poor and walk in integrity than to be crooked in one's ways even though rich" (Prov 28:6). The insight generated by this proverb resonates within the human heart and imparts some of God's infinite wisdom to those willing to learn.

The psalms were another important collection of writings within the broader category of wisdom material. One particular type of psalm captured another element of the biblical tradition's understanding of revelation. The opening verse of Psalm 19 proclaims, "The heavens are telling the glory of God; / and the firmament proclaims his handiwork." The created world bears witness to the Creator. The breathtaking beauty of the world can propel the mind's ascent to God. This notion of revelation of God through nature has had its supporters and detractors down through the centuries. Some Christian thinkers have insisted that such knowledge of God is indeed attainable and quite useful as a preparation for the fullest revelation of God in Christ. Other Christian theologians have vigorously opposed this line of reasoning, insisting that any discussion of God's revelation must focus exclusively on Christ.

THE NEW TESTAMENT

Many of the same themes we have reviewed in the Old Testament continue throughout the New Testament. The obvious new feature will be the central contention of the New Testament writings that a new definitive revelation has taken place in the person of Jesus. The New Testament writings, however, differ in terms of form (e.g., gospel, letter, sermon), audience (e.g., Jewish-Christians, Gentiles), and emphasis. This diversity will help us understand more completely the New Testament's contribution to the various understandings of mystery, faith, and revelation in Christian theology.

The Gospels are sometimes called "faith documents," meaning that they were written by those who had faith in Jesus and were intended as invitations to others to share in that faith. It is not surprising, therefore, that we find the theme of faith highlighted in many of the gospel stories.

In the Gospel of Mark, a contrast is drawn between those who *should* have genuine faith, but do not, and those who by the cultural standards of the day (i.e., sinners, tax collectors, prostitutes) would probably not have faith, but actually do. For example, the disciples in Mark's Gospel—who should have had faith as Jesus' close companions—were notoriously thick-headed when it came to understanding his teachings. In Mark 4—6, for example, Jesus calmed the sea, and then calmed the fears of the disciples, asking them, "Why are you afraid? Have you still no faith?" (4:40). In the following chapter, a woman with a flow of blood who merely touched the hem of Jesus' garment was healed ("Daughter, your faith has made you well..." 5:34); and the daughter of the synagogue official named Jarius was raised from the dead after Jesus told her father, "Do not fear, only believe" (5:36). In the next story, however, Jesus returned to his hometown—a place where one might expect he would receive a warm welcome—and he was amazed at the lack of faith in him there (6:6).

One of the most memorable stories regarding faith appeared in Matthew's Gospel. After Jesus walked on water, he summoned Peter to walk on the water too. As Peter began to fear the strong wind and choppy seas, he began to sink and cried out to Jesus to save him. Jesus reached out his hand to save Peter and said, "You of little faith, why did you doubt?" (Matt 14:31). The obvious symbolism of keeping one's faith in Jesus through turbulent times has inspired Christians down through the ages.

In John's Gospel, Jesus called his disciples to have faith specifically in him as the Son of God. In the final sign (or miracle) in John's Gospel, Jesus raised Lazarus from the dead. The exchange between Jesus and Martha, the sister of Lazarus, illustrated John's understanding of faith:

> Jesus said to her, "I am the resurrection and the life. Those who believe in me, even though they die, will live, and everyone who lives and believes in me will never die. Do you believe this?" She said to him, "Yes, Lord, I believe that you are the Messiah, the Son of God, the one coming into the world." (John 11:25–27)

In John's Gospel, the Judgement Day is not so much a future event, as a present choice to believe or not to believe in Jesus as the Son of God. "Those who believe in him are not condemned; but those who do not believe are condemned already, because they have not believed in the name of the only Son of God" (John 3:18).

The theme of revelation continues in two of the most significant episodes in Acts of the Apostles. The first is Peter's speech following Pentecost (2:14–40), which captures the theology of Acts: Through the death and resurrection of Christ, the promise of a new age in which God's Spirit would be poured out on all people is now being fulfilled. The second significant episode is the conversion of Paul, who was blinded by heavenly light on the road to Damascus as he set out to arrest Christians (9:1–20). Paul went on to become the early church's leading missionary. In his Letter to the Galatians, Paul defended his authority on the basis of his experience on the road to Damascus. "For I want you to know, brothers and sisters, that the gospel that was proclaimed by me is not of human origin; for I did not receive it from a human source, nor was I taught it, but I received it through a revelation of Jesus Christ" (Gal 1:11–12).

Paul's letters have exercised a profound influence on Christian thought, and figure prominently in numerous controversies throughout Christian history, regarding such topics as predestination, indulgences, and the relationship of faith and reason. But throughout all his letters, he conveyed what he regarded as the glorious content of the Gospel: that Christ broke the power of sin by his death and resurrection, and that by faith in Christ (and not by any works of the Law, such as circumcision), we too can stand in right relationship with God. In his Letters to the Galatians and Romans, Paul outlined the universal scope of the Gospel: "In Christ Jesus you are all children of God through faith" (Gal 3:26, see also Rom 1:16). The crucifixion was the central event of Christianity. While Paul acknowledged that the cross was a "stumbling block" and "foolishness" to those who do not believe (1 Cor 1:23), he also regarded the wisdom of this world as vastly inferior to the truth revealed by the death and resurrection of Christ. Christians live by that truth. We now see "dimly," or "indistinctly," what at the end of time we will know fully and completely (1 Cor 13:12).

We conclude this section with a brief preview of where some of the other New Testament writings dealing with mystery, faith, and revelation will resurface in later discussions.

The concept of mystery—the mystery of God's plan, the mystery of Christ—figured prominently in Colossians and Ephesians. The author of Colossians spoke of the mission to the Gentiles as "the mystery that has been hidden throughout the ages and generations but has now been revealed to his saints" (1:26). A similar use of the word *mystery* appeared in Ephesians: "In former generations this mystery was not made known to humankind, as it has now been revealed to his holy apostles and prophets by the Spirit: that is, the Gentiles have become fellow heirs, members of the same body, and sharers in the promise of Christ Jesus through the gospel" (3:5–6). In these two letters, the concept of mystery was joined with the concept of revelation. The life, death, and resurrection of Christ unlocked the mystery of God's plan for the world. This insight that Christ "sums up" and brings to completion all that has preceded him will reappear in our discussion of Christology in the early church.

In the Pastoral Epistles (1 Tim, 2 Tim, Titus) the meaning of the term *faith* shifted from a sense of trust to correct belief. As the scripture scholar Bart D. Ehrman explained, "the term 'faith,' which for Paul refers to a trusting acceptance of the death of Christ for salvation, now refers to the body of teaching that makes up the Christian religion (e.g., Titus 1:13)."[15] Likewise, in Hebrews, we find the classic definition of faith: "Now faith is the assurance of things hoped for, the conviction of things not seen" (11:1). As Monika K. Hellwig has noted, the Greek word translated as "assurance" can also be translated as "substance." If translated as assurance, "the emphasis would be on faith in the trustworthiness of God," while "substance" "might well accentuate faith as belief."[16] This difference in emphasis on faith as trust or belief will resurface at various times in the course of Christian thought.

The Book of Revelation praised both the faithfulness of Christians during times of persecution ("the endurance and faith of the saints" Rev 13:10) and the faithfulness of God to those who did not surrender the faith. Like all apocalyptic literature, Revelation bore witness to the hope that God had not abandoned the holy ones, despite the fact that they were suffering horrible persecution for their faith. This conviction will inform Christian engagements with the problem of evil, and inspire Christian speculations about the last things (i.e, eschatology).

Mystery, Faith, and Revelation in the Christian Tradition

In this section we will examine some of the leading thinkers and events in the Christian tradition surrounding the issues of mystery, faith, and revelation. We will again explore four eras in Christian history: the ancient church, the medieval period, the Protestant and Catholic Reformations, and the modern age.

THE ANCIENT CHURCH

In our earlier discussions of scripture (chapter two) and church history (chapter three), we examined how church thinkers tackled problems on two fronts. First, they responded to the charges leveled against them by adherents of the established pagan religions and philosophies. Second, they had their own "in-house" problems concerning the content and interpretation of scripture, correct christological doctrine, and the proper system of church authority.

The Christian apologists such as Justin Martyr (d. ca. 165) crafted rebuttals to the arguments of their Roman critics. Justin's response was particularly noteworthy. Justin's starting point was a Greek word shared by both Christians and various ancient philosophical traditions: *logos*. The concept of Logos will also be vitally important in the development of early Christology. Logos can be translated "Word," but it is also the root word for English terms such as *theology, biology, psychology*—"*the study of*," or "*the orderly examination of*," both of which convey a sense of activity. As the theologian William C. Placher noted, "The Logos usually meant a rational principle that orders the universe and, when we think properly, guides our understanding."[17] The ancients conceived of the Logos as a principle that gave order to the cosmos; because human nature possessed a spark or seed of that Logos, we could create order and balance in ourselves if we lived according to its dictates. In their quest for eternal wisdom, Plato and the other great philosophers and poets were, according to Justin, arriving at different facets of the Logos that Christians believe became flesh (see John 1:14) in the person of Jesus. It should not be surprising, therefore, that important elements of ancient philosophy agreed with the essential teachings of Christ: Socrates, Plato, and others were searching for the truth that Christ embodied. What Plato grasped partially, Christ revealed fully. Christianity, therefore, is the true philosophy. The concept of the Logos allowed Justin and other Christian thinkers to speak of revelation in universal terms, while at the same time insisting that Christ represents the fullest expression of God's revelation to humanity.

Irenaeus of Lyons (d. ca. 200) confronted a different set of problems. As we discussed earlier, Gnostic Christians claimed that Christ taught a secret revelation that a select number of enlightened Christians could discern when reading the scripture. They also held a dualistic view of reality—contrasting the material world with the immaterial world, darkness with light, and so on—that pitted the God of the Old Testament against the God of the New. Irenaeus faced a difficult theological challenge. He had to acknowledge the sense of mystery of the Christian revelation that the Gnostic Christians highlighted and had to concur with their claim that scripture had a spiritual meaning beyond the literal words; at the same time he had to do this without supporting the Gnostics' elitism or their denigration of the Old Testament.

Irenaeus responded to the Gnostics by developing a theory of revelation grounded in the grand sweep of history. The contemporary Jesuit theologian and cardinal, Avery Dulles, SJ, explained that

> Irenaeus of Lyons sought to defend, against various Gnostic sects, the harmony between the Old and New Testaments. In his *Adversus Haereses* he sketches the outlines of a dynamic theology of history which vies with the best in biblical theology. God, in his view, gradually educates the human race through the eternal Logos, and prepares men [i.e., humanity] by stages to receive the "solid food" of Christian revelation. Irenaeus recognizes three distinct Testaments prior to Christ; those of Adam,

Noah, and Moses. In the fourth Testament, as he calls it, the divine Word himself becomes visible, appearing in the flesh....After the Ascension, Christ's visibility is perpetuated in the Church which, though dispersed over the whole earth, believes in one heart and one soul the revelation handed down from the apostles.[18]

In Irenaeus' response to the Gnostics, he contributed a number of ideas that would inform the tradition until the present day. For our study, two of them are particularly noteworthy. First, Irenaeus sought a principle for reading the Bible that would allow for spiritual interpretations of passages without endorsing Gnosticism. He found this regulative principle in the "rule of faith"—those beliefs taught by the apostles and held by the universal church (e.g., the beliefs that will later comprise the Nicene creed). In this way, scripture, revelation, and church authority became inseparable. Second, Irenaeus grounded his theology in the concept of an unfolding mystery as found in the Letters to the Colossians and the Ephesians. Irenaeus coupled this idea, however, with the conviction that Christ's revelation cannot in any way be surpassed. There can be no greater or additional revelation to that which Christ imparted. A principle later developed in Christian thought stated that revelation ceased with the death of the last apostle. This tension between these two positions—that revelation is closed, but that the life of the Spirit-filled church continues to expand its knowledge—erupted in numerous controversies throughout Christian history, but the one closest to Irenaeus's time was Montanism.

In our earlier discussion of the development of the canon (chapter two), we mentioned Montanism, the mid-second-century apocalyptic movement whose proponents claimed that they had experienced the direct inspiration of the Holy Spirit. The most famous convert to Montanism was a brilliant thinker in Carthage named Tertullian. Before his conversion, Tertullian wrote a number of treatises in defense of orthodox belief. In one of those works, he penned the famous question, "What indeed has Athens have to do with Jerusalem?" Here Tertullian parted ways with Justin Martyr. For Justin, God's revelation was discovered by the great philosophers of Athens and elsewhere, and reading their works could indeed provide great insight into the Christian way of life. Tertullian categorically rejected this view. In fact, Tertullian once declared, "And the Son of God died; it is by all means to be believed, because it is absurd. And He was buried, and rose again; the fact is certain, because it is impossible."[20] As the theologian Roger E. Olson explained, "While Tertullian did not disallow questioning and seeking *within* Christian faith and belief—that is, within the bounds of apostolic succession and the 'apostolic rule of faith'—he did reject any study of nonbiblical, nonapostolic sources to supplement or even interpret that witness to truth that transcends all human inquiry and investigation."[21] For Tertullian, the reliance upon reason apart from revelation can easily lead us away from Christ, while faith in the things that we do not understand will keep us close to Christ.

The most influential theologian of the ancient Western church was Augustine, whose sheer volume of work allows modern readers to find passages supporting any number of positions regarding the relationship between faith and reason, or Christianity and philosophy. We will do no more than cite a few selections from his works. First, Augustine drew upon Plato's description of knowledge as "illumination." In his *Confessions* Augustine addressed God in the following way,

> Being thus admonished to return to myself, under your leadership, I entered my inmost being. This I could do because you are my helper. I entered there, and by my soul's eye, such as it was, I saw above that same eye of my soul, above my mind, an unchangeable light....It was above my mind, because it made me, and I was beneath it, because I was made by it. He who knows the truth, knows that light, and he who knows it knows eternity.[22]

Second, in addition to this emphasis on interior illumination, Augustine also spoke of the need for an external authority in both the process of learning and in the life of the church. If we are to learn a new language, for example, we must place our trust in a teacher who speaks that language and submit to his or her instruction in order to learn how to speak the language properly. Similarly,

Augustine asserted, "For my part, I should not believe the gospel except as moved by the authority of the Catholic Church."[23] Third, Augustine left us two aphorisms that tease our minds when pondering the relationship between faith and reason: "understand that you may believe," and "believe that you may understand."[24]

THE MEDIEVAL PERIOD

While Augustine's thought pervaded medieval theology, the leading theologians of the Middle Ages did not incorporate his ideas into their own theology in exactly the same way. We can, for example, easily detect Augustine's profound influence on two of the towering figures in medieval theology, Thomas Aquinas and Bonaventure, while also taking note of the significantly different directions each of them took when constructing their own theological works.

Thomas Aquinas absorbed not only Augustine's theology, but also Aristotle's philosophy. Aristotle held that things in nature move toward a natural goal or end. Observations of things in nature yield reliable data about the process of development that they undergo, and the end-result they will achieve, provided they have the proper environment in which to flourish. Acorns become oak trees; fertilized human eggs become babies, and so on. Aquinas shared Aristotle's positive regard for the autonomy of reason and his optimism that the use of reason will lead us to our natural ends. As a theologian, Aquinas believed that our natural end is to be with God. God's activity, which he called grace, builds upon our rational nature. In terms of our present discussion, therefore, Aquinas had confidence that reason and faith, philosophy and theology, and nature and grace existed in a harmonious relationship. Faith built upon reason; theology supplemented philosophy; and grace elevated nature. Aquinas wrote,

> As sacred doctrine is based on the light of faith, so is philosophy founded on the natural light of reason. Hence, it is impossible for items that belong to philosophy to be contrary to those that pertain to faith; but the former may be defective in comparison with the latter. Yet, they

contain some likenesses and some prolegomena [i.e., introductory discussions] to the latter, just as nature is a preamble to grace. If any point among the statements of the philosophers is found contrary to faith, this is not philosophy but rather an abuse of philosophy, resulting from a defect in reasoning.[25]

Philosophy, continued Aquinas, served three purposes in theology. It can demonstrate beliefs that are "preambles to faith" (e.g., that God exists). It can "make known those items that belong to the faith by means of certain similitudes; thus Augustine (in his book *On Order*, 9–12) uses many likenesses taken from philosophical teachings to show something about the Trinity." Finally, philosophy can refute arguments made against the faith.[26]

Bonaventure (1217–74) combined his appreciation of Augustine with a love for the compelling vision of Francis of Assisi, the founder of the order to which he belonged. In his work entitled the *Breviloquium*, Bonaventure invoked both Augustine's theology and Francis's love of creation.

Further, in regard to the requirement of faith that we have a concept of God of the loftiest order, this is proved not only by Holy Scripture, but also by the whole of creation. As Augustine writes in chapter four of the fifteenth part of his work "On the Trinity": "The proof of God's existence is founded not only upon the authority of the divine books, but also upon the entire natural universe around us, to which we ourselves belong, and which proclaims that it has a transcendent Creator…"[27]

Bonaventure spoke of the two books touched by the hand of God: the scriptures and the book of nature. God created nature as a "means of self-revelation so that, like a mirror of God or a divine footprint, it might lead man to love and praise his Creator."[28]

Bonaventure also shared Augustine's belief in the necessity of authority. In the opening chapter of the *Breviloquium* Bonaventure quoted approvingly from Augustine: "Faith is founded on authority; understanding on reason."[29] Here we can begin to see how

Aquinas and Bonaventure differed in their understanding of faith and reason. Aquinas's optimism was based on his understanding of humans as rational creatures who were naturally drawn to their Creator. Bonaventure shared the older Augustine's deep concern that unguided human speculation and philosophical reflection can easily lead the believer down the wrong path.

If Aquinas and Bonaventure set the debate for subsequent Catholic theology, two Franciscan philosophical theologians of the medieval period, John Duns Scotus (ca. 1266–1308) and William of Ockham (ca. 1285–1347), moved theology in a direction that could be more congenial to Protestant thinkers. Whereas Aquinas balanced faith and reason, Dun Scotus shifted the weight to faith. Aquinas shared Aristotle's high regard for human rationality and believed that, through the use of reason, knowledge of universal principles could be attained. The existence of these universal principles indicated in some partial, yet reliable, fashion the rational nature of God. Scotus, by contrast, believed that the human will, not human reason, was the highest faculty possessed by humans. It was, for example, more important to love God than to know God. Likewise, God's actions in the world do not result from God's *reason* as much as God's *will*. Faith in what God has done is paramount, whereas looking for the logic behind those actions is futile.

William of Ockham, whose name has been commonly attached to the philosophical movement known as nominalism, stressed the freedom of God and the faith of believers. William A. Herr offered a very straightforward account of Ockham's theological commitment to the freedom of God.

> Ockham certainly was not the first one to describe God as omnipotent. But usually we begin to qualify—and therefore deny—this description almost as soon as we make it. Yes, we say, God is almighty, but he is also all-wise and all-just and thus cannot do anything unjust or foolish. To all intents and purposes the scholastics, implicitly at least, invented a new attribute: God as all-rational.
>
> Perhaps we do this because we cannot bear to think about what omnipotence really implies. Part of Ockham's

originality lay in drawing out and accepting these implications.

For Ockham, divine omnipotence meant precisely
what it said: God is totally unlimited, totally unre-
stricted; God can literally do absolutely anything. And
just as Scotus had focused on human will rather than the
intellect, so Ockham focused on the divine will. God can
do whatever he pleases; he is not bound by such human
concepts as wisdom or rationality.[30]

If God can do anything, then philosophical inquiry into theological
matters is of little use to the believer. Ockham's critics would charge
that his supporters portrayed God as inconsistent and irrational.

THE PROTESTANT AND CATHOLIC REFORMATIONS

We will now focus our attention on the differences between
the theology of Luther and the positions endorsed by the bishops
at Trent. We will reserve our discussion of Calvin's thought for the
chapter on God, and we will defer our discussion of the Radical
Reformers until the chapter on sacraments.

The central theme of Luther's theology, as we discussed in the
previous chapter, was justification by faith. Luther carried forward
Scotus and Ockham's strong emphasis on faith as trust, and shared
their general disdain for Thomas Aquinas's strong reliance on philosophy. As Luther commented in his "Preface to the Epistle of St.
Paul to the Romans,"

Faith is not something dreamed, a human illusion,
although this is what many people understand by the
term. Whenever they see that it is not followed either by
an improvement in morals or by good works, while
much is still being said about faith, they fall into the
error of declaring that faith is not enough, that we must
do "works" if we are to become upright and attain salvation. The reason is that, when they hear the gospel, they
miss the point; in their hearts, and out of their resources,
they conjure up an idea which they call "belief," which

they treat as genuine faith. All the same, it is but a human fabrication, an idea without a corresponding experience in the depths of the heart. It is therefore ineffective and not followed by a better kind of life.

Faith, however, is something that God effects in us. It changes us and we are reborn from God, John 1 [:13]. Faith puts the old Adam to death and makes us quite different men in heart, in mind, and in all our powers; and it is accompanied by the Holy Spirit...

Faith is a living and unshakeable confidence, a belief in the grace of God so assured that a man would die a thousand deaths for its sake.

In each of the three paragraphs in this extended excerpt, Luther mentioned a common theme in his theology: first, faith alone is sufficient for salvation; second, God alone brings about faith; and third, faith brings assurance of one's salvation.

In their "Decree on Justification," the bishops at Trent responded to Luther's account of faith. In response to Luther's exclusive focus on faith as the basis of salvation, the bishops asserted the need for faith, hope, and love. Second, where Luther emphasized that justification is solely the work of God, the bishops spoke of believers "freely assenting to and cooperating with that grace. In this way, God touches the heart of man with the illumination of the Holy Spirit, but man himself is not inactive while receiving that inspiration, since he can reject it; and yet, without God's grace, he cannot by his own free will take one step towards justice in God's sight."[32] Third, Luther spoke of the assurance that faith gives of one's own personal salvation. The bishops insisted that "no one can know with a certitude of faith which cannot be subject to error, that he has obtained God's grace."[33]

THE MODERN AGE

With the rise of modern science, the concept of mystery became problematic. Was a "mystery" simply a problem that science had not yet solved? Was belief in miracles a remnant of an outmoded, prescientific outlook? Shouldn't reason dictate belief, especially religious belief? The deists of the seventeenth and eighteenth centuries sought either to critique Christian belief according to the standards of reason, or to confirm the truth of the central Christian beliefs according to the standards of reason. Many thinkers fall into the category of "deists," but we will confine our study to the work of the British theologian John Toland (1670–1722). In 1696 Toland published *Christianity not Mysterious*, that contained a number of ideas relevant to our present discussion. First, "mystery" in Toland's sense of the term meant "incomprehensible," and Toland rejected the idea that we are "to adore what we cannot comprehend."[34] A revelation of any kind, whether from God or another human, must be understood if it is to be believed. Second, Toland equated faith with knowledge. Faith is "a firm persuasion built upon substantial reason."[35] Third, Toland believed that "religion must necessarily be reasonable and intelligible."[36] There was a common expression circulated among the deists: "Where mystery begins, religion ends."[37] Christianity, as Toland's book title indicates, should disassociate itself in any way possible from the concept of mystery.

Deism had placed the question of the relationship between faith and reason on the theological agenda, and it became a topic of great interest among thinkers in the Enlightenment. In one of his more memorable lines, the great Enlightenment philosopher Immanuel Kant (1724–1804) declared, "Thus I had to deny knowledge in order to make room for faith…"[38] Kant insisted that our minds are limited in terms of the type of reality they can process. The nature of God is a concept simply beyond our human comprehension. Statements about God could, on the basis of what Kant called "pure reason," be neither proved nor disproved. This might at first seem to lead to agnosticism. However, Kant grounded the belief that God exists in the human experience of moral duty or obligation. Rational human beings, Kant argued, share the common human experience of having one's conscience deliver moral commands. For the religious believer, these ethical decrees are understood to be commands from God. The religious person also believed that in the afterlife those who obeyed those commands would be justly rewarded, and those who disobeyed those commands would be justly punished. Christ, in turn, embodied this moral perfection as an individual "who yielded unqualified obedience to this law." Christ provided an example of "a person morally well-pleasing to God."[39] For Kant, the truth that Christ embodied was more important to Christian faith than the historical details of his earthly existence.

Gotthold Lessing (1729–81) also believed that historical claims were a shaky foundation on which to base claims about eternal truths. In his essay "On the Proof of the Spirit and of Power," Lessing argued,

> If on historical grounds I have no objection to the statement that Christ raised to life a dead man; must I therefore accept it as true that God has a Son who is of the same essence as himself? What is the connection between my inability to raise any significant objection to the evidence of the former and my obligation to believe something against which my reason rebels?[40]

Lessing has raised two problems. First, how can we judge the historical accuracy of accounts of events that occurred two thousand years ago? How can we know that Christ actually raised from the dead Lazarus (John 11) or the widow's son in Nain (Luke 7)? Second, even if one could have some assurance that these stories are accurate, does that justify the leap to saying that Jesus was God incarnate? Lessing preferred to speak of revelation as the education of the human race: "Education is revelation coming to the individual man; and revelation is education which has come, and is still coming, to the human race."[41]

This understanding of revelation as a progressive unfolding of God's rational nature through the course of history would find its most influential expression in the philosophy of G. W. F. Hegel (1770–1831). The central concept in Hegel's thought was *Geist*— a word that can be translated as "Spirit" or "Mind." This unfolding of Spirit or Mind in history followed a dialectical pattern, commonly described as a process of thesis—antithesis—synthesis. As the theologian Robert H. King explained, Hegel's dialectic was "a process of thought whereby each assertion generates a contrary assertion, and out of this tension there arises an encompassing and transforming synthesis."[42] Through the tensions and conflicts of human history, therefore, Spirit reached increasingly fuller expression. In theological language, the dialectical pattern of historical development was the vehicle for God's revelation. One of Hegel's colleagues at the University of Berlin, Friedrich Schleiermacher, located revelation not in the grand sweep of history, but in the depths of the individual. In doing so, he charted an alternate course for Christian theology.

TWO MODERN THEOLOGICAL REACTIONS TO THE ENLIGHTENMENT

In the work of two nineteenth-century Protestant thinkers, Friedrich Schleiermacher (1768–1834) and Søren Kierkegaard (1813–55), we can see divergent theological responses to the Enlightenment.

Schleiermacher's originality as a theologian lay in his attempt to relocate the very object of the theologian's inquiry. Unlike those who argued that religion was primarily a matter of holding the right beliefs, or those who held that religion was essentially morality, Schleiermacher held that religion was primarily a matter of "feeling." Theologians Stanley J. Grenz and Roger E. Olson offered the following point of clarification: "It is important to understand correctly Schleiermacher's equation of religion with 'feeling.' The German original, *Gefuhl*, does not connote a sensation, as its English rendering would suggest, but a deep sense or awareness."[43] As Schleiermacher commented in his *Speeches on Religion*, "true religion is sense and taste for the Infinite."[44] Religious awareness involves a sense of dependence on a greater power not of our own making, a sense of, as Schleiermacher described, absolute dependence.

Theology and church doctrine give expression to this preconceptual awareness. Like two streams of lava beneath a volcano, the Spirit of God and human creativity merge and erupt into human consciousness. God's revelation, in other words, arises from within human consciousness and finds expression in language, either in the personal accounts of individuals or in doctrinal statements of the church. This requires a reformulation of the concept of "revelation." Revelation is not understood as beliefs or moral commands, but as an experience of the greater power that sustains our lives. The theologian Hugh Ross Mackintosh once commented that "it would be roughly true to say that he [Schleiermacher] has put discovery in place of revelation."[45] The Christian life is the discovery of a treasure that we possessed for a long time before we became aware of its existence.

Søren Kierkegaard also distanced himself from the Enlightenment project of finding a thoroughly rational religion. Kierkegaard was particularly put off by Hegel's grand theory of history. For Kierkegaard, this philosophy subverted the importance of the individual, especially the element of human decision. The absolute necessity of decision is critically important for Kierkegaard. Transitions (or stagnations) in our lives are brought about by our decisions. The transition to the religious stage of life did not depend on the stage of history in which one lived, and it did not emerge from the depths of our being. For Kierkegaard, the beginning of Christian faith is found in the hearing of the Gospel, the good news that teaches the paradoxical message that the Son of God was born in a manger in Bethlehem. When confronted with such a message, reason cannot help us. We must make a "leap of faith," demonstrated in the biblical story of Abraham when he was about to kill his son Isaac at the command of God. Such a situation defied all logic, and represented a suspension of the ethical commands that form the basis of Christian morality. And yet, Abraham was willing to go forward in faith.

Schleiermacher and Kierkegaard conceived of the Christian life in radically different ways. For Schleiermacher, religion begins deep within the individual, and is given expression by the believing community. Schleiermacher would agree with the psychologist Carl Jung's observation:

Life has always seemed to me like a plant that lives on its rhizome. Its true life is invisible, hidden in the rhizome. The part that appears above ground lasts only a single summer. Then it withers away—an ephemeral apparition. When we think of the unending growth and decay of life and civilizations, we cannot escape the impression of absolute nullity. Yet I have never lost a sense of something that lives and endures underneath the eternal flux.

What we see is the blossom, which passes. The rhizome remains.[46]

For Kierkegaard, the Gospel dropped like an unpredicted meteorite from heaven. We are confronted by the paradox of the Gospel, and in faith we allow the truth of the Gospel to become the truth by which we live out our lives.

John Henry Newman (1801–90), a convert to Roman Catholicism who later became a cardinal, concerned himself with many of the same issues that plagued nineteenth-century Protestant thinkers. First, he sought to find a theological framework in which we could understand the development of doctrine while at the same time ensuring doctrine's continuity with the original scriptural and apostolic traditions. Second, Newman drove a middle course between those who argued that revelation is to be equated strictly with church doctrines, and those who argued that church doctrines were secondary, dispensable expressions of religious experience. Ian Ker, a leading authority on Newman's thought, has argued that Newman believed that while "verbal formulations" of the faith were necessary, so too was a recognition of the "inadequacy of human language."[47] Third, Newman wanted to strike the right balance between faith and reason. While reason played a significant role in religious faith, it could not, for Newman, be the sole guide in human decision-making. As Newman wrote, "Life is for action. If we insist on proofs for everything, we shall never come to action; to act you must assume and that assumption is faith…"[48] Life offers probabilities, not certainties. Our commitments—whether friendships, business partnerships, or religious beliefs—are formed, tested, and confirmed over a period of time. "Revelation…is not a revealed system, but consists of a number of detached and incomplete truths belonging to a vast system unrevealed, of doctrines and injunctions mysteriously connected together…"[49]

VATICAN I AND VATICAN II

Vatican I ended abruptly with the outbreak of the Franco-Prussian War. One of the few documents to be promulgated before the council's suspension was the "Dogmatic Constitution on the

Catholic Faith" (*Dei Filius*, 1870). Avery Dulles has provided a succinct summary of the main points contained in the Constitution regarding faith and reason in relation to revelation.

> The Council taught that faith and reason, having their source in the same God, can never disagree; that the act of faith, while essentially the gift of God, is consonant with reason, inasmuch as God has adorned his revelation with many external signs and proofs, especially miracles and prophecies; and that the contents of revelation, while surpassing everything that reason can properly demonstrate or fully comprehend, have a certain intelligibility when pondered by reason under the guidance of faith itself.[50]

The bishops operated with a two-level view of revelation: Some truths can be known through the use of natural reason, but there are "some mysteries that are hidden in God, which can never be known unless they are revealed by God."[51]

In 1965 the bishops at Vatican II issued "The Dogmatic Constitution on Divine Revelation" (*Dei Verbum*). Two shifts in emphasis can be detected from Vatican I to Vatican II. First, the language in the Vatican II Constitution is far more biblical. As Gerald O'Collins, SJ, has noted, "Unlike *Dei Filius*, the First Vatican Council's Constitution on Faith (1870), *Dei Verbum* is profoundly biblical in its language and mentality. The document makes seventy-three references to scripture and quotes three passages from the Bible." Second, the bishops spoke less of revelation as a set of truths to which believers must give intellectual assent, and more of revelation as "God's self-disclosure," as O'Collins put it, to which each person is called to commit his or her entire self (cf. *Dei Verbum*, 5). O'Collins continued, "God's communication is not merely cognitive but constitutes a *real* self-communication of God which not only makes salvation known but actually brings it in person."[53]

In his work *Catholicism*, the ecclesiologist Richard P. McBrien argued that while *Dei Verbum* reaffirmed many of the traditional Catholic positions on revelation, the church brought a fresh perspective to the concept of revelation. For example, "It speaks of revelation as the divine 'mystery' (singular) disclosed in Christ, i.e., as God's final plan of salvation for all human beings (n. 2), rather than a cluster of 'mysteries' (plural), as Vatican I spoke of it."[54] Second, the bishops speak of scripture and tradition in a manner that emphasized their unity rather than their separation. "Although the Church authentically interprets the word of God, the teaching office is 'not above the word of God, but serves it, teaching only what is handed on, listening to it devoutly, guarding it scrupulously and explaining it in accord with a divine commission and with the help of the Holy Spirit...' (n. 10)."[55] Third, the "deposit of faith is not simply a static entity; there is true growth of understanding on the part of the Church."[56] Here we can detect the influence of Newman who had struggled a century earlier with the question of how to preserve both the truth of doctrine and the development of doctrine.

Conclusion

How do we speak of God's revelation in our current situation? Do the traditionalists, liberals, or radicals best approach the issues of mystery, faith, and revelation? As we begin to offer our positions on these fundamental questions of theology, we notice that some questions are particular to our own time and place, and others seem to be recurring themes in Christian thought. Our historical survey suggests that there are at least five such recurring issues that inform our current theological deliberations. First, there constantly arose the issue of the relationship of faith and reason, and the question of what weight should properly be given each of them in Christian theology. Second, there was a healthy tension between those who conceive of revelation as doctrine that calls for our belief, and those who see revelation as an experience of God that calls for our trust. Third, the "open-ended" and "closed" meaning of the term *revelation* surfaced frequently. In what sense has revelation found its definitive and unsurpassable expression in Christ, and in what sense does the progression of human history and the ongoing life of the church yield revelation? Fourth, what role does the church play in the transmission of revelation? Does Christian faith consist primarily of a personal relationship with Jesus? Fifth, does revelation arise from the depths of our being, or does it stand outside ourselves as the standard by which all human thought and action are measured?

The nineteenth-century philosopher W. K. Clifford (1845–79) once proposed the following principle: "It is wrong always, everywhere, and for anyone, to believe anything upon insufficient evidence."[57] In terms of our present discussion, is Clifford's principle a sound one for Christian theology? What counts as a "sufficient reason" for faith in God or belief in specific religious doctrines? Should we ever believe something despite compelling evidence against it? It is with these questions in mind that we turn to the topic of God.

Discussion Questions

1. What are the advantages and disadvantages of living in a highly pluralistic society?
2. How would you define "mystery"?
3. Is it wise or foolish to "simply have faith"?
4. Which stories in the Bible are especially relevant to a discussion of faith?
5. Do you believe that revelation was closed at the death of the last apostle?
6. How helpful is philosophy for doing theology?
7. Does the beauty of the natural world reveal something about God?
8. Should Christianity be "reasonable"?
9. Is the inspiration experienced by poets and songwriters different from the inspiration experienced by the biblical writers?
10. What are some religious beliefs that you hold to be true? What are some beliefs about the meaning of human existence that you hold to be true?

Suggested Readings

Two works by Avery Dulles are especially helpful: *Revelation Theology* (New York: Herder and Herder, 1969), and *Models of Revelation* (Maryknoll, NY: Orbis Books, 1992). See also the entries "Faith, "Mystery," and "Revelation," in Joseph A. Komonchak, Mary Collins, and Dermot A Lane, editors, *The New Dictionary of Theology* (Wilmington, DE: Michael Glazier, 1987). Chapters one, two, and three of Paul Avis, editor, *Divine Revelation* (London: Darton, Longman, and Todd, 1997) provide a very solid overview of the biblical concepts of revelation (by James D. G. Dunn), of Roman Catholic theology (by Gabriel Daly), and of modern Protestant theology (by Paul Avis). See also George Stroup, "Revelation," in Peter C. Hodgson and Robert H. King, editors, *Christian Theology* (Philadelphia: Fortress, 1982).

For two helpful discussions of the concept of faith, see chapter one of Berard Marthaler, *The Creed*, rev. ed. (Mystic, CT: Twenty-Third Publications, 1993), and Monika K. Hellwig, "A History of the Concept of Faith," which appears as chapter one of James Michael Lee, editor, *Handbook of Faith* (Birmingham, AL: Religious Education Press, 1990).

In addition, Pope John Paul II addressed the question of the relationship between faith and reason in his 1998 encyclical *Fides et Ratio*.

Notes

1. Peter L. Berger, *The Heretical Imperative* (Garden City, NY: Anchor Books, 1979), xi.

2. Peter L. Berger, "Protestantism and the Quest for Certainty," in *The Christian Century* 115, no. 23 (1998): 782.

3. Ibid.

4. Frederick Crews, *Skeptical Engagements* (New York: Oxford University Press, 1986), 122. I discovered this quotation in John S. Mehane, "Pluralism, Relativism, and Evidence in Shakespearean Studies," *College English* 58, no. 5 (1996): 518.

5. Kenneth Baker, *Fundamentals of Catholicism*, vol. 1 (San Francisco: Ignatius Press, 1982), 60.

6. Lesslie Newbigin, *Proper Confidence* (Grand Rapids: Wm. B. Eerdmans, 1995), 103–4.

7. This is the title of Sidney H Griffith's Pere Marquette Theology Lecture on St. Ephraem the Syrian, *Faith Adoring Mystery* (Milwaukee: Marquette University Press, 1997). He credits Robert Murray for the description (see Griffith's footnote #1).

8. Quoted in William Harmless and Raymond R. Fitzgerald, "The Sapphire Light of the Mind: The *Skemmata* of Evagrius Ponticus," in *Theological Studies* 62, no. 3 (2001): 513.

9. Quoted in Frederick Copleston, *A History of Philosophy*, vol. 9 (Garden City, NY: Image Books, 1985), 332.

10. Gordon D. Kaufman, *In Face of Mystery* (Cambridge: Harvard University Press, 1993), 64.

11. Mary Daly, *Beyond God the Father* (Boston: Beacon Press, 1973), 13.

12. Aylward Shorter, *Revelation and Its Interpretation* (London: Geoffrey Chapman, 1983), 209.

13. Bernhard W. Anderson, *Understanding the Old Testament*, 4th ed. (Englewood Cliffs, NJ: Prentice-Hall, 1986), 9.

14. R. B. Y. Scott, *The Way of Wisdom* (New York: Macmillan, 1971), 3.

15. Bart D. Ehrman, *The New Testament*, 2nd ed. (New York: Oxford University Press, 2000), 358.

16. Monika K. Hellwig, " A History of the Concept of Faith," in James Michael Lee, ed., *Handbook of Faith* (Birmingham, AL: Religious Education Press, 1990), 5.

17. William C. Placher, *A History of Christian Theology* (Philadelphia: Westminster Press, 1983), 41.

18. Avery Dulles, *Revelation Theology* (New York: Herder and Herder, 1969), 33–34.

19. Quoted in Justo L. Gonzalez, *A History of Christian Thought*, vol. 1 (Nashville: Abingdon Press, 1970), 179.

20. Ibid.

21. Roger E. Olson, *The Story of Christian Theology* (Downers Grove, IL: InterVarsity Press, 1999), 94.

22. *Confessions*, VII, 10, John K. Ryan, trans. (Garden City, NY: Image Books, 1960), 170–71.

23. Quoted in Jaroslav Pelikan, *Reformation of Church and Dogma* (1300–1700), vol. 4 of The Christian Tradition (Chicago: University of Chicago Press, 1984), 263.

24. Quoted in Yves M. J. Congar, *A History of Theology* (Garden City, NY: Doubleday, 1968), 46.

25. Quoted in Vernon J. Bourke, ed., *The Pocket Aquinas* (New York: Washington Square Press, 1960), 292–93.

26. Ibid., 293.

27. Bonaventure, *Breviloquium*, I.2.5, Jose de Vinck, trans. (Paterson, NJ: St. Anthony Guild Press, 1963), 36.

28. Ibid., II.11.2 (p. 101).

29. Ibid., I.1.4 (p. 34).

30. William A. Herr, *Catholic Thinkers in the Clear* (Chicago: Thomas More Press, 1985), 129–30.

31. Martin Luther, "Preface to the Epistle of St. Paul to the Romans," in John Dillenberger, ed., *Martin Luther* (Garden City, NY: Anchor Books, 1961), 23–24.

32. "Decree on Justification," in J. Neuner and J. Dupuis, eds., *The Christian Faith* (New York: Alba House, 1982), 557.

33. Ibid., Chapter IX, 560.

34. Quoted in James C. Livingston, *Modern Christian Thought* (New York: Macmillan, 1971), 21.

35. Quoted in H. D. McDonald, *Theories of Revelation* (Grand Rapids: Baker Books, 1979), 44.

36. Ibid.

37. Ibid., 229.

38. Immanuel Kant, *Critique of Pure Reason*, translated by Paul Guyer and Allen W. Wood (Cambridge: Cambridge University Press, 1998), 117.

39. Immanuel Kant, *Religion Within the Limits of Reason Alone*, Theodore M. Greene and Hoyt H. Hudson, trans. (New York: Harper and Row, 1960), 56.

40. Gotthold Lessing, "On the Proof of the Spirit and of Power," in Henry Chadwick, ed., *Lessing's Theological Writings* (Stanford, CA: Stanford University Press, 1956), 54.

41. Lessing, "The Education of the Human Race," in Chadwick, 83.

42. Robert H. King, "The Task of Systematic Theology," in Peter C. Hodgson and Robert H. King, eds., *Christian Theology* (Philadelphia: Fortress Press, 1982), 15.

43. Stanley J. Grenz and Roger E. Olson, *Twentieth-Century Theology* (Downers Grove, IL: InterVarsity Press, 1992), 44.

44. Frederich Schleiermacher, *On Religion*, John Oman, trans. (New York: Harper and Row, 1958), 39.

45. Hugh Ross Mackintosh, *Types of Modern Theology* (London: Nisbet and Co., 1937), 100.

46. C. G. Jung, *Memories, Dreams, and Reflections*, rev. ed., Aniela Jaffe, ed. (New York: Pantheon Books, 1973), 4.

47. Ian Ker, "Introduction," to *Newman the Theologian: A Reader*, Ian Ker, ed. (Notre Dame, IN: University of Notre Dame Press, 1990), 15.

48. Quoted in Placher, *A History of Christian Theology*, 284.

49. Quoted in Ker, *Newman the Theologian: A Reader*, 16.

50. Avery Dulles, *Models of Revelation* (Garden City, NY: Doubleday, 1983), 249.

51. *Dei Filius*, chapter 4, quoted in J. Neuner and J. Dupuis, eds., *The Christian Faith* (Staten Island, NY: Alba House, 1982), 45.

52. Gerald O'Collins, *Retrieving Fundamental Theology* (Mahwah, NJ: Paulist Press, 1993), 51.

53. Ibid., 53.

54. Richard P. McBrien, *Catholicism*, new ed. (San Francisco: HarperCollins, 1994), 247.

55. Ibid.

56. Ibid.

57. Quoted in Michael Peterson et al., *Reason and Religious Belief* (New York: Oxford University Press, 1991), 34.

5

THE CONCEPT OF GOD IN PATRISTIC AND MEDIEVAL THEOLOGY

In the previous chapter we delved into the issues of mystery, faith, and revelation. One of the greatest mysteries of the Christian faith is the Trinity. In this chapter we will explore the biblical roots and historical development of the doctrine of the Trinity up to the Middle Ages. More specifically, we will examine the various theological moves that made up the developments, explore the logic behind each move, and determine the reasons why alternative approaches were rejected. As difficult as the theological history of the doctrine of the Trinity can be, it can also serve as a very useful guide for studying the craft of theology. As we move into a discussion of the medieval period, we will focus attention on the question of the ability of humans to know God, and investigate the traditional arguments for the existence of God found in Thomas Aquinas's *Summa Theologiae*.

The Task of Making Distinctions in Critical Thought

The doctrinal development of the Trinity is a story filled with thinkers offering theological distinctions. Some of these distinctions were rejected and others were incorporated into the orthodox Christian creeds. This practice of making distinctions can unintentionally generate a great deal of confusion. It might be helpful, therefore, to begin with an example from another field of study.

In high school geometry, we were introduced to different shapes and learned the definition for each of them. For example, a polygon is any closed shape with three or more straight lines. Triangles are three-sided figures; squares are four-sided figures; pentagons are five-sided figures. All triangles, therefore, are polygons, but not all polygons are triangles. We later learned to differentiate various types of triangles: right triangles (one angle is equal to 90 degrees), acute triangles (all angles are less than 90 degrees), and obtuse triangles (one angle is greater than 90 degrees). This reminder of high school geometry serves as an illustration of how distinctions are drawn in order to help us better conceptualize and more accurately define different shapes.

To push this example one final step, recall the Pythagorean theorem that: the square of the hypotenuse of a right triangle is equal to the sum of the squares of the other two sides ($a^2+b^2=c^2$). This theorem captures a universal property of right triangles in a very concise, understandable formula. If one side of a triangle is three inches and the other side is four inches, then the hypotenuse is always five inches. The human discovery and formulation of that fact appeared at some point in human history, but the truth of that theorem existed long before that discovery. In other words, we need to differentiate between the truth of a concept and the history of human inquiry concerning that concept.

The Old Testament

The most famous passage in the Old Testament regarding the nature of God occurs when God speaks to Moses from the burning bush and orders him to return to Egypt to demand that Pharaoh release the Israelite slaves. At this point in the narrative, Moses and God exchange a question and answer.

> But Moses said to God, "If I come to the Israelites and say to them, 'The God of your ancestors has sent me to you,' and they ask, 'What is his name?' what shall I say to them?" God said to Moses, "I AM WHO I AM." He said further, 'Thus you shall say to the Israelites, 'I AM has sent me to you.'" (Exod 3:13–14)

The translations of the divine name given to Moses vary, but two general observations can be made about this crucial passage. The concept of "name" figures prominently in the biblical writings. A name is not an arbitrary designation, but in some sense is a means of revelation about the nature of the person or the role he or she plays in God's history of salvation (e.g., Gen 17:5; see also Mark 5:9). Second, God reveals the divine name to Moses, and in doing so, establishes a special bond with him. But God's name is also shrouded in mystery. The divine name stems from the "to be" verb form, and consequently has a sense of past, present, and future all at the same time. The God presently speaking to Moses from the burning bush is the same God who in the past called Abraham, Isaac, and Jacob, and who promises to be with Israel in the future. The name does not reveal God's nature as much as offer an assurance that God has been, and always will be, in a special covenant relationship with Israel.

The central theological claim about God that emerges from the Old Testament writings is that there is only one God. The belief in a strict, absolute monotheism (i.e., the belief that only one God exists) seems to have been a notion that gradually developed over the course of Israelite history. The First Commandment reads: "I am the Lord your God, who brought you out of the land of Egypt, out of the house of slavery; you shall have no other gods before me" (Exod 20:2). This commandment reflects the ambiguity of earlier Israelite thought in that it suggests the existence of lesser deities. Similar indications of belief in the existence of lesser gods can be detected in Joshua's farewell speech (see Josh 24:14–15) and in various psalms (e.g., "For the Lord is a great God, / and a great King above all gods" (Ps 95:3). This belief that there are many gods, but that one's own particular deity is supreme over all the others, is known as henotheism.

Later Old Testament writers were not content to say that Yahweh is the supreme deity among other gods. In what is commonly called Second Isaiah (Isa 40–55), we find a clear, unambiguous affirmation that Yahweh is the one and only true God. All other supposed gods do not exist. "I am the first and I am the last; / besides me there is no god" (Isa 44:6). As the scripture scholar J. Alberto Soggin observed, "For the first time here we find two concepts of the faith of Israel which were soon to become fundamental: the proclamation of an absolute monotheism, which did not compromise with Canaanite polytheism and had no henotheistic elements, and the confession of God the creator, a feature which had hitherto had a low profile in the biblical proclamation."[1]

The confession of God as Creator added one more aspect of God's activity to the Old Testament portrait of the Lord. The Old Testament God is a God who acts: God created, God called Abraham, God freed the Israelite slaves, God sent the prophets, and so on. In the Bible there are numerous messengers, such as angels or prophets who do God's bidding, but there are also passages that speak of God's Word, God's Spirit, or God's Wisdom at work in world. The concept of the "word of God" appears most frequently in the prophetic writings.

> For as the rain and the snow come
> > down from heaven
> and do not return there until
> > they have watered the
> > earth,
> making it bring forth and sprout,
> > giving seed to the sower and
> > bread to the eater,
> so shall my word be that goes out
> > from my mouth;
> > it shall not return to me empty,
> but it shall accomplish that which
> > I purpose,
> and succeed in the thing for
> > which I sent it. (Isa 55:10–11)

The concept of God's Spirit makes an early appearance in the Bible. In the second verse of the opening chapter of Genesis, we read that a "wind from God" or "the spirit of God" swept over the waters. The Wisdom of God is personified as a woman named "Sophia" (a name that simply means "Wisdom"). In the Book of Wisdom (one of the seven works in the Old Testament regarded as canonical by Catholics, but not by Protestants), Wisdom is

a breath of the power of God,
and a pure emanation of the glory of the Almighty;
therefore nothing defiled gains entrance into her.
For she is a reflection of eternal light,
a spotless mirror of the workings of God,
and an image of his goodness. (Wis 7: 25–26)

While the classic doctrine of the Trinity was certainly not enunciated in any of the Old Testament writings, the theologian Gerald O'Collins, SJ, has argued, "The vivid personifications of Wisdom / Word and Spirit, in as much as they were *both* identified with God *and* the divine activity and distinguished from God, opened up the way toward recognizing God to be tripersonal."[2] We need to turn our attention to the New Testament and see how the unwavering belief in monotheism was related to the activity of the Wisdom, Word, and Spirit of God.

The New Testament

The strict absolute monotheism found in the later Old Testament writings carried over into the New Testament, as did the belief in God's active presence in the world. The New Testament writers continued to speak of God's Wisdom, Word, and Spirit. The concepts of Wisdom and Word were frequently used to discuss the identity and mission of Jesus of Nazareth. In a few instances, the New Testament declared that Christ was God. The early Christians identified the Spirit as the animating, inspiring, and empowering agent in both the career of Jesus and the church, as well as the provider of gifts necessary to live the Christian life. For the early Christians, the God of their ancestors who created the world, the man Jesus who lived among them, and the Spirit who continued to guide their church all played an indispensable role in their understanding of God.

The early Christian communities began to speak of the Father, Son, and Spirit in formulaic expressions in their public prayer and liturgy. These early trinitarian expressions appear in the New Testament, but they are not explained (e.g., 2 Cor 13:13).

Later theologians will regard them as early expressions of the official doctrine of the Trinity.

The New Testament contains several passages in which the Old Testament concept of Wisdom is used to describe Christ's identity. In some passages, Christ is Wisdom. For example, Paul describes Christ as "the power of God and the wisdom of God" (1 Cor 1:24). Scripture scholars Reginald H. Fuller and Pheme Perkins argued that, in certain passages in Matthew's Gospel (11:19; 11:25–30; 23:34; 23:37–39), "Jesus is clearly presented as Wisdom herself speaking."[3] In other passages, while Jesus is not directly referred to as Wisdom, the categories of thought used to describe Jesus are derived from the wider wisdom tradition of the Old Testament. For example, in Colossians, Christ is called "the firstborn of all creation," a designation that echoes Wisdom's statement in Proverbs: "The Lord created me at the beginning of his work, / the first of his acts long ago" (Prov 8:22).

We discussed the concept of the Word (Logos) in the previous chapter when we reviewed the theology of Justin Martyr, and we will return to this concept when we discuss Christology in the early church. We are also introduced to the Word in the very opening verse of John's Gospel: "In the beginning was the Word, and the Word was with God, and the Word was God" (1:1). The phrase "In the beginning" recalls the opening verse of Genesis when God created the world. The central claim of the prologue of John's Gospel (1:1–18) is that the Word of God took on human flesh in the person of Jesus Christ.

The late scripture scholar Raymond E. Brown, SS, argued that in three New Testament passages, Christ is clearly called God: Heb 1:8–9, John 1:1, and John 20:28. In John 20:28, the apostle Thomas, who earlier had not been present when the Risen Lord appeared to the disciples and who doubted the veracity of his fellow disciples' account, confronts the resurrected Jesus and exclaims, "My Lord and my God!" Brown wrote, "This is the clearest example in the NT [New Testament] of the use of 'God' for Jesus."[4] This passage also served as a corresponding bookend to this same gospel's prologue. As the scripture scholar D. Moody Smith, Jr, has argued,

Thomas's response is exactly appropriate, as he utters the confession of Jesus as Lord *(kyrios)* and God *(theos)*. This confession is typical of early Christian theology and language as far as Lord *(kyrios)* is concerned, but uniquely Johannine in its ascription of the name God *(theos)* to Jesus as well. In 1:1 the preexistent word *(logos)* is called God *(theos)* and at the end of the prologue this most exalted title is repeated, after the incarnation of the Word in Jesus has been confessed. For the most part John withholds the designation *theos* from Jesus, but in the course of the narrative makes clear that this ascription of deity to Jesus is indeed correct and unavoidable (5:18; cf. 5:19–24; 10:30; 14:8–11). While Thomas may have once doubted, he has now made the confession that is essential and true. Jesus is Lord and God.[5]

This straightforward description of Christ as God necessitated a theological explanation that preserved both monotheism and Christ's divinity. These passages added one more piece of data that needed to be factored into a Christian understanding of God.

In addition to the Wisdom and Word of God, the concept of the Spirit of God carried over from the Old Testament, where it had moved over the waters at creation, rushed upon King David, and inspired the prophets. In the New Testament, the Holy Spirit filled Mary and Elizabeth, descended upon Christ at his baptism, and empowered the apostles at Pentecost. In his various letters, Paul describes how the Holy Spirit equips the church with the gifts that are needed for its organization and vitality (1 Cor 12), and enables the individual believer to live as a new creation in Christ with love, joy, peace, patience, kindness, generosity, faithfulness, gentleness, and self-control (Gal 5:22–23). As Paul explains, "Now we have received not the spirit of the world, but the Spirit that is from God, so that we may understand the gifts bestowed on us by God" (1 Cor 2:12). In John's Gospel, Jesus promises his disciples that "the Holy Spirit, whom the Father will send in my name, will teach you everything, and remind you of all that I have said to you" (14:26).

In addition to speaking of Christ as the embodiment of God's Wisdom or Word, or of their own experience of God's Spirit being poured out into their hearts, the early Christians offered benedictions such as, "The grace of the Lord Jesus Christ, the love of God, and the communion of the Holy Spirit be with all of you" (2 Cor 13:13). The most famous of these early trinitarian expressions appears at the conclusion of Matthew's Gospel. The Risen Lord appears to his disciples and instructs them, "Go therefore and make disciples of all nations, baptizing them in the name of the Father and of the Son and of the Holy Spirit" (Matt 28:19). An early handbook of Christian teachings and practices known as *The Didache* reflects the early use of the trinitarian formulas in baptism. "The procedure for baptizing is as follows. After rehearsing all the preliminaries, immerse in running water 'In the Name of the Father, and of the Son, and of the Holy Ghost.'"[6]

The rudimentary elements of the doctrine of the Trinity are, therefore, scattered throughout the New Testament. First and foremost, there is one and only one God. Second, there is a practice begun in the Old Testament and continued in the New Testament of speaking of God's Wisdom, Word, and Spirit as God's agents in creation, without suggesting that these are some type of lesser gods. Third, Christ is called God. Fourth, the New Testament speaks of the Father and the Son and the Holy Spirit, though there is no deliberate attempt in the New Testament to define the precise relationship among the three. The task of finding a conceptual framework that would incorporate these four pieces of data would fall to the theologians of the early church.

The Ancient Church

As we have discussed earlier, the apologists of the ancient church took up the challenge of rebutting the common charges leveled against Christians by their pagan and Jewish critics. The apologist Justin Martyr was one of the first Christian writers to tackle the question of how Christians could maintain a commitment to monotheism while at the same time claiming that Christ is divine. Justin's first step was to express his absolute, unwavering commitment to monotheism. As the biblical theologian Gerard Sloyan explained, "God is *'agennetos'* for Justin, *meaning for him unoriginated, in contrast to creatures who have a beginning* (1 Apology, 14.1). *The importance of this Greek term cannot be overstressed.* It will recur constantly in the discussion of the mystery of the Trinity."[7] Justin's second foundational claim was that Christ was the Word (Logos) of God in the flesh. On this second point, Justin searched for an appropriate analogy to describe the relationship between God and the Logos. Justin strained to find a figure of speech that avoided any suggestion that the essence (*ousia* in Greek) of God was in any way divided. Such a division would threaten Justin's first tenet of monotheism. It was, Justin offered, like an utterance that expresses a thought, or like the sun and its rays that illuminate our world.

Justin's theology was not without its deficiencies. He would occasionally lapse into troubling expressions, such as when he referred to the Word as "another God." Even the very influential analogy of the sun and its rays raised questions about the relationship of the Word to the Father. A bright candle placed in a very large room will illuminate the space closest to it very nicely, but the light may not carry to the far reaches of the room. In the same way, does the divine power of the Father suffer a diminution of any kind in the Word-made-flesh as he lived among us? In addition to these christological points, the Holy Spirit did not figure prominently in Justin's writings. These features of Justin's thought result in a tendency to view the Holy Spirit as subordinate to the Son, who in turn is subordinate to the Father. In his *First Apology* Justin wrote,

> We worship the Creator of the universe…with the word of prayer and thanksgiving…expressing our thanks to him in words, with solemn ceremonies and hymns.…The Master, who taught us this worship and who was born to this end, was crucified under Pontius Pilate.…We are sure that he is the Son of the true God, and hold him the second in order, with the Spirit of prophecy in the third place.[8]

This subordinationism, as it became known, was ultimately rejected in the creedal formulations of the church, but for many thinkers in the ancient church, a commitment to monotheism required assigning the Word a subordinate role to the Father. For these thinkers, if the Word had equal divine status to the Father, then Justin's comment about the Word being "a second God" might not be too far off the mark. Another name for this approach is monarchianism, meaning that God is a monarch—one authority whose power is not shared by others, except those to whom the monarch assigns it. Not only will this argument reappear frequently in the development of the doctrine of the Trinity, we will revisit it when we study the christological debates of the early church.

Irenaeus, the great opponent of Gnostic thought, spoke of God's progressive revelation in human history through a series of covenants with Adam, Noah, Moses, and Christ. In Greek theological parlance, this history of God's interaction with the world is God's "economy." In English, the term is associated with matters of finance. While the two meanings of the term *economy* may seem at first to be completely unrelated, the word *economy* originally referred to the organization and management of a household. The economy of a nation therefore refers to the well-ordered production and exchange of its goods; the economy (or in Latin, "dispensation") of God refers to "God's providential management of the household of creation, redemption, and consummation."[9] Irenaeus memorably described the Word and the Spirit as the "two hands of God" at work in God's economy of salvation.

For Irenaeus, the history of God's covenants is therefore the clue for understanding the nature of God and God's intentions for humanity. Irenaeus, however, did not claim that God *became* triune over the course of history. God *always was* triune, but the full revelation of that reality occurred over time. This is the origin of the theological distinction between "the economic Trinity," meaning the nature of God as revealed through time, and "the immanent Trinity," meaning the nature of God as it has always existed. This distinction would gradually become part of the common theological terminology regarding the Trinity, but the distinction should not be drawn too starkly. There is only one God. The distinction between the economic Trinity and the immanent Trinity amounts to two approaches to the same reality. As the Jesuit theologian Karl Rahner reminded us, "The economic Trinity is the immanent Trinity and the immanent Trinity is the economic Trinity."[10]

Some theologians at the time believed that they had a simple way to reconcile their commitment to monotheism with the Christian conception of "the economy" of salvation, or the revelation of God as it unfolded in history. They proposed that Christians should hold that the one God appeared in different roles, or modes, throughout history. God appeared as Father, as Son, and as Spirit. This belief, known as modalism, gained support among a number of thinkers in the early church, but it too was ultimately rejected in the church's creeds. The theological impulse behind both subordinationism and modalism was to preserve monotheism. Subordinationism did so by denying equal divine status to both the Father and the Word. Modalism did so by emphasizing the distinction, saying God was, in turn, Father in the Old Testament, Son in the New Testament, and Holy Spirit now. A theological vocabulary was needed that could express the oneness of God, while preserving the distinct and equal identities for the Father, Son, and Spirit in the economy of salvation. This need was met in large part by the African, Latin-speaking theologian Tertullian.

Tertullian's theology advanced the discussion of the development of the doctrine by providing the categories of thought that would continue to shape all subsequent trinitarian thought. Tertullian introduced the very word *Trinity* into the Christian vocabulary regarding God. As Alister McGrath noted.

> Tertullian gave the theology of the Trinity its distinctive vocabulary...he also shaped its distinctive form. God is one; nevertheless, God cannot be regarded as something or someone totally isolated from the created order. The economy of salvation demonstrates that God is active in creation. This activity is complex; on analysis, this divine action reveals both a *unity* and a *distinctiveness*. Tertullian argues that *substance* is what unites the three aspects of the economy of salvation; *person* is what distinguishes them. The three persons of the Trinity are distinct, yet not divided *(distincti non divisi)*, different yet not separate or independent of each other *(discreti non separti)*. The complexity of the human experience of redemption is thus the result of the three persons of the Godhead acting in distinct yet coordinated manners in human history, without any loss of the total unity of the Godhead.[11]

As McGrath mentioned, there was a theological need to speak about God's unity *and* distinctiveness at the same time. In order to meet this need, Tertullian spoke of substance and persons. Substance is what the Father, Son, and Spirit share. Personhood is what sets them apart, so to speak. "The primary sense of *persona*," according to the patristics scholar J. N. D. Kelly, "was 'mask,' from which the transition was to the actor who wore it and the character he played."[12] Theologians in the modern age would come to express an uneasiness with the use of the term *person*, believing that to modern ears *person* suggests a distinct individual with a unique center of consciousness. This would convey a sense of tritheism (three Gods) rather than monotheism. Whatever its drawbacks, Tertullian's formulation exercised a pervasive and long-lasting influence on Christian thought: God is one substance in three persons.

Origen, a younger, Greek-speaking contemporary of Tertullian, was crafting his own highly original theological system of thought in Alexandria. He drew upon the storehouse of ideas that had developed within the Platonic tradition that predated Jesus. Plato himself died in the fourth century BC, and as the succeeding generations of Platonic scholars developed his ideas, new questions were asked and new trails were blazed. One of the most influential interpreters of Plato was Plotinus (205–70) whose Neoplatonic work influenced a considerable number of early Christian thinkers. Plotinus conceived the created world as the final emanation from a divine hierarchy consisting of the "One," which emanated into the "Mind," which in turn emanated into the "World Soul," which mixed with matter to create the world in which humans live. This divine Triad was described as three *hypostases*. As the patristics scholar Maurice Wiles wrote,

> To Origen this ground plan must have appeared heaven-sent. The most naturally congenial of the non-Christian philosophical traditions had been led to the conclusion that the divine must exist in three "hypostases." Christian tradition spoke quite independently of three divine beings, the three "hypostases" of Father, Son and Holy Spirit. Where philosophy provided the form, revelation could supply the content.[13]

151

Origen's combination of Christian theological claims and Neoplatonic categories of thought was highly influential, but Origen was
not always consistent in his writings. Some passages in his writings
suggested subordinationism; others seemed to oppose it. Even the
theological giants of the early church differed in their verdict. The
biblical scholar Jerome (d. ca. 420) believed Origen was a subordina-
tionist; Athanasius (d. 373), bishop of Alexandria, did not.[14]

Origen's use of the Neoplatonic concept of emanation produced conflicting statements regarding the relationship among the
Father, Son, and Spirit. On the one hand, Origen thought of the
Trinity in hierarchical terms, in a manner similar to Plotinus's divine
Triad. The Father stands at the apex of the hierarchy, like the highest point on a grand waterfall where the torrents begin to pour down
the mountainside. "But the Son and the Spirit are also in their
degree divine, possessing, though derivatively, all the characteristics
of deity; distinct from the world of creatures, they cooperate with
the Father and mediate the divine life flowing from Him."[15] The
unity of the Father, Son, and Spirit consists of the fact that all three
are united in their will, or mission. Origen saw the unity of the three
as analogous to the unity of husband and wife in marriage.

On the other hand, Origen rejected the idea that the Word
had a beginning, and it is on this point that Origen's work anticipated theological debates to come. For Origen, the Word always
existed with the Father. As the theologians Roger E. Olson and
Christopher A. Hall explained, "To assert that there was ever a time
when the Son did not exist would be to contend 'there was once a
time when He was not the Truth, nor the Wisdom, nor the Life,
although in all these He is judged to be the perfect essence of God
the Father, for these things cannot be severed from Him, or even
be separated from His essence...'"[16] The essence of the Father and
the essence of the Son are one and the same, in Greek *homoousios*
(*homo* means "same," *ousios* means "being, or substance"). The eternal nature of the Word, and the belief that the Father and the Word
share the same being or substance, would be officially sanctioned
by the bishops at the Council of Nicaea in 325.

Before we turn to Nicaea, we need to address one very technical aspect of this discussion about the eternal nature of the Word
that became flesh in Christ Jesus. Early church thinkers spoke of

the "generation" of the Word or the Son from the Father, but many, including Origen, insisted that the Word's generation was "an eternal generation." Here our commonsense understanding of generation fails us. Human generation is a very temporal affair—people are born on a specific day in a given year. But if someone wants to argue for the coeternal existence of the Father, Son, and Spirit, then the word *generation* as it is commonly used does not apply. Irenaeus admitted that he did not know how the Son was generated from the Father. Tertullian offered the analogies of the root, the shoot, and the fruit of a plant, or a source of a river and the river itself for ways of thinking about how the Father, Son, and Spirit are one in substance.[17] As Olson and Hall observed, Origen recognized the problem.

> Origen understands that the generation of the Son cannot possibly be a corporeal generation. "For we do not say, as the heretics suppose, that some part of the substance of God was converted into the Son, or that the Son was procreated by the Father out of things nonexistent, i.e., beyond His own substance, so that there was a time when He did not exist." No, Origen insists, corporeal constructions will lead nowhere.[18]

According to Origen, the Son is generated from the Father, but this generation should not be taken to mean that the Son had a beginning in time. Nor should we think of the immaterial substance of God as we would a quantity of some material substance here on Earth. These are, to be sure, very difficult concepts to grasp, but they play a critical role in the deliberations of the bishops at the first ecumenical council of the church, the council of Nicaea.

The Council of Nicaea and Post-Nicene Developments

The importance of the Council of Nicaea will be discussed in greater length in the Christology chapter, but for our present discussion, the Council played a vital role in the development of the doctrine of the Trinity. The bishops rejected the position of a thinker named Arius who argued that the Son was not of the same substance as the Father, and instead they accepted the case championed by a deacon named Athanasius, who soon after the council became bishop of Alexandria. Nicaea represented an important step in the history of the church's official declaration of the doctrine of the Trinity. Following the lead of Athanasius, the bishops stated that the Father and the Son are "of the same essence" or "one in being" *(homoousios)*.

The creed composed at Nicaea in 325, however, did not have much to say about the Holy Spirit. But the logic of Christian belief and practice (e.g., the baptismal formula) required that due consideration be given the Holy Spirit. In the same way that earlier theologians had to clarify the "generation" of the Son, theologians now had to determine the "procession" (see John 15:26, NAB) of the Spirit. This period of Christian thought will conclude with the official declaration at the second ecumenical council, held in Constantinople in 381, that the Holy Spirit is "the Lord and Giver of life, who proceeds from the Father, who together with the Father and the Son is worshipped and glorified, who has spoken through the prophets."[19]

In the course of the debates regarding the divinity of the Holy Spirit that took place from 325 to 381, between the two Councils, the final building blocks for the doctrine of the Trinity were put in place. The three thinkers most responsible for this final stage of development are known as the Cappadocian fathers. The title is derived from the region of Cappadocia in present-day Turkey where Basil (ca. 330–79), Gregory of Nazianzus (330–89), and Gregory of Nyssa (ca. 335–94) lived. These three thinkers devoted much preaching, public debate, and scholarly writing to their defense of the divinity of the Holy Spirit and their formulation of a precise terminology about the Trinity that avoided subordinating either the Son or the Spirit to the Father, and also avoided falling into language that suggested tritheism rather than monotheism. According to the late theologian Catherine Mowry LaCugna, the Cappadocians were able to accomplish this feat by making three crucial distinctions.

First, the Cappadocians very clearly differentiated between the concepts of *ousia* and *hypostasis*. God is one *ousia* in three *hypostases*—one substance in three persons. The *ousia* refers to the universal, to what the three share; the *hypostasis* to the particular, to what makes each distinctive. As LaCugna explained, for the Cappadocian thinker Gregory of Nyssa,

> some nouns can be predicated of more than one individual, such as the noun humanity, which refers to the common nature of several individuals. Andrew, James, and John can be equally human. This common nature is the *ousia*. Other nouns refer to particular individuals such as Paul and Timothy. Each individual is a *hypostasis* of an *ousia*. In the case of Paul and Timothy, these two *hypostases* share the same *ousia*.[20]

Second, "a new distinction emerged between Fatherhood and Godhood; they were no longer synonyms. It was now possible to think of 'God' as self-differentiated: the Father is God, and the Son is God."[21] Third, the concept of person became primary over the concept of substance. For the Cappadocians, *person* is a relational term. The theologian Gerald O'Collins, SJ, explained, "At the heart of God, the Cappadocians saw an interpersonal communion or *koinonia*, with communion as the function of all three divine persons and not simply the Holy Spirit. For this interpersonal model of the Trinity, God's inner being is relational, with each of the three persons totally related to the other two in 'reciprocal delight'—to borrow an Athanasian expression..."[22]

The work of the Cappadocians provided the church with the terminology and conceptual framework to construct the orthodox confession of the Triune God as one nature in three persons. Even with such a consensus finally hammered out, there was one problem that remained. In the West, Christians spoke Latin and in the East Christians spoke Greek. Using Greek terms, Eastern Christians would state that there is one *ousia* (nature) in three *hypostases* (persons). Finding a suitable Latin translation presented certain difficulties. Tertullian had used the language of "one substance in three persons." The problem was that the Latin word *substantia* was frequently translated into Greek as *hypostasis*[23] creating the impression in the West that the Greeks spoke of three "substances" of God, which to Western ears sounded like tritheism. Despite these linguistic hurdles, the church had found the language it believed preserved the unity of God and the distinctiveness of the three divine persons. This is not to suggest that within that framework further theological speculation did not occur, but rather that the boundaries of the debate had been fixed.

One of the most creative thinkers to work within those boundaries was Augustine of Hippo (354–430), whose reflections on the subject appeared in *On the Trinity*, a work written over the course of twenty years. Scholars debate whether Augustine's approach differed significantly from the Cappadocians. Maurice Wiles has defended the claim that we can speak of an Eastern and a Western approach to the Trinity.

> The East (with the important exception of Athanasius) tends to approach from the side of the three, the West from the side of the one. When an Easterner spoke of God he thought most naturally of the Father, with whom the Son and the Spirit must somehow be joined in coequal godhead. When a Westerner spoke of God he thought most naturally of the one triune God, within whose being real distinctions of person must somehow be admitted.[24]

Augustine placed great emphasis on the essential unity of the three persons, seeing the Trinity as a divine communion of mutual indwelling love. He often pictured the Spirit as the love that unites Father and Son.

One of Augustine's most distinctive contributions to the discussion of the Trinity was his search for traces or vestiges of the Trinity in the human soul. Augustine offered various examples of the trinitarian composition of the human psyche, but the most famous was the trio of memory, intellect, and will. Augustine's insight, as the theologian William J. Hill explained, was "that each of these activities is identical with the one self which is acting and yet relationally distinct from the other two activities."[25] In other words, we know from personal experience that we are one person, yet our personalities have many dimensions that can act simultaneously. Such analogies served not only a didactic purpose, but also laid the foundation for a Christian spirituality that saw the nature of God revealed not only in the divine economy, but also in the depths of the individual and in the human experience of love.

Before tackling the issues raised in the medieval discussions of God, we need to return to our initial discussion of the importance of distinctions in such fields of study as geometry. The purpose of the distinctions there is to clarify our understanding and discussion of various shapes; for example, squares and rectangles, equilateral triangles and isosceles triangles. In Christian discourse about God, certain distinctions arose and eventually became part of the shared vocabulary of the church: the immanent Trinity and the economic Trinity, substance and person, generation of the Word and creation of the Word. Such distinctions can often be confusing, but they are intended to help Christians understand more precisely what they mean when they say, "Glory be to the Father, the Son, and the Holy Spirit." In this way, the history of Christian thought regarding the Trinity demonstrates the wisdom of the ancient principle *lex orandi, lex credendi* ("the law of worship is the law of belief").[26]

Human Knowledge of God

The distinction between the economic Trinity and immanent Trinity balances two claims within Christian faith. On the one hand, God's intentions for humanity have been made known "to our ancestors in many and various ways" (see Heb 1:1), culminating in the appearance of Christ among us. Because of this way, we can possess reliable knowledge about God. On the other hand, humans cannot comprehend the nature of our God, "who dwells in unapproachable light, whom no one has ever seen or can see" (see 1 Tim 6:16). This question of the extent to which humans can comprehend God or possess genuine knowledge of God is directly related to many of the issues we discussed in the previous chapter concerning mystery, faith, and revelation. In the trinitarian and christological debates in the early church, theologians were acutely aware that they confronted a theological problem: either we cannot know God, in which case we would be unable to speak reliably at all about God, or we can know God, in which case we would seem to be treating God as a physical object that could be examined. As the late Orthodox scholar John Meyendorff explained, "A known God is necessarily limited, since our created intelligence is limited by its very creation."[27]

This creative tension between God as the One who reveals, or who can be known (as emphasized in the concept of the economic Trinity) and God as the One who remains unknowable (as emphasized in the concept of the immanent Trinity) produced two theological traditions in the ancient world: the affirmative way (or cataphatic tradition), and the negative way (or apophatic tradition). Not only are these two ways of thinking about knowability of God, but they are also basic differences between the Western and the Eastern Church.

THE CATAPHATIC AND THE APOPHATIC TRADITIONS

Harvey Egan, SJ, a theologian who specializes in the study of Christian mysticism, offered the following contrast between these two traditions, beginning with the affirmative way:

> As a philosophical-theological position, the affirmative way stresses what the First Vatican Council (1870) formally declared as a truth of faith, namely, that "God...may be certainly known by the natural light of human reason, *by means of created things*, because 'ever since the creation of the world his invisible nature, namely his eternal power and deity, has been clearly perceived in the things that have been made' (Rom 1:20); but that it pleased his wisdom and bounty to *reveal himself* and the eternal decrees of his will to mankind by another and a supernatural way [i.e., through Christ].[28]

In the affirmative way, there is a confidence that humans can recognize and comprehend God's revelation. By contrast, according to Egan, "As a philosophical-theological position, the negative way emphasizes that the all-transcendent God is ineffable, incomprehensible, and 'wholly other.'"[29] In the negative way, there is sense of the inadequacy of human thought and language, and a heavier emphasis on the awesome, overwhelming, and indescribable nature of God.

The affirmative and negative ways are indispensable, mutually corrective impulses in the Christian way of life. The affirmative way celebrates the power of human language to illuminate human experience. In this approach, good theology is like good poetry in that both open up ways of seeing the world or expressing elusive ideas. The negative way, by contrast, reminds us of the inadequacy of our language and retains an appreciation for the religious insights expressed in paradoxical form (e.g., "the brilliant darkness" of God[30]). The negative way reminds us of the mystery and incomprehensibility of God. As Augustine once reminded his congregation in a sermon, "If you have understood, then what you have understood is not God."[31] The affirmative way searches for the right words to say; the negative way waits in silence for God's response.

The writings of an anonymous fifth- or sixth-century monk known to us as Pseudo-Dionysius (or Denys the Areopagite) illustrate beautifully the dynamic interplay of the affirmative and negative ways. In his work "The Divine Names," he posed the following question:

> How then can we speak of the divine names? How can we do this if the Transcendent surpasses all discourse and all knowledge, if it abides beyond the reach of mind and of being, if it encompasses and circumscribes, embraces and anticipates all things while itself eluding their grasp and escaping from any perception, imagination, opinion, name, discourse, apprehension, or understanding?[32]

In responding to his own questions, Dionysius drew upon the insights of both the affirmative way and the negative way. In typically affirmative fashion, Dionysius confidently asserted that God is "a Source which has told us about itself in the holy words of scripture."[33] In reference to this aspect of his theology, the theologian Seely J. Beggiani observed, "Although Scripture is limited to the use of veiled images and symbols, it does furnish us with some intimation of God by providing us with divine names. These names are not the result of human speculation but have been fashioned through the inspiration of the Spirit."[34] Dionysius, however, tempered his claims with an accent on the negative way, speaking of God as "the Inscrutable One [who] is out of the reach of every rational process. Nor can any words come up to the inexpressible Good."[35] For Dionysius, to progress in the spiritual life we must discard our images of God and enter more and more completely into an awareness of the utter incomprehensibility of God. It is in this spirit that the Orthodox scholar Vladimir Lossky commented that apophaticism (i.e., the negative way) "constitutes the fundamental characteristic of the whole theological tradition of the Eastern Church."[36]

THE USE OF ANALOGY

The Scottish theologian Ian A. McFarland once commented, "Good theology begins and ends with a recognition that we can never know God completely....The good theologian (literally, one who talks about God) thus emerges as a person who strikes the right balance between saying too much and saying too little."[37] When we say too much about God, we often enlist God as a supporter for our own causes (e.g., "God certainly does not approve of..."). We presume too quickly to know the mind of God. When we say too little about God, we fail to offer our neighbors the consolation of our deepest religious convictions. We do not embrace the insight Paul conveyed to the church at Corinth; namely, that while it is certainly true that we see (i.e., understand) God "dimly" or "indistinctly" (1 Cor 13:12), nevertheless, we do in fact see. We *can* have knowledge of God, imperfect though it may be. The balancing act of not saying too much and not saying too little about God is the hallmark of sound theology. In order to accomplish this feat, theologians employ the concept of analogy.

Before turning to the definition of the term *analogy*, let us consider two verses taken from the Book of Psalms. The first is the opening verse of Psalm 23, "The Lord is my shepherd, I shall not want." The second is taken from Psalm 18, "The Lord is my rock, my fortress, and my deliverer, / my God, my rock in whom I take refuge, / my shield, and the horn of my salvation, my stronghold" (18:2). In both verses, the psalmist conveys an insight into the nature of God through the use of imagery. The reader knows that the language is not intended to be taken literally. God is, however, a shepherd, in the sense of One who guides and protects us. God is obviously not literally a rock, or a shield, but the Lord is a secure foundation and a source of protection. As proponents of the negative way remind us, it is easier to know what God *is not* rather than what God *is*. For Aquinas, it is easier for humans to know that God is not finite than it is to grasp the eternal nature of God.

Theologians label images, such as the ones we find in the psalms, analogies. An analogy is a comparison in which two elements being compared are both similar and dissimilar in significant aspects. For example, the Lord is like a shepherd in terms of God's care and concern for humanity, and unlike a shepherd in terms of having a body. In more technical terms, analogous statements are neither univocal or equivocal statements. As the philosopher Ed. L. Miller explained in his work *God and Reason*, "We speak univocally (literally 'naming in one way') when we apply a word with the same meaning to different things. Thus when we say, 'Peter is a man, and James and John also,' we predicate exactly the same thing of James and John as we do of Peter. Here we are using the word 'man' univocally."[38] To speak univocally about God would require that we know the nature of God to such a degree that we could be certain that our concepts of goodness and wisdom apply to God in exactly the same way as they apply to humans. This seems to be saying too much about God.

However, as Miller continued, "We speak equivocally (literally, 'naming in like ways') when we employ a single word but intend completely different meanings, as when we use the word 'pen' to mean at one time an instrument for writing and at another time a place for pigs."[39] If our religious language were equivocal, we could not speak assuredly about God's goodness, wisdom, or power. Our concepts of goodness, wisdom, or power would bear no relation at all to God's attributes. Here we would be saying too little about God. An analogy, therefore, is the middle way between univocal and equivocal statements. It claims that God is like—yet also unlike—a shepherd, a fortress, a shield, and so on.

AQUINAS'S FIVE WAYS

The theologian Thomas Aquinas (ca. 1225–74) had a deep appreciation for the insights of the affirmative and the negative ways, as well as a profound awareness of the analogical nature of our language about God. Aquinas also regarded human reason as a capacity given to us by our Creator. Consequently, Aquinas valued the insights of both Christian and non-Christian thinkers, including those of Aristotle, whose works were being reintroduced in the West in thirteenth-century universities. Aquinas's theological writings displayed his remarkable ability to synthesize a vast array of theological and philosophical sources into a comprehensive system. His intellectual power of integration was no more clearly displayed than in his lengthy, yet orderly, exposition of theology entitled *Summa Theologiae.*

In one of the most widely debated passages from the *Summa* (I, Q. 2, article 3), Aquinas offered five arguments for God's existence—or, more precisely, he offered five "ways" of thinking about God's existence. Before we examine these five arguments, it is important to make a few observations about the common designation of Aquinas's Five Ways as "proofs" for the existence of God. Aquinas was a medieval religious scholar and member of the Dominican Order who conceived of the *Summa* as an introductory text for the study of theology. He was not attempting to prove the existence of God to either himself or his audience. While for Aquinas it could be reasonably demonstrated through the use of human reason that God exists, he did not dwell on the question, and the Five Ways take up only a few pages. Aquinas also was aware that Aristotle arrived at conclusions contrary to his own. Aristotle, for example, believed the universe was eternal, whereas Aquinas asserted that God created the universe from nothing. For Aquinas, the question "Who is God?" was far more interesting than the question "Does God exist?"

In the First Way, Aquinas began with the observation that things in this world are in constant motion. Aquinas accepted Aristotle's definition of motion (*motus* in Latin, which can be translated as "motion" or "change") as a transition from a state of potentiality to actuality. Potentiality refers to what something can become;

actuality refers to what something currently is. For example, an acorn is in potentiality an oak tree, but in actuality is still an acorn. But, as the philosopher Milton K. Munitz has explained, motion refers broadly to "(a) a change of *quantity*, as when something grows or diminishes in size; (b) a change in *quality*, as when something changes color, or changes from cold to hot; (c) a change of *place*, as when something moves from one spatial position to another."[40]

How, then, do we account for this motion? Aquinas argued that "Now anything in process of change is being changed by something else."[41] In other words, motion (broadly conceived) requires a mover, which itself needs a mover, and so on. "Now," continued Aquinas, "we must stop somewhere, otherwise there will be no first cause of the change....Hence one is bound to arrive at some first cause of change not itself changed by anything, and this is what everybody understands by God."[42] In the more technical language of Aristotle and Aquinas, there must be a pure Actuality with no potentiality (hence, not itself subject to change) to account for the motion in the world. One further note needs to be made here. Aquinas did not seem to be thinking in terms of motion in a linear sense: a child requires the existence of a parent, who in turn requires a child's grandparent, and so on back in time. Rather as the great twentieth-century Jesuit philosopher F. C. Copleston noted, "We have to imagine, not a lineal or horizontal series, so to speak, but a vertical hierarchy, in which a lower member depends here and now on a causal activity of the member above it. It is the latter type of series, *if prolonged to infinity*, which Aquinas rejects."[43]

In the Second Way, Aquinas focused on the nature of causality. Like the idea of motion, causality was defined more broadly by both Aristotle and Aquinas than by us. Aristotle spoke of an object having four causes: a material cause, a formal cause, an efficient cause, and a final cause. Take, for example, a marble bench in a park. The material cause is marble; without marble, such a bench would not exist, so Aristotle labeled this the material cause of its existence. The formal cause is the shape given the material. A block of marble could be cut into any number of objects (a statue, an altar, or a pedestal). The one who carved the bench is the efficient cause, and the purpose for which it was constructed is the final cause. Effects (the presence of a marble bench in a park) require causes to account for their existence.

As he reasoned in the First Way, Aquinas concluded that there must be a first cause, which is itself uncaused.

In the Third Way, Aquinas distinguished between necessary and contingent beings. A necessary being must exist. A contingent being does not have to exist. It could be or could not be. A contingency plan would be, "In the event this happens, do x. If it doesn't happen, do y." Suppose someone is stuck in traffic on a highway leading to the airport. She may call her friend and say, "If I am able to make my flight, I will meet you at noon. If I miss my flight, I will take the later flight and meet you for dinner." She may catch her flight or miss it. She may get to the airport, only to find her flight has been delayed or canceled. Some possible scenarios will occur and others will not. A contingent event depends on something else for its occurrence.

Aquinas's reasoning at this point closely resembles the reasoning he employed in the first two ways. We observe that all things in the world are contingent. There is no necessity for anything to exist. We could certainly imagine a room without desks, an Earth without people, or a universe without our solar system. The eighteenth-century philosopher G. W. Leibniz once asked, "Why is there something rather than nothing?"[44] Aquinas's Third Way posed the same question: Why is there anything at all? Aquinas concluded that there must be one Necessary Being to account for the existence of the contingent universe.

Aquinas's Fourth Way is commonly called the "scale of perfection" argument. We offer comparative analyses of things: some actions are morally better than others; some accounts of events are truer than others. Such language only makes sense if there is some scale of perfection. A truer statement implies that "Truth" exists and that one statement more closely approximates Truth. A better moral action requires "Goodness" to exist so that one action can be judged as more moral than another. The standard modern objection would assert that such judgments are culturally determined; there is no one universal standard of Truth or Goodness, any more than there is one definition of Beauty. Beauty is in the eye of the beholder.

In the Fifth Way, Aquinas asserted that things in nature display purpose or design. Aristotle spoke of the *telos*, or the goal or purpose of things in nature; for this reason, Aquinas's Fifth Way is technically called the teleological argument, but it is commonly known as "the argument from design." The created order displays design. Take as an example the intricate composition of the human eye or the complexity of the human brain. In modern terms, we can ask, "Do such systems exist as a fluke of evolution or do they reflect the work of an intelligent designer?" Aquinas would say the latter, and he concluded, "Everything in nature, therefore, is directed to its goal by someone with understanding, and this we call 'God.'"[45]

Before we move on from consideration of Aquinas's Five Ways, we need to mention one other argument for the existence of God that predated Aquinas, but that he does not include in the *Summa*. Anselm of Canterbury (ca. 1033–1109), who gave us the famous description of theology as "faith seeking understanding," is often credited with the formulation of the ontological argument for the existence of God. Aquinas preferred arguments that were grounded in a consideration of some characteristic of the universe (e.g., motion, change, design). These kinds of argument are cosmological, meaning that they are based on the universe (i.e., the cosmos). Anselm's argument, by contrast, is based on the idea of God itself. It moves from ideas to reality and is called the ontological argument, from the Greek *on-logos*, "the study of being" or "the study of that which is."[46]

Anselm's starting point is the definition of God as "a being than which none greater can be thought." Anselm argued that once we properly understood that definition, we realize that such a being, by necessity, exists. Anselm uses the example of a painter, so we will follow his lead, and think about Leonardo da Vinci's portrait, the *Mona Lisa*. Before committing the portrait to canvas, da Vinci had a mental image in his mind. After completing the painting, the idea exists in reality as well as in his mind. Something that exists in the mind and reality is better, says Anselm, than something that exists only in the mind. The idea of God exists at least in the human mind. But if God is a being greater than which none can be conceived, then God must exist not only in the mind, but in reality as well. Therefore, God exists. The controversy regarding the validity of this argument continues to the present time, with respected thinkers on both sides of the issue.

Two Modern Responses
to Aquinas's Arguments

The modern philosopher of religion Basil Mitchell began *The Justification of Religious Belief* with these words: "The question I want to discuss is whether religious belief requires or admits of rational support; if so, of what sort and to what extent."[47] Mitchell's question, which he answers in the affirmative, is representative of the type of inquiry undertaken by scholars in the field of philosophical theology. Mitchell himself argued for the "cumulative case" for traditional Christian theism, insisting: "Thus the debate between theists and atheists is unlikely to make progress, so long as it is confined to a single argument, such as the cosmological argument, or, indeed, to a whole series of arguments, if these are to be taken piecemeal without at any stage being brought into relation to one another."[48] In other words, Mitchell would argue that any one of Aquinas's Five Ways, or any other single argument for the existence of God, does not establish beyond a shadow of a doubt that God exists. However, the cumulative effect of many, very strong arguments provides a convincing, coherent argument in favor of theism. Not all thinkers, however, find Mitchell's project to be a useful one for Christian theology.

The twentieth-century Protestant theologian Karl Barth delivered a sermon in 1933 titled "The First Commandment as a Theological Axiom." Barth's sermon began: "An axiom is a statement which cannot be proven by other statements. Indeed it is not in need of being proven by other statements."[49] Barth insisted that theology—like mathematics, physics, and logic—rests on a bedrock principle (or set of principles). For example, it is an axiom in logic that a thing cannot be and not be at the same time. This would be a logical contradiction. Barth continued:

> If there is also an axiom of *theology*, as the title of this address implies, then what is meant is this: theology too rests in regard to the proof of its statements on an ultimate and decisive presupposition. As such, it can neither be proven nor is it in need of proof. It contains in itself everything which is necessary for its proof. It can be

stated just as the axiom or axioms of any other discipline. The statements of theology are measured by the axiom every bit as rigorously as the statements of every other discipline are measured by its axioms.[50]

As the title of his sermon suggests, Barth insisted that the First Commandment is the axiom of all Christian theology: "I am the Lord your God, who brought you out of the land of Egypt, out of the house of slavery; you shall have no other gods before me" (Exod 20:2–3).

Barth's thesis carries with it a number of implications about the nature of theology and revelation and a number of other theological areas of concern. In the context of our present discussion, Christian theology, according to Barth, does not best serve the needs of the Christian community if it is overly preoccupied with proving God's existence. While other theologians would certainly disagree with Barth's contention, he would insist that Christian theology takes the existence of God as axiomatic. Our energies are more profitably spent exploring the implications of God's existence for our way of life, or examining how Christ discloses the nature of God, or celebrating the presence of God in our lives through liturgy. Some theologians applaud Barth's declaration of the axiomatic status of the Christian belief in God's existence. Others believe he prematurely ends a conversation that would be rewarding for believer and nonbeliever alike.

This divergence in approaches to the project of philosophical theology will resurface in our next chapter dealing with the question of God in the modern age. How do Christians best offer their "defense to anyone who demands from you an accounting for the hope that is in you" (1 Pet 3:15)? What role does reason play in this endeavor? Does Christianity embody a universal truth that could be realized through methods and means other than the Gospel? Does Christianity call us to make a leap of faith that is separate and apart from reason? These are some of the questions that will occupy the great theological minds in the modern age.

Discussion Questions

1. What is the depiction of God in the Bible? Is this your understanding of God?
2. What is the Wisdom, Word, or Spirit of God? How is it active in the world?
3. What is your evaluation of Irenaeus's description of the Word and Spirit as "the two hands of God?"
4. What does it mean to say that God is one substance in three persons?
5. What analogies could you give to express the mystery of the Trinity?
6. What are some useful analogies or images to speak of the mystery of God?
7. To what extent can we know the nature of God? What implications follow from your position?
8. What is your evaluation of Aquinas's Five Ways? Do the findings of modern science confirm or undermine the arguments?
9. Is it possible to offer reasonable arguments for the existence of God?

Suggested Readings

Three very helpful introductions to the Trinity are Roger E. Olson and Christopher A. Hall, *The Trinity* (Grand Rapids: William B. Eerdmans, 2002); William J. La Due, *The Trinity Guide to the Trinity* (Harrisburg, PA: Trinity Press International, 2003); and Gerald O'Collins, *The Tripersonal God* (Mahwah, NJ: Paulist Press, 1999). For an excellent introduction to the patristic debates, see William G. Rusch's Introduction to *The Trinitarian Controversy*, William G. Rusch, ed. (Philadelphia: Fortress Press, 1980). See also Christopher B. Kaiser, *The Doctrine of God* (Westchester, IL: Crossway Books, 1982). For a discussion of the negative way, see Vladimir Lossky, *The Mystical Theology of the Eastern Church* (Crestwood, NY: St. Vladimir's Seminary Press, 2002). For a review of arguments for the existence of God, see chapter three of

Peter Kreeft and Ronald K. Tacelli, *Handbook of Christian Apologetics* (Downers Grove, IL: InterVarsity Press, 1994); and chapters four to six of Brian Davies, *An Introduction to the Philosophy of Religion*, 2nd ed. (Oxford: Oxford University Press, 1993).

Notes

1. J. Albert Soggin, *Israel in the Biblical Period* (Edinburgh: T & T Clark, 2001), 51.

2. Gerald O'Collins, *The Tripersonal God* (Mahwah, NJ: Paulist Press, 1999), 34.

3. Reginald H. Fuller and Pheme Perkins, *Who Is This Christ?* (Philadelphia: Fortress, 1983), 55.

4. Raymond E. Brown, *An Introduction to New Testament Christology* (Mahwah, NJ: Paulist Press, 1994), 188.

5. D. Moody Smith, Jr, *John* in the Abingdon New Testament Commentaries Series (Nashville: Abingdon, 1999), 383.

6. *The Didache*, 2.7, in Maxwell Staniforth, trans. *Early Christian Writings* (New York: Penguin Books, 1968), 230-31.

7. Gerard S. Sloyan, *The Three Persons in One God* (Englewood Cliffs, NJ: Prentice-Hall, 1964), 33. Italics are Sloyan's.

8. Quoted in O'Collins, *The Tripersonal God*, 90-91.

9. Catherine M. LaCugna, "Economy, Divine," *The HarperCollins Encyclopedia of Catholicism*, Richard P. McBrien, ed. (San Francisco: HarperCollins, 1995), 451.

10. Karl Rahner, *The Trinity* (New York: Herder and Herder, 1970), 22.

11. Alister McGrath, *Christian Theology* (Cambridge, MA: Blackwell, 1994), 252.

12. J. N. D. Kelly, *Early Christian Doctrines*, rev. ed. (San Francisco: Harper and Row, 1978), 115.

13. Maurice Wiles, *The Christian Fathers* (New York: Oxford University Press, 1982), 35.

14. William J. La Due, *The Trinity Guide to the Trinity* (Harrisburg, PA: Trinity Press International, 2003), 38.

15. Quoted in Kelly, *Early Christian Doctrines*, 131.

16. Roger E. Olson and Christopher A. Hall, *The Trinity* (Grand Rapids: Wm. B. Eerdmans, 2002), 24.

17. Kelly, *Early Christian Doctrines*, 113.

18. Olson and Hall, *The Trinity*, 24.

19. J. Neuner and J. Dupuis, eds., *The Christian Faith*, rev. ed. (New York: Alba House, 1982), 9.

20. Catherine Mowry LaCugna, *God For Us* (San Francisco: HarperCollins, 1991), 67.

21. Catherine Mowry LaCugna, "God in Communion with Us," in *Freeing Theology*, La Cugna, ed. (San Francisco: Harper-Collins, 1993) 86.

22. O'Collins, *The Tripersonal God*, 132.

23. See Olson and Hall, *The Trinity*, 30; and Giles Hibbert, OP, "Trinity—One God or Many?" at www.bfpubs.demon.co.uk/trinity.htm.

24. Maurice Wiles, *The Christian Fathers*, 49-50.

25. William J. Hill, *The Three-Personed God* (Washington, DC: The Catholic University of America Press, 1982), 56.

26. "Lex orandi, lex credendi," in *The HarperCollins Encyclopedia of Catholicism*, Richard P. McBrien, ed. (San Francisco: Harper San Francisco, 1995), 767.

27. John Meyendorff, *Christ in Eastern Christian Thought* (Crestwood, NY: St. Vladimir's Seminary Press, 1975), 93.

28. Harvey D. Egan, "Affirmative Way," in Michael Downey, ed., *The New Dictionary of Catholic Spirituality* (Collegeville, MN: Liturgical Press, 1993), 14.

29. Egan, "Negative Way," in *The New Dictionary of Catholic Spirituality*, 700.

30. Pseudo-Dionysius, "The Mystical Theology," in Colm Luibheid, trans., *Pseudo-Dionysius: The Complete Works* (Mahwah, NJ: Paulist Press, 1987), 135.

31. Quoted in Elizabeth Johnson, *She Who Is* (New York: Crossroad Publishing Co., 1992), 105. The quotation is taken from Augustine's Sermon #52.

32. Pseudo-Dionysius, "The Divine Names," in *Pseudo-Dionysius: The Complete Works*, 53.

33. Ibid., 51.

34. Seeley J. Beggiani, "Theology at the Service of Mysticism: Method in Pseudo-Dionysius," *Theological Studies* 57, no. 2 (1996): 216.

35. Pseudo-Dionysius, "Divine Names," 49-50.

36. Vladimir Lossky, *The Mystical Theology of the Eastern Church* (Crestwood, NY: St. Vladimir's Seminary Press, 2002), 26.

37. Ian A. McFarland, "Developing an Apophatic Christocentrism," in *Theology Today* 60 (2003): 201.

38. Ed. L. Miller, *God and Reason*, 2nd ed. (Englewood Cliffs, NJ: Prentice Hall, 1995), 215.

39. Ibid.

40. Milton K. Munitz, *The Ways of Philosophy* (New York: Macmillan Publishing Co., 1979), 132.

41. St. Thomas Aquinas, *Summa Theologiae* I, q. 2, art. 3, translated by the Blackfriars, vol. 2 (New York: McGraw-Hill Book Company, 1964), 13.

42. Ibid., 15.

43. F. C. Copleston, *Aquinas* (New York: Penguin Books, 1955), 123, emphasis added.

44. G. W. Leibniz, "The Principles of Nature and Grace, Based on Reason," at www.earlymoderntexts.com/f_leibniz.html, accessed 10/10/06. The link for the text of "Principles" is toward the bottom of the page.

45. St. Thomas Aquinas, *Summa*, I, q, 2, art. 3, p. 17.

46. "Ontology," in *The HarperCollins Encyclopedia of Catholicism*, Richard P. McBrien, ed. (San Francisco: HarperCollins, 1995), 934.

47. Basil Mitchell, *The Justification of Religious Belief* (New York: Oxford University Press, 1981), 1.

48. Ibid., 45.

49. Karl Barth, "The First Commandment as an Axiom of Theology," in *The Way of Theology in Karl Barth*, H. Martin Rumscheidt, ed. (Allison Park, PA: Pickwick Publications, 1986), 63.

50. Ibid., 63.

6

THE CONCEPT OF GOD
IN REFORMATION AND MODERN
THEOLOGY

In this chapter we continue our investigation of the concept of God in the history of Christian thought. We begin with the sixteenth-century Protestant Reformers, and follow the twists and turns in the Christian tradition until we arrive at the Second Vatican Council (1962–65). In each of the intervening centuries we find a set of concerns and issues dominating the discussion: in the seventeenth century, it was the emergence of modern scientific thought and its impact on Christian theology; in the eighteenth century, it was the Enlightenment's promotion of reason in all aspects of human existence; in the nineteenth century, it was the rise of modern atheism; and in the twentieth century, it was the challenge of finding a meaningful expression of Christian thought in a secularized world.

The Sixteenth Century

MARTIN LUTHER

The turning point in the personal life of Martin Luther (1483–1546), and the decisive moment in his career as a theologian, occurred when he realized that the "righteousness of God" was not a teaching to be feared, but rather the heart of the good news that should be embraced in faith. Earlier in his life, Luther understood the righteousness of God to mean the moral demands God placed upon humans, and the eternal punishment that awaits sinners who fail to live up to those demands. As a young scripture professor at the University of Wittenberg, Luther was assigned to lecture on Psalms, Hebrews, and Paul's Letters to the Galatians and the Romans. In Paul's Letter to the Romans Luther read a verse (1:17) that decisively altered his understanding of God. Luther recounted this realization in the preface to the complete collection of his Latin writings, published in 1545.

> Though I lived as a monk without reproach, I felt that I was a sinner before God with an extremely disturbed conscience. I could not believe that he was placated by my satisfaction. I did not love, yes, I hated the righteous God who punishes sinners, and secretly, if not blasphemously, certainly murmuring greatly, I was angry with God, and said, "As if, indeed, it is not enough, that miserable sinners, eternally lost through original sin, are crushed by every kind of calamity by the law of the decalogue, without having God add pain to pain by the gospel and also by the gospel threatening us with his righteousness and wrath!" Thus I raged with a fierce and troubled conscience...
>
> At last, by the mercy of God, meditating day and night, I gave heed to the context of the words, namely, "In it the righteousness of God is revealed, as it is written, 'He who through faith is righteous shall live.'" There I began to understand that the righteousness of God is that by which the righteous lives by a gift of God, namely by faith....Here I felt I was altogether born again and had entered paradise itself through the gate.[1]

In his biography of Luther, the historian Richard Marius described Luther's critical insight into the nature of God. "As he examined the joining of the words 'righteousness of God,' he saw that this righteousness or 'justice' was not something that God did *against* sinners; it was something that God gave *to* Christians... *Iustitia*—justice, righteousness—did not mean that God judged people according to the Ten Commandments; rather *iustitia* was equity, a favorable verdict given by the judge because of special circumstances, the circumstances here being helplessness and faith on the part of the Christian....God becomes righteous because he is merciful—demonstrating the kind of God he is."[2]

Because the mercy of God is given as a gift, and not as an entitlement, Luther believed that the Christian's life should be imbued with a sense of gratitude. In a sermon he delivered in 1528, Luther offered the following commentary on the first article of the Apostles' Creed.

> The first article teaches us that God is the Father, the creator of heaven and earth. What is this? What do these words mean? The meaning is that I should believe that I am God's creature, that he has given to me body, soul, good eyes, reason, a good wife, children, fields, meadows, pigs, and cows, and besides this, he has given to me the four elements, water, fire, air, and earth. Thus this article teaches that you do not have your life of yourself, not even a hair...
>
> But if everything is a gift of God, then you owe it to him to serve him with all these things and praise and thank him, since he has given them and still preserves them.[3]

JOHN CALVIN

While Luther stressed the concept of justification, a second-generation Protestant reformer's treatment of God's grace has forever linked Luther with the theory of predestination. John Calvin (1509–64) was not the first thinker in the Christian tradition to speak of predestination, but he is the one thinker most commonly associated with the doctrine. Predestination is the belief that God has elected some people for salvation, and others for damnation; this is called, more specifically, "double predestination" because God predestines both the saved and the damned. Because this decree was issued "before the foundation of the world" (Eph 1:4), the number of the elect (i.e., those chosen to be with God for all eternity) was fixed by God before any humans lived on Earth. Furthermore, because this is an eternal decree, humans are unable by their actions to alter their status as either saved or damned.

Calvin defended this doctrine in a number of ways. First, Calvin believed that it was plainly taught in scripture. Not only is the notion of God's election of Israel a dominant theme in the Old Testament, but the New Testament writings also speak of God's "elect" (see Rom 8:33, Matt 24:22). In his Letter to the Romans, Paul declared:

> We know that all things work together for good for those who love God, who are called according to his purpose. For those he foreknew he also predestined to be conformed to the image of his Son, in order that he might be the firstborn within a large family. And those whom he predestined he also called; and those whom he called he also justified; and those whom he justified he also glorified. (8:28–30)

For Calvin, a doctrine that is clearly stated in scripture, no matter how jarring to human sensibilities, must be held as true by Christians.

Second, the doctrine of predestination, Calvin insisted, followed logically from the central Protestant principle that salvation comes from God's grace alone. "For by grace you have been saved through faith, and this is not your own doing; it is a gift of God—not the result of works, so that no one may boast" (Eph 2:8–9). Salvation is a gift freely given by God, not a reward bestowed on those who "earned" it.

Third, Calvin emphasized both the lowly state of humanity and the majesty of God. In his magnum opus, *Institutes of the Christian Religion*, Calvin wrote,

> Hence that dread and wonder with which Scripture commonly represents the saints as stricken and overcome whenever they felt the presence of God. Thus it comes about that we see men who in his absence normally remained firm and constant, but who, when he manifests his glory, are so shaken and struck dumb as to be laid low by the dread of death—are in fact overwhelmed by it and almost annihilated. As a consequence,

we must infer that man is never sufficiently touched and affected by the awareness of his lowly state until he has compared himself with God's majesty.[4]

The sovereign and majestic power of God functioned as the organizing principle in Calvin's theology, and it was this biblical standard by which all theological claims were to be judged. For Calvin, then, predestination was scripturally sound and theologically appropriate in that it rightly attributed all glory to God.

While the doctrine of double predestination became the hallmark of traditional Calvinist theology, it has received a mixed review within the wider Christian community. Those who object to Calvin's position believe that predestination reduces human existence to a puppet show with God as the grand puppeteer pulling all the strings. Others fear the rejection of human freedom also eliminates the critical Christian concepts of sin, repentance, and moral responsibility. How can people be held responsible for actions they were predestined by God to perform? If sin is defined as a human action that violates the will of God, how can a proponent of predestination say anything is sinful? Why preach the Gospel and call those assembled to conversion if both their lives (and afterlives) are already determined?

Though aware of these difficulties, Calvin never wavered in his insistence on predestination being an essential component of Christian belief. While predestination naturally raised the agonizing question in the mind of the individual of whether he or she was part of the elect or the damned, Calvin frequently emphasized the more consoling aspects of the doctrine. As the historian William J. Bouwsma noted,

> Predestination, for Calvin, can be understood only within the context of faith; then, "treated properly and soberly, no doctrine is more useful." It promotes zeal and industry to live purely, and to stimulate us "to glorify God's judgments and to exclaim with Paul, Oh deep and incomprehensible abyss!" Teaching "that our salvation is grounded only on the goodness of God" and "that we shall always be safe," it evokes gratitude and inspires confidence. This explains

why, although earlier editions of the *Institutes* had treated predestination as part of the doctrine of providence, in the final edition Calvin discussed it in connection with salvation. In this context, and only here, is it edifying.[5]

The salvation promised in scripture stemmed from God's power and knowledge, but also God's mercy. A just God could certainly condemn the whole of humanity to damnation, so the promise that God has chosen some to be saved should be the cause for rejoicing.

Like Luther, Calvin insisted that scripture is the supreme authority in matters of Christian belief and practice. But Calvin was almost adamant that the power of scripture is experienced in the hearts of believers. Indeed, "Scripture will ultimately suffice for a saving knowledge of God only when its certainty is founded upon the inward persuasion of the Holy Spirit."[6] In a similar vein, Calvin spoke of faith as "firm and certain knowledge of God's benevolence toward us, founded upon the truth of the freely given promise in Christ, both revealed to our minds and sealed upon our hearts through the Holy Spirit."[7] Calvin placed great emphasis on the interiority of the person, on the "inward persuasion" of the Holy Spirit and its effect on the heart of the individual. Calvin balanced this with a conviction that the history recounted in the Bible was accurate and the precepts taught in scripture needed to be obeyed (e.g., baptism should be administered).

THE SPIRITUALISTS

A third group of sixteenth-century Protestant reformers—after those following Luther and Calvin—took what they believed was the logical next step in the Protestant reclaiming of the Gospel. In doing so, they focused their attention exclusively on the interiority of the person, and denied the need for any external rituals. This third group within Protestantism, known as the Spiritualists, rejected any eternal signs of Christian faith. Rather, as the historian R. Emmet McLaughlin described, the Spiritualists

saw the root of the Protestant malaise in the reliance on externals such as the sacraments, the church, and scripture.

They argued that the Spirit could directly inspire faith and remake the sinner into a true Christian. An inner Lord's Supper, an inner baptism, and an inner word all took precedence over outward rituals and the Bible, thereby rendering the latter superfluous.[8]

The Spiritualists took their inspiration from various New Testament passages. For example, Paul distinguished between the letter and the spirit of the law (2 Cor 3:1–6) and asserted that Christ lives within us (Rom 8:9; Gal 2:20). In John's Gospel Jesus spoke of being born of the Spirit (3:8) and of worshipping God in spirit and truth (4:24). In Luke's Gospel, Jesus taught that the kingdom of God is within you (Luke 17:21, now more commonly translated as "among you").[9] The Spiritualist Valentin Weigel (1533–88) captured this theological sentiment in his 1578 work "The Golden Grasp" when he declared: "Oh Lord God and Father, you have indeed written for us with your finger in the book of life, so that we should not seek it externally, on paper or in the flesh in this place or that, but rather await it in us."[10]

Our final sixteenth-century thinker also focused on the interiority of the person, but combined that approach with a strict obedience to the teachings of the Catholic church. One of the leading figures in the sixteenth-century Catholic Reformation was Ignatius of Loyola (ca. 1491–1556), who founded the Society of Jesus, a religious order commonly known as the Jesuits. Ignatius's motto of "finding God in all things" suggested that God was intimately present in each and every aspect of human existence, from mundane chores to meditative prayer. According to the two Jesuit scholars, Thomas M. Gannon, SJ, and George W. Traub, SJ,

> The revolution in spiritual thinking and practice initiated by Ignatius of Loyola consisted, then, in a shift of emphasis in the idea of God—where he is, how he acts in the world, and how he might be found....If previous writers conceived of the spiritual life as a union with God principally through interior prayer, Ignatius, so impressed with God's continuous saving action in the

world, was convinced that a person could achieve union with God in action.[11]

The Jesuits, inspired by Ignatius's vision of finding God in the midst of worldly activity, traveled around the globe doing missionary work, and founding schools, universities, and seminaries. Indeed, it was a controversy between a Jesuit cardinal and a young mathematician and astronomer that begins our study of seventeenth-century Christian thought on God.

The Seventeenth Century

In what would eventually become one of the most notorious episodes in the church's intellectual life, the Jesuit cardinal and theologian Robert Bellarmine wrote a letter in 1615 to Galileo Galilei (1594–1642) and to a Carmelite priest named Foscarini who had recently published a work endorsing Galileo's theories. Bellarmine warned that "to affirm that the sun is really fixed in the center of the heavens and merely turns upon itself without traveling from east to west, and that the earth is situated in the third sphere and revolves very swiftly around the sun, is a very dangerous thing, not only by irritating all the theologians and Scholastic philosophers, but also injuring our holy faith and making the sacred Scripture false."[12] Galileo's clash with church authorities ultimately resulted in his being sentenced to house arrest in 1633 (though he continued to publish). The ecclesiastical trial of Galileo has become a symbol of an outdated, entrenched authority attempting to squelch creative, innovative thought.

The seventeenth century saw a string of remarkable achievements in the fields of mathematics, physics, and astronomy, culminating with Isaac Newton's publication of the *Principia Mathematica* in 1687. As a result of the various scientific advances over the course of the seventeenth century, a new conception of the universe replaced the medieval worldview that had its origins in the philosophy of Aristotle. The universe became understood along the lines of a machine, a grand assembly of interconnected parts working in harmony. The question became, Where did God fit into the machine?

Two thinkers in the seventeenth century took differing approaches in this new scientific climate. The first, René Descartes (1596–1650), became known as the father of modern philosophy; the second, Blaise Pascal (1623–62), gained fame for a theological work that he had only begun at the time of his death.

RENÉ DESCARTES

Seventeenth-century thinkers literally began to see the world in an entirely new way. The rising and the setting of the sun around the Earth seemed the most indisputable commonsense observation that anyone could make. But if Copernicus and Galileo were right, and the Earth actually moved while the sun remained still, what other assumptions about the universe could be mistaken? The scientific theories of Aristotle that had been accepted for centuries were now being rejected. The Protestant Reformation of the prior century had already divided Christians on fundamental questions of doctrine. In this fractured intellectual world, French, Jesuit-trained scholar René Descartes set out to find a secure, indisputable foundation for all knowledge. Descartes was confident that such a foundation existed and that his method of reasoning had identified it. On this foundation could be built the superstructure of human knowledge, and this foundational idea would be apparent to any reasonable person, apart from his or her religious, philosophical, or political convictions.

The approach Descartes prescribed and the results he believed it yielded ultimately appeared in print in his works *Discourse on Method* (1637) and *Meditations on First Philosophy* (1641), though he had begun formulating those ideas as early as 1619. In these two works, Descartes outlined his "method of doubt." He began by recognizing that he had at times in his life held erroneous beliefs. He also acknowledged that our senses do on occasion deceive us. A modern example is how railroad tracks appear to move closer to each other in the distance, though we know that is obviously not so. Descartes also noted that he had experienced very vivid dreams that, at the time, he would have easily mistaken for reality. How, then, can we know that the beliefs we presently hold are in fact correct? How can we be sure that our senses are not deceiving us? How, finally, can we know that we are not at the present moment dreaming? Descartes' famous resolution of these questions is that even if *I* do hold false beliefs, or if *I* am being deceived by my senses, or if *I* am in a dream, then one absolute truth which *I* cannot doubt is that *I* exist: "I think, therefore I am," or in Latin, *Cogito, ergo sum.*

Descartes' method of doubt held important implications for Christian theology. First, he called into question any authority other than human reason and its ability to recognize clear and distinct ideas. Traditional sources of authority (e.g., the Bible, church) were displaced by the self. This "turn to the subject," as it is called, represented a fundamental change in the way people argued. As the theologian Hans Küng observed,

> With Descartes, European consciousness in a critical development reached an *epochal turning point.* Basic certainty is no longer centered on God, but on man. In other words, the medieval way of reasoning from certainty of God to certainty of self is replaced by the modern approach: from certainty of the self to certainty of God.[13]

Second, Descartes divided reality into material substance (or "extended" substance) and thinking substance. The material substance obeyed the physical laws of nature; thinking substance was undetermined by any external force. This raised troubling questions not only for how the body and the soul were united in the human person, but also for God's activity in the physical world. Theologian Jeffrey Hopper summarized in this way:

> The universe that Descartes described was not, however, as much mathematical as mechanical, at least in his later writings. In his mechanical universe Descartes sought to account for all effects in terms of the impact of bodies upon bodies. There were no natural motions such as bodies falling toward the center, nor any effects of "intelligences" such as had moved the planets according to earlier theories. Nor did God "interfere." God had established the laws of this mechanical world and maintained them as well

181

as the constancy of the total amount of motion, but no special appeals to divine intervention were appropriate.[14]

As Hopper noted, Descartes' God does not interfere with the laws of nature. Whether he intended to do so or not, Descartes was underwriting a new theological movement—deism—that would take as its fundamental principle the noninterference of God in the physical world.

Deism accepted the modern scientific model advanced by Descartes that saw the universe as a machine, or, as the deists generally preferred, a watch. The deistic God was the Watchmaker who created the universe and set in place immutable laws that seventeenth-century scientists were just beginning to express mathematically. Because God did not interfere in the creation, miracles were excluded. The deists insisted that any reasonable person who objectively viewed the evidence would conclude that God exists. The design of the universe made that plain to see. God also implanted in the minds of all humans a set of ethical precepts that all people should obey. In a world filled with bloodshed in the name of religion, these universal ethical laws provided the basis for social harmony. (On a side note, Thomas Jefferson was deeply influenced by deism, and the American political system's separation of church and state followed logically from the premises of deism.) In short, the deists viewed the world as orderly. There were no interruptions by God in the physical world in the form of miracles, or deviations in the dictates of reason in matters of religion, ethics, or politics.

In 1624 Lord Herbert of Cherbury (1583–1648) published *De Veritate* (On Truth), one of the foundational works in deism. In this work, Lord Herbert outlined five principles that were the basis for a natural religion, a religion whose central tenets neither required a divine revealer to impart them, nor offended the common sense of its adherents. Religious studies scholar James C. Livingston summarizes these five principles:

1. That one God exists
2. That God ought to be worshipped
3. That the practice of virtue is the chief part of the worship of God

4. That humans have always had an abhorrence of evil and are under an obligation to repent of their sins

5. That there will be rewards and punishments after death[15]

Lord Herbert's work stands as a testament to the seventeenth century's desire for a rational, universal, and ethical religion, and the century's overwhelming confidence that such a religion existed. There was one seventeenth-century intellectual, however, who warned that the age's fascination with reason was overlooking an essential component of human existence in general, and Christianity in particular.

BLAISE PASCAL

Blaise Pascal was a brilliant seventeenth-century scientist and mathematician who pioneered advances in geometry, probability theory, and hydraulics. He also invented one of the first calculating machines. By his own account, the turning point in his short life of thirty-nine years occurred on the night of November 23, 1654, when he underwent a mystical experience of God. Pascal recorded a cryptic account of that event on a piece of parchment, which he sewed on the inside of his coat. This "Memorial," which was discovered only after Pascal's death, began:

> The year of grace 1654.
> Monday, 23 November, feast of Saint Clement, Pope
>   and Martyr, and of others in the Martyrology.
> Eve of Saint Chrysogonus, Martyr and others.
> From about half past ten in the evening until half past
>   midnight.
> Fire
> "God of Abraham, God of Isaac, God of Jacob," not of
>   philosophers and scholars.
> Certainty, certainty, heartfelt, joy, peace.
> God of Jesus Christ.
> God of Jesus Christ.[16]

It is this contrast between the God of Abraham, Isaac, and Jacob and the God of philosophers and scholars that sheds light on Pascal's most famous theological work, an apologetic work that he began in 1658 and left unfinished at the time of his death. His preparatory notes or thoughts (in French, *pensees*) were published posthumously and contain observations and aphorisms that have captivated generations of readers seeking insights into the Christian faith.

Given his own intellectual gifts, Pascal easily recognized the potential of human reason to solve problems of physics and mathematics, but he also was keenly aware of the vital role the heart plays in human decision-making. When confronting our major life-decisions, Pascal reminded us, we do not rely—and should not rely—exclusively on reason. How does someone choose which college to attend? Why does someone choose to marry one person rather than another, or marry at all? These decisions are obviously to a large degree rational choices, but they are not solely rational. Our decisions are not purely analytical calculations; they involve intuition and a level of human understanding that can not be verbalized. As Pascal penned in his most famous *pensee*, "The heart has its reason, which reason does not know."[17]

Pascal's analysis of the human condition and the critical role of the heart converged in his famous argument, commonly known as Pascal's Wager. We are confronted in life with questions of great importance, and we must choose which response to make (e.g., to propose marriage). The choice is unavoidable, for to say, "I will not make a decision today," is itself a choice. We also sometimes need to make the choice without seeing all the evidence or knowing the results. This is no more clearly evident than when we face the question of God's existence. God, as Pascal noted, is hidden from our view. "God being thus hidden, any religion that does not say that God is hidden is not true, and any religion which does not explain why does not instruct."[18] Reason alone cannot settle the question of God's existence, yet the question must be answered. Our lives are of necessity, then, bets or wagers on the question of whether God exists or not.

Pascal's Wager followed from his insight that our lives are bets or wagers whose outcomes cannot at this time be determined. We are faced with a choice: to live our lives in a manner that would be fully consonant with the belief that God exists, or to live as if God does not exist. There are four possible outcomes of our decision. First, we could bet that God exists and be right. Second, we could bet that God exists and be wrong. Third, we could bet that God does not exist and be right. Fourth, we could bet that God does not exist and be wrong. In order to bet wisely, the gambler must consider the expected winnings in relation to the risk being assumed. In the first scenario, if we bet with our lives that God exists and we are right, we win eternal life with God. In the second scenario, if we bet that God exists and we are wrong, we have lost nothing. In the third scenario, if we bet that God does not exist and we are right, we win nothing. In the fourth scenario, if we bet that God does not exist and we are wrong, we could lose eternal life with God. The wiser bet, therefore, is to live as if God exists. Since the time of Pascal, there has been a lively discussion over whether this argument is clever or crude, and much speculation over what place it would have had if Pascal had completed his final work. In the century following Pascal's death, Western thought became increasingly skeptical not only of questions of God's existence, but of the possibility of knowledge itself.

The Eighteenth Century

Two of the leading thinkers of the eighteenth century were the philosophers David Hume (1711–76) and Immanuel Kant (1724–1804). Both were in their own ways embodiments of the spirit of the Enlightenment, the period of Western thought from approximately 1650 to 1800. Kant captured the mood of the Enlightenment when he declared its motto to be "Have the courage to use your own intelligence!"[19] Hume and Kant both lived by that motto, but it led them in two different directions. In many ways, Hume represents the Enlightenment's impulse to call into question all that had been previously accepted as true, while Kant represents the Enlightenment's drive to chart a new course for Western thought.

DAVID HUME

Hume published influential works in the fields of history, politics, and philosophy, but his importance for Christian theology lies in his thorough-going skepticism. Hume opposed dogmatic stances, whether it was the religious dogmatism of Scottish Calvinists or the equally adamant stance of atheists such as Baron d'Holbach.[20] Hume's skepticism is no more clearly displayed than in his 1748 work *An Enquiry Concerning Human Understanding*. In his *Enquiry* Hume asserted that while we can make certain reasonable assumptions about the world based on our experience, we are unable to speak with certainty about a wide range of questions that have preoccupied philosophers since the time of the Greeks. "The only method of freeing learning, at once, from these abstruse questions, is to enquire seriously into the nature of human understanding, and show, from an exact analysis of its powers and capacity, that it is by no means fitted for such remote and abstruse subjects."[21]

In Section X of the *Enquiry*, Hume dealt specifically with the question of miracles. Hume did not outright deny the possibility of miracles, though he certainly questioned the probability that they occurred. Hume defined a miracle as "a violation of the laws of nature," and "*a transgression of a law of nature by a particular volition of the Deity, or by the interposition of some invisible agent.*"[22] Is it reasonable, then, to believe in miracles? Hume's response is characteristically skeptical. Wise individuals should always proportion their beliefs to the evidence (X.4). What is the evidence? Is the evidence great enough to conclude that a suspension of the regular laws of nature took place at a particular moment in time? Hume concludes that it was highly unlikely. First of all, we must consider the source of the testimony. According to Hume,

> there is not to be found, in all history, any miracle attested by a sufficient number of men, of such unquestioned good sense, education, and learning, as to secure us against all delusions in themselves; of such undoubted integrity, as to place them beyond all suspicion of any design to deceive others; of such credit and reputation in the eyes of mankind, as to have a great deal to lose in case

of their being detected in any falsehood; and at the same time, attesting facts, performed in such a public manner, and in so celebrated a part of the world, as to render the detection unavoidable...[23]

This lack of independent confirmation of miracles by neutral observers, the human inclination to exaggerate claims, and other factors all suggest that miracles are highly improbable.

Hume's discussion of miracles in the *Enquiry* created a stir, but he soon began writing a short work devoted exclusively to religious belief. Though Hume completed the first draft of *Dialogues Concerning Natural Religion* in the 1750s, his friends convinced him that its publication would generate too much controversy. Hume left instructions for the work to be published after his death, and in 1779 the *Dialogues* appeared in print.

Modeled on the dialogues of Cicero, Hume's *Dialogues* involve three characters: Demea, Cleanthes, and Philo. In his introduction to a recent edition of the *Dialogues*, Martin Bell outlined the relevant questions addressed by the three characters: "Can reason establish the existence of God? What can be known by reason of the nature and attributes of God? Can there be a reasoned solution to the conflict between divine goodness and divine power, given the existence of moral evil and natural suffering?"[24] In Hume's work, Demea offers the orthodox Calvinist position; Cleanthes advocates positions representative of the natural religion movement; and Philo is the skeptic who questions the validity of the arguments proposed by his two conversation partners.

The perspectives of the three characters can be more clearly defined if we focus on one topic of their conversation: What can we reasonably conclude about the nature of God based on an objective observation of the world? Demea is reluctant to consider the question. Given "the infirmities of human understanding," the nature of God is "altogether incomprehensible and unknown to us." Consequently, "we ought to humble ourselves in his august presence, and, conscious of our frailties, adore in silence his infinite perfections which eye hath not seen, ear hath not heard, neither hath it entered into the heart of man to conceive." In reply, Cleanthes confidently offers the argument from design to support the claim that reason will lead a thoughtful person to realize that God exists.

> Look round the world, contemplate the whole and every part of it: you will find it to be nothing but one great machine, subdivided into an infinite number of lesser machines, which again admit of subdivisions to a degree beyond what human senses and faculties can trace and explain....Since therefore the effects resemble each other, we are led to infer, by all the rules of analogy, that the causes also resemble, and that the Author of nature is somewhat similar to the mind of man, though possessed of much larger faculties, proportioned to the grandeur of the work which he executed.[26]

Philo offers the following rejoinder: "This world...is very faulty and imperfect, compared to a superior standard, and was only the first rude essay of some infant deity who afterwards abandoned it, ashamed of his lame performance."[27] Later Philo comments, "The world plainly resembles more an animal or a vegetable than it does a watch or a knitting loom. Its cause, therefore, it is more probable, resembles the cause of the former."[28] For Philo, a reasonable person cannot conclude that the world was created by a perfect God. If we accept the principle that the cause is known by its effects, then we cannot conclude that an imperfect world was created by a perfect God. Nor can we reasonably conclude that the world was created by one God, and not many gods and goddesses.

IMMANUEL KANT

Prussian philosopher Immanuel Kant, by his own account, credited Hume with "waking him from his dogmatic slumber." Hume enabled Kant to realize that the mind is not a tabula rasa, a blank slate or passive receptacle of the data collected by the human senses. Rather, the mind is active; it organizes and catalogues the data. The corollary to this is that the mind is also limited in the type of data it can receive. It is equipped to handle only data within time and space. For example, as we sit alone in a quiet reading room in the library, we are oblivious to certain sound waves (e.g., radio waves) bouncing around the room. These waves travel at frequencies beyond the range of the human ear to detect. In a similar way, the human mind is structured in ways that allow it to register certain types of perceptions, but not others.

This understanding of the mind as both active and limited gives rise to two important distinctions in Kant's philosophy. First, Kant distinguished between phenomenal and noumenal reality. Phenomenal reality exists within the confines of time and space; that is, it is a reality that our senses can perceive. Our minds are extremely adept at interpreting this type of data. This is why humans have enjoyed such success in the physical sciences. Noumenal reality, by contrast, is not confined by time and space; that is, it is a reality that our senses can't perceive. Our minds are unable to process or relay to us this type of knowledge. This noumenal reality would include, above all, the nature of our God who transcends time and space.

Kant also distinguished between a proof and a postulate. A proof provides irrefutable evidence to confirm the truth of a claim. No such evidence is available to prove God's existence. However, the moral experience of humans allows us to offer postulates of reason. A postulate is something that reasonable persons accept as true, even though the proposition is not proven. For example, in Euclidean geometry we accept as true the claim that the shortest distance between two points is a straight line. Kant rejected the traditional proofs for the existence of God, but did accept the existence of God as a postulate of moral reasoning (what Kant called "practical reason").

Kant's moral argument for the existence of God is based on the human experience of moral duty or obligation. Kant believed that all rational persons have an innate sense of moral duty or obligation. If we saw a frail person slip and fall, as rational agents we would realize that it was our duty to offer assistance to that person. We, of course, are not forced to do so. Other considerations, whether they be legitimate or selfish, might override the command of our conscience. However, the thought should cross our minds to help the person. From this experience of moral duty, common to all rational human beings, Kant believed we were justified in accepting three postulates as true.

First, we do not always act on the moral command. We praise those who obey the command of duty, and we blame those who disobey the command. Given our rational nature, we know what we ought to do, but we do not always act accordingly. It makes sense, therefore, to believe that we have genuine free will.

Second, in a just universe, those who obey the moral law should be the happiest people in life, and conversely, those who disregard the moral law should be the most unhappy. Unfortunately, human experience teaches us that the good are often persecuted and the wicked often prosper. Those who commit horrible deeds are often not caught and never have to suffer the consequences of their actions, while the victims and their families experience great suffering. If the universe is fair, Kant reasoned, there must be a life after the present one in which those who were persecuted for their moral uprightness will be rewarded, and those who profited from their immoral actions will receive their just punishment. The second postulate, therefore, is the immortality of the soul.

Third, in order for the scales of justice to be balanced, there would need to be a source who knows all of the internal desires and external actions of every single individual in human history. This source would also need to have the ability to assign the respective rewards and punishments. We would, in short, need an omniscient and omnipotent God who could perform this monumental task. Hence, the existence of God is the third postulate. Kant's system preserved a role for God as the guarantor of the moral stability of the universe. A number of nineteenth-century atheists did not share Kant's confidence that the universe is just, and insisted that belief in God was impeding the pursuit of justice, not hastening its arrival.

The Nineteenth Century

In our earlier chapter on revelation, we already mentioned three nineteenth-century believers: Friedrich Schleiermacher, Søren Kierkegaard, and John Henry Newman. We will, therefore, focus our attention in this section on three leading atheists of the nineteenth century: Ludwig Feuerbach (1804–72), Karl Marx (1818–83), and Friedrich Nietzsche (1844–1900). We will also take note of the work of Charles Darwin (1809–82) and the controversy generated by his theory of evolution.

Feuerbach and Marx drew much of their language and inspiration from Hegel, a philosopher who, ironically, argued that the uniting of the divine and human nature of Christ provided the key to human history. Hegel spoke of an ongoing dialectical movement of history in which present alienation would be overcome in a final reconciliation of matter and spirit. The dialectical unfolding of truth, the present alienation of humanity from its source of enrichment, and the reconciliation that would be brought about at the end of human history are themes that Hegel included in his philosophical effort to show the inherent rationality of Christian belief. But, as noted by Alister McGrath, Hegel's work was interpreted in two fundamentally different ways by his followers. Some saw Hegel as a "major ally in the church's struggle against unbelief." Others feared that Hegel had "reconstructed and redefined central theological ideas—such as incarnation—until they virtually disappeared from view, having been replaced by secular philosophical notions.[29]

Ludwig Feuerbach

One of Hegel's former students, Ludwig Feuerbach, employed Hegel's dialectic to argue for the inherent irrationality of theism in his work *The Essence of Christianity* (1841). Feuerbach's Hegelian style of atheism took the following form. First, "the historical progress of religion consists in this: that what by an earlier religion was regarded as objective, is now recognized as subjective; that is, what was formerly contemplated and worshiped as God is now perceived to be something *human*."[30] In other words, Christians regard the ancient Greek and Roman mythologies with their gods and goddesses as brilliant literary expressions of human experience, but they obviously do not believe that such gods or goddesses exist. There is no Cupid, but there is a powerful human experience of being struck, as though by an arrow, by the beauty of another human person. Second, for Hegel human consciousness has a dynamic quality whereby it reaches beyond itself to an object. McGrath explained, "The Hegelian analysis of consciousness requires that there be a formal relation of subject to object. The concept of 'consciousness' cannot be isolated as an abstract idea, in that it is necessarily linked with an object: to be 'conscious' is to be conscious of something...”[31] This inevitable “objectification” or “externalization”[32] (terms borrowed from Hegel) of human consciousness generates a sense of human alienation.

> Religion is the disuniting of man from himself; he sets God before him as the antithesis of himself. God is not what man is—man is not what God is. God is the infinite, man the finite being; God is perfect, man imperfect; God eternal, man temporal; God almighty, man weak; God holy, man sinful. God and man are extremes...[33]

Third, the reconciliation comes when we realize that the object of our consciousness is not something outside the self (e.g., Absolute Spirit, God), but our own human nature. Human descriptions of God are actually statements about the ideal human nature, in which human virtues abound, and human vices are nonexistent. We realize that “the secret of theology is nothing else than anthropology” and “the knowledge of God nothing else than a knowledge of man!”[34]

When Feuerbach advocated atheism, he did not do so in order to promote a selfish lifestyle or a social policy that overlooked the needs of the poor. Rather, Feuerbach advocated atheism as a form of human liberation.

> Anyone who knows me only as an atheist does not really know me at all....“I deny God”? Yes, but for me this means that I deny the negation of man; I replace the illusionary, fantastic, heavenly state of man, which in real life inevitably leads to the denial of man, with the sensible, real, and therefore necessarily political and social state of man. For me the question of the existence or non-existence of God is the question of the existence or non-existence of man.[35]

Feuerbach regarded religion as the negation of humanity, and believed that atheism focused our attention properly on the political and social conditions in which we live.

192

The challenge Feuerbach presents to contemporary theologians centers on our language about God. How can we be sure that the language we use about God is accurate, that it refers to the actual nature of God, and is not simply an expression of our deepest wishes? Feuerbach once wrote, "If God were an object to the bird, he would be a winged being: the bird knows nothing higher, nothing more blissful, than the winged condition."[36] Do we create an image of God in our own image and likeness? The great twentieth-century Protestant theologian Karl Barth grappled with Feuerbach's position, and concluded that Christian theology cannot be based on human experience, but rather solely on the Word of God. He once quipped that "one can *not* speak of God simply by speaking of man in a loud voice."[37]

KARL MARX

Karl Marx also adopted Hegel's dialectical view of world history. According to Marx, the driving force behind human history was economics and the social classes it produced. As Marx and his associate Friedrich Engels wrote in the opening lines of their work *The Communist Manifesto*, "The history of all hitherto existing society is the history of class struggles."[38] The economic arrangement determined the social relations of people. A change in the economic system would therefore alter the social relations among people.

Marx envisioned the progress of history as a movement from capitalism to socialism to communism. In capitalism, there is private ownership of the means of production. "The means of production" refers to how goods are produced. In modern industrialized society, the primary ways in which goods are produced on a wide-scale basis is through factories. The owners, who in Marxist terminology are called the bourgeoisie, control the factories and hence have a domineering influence over the lives of the workers, who in Marxist terminology are called the proletariat. For example, the population of Manchester, England, swelled from 25,000 in 1770 to 455,000 in 1850.[39] People could no longer survive as farmers, so they flooded into the cities looking for work in the factories. In their desire to maximize profits, factory owners sold their products at the highest price, and kept their labor costs as low as possible. As a result, the poor stayed poor, and the rich stayed rich. The inevitable consequence of this class struggle, said Marx, would be for the workers to rise up in revolt and overthrow the owners. The state would then assume ownership of the means of production, and usher in a new stage in human history known as socialism. The function of the state would be to redistribute the wealth. The state, however, would eventually pass out of existence. Human history would enter its final stage, communism. The class struggle would finally be overcome. There would be no private property; all things would be held in common. People would work according to their ability, and receive according to their need.

Marx's atheism followed from his perception that religion slowed the pace of history's inevitable drive to communism by functioning as an ideology that promoted the interests of the powerful. For example, if people are believed to be naturally selfish, then an economic theory based on competition (i.e., capitalism) would be the "natural" economic system. Any other system—for instance, one based on cooperation (i.e., communism)—would "naturally" be doomed to failure. If a religion promoted the idea that this life is merely a prelude to an eternity of bliss or punishment, and that we should suffer in this life in order to be rewarded in the next, then that religion would be advocating a worldview that discouraged social revolution. In this context, Marx penned his famous claim that religion is the "opium of the people."[40] Religion numbed people to the reality of their socio-economic plight.

For this reason Marx believed that the *criticism of religion* is in the main complete, and criticism of religion is the premise of all criticism."[41] In order to demolish a socioeconomic system, Marx suggested, first attack the ideology that protects and promotes the interests of the socioeconomic elite. The primary ideology is religion, and once that impediment is removed, the march towards communism will proceed at a much greater pace. For Marx, the disclosure and elimination of capitalist ideology, including religion, was the task of philosophy. As he wrote in his "Theses on Feuerbach," "The philosophers have only *interpreted* the world, in various ways; the point, however, is to *change* it."[42]

FRIEDRICH NIETZSCHE

In the work of Friedrich Nietzsche we find someone who wanted his readers to realize just how much the world had already changed. This is most clearly evident in his parable of the Madman.

> *The Madman.* Have you not heard of that madman who lit a lantern in the bright morning hours, ran to the market place, and cried incessantly, "I seek God! I seek God!" As many of those who do not believe in God were standing around just then, he provoked much laughter. Why, did he get lost? said one. Did he lose his way like a child? said another. Or is he hiding? Is he afraid of us? Had he gone on a voyage? or emigrated? Thus they yelled and laughed. The madman jumped into their midst and pierced them with his glances.
>
> "Whither is God" he cried. 'I shall tell you. We have killed him—you and I. All of us are his murderers....Do we not hear anything yet of the noise of the gravediggers who are burying God? Do we not smell anything yet of God's decomposition? Gods too decompose. God is dead. God remains dead. And we have killed him.[43]

After his speech, the madman and the crowd fell silent. The madman threw his lantern down to the ground, and walked away. Nietzsche continued, "'I come too early,' he [the madman] said then; 'my time has not come yet. This tremendous event is still on its way, still wandering—it has yet reached the ears of man...'"[44] Interpreters of Nietzsche differ as to the meaning of this scene. For the Nietzsche scholar Walter Kaufmann, this passage is "a declaration of what he takes to be a historical cultural fact. 'God is dead'; 'we have killed him'; and 'this tremendous event...has not yet reached the ears of man'—that is an attempt at a diagnosis of contemporary civilization, not a metaphysical speculation about ultimate reality."[45] In other words, Nietzsche's declaration that God is dead should not be taken as a statement that God once existed but no longer does. Rather, the Western world has passed into an era in which belief in God is no longer the central organizing principle of personal or social life.

Nietzsche did not bemoan "the death of God," but rather saw that event as the birth of a new age in which true human fulfillment would be actualized. Christianity was, for Nietzsche, part of the problem, not part of the solution. Christianity offered a slave morality, one borne of the resentment that those who lack social, economic, and political influence feel toward those in power. In a sour-grapes scenario, the weak realize that they cannot possess power, and consequently label the human drive and impulses towards powerful as immoral. This frustration of human nature is embodied in the ethos of Christianity. With the death of God, however, a new human ideal can be realized.

The new vision for human fulfillment that Nietzsche proposed was based on what Nietzsche called "the will to power." Nietzsche labeled those who acted upon this will to power the masters; those who did not were slaves. This assertion of the will to power was not tied to any universal moral code; such a code did not exist for Nietzsche. This expression of the human personality was purely a matter of self-creativity and self-expression, bound by no moral or religious code. The philosopher Alasdair MacIntyre noted, "Sympathetic interpreters of Nietzschean 'will to power' have insisted that by power Nietzsche does not mean power over others; he saw the ideal expression of power in the type of personality in which the limitations of self-love have been overcome, but which nonetheless affirms itself."[46] Less sympathetic interpreters see in Nietzsche the intellectual foundation for twentieth-century Nazism.

The new ideal of human fulfillment presented by Nietzsche was called the Overman or Superman (*Ubermensch* in German): the one who acts on self-determined values in accordance with his or her will to power. The philosopher Samuel Enoch Stumpf summed up Nietzsche's perspective: "The superman will be rare, but he is the next stage in human evolution. History is moving not toward some abstract developed 'humanity' but towards the emergence of some exceptional men: 'Superman is the goal,' says Nietzsche."[47]

CHARLES DARWIN

The issue of human evolution and its eventual outcome was another topic that surfaced in the nineteenth century. The controversy was sparked by the naturalist and former divinity student named Charles Darwin. Charles Darwin's work *The Origin of Species* (1859) synthesized the results of Darwin's own research, the studies on population growth by the economist Thomas Malthus (1766–1834), and the findings of geologists (e.g., Charles Lyell 1797–1875) and biologists (e.g., Lamarck 1744–1829) of his day. Darwin's research was based in large part on the observations he made and the specimens he collected during his five-year expedition (1831–36) aboard the ship the *Beagle*. His most famous stop on the voyage was at the Galapagos Islands off the coast of South America, where he made detailed observations about the different species of finches found on the different islands. He made note of the differences in the size and shape of the finches' beaks. For Darwin, these differences confirmed Malthus' theory that given an abundant food supply, a population of a given species would increase, precipitating an eventual crisis in which population would outrun food supply. Using that model, Darwin concluded that the differences in the finches' beaks resulted from a process of natural selection in which those finches that had the physical characteristics to eat whatever food was available flourished on that island. In *The Descent of Man* in 1871, he applied the same logic to the human species and included humans in the overall scheme of natural selection.

Darwin's work had a number of consequences for Christian thought. First and most obvious was that Darwin's theory contradicted the literal seven-day creation story. Darwin's theory also challenged the belief that scientists could determine the age of the earth by counting back the generations from Christ to Adam. Second, the world Darwin presented was a cruel world in which weak and maimed creatures were crushed out of existence. Extinction, a foreign notion to medieval people, was now recognized as a distinct possibility for any species, including humans. Third, the status of humans as a unique creation of God, endowed with a soul and intellect reflective of their status as creatures made in the image of God, was revoked. In his history of Western thought, the scholar Richard Tarnas described the change in thinking brought about by Darwin's work.

> Any remaining theological assumptions concerning the world's divine government and man's special spiritual status were severely controverted by the new theory and evidence: Man was a highly successful animal. He was not God's noble creation with a divine destiny, but nature's experiment with an uncertain destiny. Consciousness, once believed to rule the universe and permeate it, was now understood to have arisen accidentally in the course of matter's evolution, to have been in existence a relatively brief time, and to be characteristic of a limited and relatively insignificant part of the cosmos—Homo sapiens— for which there was no guarantee its ultimate evolutionary fate would be any different from that of thousands of now extinct species.[48]

Some thinkers equated Darwin's concept of evolution with human progress, and saw human history as moving toward a future utopian state. Others saw in Darwin a confirmation of the bestial nature of humanity which no form of civilization could ever completely disguise. The twentieth century provided ample evidence for both points of view.

The Twentieth Century

Among the more significant developments in twentieth-century thought regarding God were the philosophical discussions about the meaningfulness of religious language, the psychological atheism of Sigmund Freud (1856–1939), and the creative theological syntheses produced by, among others, Paul Tillich (1886–1965) and Karl Rahner (1904–84).

LOGICAL POSITIVISM

A group of philosophers working in Vienna shortly after World War I initiated a movement known as logical positivism that would exert a tremendous influence on philosophical and theological discussions about God for the next fifty years. In 1936 the movement gained momentum when the British philosopher A. J. Ayer published *Language, Truth, and Logic*, the definitive statement of logical positivism. At the heart of Ayer's philosophical enterprise was the verification principle. Ayer wrote, "The principle of verification is supposed to furnish a criterion by which it can be determined whether or not a sentence is literally meaningful. A simple way to formulate it would be to say that a sentence had literal meaning if and only if the proposition it expressed was either analytic or empirically verifiable."[49] An analytic statement, which is also known as a tautology, is a statement that is true by definition: "A bachelor is an unmarried man." An empirically verifiable statement can be confirmed or denied through sense experience: "Water freezes at thirty-two degrees Fahrenheit." Any statement that is not analytic or empirically verifiable is, according to the verification principle, not meaningful. As Ayer himself concluded, "For to say that 'God exists' is to make a metaphysical utterance which cannot be either true or false. And by the same criterion, no sentence which purports to describe the nature of a transcendent god can possess any literal significance."[50]

Logical positivism spawned a number of related discussions concerning the meaningfulness of religious language. One of the most important debates took place among British philosophers in the 1950s. The British debate involved a rare combination of factors: high-powered influential philosophers writing brief essays in a style and language that was scholarly yet accessible to the general reader. Out of this fertile period in British thought came a collection of essays by sixteen different thinkers entitled *New Essays in Philosophical Theology* (1955). The work remains today one of the most important, readable modern studies of religious language.

In this collection, atheist Antony Flew presented a challenge to religious believers (in his essay "Theology and Falsification"). What would it take, Flew asked, for religious believers to retract the statement "God loves us" or "God exists"? If the religious believer is unwilling, under any conditions, to withdraw his or her support for either statement, then such statements are not really meaningful assertions as much as stubbornly held beliefs that will never be surrendered, no matter what evidence is marshaled against them.

Flew invoked the problem of evil to bolster support for his claim that religious believers are simply unwilling to retract their statements. He cited the example of a child dying of inoperable cancer of the throat. Even in this horrible situation where the love or existence of God could be most obviously called into question, the religious believer refuses to do so. The problem of evil has long challenged Christian claims about God. If God is all-knowing, all-loving, and all-powerful, then God should *know how* to create a world without evil, should *want* to create such a world, and should *be able* to create such a world. Nonetheless, evil still exists. Therefore, an all-knowing, all-loving, all-powerful, God must *not* exist.

The most common defense would be the free-will defense that argues that God endowed each person with genuine free will, and that the misuse of that gift results in evil actions being performed. This accounts for moral evil, evil that results from human choice. But what about natural evil, the misery that results from nonhuman causes such as earthquakes, tidal waves, and disease? The concern to articulate the proper Christian response to the problem of evil generated a great deal of attention to another philosophical movement of the twentieth century: process philosophy.

PROCESS PHILOSOPHY

The leading twentieth-century representative of process thought was Alfred North Whitehead (1861–1947), a mathematician and philosopher whose book *Process and Reality* was the seminal work in the field. Process philosophy represented a fundamental shift in the outlook of Western philosophy. Whereas the prevailing Western view since the time of Plato had been that the highest principle in the universe must be unchanging being, Whitehead believed that the process of becoming was superior. As Whitehead argued, "God is not to be treated as an exception to all metaphysical principles, invoked to save their collapse. He is their chief exemplification."[51]

Following the lead of Whitehead, process theologians offered an alternative account of the nature of God and of God's relation to the world. First, process theologians rejected the traditional idea that God created the universe from nothing *(ex nihilo)*. God plays a critical role in the universe's movement from chaos to order. This grand cosmic evolutionary process, argued the process theologian John B. Cobb Jr., provides the context in which Christians can make sense of natural evil.

> In this context the problem of natural evil in the usual sense is not acute. The destruction of living things by earthquakes and volcanoes could have been avoided only by vast postponement of the creation of life until a much higher degree of physical order was attained. But in spite of occasional destructive outbreaks there is far more value in a world teeming with life than in a dead one. And perhaps if life had waited for a safer environment, the only moment when the emergence of life on our planet was possible would have long since been past.[52]

Second, process theologians insist that God's love is persuasive, not coercive. God does not force humans to do anything. Consequently, humans may choose to act in ways that grieve God. Third, God is affected by the world, and the world contributes something to God's nature. For this reason, process theologians speak frequently in emotional terms about God: God grieves with victims of violence, God rejoices when humans turn away from sin, and so on. In the words of Whitehead, "God is the great companion—the fellow-sufferer who understands."[53]

SIGMUND FREUD

Whereas process philosophers and theologians reserved an essential, albeit unconventional, role for God in human evolution, the founder of psychoanalysis, and one of the most influential figures of the twentieth century, regarded belief in God as an illusion borne out of humanity's deepest fears. Sigmund Freud offered the following psychological explanation for religious belief in *The*

Future of an Illusion (1927): "The gods retain their threefold task: they must exorcize the terrors of nature, they must reconcile men to the cruelty of fate, particularly as it is shown in death, and they must compensate them for the sufferings and privations which a civilized life in common has imposed on them."[54] Each of these three purposes figured prominently in Freud's many works devoted to religious belief.

Freud viewed religion as a coping mechanism to deal with the anxiety produced by an awareness of the precariousness of human existence, the mystery of death, and the societal demand to repress human drives. The power of natural forces and the mystery of death impressed upon the human psyche a sense of helplessness.

> There are the elements, which seem to mock at all human control: the earth, which quakes and is torn apart and buries all human life and its works; water, which deluges and drowns everything in a turmoil; storms, which blow everything before them; there are diseases, which we have only recently recognized as attacks by other organisms; and finally there is the painful riddle of death, against which no medicine has yet been found, nor probably will be. With these forces nature rises up against us, majestic, cruel and inexorable; she brings to our mind once more our weakness and helplessness, which we thought to escape through the work of civilization.[55]

In order to increase their chances for survival in this uncertain world, humans lived in groups. Groups, however, imposed certain codes of behavior to ensure their stability. Sexual behavior and acts of aggression needed to be regulated. Freud regarded civilization as a practical necessity that nonetheless exacts a psychological toll on the human psyche. Freud developed this theme at length in *Civilization and Its Discontents* (1929), but it also appeared earlier in *The Future of an Illusion*: "It is remarkable that, little as men are able to exist in isolation, they should nevertheless feel as a heavy burden the sacrifices which civilization expects of them in order to make communal life possible."[56] The anxiety produced by the human fear of the unknown and the repressive nature of human civilization exert tremendous pressure on the human psyche. Humans develop various forms of neurotic behavior to cope with the anxiety. For Freud religion displays this psychological process on a collective scale, and so he labeled religion "a universal obsessional neurosis."[57]

PAUL TILLICH AND KARL RAHNER

Other twentieth-century thinkers who shared Freud's interest in the human psyche did not concur with his conclusions about God. Two theologians, one Protestant and the other Catholic, wrote poignantly about discovering God in the depths of our consciousness. The Protestant theologian Paul Tillich spoke movingly of finding God in the depth of our being in his sermon "The Depth of Existence."

The wisdom of all ages and all continents speaks about the road to our depth. It has been described in innumerably different ways. But all those who have been concerned—mystics and priests, poets and philosophers, simple people and educated people—with that road through confession, lonely self-scrutiny, internal or external catastrophes, prayer, contemplation, have witnessed to the same experience. They have found that they were not what they believed themselves to be, even after a deeper level had appeared to them below the vanishing surface. That deeper level itself became surface, when a still deeper level was discovered, this happening again and again, as long as their very lives, as long as they kept on the road to their depth....

The name of this infinite and inexhaustible depth and ground of all being is *God*. That depth is what the word *God* means. And if that word has not much meaning for you, translate it, and speak of the depths of your life, of the source of your being, of your ultimate concern, of what you take seriously without reservation. Perhaps, in order to do so, you must forget everything traditional that you have learned about God, perhaps even that word itself. For if you know that God means depth, you know much about Him. You cannot then call yourself an atheist or unbeliever. For you cannot think or say: Life has no depth! Life itself is shallow. Being itself is surface only. If you could say this in complete seriousness, you would be an atheist; but otherwise you are not. He who knows about depth knows about God.[58]

The Jesuit theologian Karl Rahner did more than any other thinker in twentieth-century Catholic theology to reclaim the mysterious sense of God's presence in human consciousness. He wrote,

Our existence is embraced by an ineffable mystery whom we call God. We can exclude him from our day-to-day awareness by the concerns and activity of our daily lives; we can drown the all-pervading silence of this mystery. But he is there: as the one comprehensive, all-bearing ground of all reality; as the comprehensive question that remains when all individual answers have been given....

This ultimate mystery at the root of reality and of our lives is nameless, impenetrable, something we cannot dominate with our concepts and life calculations, something that gives itself only when we yield to it in worship. We call it God.[59]

Rahner served as an adviser during the Second Vatican Council to the bishops who addressed the issue of modern atheism in their "Pastoral Constitution on the Church in the Modern World" (Gaudium et spes). The bishops acknowledged that often "atheism is born from a violent protest against the evil in the world" and conceded that when believers "fail in their religious, moral, or social life, they must be said to conceal rather than to reveal the true nature of God and of religion."[60] In language reminiscent of Rahner's, the bishops continued,

Meanwhile, every man remains a question to himself, one that is dimly perceived and left unanswered. For there are times, especially in the major events of life, when no man can altogether escape from such self-questioning. God alone, who calls man to deeper thought and to more humble probing, can fully and with complete certainty supply an answer to this questioning.[61]

For Christians the answers to our deepest questions can be found in the life, death, and resurrection of Jesus Christ, and it is to Christian reflection on these decisive events that we now turn.

Discussion Questions

1. Do you accept Calvin's theory of predestination? Why? Why not?
2. Is Pascal's Wager a solid argument? Is his discussion of the heart as an essential element in human decision-making convincing?
3. What is your evaluation of Philo's critique of the argument from design in Hume's *Dialogues Concerning Natural Religion*?
4. Is Kant's moral argument for the existence of God compelling? Why? Why not?
5. Is Feuerbach right when he states that we create God in our own image? What is the best theological response to Feuerbach's position?
6. Is Marx correct when he labels religion "the opium of the people"?
7. What is your interpretation of Nietzsche's claim that God is dead?
8. Does evolution undermine Christian beliefs about creation?
9. What would you respond to Flew's challenge?
10. What is your assessment of Freud's view of religion?
11. Does process theology present a sound view of God?
12. What does Tillich mean by the "depth of being"?

Suggested Readings

For a very helpful introduction to modern theology, see James C. Livingston, *Modern Christian Thought*, Volume One, Second Edition (Upper Saddle River, NJ: Prentice Hall, 1997), and James C. Livingston and Francis Schüssler Fiorenza, *Modern Christian Thought*, Volume Two, Second Edition (Upper Saddle River, NJ: Prentice Hall, 2000). For another useful volume, see James M. Byrne, *Religion and the Enlightenment* (Louisville, KY: Westminster John Knox Press, 1996). Karen Armstrong's *A History of God* (New York: Ballantine Books, 1993) is a very readable survey. Hans Kung's *Does God Exist?* (Garden City, NY: Doubleday, 1980) is a lengthy, but interesting work. For a fine collection of primary sources, see Timothy A. Robinson, ed., *God* (Indianapolis: Hackett Publishing Co., 1996). For works in philosophical theology, see Ronald H. Nash, *The Concept of God* (Grand Rapids: Zondervan, 1983), and C. Stephen Evans, *Philosophy of Religion* (Downers Grove, IL: InterVarsity Press, 1985).

Notes

1. Martin Luther, "Preface to the Latin Writings," in *Martin Luther: Selections from His Writings*, John Dillenberger, ed. (Garden City, NY: Anchor Books, 1961), 11.

2. Richard Marius, *Martin Luther* (Cambridge: Belknap Press, 1999), 193.

3. Luther, "Sermons on the Catechism," in Dillenberger, 208–9.

4. John Calvin, *Institutes of the Christian Religion* I, 1, 3 John T. McNeill, ed., and Ford Lewis Battles, trans. (Philadelphia: The Westminster Press 1960), 38–39.

5. William J. Bouwsma, *John Calvin: A Sixteenth-Century Portrait* (New York: Oxford University Press, 1988), 173.

6. Calvin, *Institutes* I, 8, 13. I discovered this quotation in *John Calvin: Selections from His Writings*, John Dillenberger, ed. (Missoula, MT: Scholars Press, 1975), 13.

7. Calvin, *Institutes* III, 2, 7. Quoted in Dillenberger, *John Calvin*, 15.

8. R. Emmet McLaughlin, "Preface," *Valentin Weigel* (Mahwah, NJ: Paulist Press, 2003), 2–3.

9. Andrew Weeks, "Introduction," *Valentin Weigel* (Mahwah, NJ: Paulist Press, 2003), 24.

10. Valentin Weigel, "The Golden Grasp," in *Valentin Weigel* (Mahwah, NJ: Paulist Press, 2003), 209.

11. Thomas M. Gannon and George W. Traub, *The Desert and the City* (Chicago: Loyola University Press, 1969), 158–59.

12. "Bellarmine's Letter to Foscarini," in Clive Morphet, *Galileo and Copernican Astronomy* (London: Butterworths, 1977), 27.

13. Hans Küng, *Does God Exist?* (Garden City, NY: Doubleday, 1980), 15, emphasis his.

14. Jeffrey Hopper, *Understanding Modern Theology*, vol. 1 (Philadelphia: Fortress Press, 1987), 34.

15. James Livingston, *Modern Christian Thought*, vol. 1, 2nd ed. (Upper Saddle River, NJ: Prentice-Hall, 1997), 16.

16. Blaise Pascal, "The Memorial," in *Pensees*, A. J. Krailsheimer, trans. (New York: Penguin Books, 1966), 309.

17. Blaise Pascal, *Pensees* #277, W. F. Trotter, trans. (New York: E. P. Dutton, 1958), 78.

18. Blaise Pascal, *Pensees* #242, A. J. Krailsheimer, trans., 103.

19. Immanuel Kant, "What is Enlightenment?" in *The Philosophy of Kant*, Carl J. Friedrich, ed. (New York: The Modern Library, 1949), 132.

20. Martin Bell, "Introduction," in David Hume, *Dialogues Concerning Natural Religion*, Richard H. Popkin, ed. (New York: Penguin Books, 1990), 5.

21. David Hume, *An Enquiry Concerning Human Understanding* I.12, Tom L. Beauchamp, ed. (New York: Oxford University Press, 1999), 92.

22. Hume, *Enquiry* X.12, 173, and 173n23; the italics are Hume's.

23. Hume, *Enquiry* X.15, 174.

24. Bell, "Introduction," 10.

25. David Hume, *Dialogues Concerning Natural Religion* (New York: Hafner Press, 1948), 15.

26. Ibid., 17.

27. Ibid., 41.

28. Ibid., 47.

29. Alister E. McGrath, *The Making of Modern German Christology 1750–1990*, 2nd ed. (Grand Rapids: Zondervan Publishing House, 1994), 55.

30. Ludwig Feuerbach, *The Essence of Christianity*, George Eliot, trans. (New York: Harper and Row, 1957), 13.

31. McGrath, *The Making of Modern German Christology*, 68.

32. Ibid.

33. Feuerbach, *The Essence of Christianity*, 33.

34. Ibid., 207.

35. Quoted in Marcel Neusch, *The Sources of Modern Atheism* (New York: Paulist Press, 1982), 50.

36. Feuerbach, *The Essence of Christianity*, 17.

37. Karl Barth, *The Word of God and the Word of Man* (New York: Harper and Brothers, 1957), 196.

38. Karl Marx and Friedrich Engels, *The Communist Manifesto* (New York: Penguin Books, 1985), 79.

39. Lloyd Kramer, Course Guidebook to his lecture series *European Thought and Culture in the 19th Century*, Part I, tape/CD/DVD (Chantilly, VA: The Teaching Company, 2001), p. 53.

40. Karl Marx, "Contribution to the Critique of Hegel's Philosophy of Right," in Karl Marx and Friedrich Engels, *On Religion* (Chico, CA: Scholar's Press, 1982), 42.

41. Ibid., 41; emphasis his.

42. Marx, "Theses on Feuerbach," in *On Religion*, 72; emphasis his.

43. Friedrich Nietzsche, *The Gay Science* [125], *The Portable Nietzsche*, Walter Kaufmann, ed., (New York: Penguin Books, 1968), 95.

44. Ibid., 97.

45. Walter Kaufman, *Nietzsche*, 3rd ed. (New York: Vintage Books, 1968), 100.

46. Alasdair MacIntyre, *A Short History of Ethics* (New York: Macmillan, 1966), 224.

47. Samuel Enoch Stumpf, *Philosophy: History and Problems*, 2nd ed. (New York: McGraw-Hill Book Company, 1977, 378–79.

48. Richard Tarnas, *The Passion of the Western Mind* (New York: Harmony Books, 1991), 327.

49. Alfred Jules Ayer, *Language, Truth and Logic* (New York: Dover Publications, 1946), 5.

50. Ibid., 115.

51. Alfred North Whitehead, *Process and Reality*, corrected ed. David Ray Griffin and Donald Sherburne, eds. (New York: The Free Press, 1978), 343.

52. John B. Cobb, Jr., *God and the World* (Philadelphia: Westminster Press, 1969), 93.

53. Whitehead, *Process and Reality*, 351.

54. Sigmund Freud, *The Future of an Illusion* (Garden City, NY: Anchor Books, 1964), 24.

55. Ibid., 20–21. I first discovered this quotation in Charles P. Henderson's helpful work *God and Science* (Atlanta: John Knox Press, 1986), 25.

56. Freud, *The Future of an Illusion*, 3.

57. Quoted in Marcel Neusch, *The Sources of Modern Atheism*, 93.

58. Paul Tillich, *The Shaking of the Foundations* (New York: Charles Scribner's Sons, 1948), 56–57.

59. Karl Rahner, *Prayers and Meditations* (New York: Crossroad, 1981), 32–33.

60. "Pastoral Constitution on the Church in the Modern World *(Gaudium et spes)* section 19, *Documents of Vatican II* Austin Flannery, ed. (Grand Rapids: Eerdmans, 1975), 919.

61. Ibid., section 21, p. 921.

7

CHRIST AND SALVATION IN SCRIPTURE AND THE FATHERS

By this stage of our survey of Christian theology, we have already noticed that no single area of Christian theology stands in isolation from any other. We have seen that the development of the New Testament canon involved questions of church authority; methods of biblical interpretation led to a consideration of revelation; revelation necessarily raised questions about the nature of God; and so on. Because any adequate Christian account of God requires talk about Christ, we turn our attention at this juncture to questions regarding what later theologians would call the "person" and "work" of Christ. The "person" of Jesus refers to his identity. This area of theological inquiry is Christology. The "work" of Jesus asks questions about what Christ accomplished through his life, death, and resurrection. This area of theological inquiry is soteriology (literally, "the study of salvation"). We begin with an overview of the biblical passages that played a significant role in the early church's christological reflection. We will then retrace the steps that led to the church's formulation of the classic christological definitions in the patristic era. We will conclude with a review of the leading soteriological theories that were proposed in both scripture and patristic theology.

New Testament Christology

The twenty-seven books of the New Testament (the four Gospels, the letters of Paul, Hebrews, the Catholic or General Epistles, and Revelation) comprise the norm by which all subsequent Christologies are measured. The New Testament, however, does not confine itself to one title or image of Jesus. Our first task, therefore, is to catalogue some of the leading christological portraits, themes, and titles in the New Testament. Although important christological data is found throughout the New Testament, the Gospels provide the bulk of the christological information, and so we will concentrate our attention on the four Gospels and Acts.

As mentioned earlier, the Gospels of Matthew, Mark, and Luke are known as the Synoptic Gospels because the broad outline of Jesus' career and the general content of Jesus' teachings are similar in these three. John's Gospel emphasizes Jesus' divinity to a far greater degree. In John, the chronology of events in Jesus' career differs from the one found in the Synoptics. Also in John, Jesus speaks in long discourses and tells no parables as he commonly does in the synoptic accounts.

The Gospels that were ultimately deemed canonical function as the standard of orthodoxy in the christological debates of the early church. However, the Gospels themselves are expressions of the christological perspectives of the four evangelists, and in this way represent a snapshot of the christological thinking of various Christian communities in the second half of the first century AD. The prevailing scholarly opinion is that Mark was the first Gospel written (ca. AD 70). Matthew and Luke used Mark as a source, but they also had access to a common source of material that scholars today identify as "Q," the first letter of the German word *Quelle* that means "source." We do not know whether Q was a written source or simply a body of material in the oral tradition of the early church. Using Mark, Q, and their own sources, Matthew and Luke composed their Gospels ca. AD 80–90. The Gospel of John was the last of the four Gospels to reach completion, sometime around the end of the first century. The gospel writers, therefore, were not merely compiling information about Jesus. Rather, they were collecting, arranging, and editing the received tradition and crafting a Gospel that spoke uniquely to the questions and concerns of their own particular communities. As a result each of the four Gospels has its own points of emphasis regarding the identity of Jesus.

THE GOSPEL OF MARK

Most scholars regard the turning point of Mark's Gospel to be the scene of the disciples on the road to Caesarea Phillippi (Mark 8:27—9:1), so we will divide that Gospel into two halves. In the climactic scene on the road to Caesarea Phillippi, Jesus asks the disciples the fundamental question of Christology, "Who do people say that I am?" (8:27). The first half of the Gospel builds up to that question, and the second half moves toward its answer.

The opening verse of Mark identifies Jesus as "Christ" and "Son of God" (although the latter is omitted in some ancient manuscripts). These are two commonly used christological titles in the Gospels. *Christ* is the Greek word for Messiah (literally "the anointed one"). Typically kings were anointed at their coronation ceremony, empowering them to function as the leader of the community. "Son of God" varied in its meaning considerably. The nation of Israel could be called God's "firstborn son" (Exod 4:22), while it can also be used in a restricted sense of God's one and only Son (John 3:16).

Jesus begins his ministry with the proclamation, "The time is fulfilled, and the kingdom of God has come near; repent, and believe in the good news" (Mark 1:15). This verse raises questions that persist to the conclusion of the Gospel. What is the hope of Israel that is now being fulfilled? What does Jesus mean by the concept of "the kingdom of God?" What exactly is the good news that we are called to believe?

Jesus' star quickly rises. He expels demons, heals the sick, and teaches with authority. In an ironic twist, the demons know the identity of Jesus. "What have you to do with us, Jesus of Nazareth? Have you come to destroy us? I know who you are, the Holy One of God" (Mark 1:24). By the end of the first chapter, "Jesus could no longer go into a town openly, but stayed out in the country; and people came to him from every quarter" (1:45).

Jesus soon encounters opposition from the religious authorities. He forgives sins, eats with sinners and tax collectors, and cures a man on the Sabbath. In reply to his critics, Jesus claims for himself the title "the Son of Man" (Mark 2:10, 28), the title of the divinely commissioned agent of judgement in the apocalyptic vision in Daniel 7. As a result of Jesus' controversial actions and teachings, leaders from two groups, the Pharisees and the Herodians, seek to eliminate him (Mark 3:16). Even at this early stage of Jesus' ministry, Mark introduces the cross—a theme that will increase in prominence over the course of the Gospel.

Preceding the scene at Caesarea Phillippi, Mark presents the continued confusion of the disciples. Failing to perceive the significance of Jesus' two feedings of the multitude (the feeding of the five thousand in 6:30–44, and the feeding of the four thousand in 8:1–9), as well as Jesus' walking on water (6:45–52), the disciples seem unable to understand the mystery Jesus seeks to reveal to them. Jesus even asks them, "Do you not yet understand?" (8:21).

In the climactic Caesarea Phillippi scene, it appears at first that Peter understands who Jesus is when he announces that Jesus is the Messiah. In a curious turn of events, Jesus orders Peter not to tell anyone about his identity (Mark 8:30), a feature of Mark's Gospel that scholars call "the messianic secret." Jesus then informs his disciples that he must go to Jerusalem to suffer and die. Peter, who earlier had seemed to provide the crucial breakthrough in the disciples' understanding of Jesus, now begins to argue with him, prompting Jesus to issue some of his harshest rebukes in the entire Gospel: "Get behind me, Satan! For you are setting your mind not on divine things but on human things" (8:33).

The bone of contention between Jesus and Peter was the notion of Messiahship. There were various expectations regarding the Messiah, but as scripture scholar D. E. Nineham noted:

> However exactly the term *Messiah* was understood at the time—and…different groups understood it in different ways—there was general agreement that the Messiah would accomplish his work by the possession and exercise of brute power in one form or another…[and] he would be a glorious and manifestly victorious figure to whom defeat and suffering would be entirely foreign.[1]

Jesus was offering a Messiahship that recalled the mysterious Suffering Servant in the Book of Isaiah. In the portion of Isaiah believed to be written during the Babylonian Exile, there are four

213

songs that speak of a Suffering Servant. The identity of that servant is unknown. Perhaps it was a figure intended to represent the Israelite people, or maybe it referred to a single righteous person. In any event, Christians were quick to make the association between the Suffering Servant (see Isa 52:13—53:12) and Jesus.

The first half of Mark's Gospel culminated in the scene at Caesarea Phillippi with the revelation of Jesus' identity as the Suffering Messiah. The second half of the Gospel moves to the cross. Jesus tells his disciples for the second (9:30–32) and third time (10:32–34) that he must go to Jerusalem to suffer and die. In chapters eleven and twelve Jesus enters Jerusalem riding on a colt, overturns the money changers' tables in the Temple, and engages the Jewish leaders in debates regarding such controversial matters as the payment of taxes to the Romans. In Mark 13 Jesus gives an apocalyptic discourse. In chapter fourteen, we read of Jesus' last days on earth. He celebrates the Passover with his disciples and after the meal goes to pray in the Garden of Gethsemane. There Jesus is arrested and brought before the Jewish court known as the Sanhedrin. He is found guilty of the charge of blasphemy. In the morning, Jesus is sent to the Roman procurator or governor, Pilate, who reluctantly sentences him to death by crucifixion on the charge that he claimed to be "the King of the Jews." While on the cross, Jesus cries out,"My God, my God, why have you forsaken me? (Mark 15:24; see Ps 22:1). After Jesus' death on the cross, the Roman centurion states, "Truly this man was God's Son" (Mark 15:39). The Gospel ends on a peculiar note. On the first day of the week, the women go to Jesus' tomb to anoint his body. To their surprise, "a young man" dressed in white is sitting in the tomb and announces to the women that Jesus has been raised from the dead. In what is generally regarded as the authentic ending of the Gospel (as opposed to the sentences after that, believed to have been tacked on years later), Mark says: the women "went out and fled from the tomb, for terror and amazement had seized them; and they said nothing to anyone, for they were afraid" (Mark 16:8).

THE GOSPEL OF MATTHEW

Scripture scholar Keith F. Nickle introduced Matthew's Gospel with the simple question, "Why expand a Gospel?"[2] In other words, why write a new Gospel? What issues did Mark's Gospel not address for Matthew? We can begin to construct a probable answer by noting what new material Matthew included. The two most obvious additions are that Matthew has an account of Jesus' birth (Mark has no birth story), and Matthew has stories of postresurrection appearances by Jesus (Mark has the empty tomb, but no appearances by the resurrected Jesus). We can further refine our answer to the question of why Matthew felt the need to write a new Gospel by noting his own particular emphases and seeing how he adapted the stories in Mark's Gospel.

While scholars disagree about the structure of Matthew's Gospel, there is a general consensus that between the birth story and Jesus' death and resurrection, Jesus delivers five discourses. Each discourses ends with a similar formulaic expression, such as "Now when Jesus had finished saying these things..." (Matt 7:28, see also 11:1, 13:53, 19:1, and 26:1). Matthew's arrangement of material into five discourses might well be intended to recall the five books of the Law. We will briefly review the content of these five discourses, as well as the birth and resurrection narratives, to undercover the points of emphasis in Matthew's Christology.

Unlike Mark, Matthew begins with Jesus' genealogy and birth narrative. The genealogy, which traces Jesus' lineage back to Abraham, consists of three sets of fourteen generations. Matthew suggests that the arrival of the Messiah was not a random event, but rather fits perfectly into the salvation history that began with Abraham, reached its political height during the reign of David, endured the low point of the Babylonian Exile, and culminated with Jesus. In the birth narrative Matthew continues to situate Jesus within the larger history of Judaism, especially the prophetic tradition. Jesus' birth, says Matthew, fulfills the promise made long ago through Isaiah the prophet: "Look, the virgin shall conceive and bear a son, / and they shall name him Emmanuel" (Matt 1:23). Especially important are the prophecies regarding the line of David. Matthew weaves together the promise of David's eternal dynasty (2 Sam 7:16), the Immanuel prophecies of Isaiah (Isa 7:14; 9:1–6; 11:1–9), and the symbolism of Bethlehem, the birthplace of David (Mic 5:2)—all to create the classic Christmas story of the virgin birth; the wise men's presentation of gold, frankincense, and myrrh to the infant Jesus; and Herod's slaughter of the innocents.

In the first of his five discourses, Jesus delivers the Sermon on the Mount (Matt 5–7). The mountain setting recalls the figure of Moses on Mt. Sinai. Matthew stresses the continuity between the Law received by Moses and the teachings of Jesus. "Do not think that I have come to abolish the law or the prophets; I have come not to abolish but to fulfill" (5:17). Jesus does, however, offer his own distinctive commentary on the Law. Jesus begins, "You have heard that it was said to those of ancient times..." and then quotes the commandments: Do not kill, do not commit adultery, an eye for an eye, etc. It is in this context that Jesus offers some of his most radical teachings: do not grow angry, do not lust, offer no resistance to evil. In this way, Jesus demonstrates both his indebtedness to the Jewish legal tradition, and his eagerness to see the deeper intent of the Law.

In the second discourse, commonly designated the missionary discourse, Jesus sends out his twelve apostles. It is important for the logic of Matthew's Gospel that the apostles go only to the Jews. "Go nowhere among the Gentiles, and enter no town of the Samaritans, but go rather to the lost sheep of the house of Israel" (Matt 10:5). Matthew sees Jesus' ministry as an offer to Judaism primarily, and then only afterwards, as a universal offer to all humanity. In the final scene of the Gospel, the Risen Lord instructs the disciples, "Go therefore and make disciples of all nations..." (28:19).

In the third discourse, Jesus teaches in parables. The parable is one of Jesus' most common methods for teaching about the kingdom of God (in Matthew, "kingdom of heaven"). The concept of the kingdom of God is central to the proclamation of Jesus in the Synoptic Gospels, but there is much debate as to what Jesus intended by it. The parables tease the listener's imagination in an act of comparison: "The kingdom of heaven is like treasure hidden in a field, which someone found and hid; then in joy he goes and sells all that he has and buys that field" (13:44).

In the fourth discourse, Jesus speaks of the church. Matthew is the only one of the four Gospels in which Jesus speaks of the church *(ekklesia)*. This discourse has teachings regarding the authority of the church, but it also expresses concern for "the little ones." God is like the shepherd who leaves the ninety-nine sheep to search for one lost sheep. "So it is not the will of your father in heaven that one of these little ones should be lost" (Matt 18:14).

In the fifth discourse, Jesus has some scathing words for the Jewish leaders known as the scribes and the Pharisees. His eschatological teaching emphasizes the need for diligence and good works as Jesus' followers await the return of the Son of Man at judgement day. In Matthew 23 Jesus pronounces seven "woes" against the scribes and Pharisees. While respecting their authority as teachers of the Law, Jesus accuses them of hypocrisy and lawlessness (23:28). The Pharisees, as we discussed earlier in the church history chapter, were the leading party in Judaism after the destruction of the Temple in AD 70. The historical-critical question is whether the intensity of Jesus' attack reflects the career of the historical Jesus, or whether Matthew has intensified the rhetoric to reflect his own community's experience of expulsion from the synagogue, which occurred when the Pharisees (or rabbis) met in the town of Jamnia and composed "the Twelfth Benediction" against "the Nazarenes" (i.e., Christians).

In the final chapters of Matthew's Gospel, we find a chronology generally similar to one found in Mark. The most significant change introduced by Matthew appears at the empty tomb. As the women approach the tomb, an earthquake occurs, an angel descends from heaven, rolls back the stone from the tomb, and sits upon it. Unlike in Mark where the women say nothing to anyone because they were afraid, Matthew reports that "they left the tomb quickly with fear and great joy, and ran to tell his disciples" (28:8). In the final scene, the Risen Lord appears to disciples on a mountain in Galilee, commissioning them to preach, baptize, and teach until the end of the age.

THE GOSPEL OF LUKE AND ACTS OF THE APOSTLES

Because Luke and Acts were originally joined as a single two-volume work, a complete account of the author's Christology must include what Jesus says and does in the Gospel, and what the early

Christians proclaim about him in the early Christian mission recorded in Acts. In both works the author structures the narrative along geographical lines. In Luke, Jesus' mission is confined to the region of Galilee until Jesus "set his face to go to Jerusalem" (9.51). In the "travel narrative" (9:51—19:27), Jesus travels to Jerusalem where he suffers, dies, and is raised from the dead. Similarly, Acts 1:8 provides the reader with the key to the course of events: "But you will receive power when the Holy Spirit has come upon you; and you will be my witnesses in Jerusalem, in all Judea and Samaria, and to the ends of the earth."

Like the Gospel of Matthew, the Gospel of Luke begins with a birth story. Both authors use their birth stories as vehicles by which to advance their respective Christologies. In Luke's Gospel, the angel appears to the shepherds keeping watch in the fields (there are no wise men in Luke's Gospel). The angel announces to them: "To you is born this day in the city of David, a Savior, who is the Messiah, the Lord" (Luke 2:11). When Mary and Joseph bring the infant Jesus to Jerusalem, the righteous and devout Simeon takes Jesus into his arms and declares, "Master, now you are dismissing your servant in peace, / according to your word, / for my eyes have seen your salvation, / which you have prepared in the presence of all peoples, / a light for revelation to the Gentiles / and for glory to your people Israel" (2:29–32). Luke emphasizes the universal scope of Jesus' mission: Jesus is the long awaited Messiah and Lord who extends the offer of salvation to Jews and Gentiles alike.

In the first scene in his public ministry, Jesus enters the synagogue in Nazareth and proclaims the reading from the prophet Isaiah: "The Spirit of the Lord is upon me, / because he has anointed me to bring good news to the poor. / He has sent me to proclaim release to the captives / and recovery of sight to the blind, / to let the oppressed go free, / to proclaim the year of the Lord's favor" (Luke 4:18). This passage captures two aspects of Luke's Christology. First, the Spirit of the Lord rests upon Jesus. The Holy Spirit figures prominently in both Luke and Acts. It inspires and guides the characters in the birth narrative (e.g., Mary in 1:35; Elizabeth in 1:41; Zechariah in 1:67); it descends upon Jesus at his baptism (3:22), and is poured out on the disciples at Pentecost (Acts 2). Second, as "the anointed one" (i.e., the Messiah), Jesus brings glad tidings to the poor. Not only is special concern given to the poor, but the rich are frequently warned that their wealth may hinder them from accepting the Gospel ("Blessed are you who are poor....But woe to you who are rich" Luke 6:20, 6:24).

Most of the material unique to Luke's Gospel is found in the travel narrative. This includes most notably the two famous parables of the Good Samaritan (10:29–37) and the Prodigal Son (15:11–32). Luke alone also preserves an important passage regarding the kingdom.

> Once Jesus was asked by the Pharisees when the kingdom of God was coming, and he answered, "The kingdom of God is not coming with things that can be observed; nor will they say, 'Look, here it is!' or 'There it is!' for, in fact, the kingdom of God is among you." (Luke 17:20–21)

In the view of the late scripture scholar Norman Perrin, "we may claim that the meaning is this: 'the Kingdom is a matter of human experience.' It does not come in such a way that it can be found by looking at the march of armies or the movement of heavenly bodies; it is not to be seen in the coming of messianic pretenders. Rather it is to be found wherever God is active decisively within the experience of an individual and [humans] have faith to recognize this for what it is."[3] Finally, Luke introduces an element of necessity into Jesus' journey to Jerusalem. "Yet today, tomorrow, and the next day I must be on my way, because it is impossible for a prophet to be killed outside of Jerusalem" (13:33).

Luke slightly alters Mark's account of Jesus' death. In Mark's Gospel, Jesus dies with the stark verse from Psalm 22 on his lips, "My God, my God, why have you forsaken me?" (Mark 15:34). Immediately after Jesus' death, the centurion standing by the cross declares, "Truly this man was God's Son" (Mark 15:39). Luke adds a conversation among Jesus and the criminals being crucified on each side of him. Compassionate and forgiving to the end, Jesus assures one of the criminals, "Truly I tell you, today you will be with me in Paradise" (Luke 23:43). Luke's last words are not the anguished cry of the psalmist, but rather, "Father, into your hands I commend my spirit" (Luke 23:46). And in Luke, the centurion asserts, "Certainly this man was innocent" (Luke 23:47). According to the scripture scholar Richard B. Hays, Luke's passion narrative sought to "demonstrate that Jesus died in accordance with the Scriptures, as the Righteous One prefigured in Isaiah, the lament psalms, and Wisdom of Solomon. His death once again confirms that the true prophet must be rejected, and it also establishes a pattern for his followers—as the martyrdom of Stephen shows."[4] The career and death of Stephen, the first Christian martyr, in Acts 7 deliberately parallels that of Jesus in the Gospel. Luke's Christology, in other words, does not end either at the cross or the resurrection, but the ascension.

The speeches of Peter and Stephen in Acts refer not only to the earthly career of Jesus, but also his present exalted, heavenly status. In the Pentecost sermon, Peter declares, "This Jesus God raised up, and of that all of us are witnesses. Being therefore exalted at the right hand of God, and having received from the Father the promise of the Holy Spirit, he has poured out this that you both see and hear" (Acts 2:32–33). Peter makes a similar point in his speech before the Sanhedrin, "The God of our ancestors raised up Jesus, whom you had killed by hanging him on a tree. God exalted him at his right hand as Leader and Savior that he might give repentance to Israel and forgiveness of sins. And we are witnesses to these things, and so is the Holy Spirit whom God has given to those who obey him" (Acts 5:30–32). The theologian Veli-Matti Karkkainen observed,

> The Pentecost speech of Peter in Acts 2 of the Book of Acts shows evidence that Jesus, having been raised from the dead, has been exalted to God's right hand, according to the prophecy of David. Peter's next speech in the following chapter is replete with christological themes: Jesus is God's servant, the holy and just one, the leader of life, the Messiah who has been designated for Israel, the prophet of whom Moses spoke.[5]

As the exalted Lord, Christ bestows the gift of the Spirit on the church as the gospel message is carried from Judea to Samaria, to the ends of the earth.

THE GOSPEL OF JOHN

John's Gospel consists of a prologue, of a section designated "the Book of Signs" that is devoted to Jesus' miracles and discourses (often occurring on key Jewish feast days), of a "Book of Glory" consisting of a farewell discourse by Jesus, and of John's account of Jesus' death and resurrection. Chapter twenty-one appears to be an epilogue.

It could very well be argued that no other eighteen verses have been more influential on the course of the church's Christology than the prologue to John's Gospel. The opening verse of the prologue, which also figured prominently in our earlier discussion of the Trinity, employs the concept of the Logos (the Word): "In the beginning was the Word and the Word was with God, and the Word was God" (John 1:1). The central christological point appears in v. 14: "And the Word became flesh and lived among us..." The eternal Word became a human person and entered into human history. To interact with Jesus while he walked among the people on the roads of Galilee was to encounter God in the flesh. In his commentary on John's Gospel, Raymond Brown noted,

> Verse 14b and the succeeding lines show that, if the Word has become flesh, he has not ceased to be God. In 14b this is given expression in the verb *shenoun* ("make a dwelling; pitch a tent") which has important OT [Old Testament] associations. The theme of "tenting" is found in Exodus xxv 8–9 where Israel is told to make a tent (the Tabernacle—*skene*) so that God can dwell among His people; the Tabernacle became the site of God's localized presence on earth....When the Prologue proclaims that the Word made his dwelling among men, we are being told that the flesh of Jesus Christ is the new localization of God's presence on earth, and that Jesus is the replacement of the ancient Tabernacle.[6]

The prologue of John is the scriptural basis for the doctrine of the Incarnation—that in Jesus, God became flesh.

John speaks of Jesus' "signs" rather than "miracles." The signs in John's Gospel have a dual function. They help the person or persons in need, but they also signify who Jesus is. For example, in the feeding of the multitudes (the only miracle that appears in all four Gospels), the hungry crowds are fed, but the sign in John is also the basis for Jesus' lengthy "Bread of Life" discourse. In the story of raising Lazarus from the dead, the seventh and final sign, Jesus assures Lazarus's sister Martha that Lazarus will rise. In reply, Martha expresses her belief in the future resurrection of the dead. Jesus answers:

> "I am the resurrection and the life. Those who believe in me, even though they die, will live, and everyone who lives and believes in me will never die. Do you believe this?" She said to him, "Yes Lord, I believe that you are the Messiah, the Son of God, the one coming into the world." (John 11:25–27)

Jesus invokes the "I am," recalling the giving of the divine name to Moses. Just as God gives life, belief in Jesus gives eternal life. To this, Martha makes the fundamental profession of faith in Jesus that John seeks from the readers of the Gospel: "Yes, Lord, I believe that you are the Messiah, the Son of God, the one coming into the world." As a result of the raising of Lazarus, the leaders decide that Jesus must die. So, in an ironic twist, by bringing Lazarus to life, Jesus brings about his own death. Jesus is the life-giving Savior who dies so that his followers may live.

The "Book of Glory" deals with the final days of Jesus, his crucifixion, and his resurrection. John's account of these events is distinctive. At the Last Supper there is no Eucharist; rather, Jesus washes the feet of the disciples. In John, the Last Supper, unlike in the Synoptics, is not a Passover meal. On noon of the preparation day for the Passover, the time at which the lambs for the Passover meal were being slaughtered, Jesus is sentenced to death (John 19:14). In this way, we now understand more fully the meaning of John the Baptist's earlier proclamation that Jesus is "the Lamb of God." The Lamb's blood would now be shed, and just as the lamb's blood had spared the Israelites' lives on the first Passover, Jesus' death creates the possibility for eternal life. Knowing that his mission is complete, Jesus simply says, "It is finished," bows his head, and dies. The resurrected Lord appears first to Mary Magdalene, then to the disciples, and finally to "doubting" Thomas.

CONCLUDING THOUGHTS ON CHRISTOLOGY IN THE FOUR GOSPELS AND ACTS

The church included four Gospels and Acts in the canon, and in doing so, enshrined a rich diversity of Christologies. Mark's Gospel emphasized that Jesus was a Suffering Messiah whose entire ministry falls under the shadow of the cross. Matthew struck the note of continuity between the hopes of Judaism and the figure of Jesus. Luke highlighted Jesus' concern for the poor and his message of mercy and forgiveness. John's Gospel spoke of Jesus as the Incarnate Word of God, and as the one who offered eternal life to those who believe.

This diversity of perspectives found in the four Gospels raises a theological question: Do the gospel portraits of Jesus complement or contradict each other? If the four Gospels present complementary ideas about Jesus, then each Gospel enriches what we learn about Jesus from the other three. Mark's emphasis on Jesus' suffering would not, therefore, contradict Luke's emphasis on Jesus' compassion. If, however, the differences among the four Gospels seem too vast, then a theological problem arises. For example, in John's Gospel Jesus declares, "The Father and I are one" (John 10:30), while in Mark's Gospel Jesus, when asked about the end of time, replies "But about that day or hour no one knows, neither the angels in heaven, nor the Son, but only the Father" (Mark 13:32). Are these sayings too far apart to be logically attributed to the same person? The challenge facing the early Christian theologians, therefore, was to construct a framework that could accommodate all four gospel Christologies.

Christology in the Early Church

The early christological debates dealt with two critical, interrelated sets of questions. The first set centered on the relationship of the Father to the Son. Was the Son divine, or was the Son the divinely chosen, supreme representative of the Father? We will focus specifically on this question when we discuss the Council of Nicaea in 325. If the Son was divine, as the church ultimately declared, then a second set of questions naturally arose. How can the human and divine natures of Christ coexist in the person of Jesus? We will take this question as our guide when we study the Council of Chalcedon in 451. Both sets of questions touch upon issues that we discussed in our earlier chapter on the development of the doctrine of the Trinity.

CHRISTOLOGY PRIOR TO THE COUNCIL OF NICAEA

The easiest way to resolve questions of Christ's humanity and divinity is simply to deny either his humanity or his divinity. While this may not be the correct way to do Christology, such explanations did develop in the early church. A group known as the Ebionites ("the poor ones") denied the divinity of Christ. As the theologian Donald McKim wrote,

> christologically, they regarded Jesus as "the elect of God," "the true prophet," but they denied that he was divine. The early history of Jesus (Matt 1–2) is deleted from their gospel, because they denied the virgin birth of Jesus, his Sonship, and his preexistence. Jesus was perceived as a man on whom the Holy Spirit descended and into whom it entered at his baptism, a view that came to be known as *adoptionism*.[7]

The adoptionists held that Christ was the adopted Son of God, not the eternal Son of God. The moment of adoption was most commonly asserted to have occurred at Christ's baptism when the heavenly voice declares, "This is my Son, the Beloved, with whom I am well pleased" (Matt 3:17). Others believed it happened at the resurrection: "…his Son, who was descended from David according to the flesh and declared to be Son of God with power according to the spirit of holiness by resurrection from the dead…" (Rom 1:3–4).

A second group, the Docetists, denied the humanity of Jesus. "Docetism" takes its names from the Greek word meaning "to seem" or "to appear." Jesus appeared to be human, but was not genuinely human. Christ did not enter fully into the human condition, but rather took on the appearance of a human in order to communicate his message. His flesh was merely a garment thrown over his divinity. Jesus, therefore, did not actually thirst, feel hunger, or experience temptation. As one might expect, the Docetists preferred the Christology of John's Gospel, which they misunderstood. Jesus was the eternal Word of God who came down from heaven and returned to heaven. "I came from the Father and have come into the world; again, I am leaving the world and am going to my Father" (John 16:28). The church came to regard both Ebionitism and Docetism as lopsided answers to the question of Christ's identity. The Ebionites had excluded Christ's divinity; the Docetists had done the same with Christ's humanity.

It is often easier in theological matters to exclude errors rather than to offer solutions. The early church's path to a consensus on Christology follows a similar course. For example, the second-century thinker Justin Martyr knew what he wanted *not* to say when he spoke of Christ as the Word of God. The theologian Gerald O'Collins offered the following description of Justin Martyr's insight.

> In his *Dialogue with Trypho* Justin explained that "God has begotten of himself a rational Power" that was called in the Scriptures by various titles: "sometimes the Glory of the Lord, at other times Son, or Wisdom, or Angel, or God, or Lord, or Word" (61.1; see 61.3). To interpret the generation of the Word, Justin appealed to the sun sending forth its rays or a fire kindling other fires. Just as in these analogies, the begetting of the Son did not mean an "amputation, as if the essence *(ousia)* of the Father were divided" (ibid., 128.3, 4).[8]

Justin Martyr realized that an adequate Christology could not threaten the unity of God; so too third-century thinker Tertullian argued that an adequate Christology could not threaten the unity of the person of Jesus. The patristics scholar Richard A. Norris, Jr., described Tertullian's theological concern:

> [Tertullian's] opponents had maintained that "Son" refers to the humanity of Jesus, his flesh, while "Father" refers to his deity. This troubled Tertullian because, while he insisted upon distinguishing Logos and Father within the sphere of the divine, he did not believe that Jesus Christ, the incarnate Logos, is two separate things or items—*personae*. There is only one of him, Tertullian argues, and he expresses this judgment by saying that Christ is one "person." Of course, he sees a duality in Christ. Jesus is constituted out of two "substances," flesh on the one hand and Spirit on the other, which are designations for human and divine ways of being. In him, these factors are mingled, though not in such a way as to react on one another and be mutually changed.[9]

While Tertullian had difficulty stating exactly how the human and divine substances coexisted in the person of Christ, he was convinced that Christ was both human and divine. Another third-century theologian, Origen, offered the image of a lump of coal that is placed in a fire to describe the unity of Jesus' soul with the Logos of God. The christological controversies of the second and third centuries provided the church with a clear sense about what constituted an insufficient christology (i.e., Ebionitism, Docetism), and a general conceptual framework and vocabulary (person, substance, Logos) for constructing an adequate christology. These steps paved the way for the Council of Nicaea.

Before we turn our attention to the Council of Nicaea, two observations deserve our attention. First, the christological positions promoted by the theologians of the second and third centuries were often framed in philosophical terms. As a result, their descriptions of Christ might seem far removed from the gospel accounts of the Jesus who walked the dusty roads of Galilee. As the Christian movement spread throughout the wider Greco-Roman world, theologians employed the philosophical language of their day. The theologian Leland White noted,

As a culture, Hellenism was shaped by a vision of the world, the cosmos, rather than a sense of history. As the Church developed within this culture, it had to explain philosophically how human beings fitted into the world instead of describing where history was leading. Its Christology, therefore, shed the historical orientation favored by Jewish Christians who saw Jesus as the answer to the question of where human events were headed, the future of God's people. Both Tertullian and Origen presented philosophically oriented Christologies, statements about Christ which also interpreted the universe.[10]

The second observation would be that of the four gospels, John's Gospel seemed to play the dominant role in the Christologies of the early church. In the view of the theologian Roger Haight, "After the New Testament period, the understanding of Jesus Christ became governed by the framework and language of the Prologue of John's gospel. The Jesus who was the subject matter of christology ceased to be the Jesus of the synoptics. Or, to put it another way, the Jesus of the synoptics became understood in Johannine terms."[11]

THE COUNCIL OF NICAEA

The Emperor Constantine, who had brought an end to the long-standing imperial policy of the persecution of Christians, was distressed when a crisis that had begun in Alexandria grew in such size and intensity to eventually threaten the unity of the church. The debate had begun in Alexandria, pitting the bishop Alexander and his eventual successor Athanasius, against the presbyter named Arius. The emperor ordered the bishops of the church to convene a meeting for the purpose of resolving this dispute. This gathering of the world's bishops, the first "ecumenical council" in Christian history, took place in the year 325 in the city of Nicaea in modern-day Turkey. The controversy that had erupted in the church centered on the christological question: Was Christ God?

Arius's position on the question was straightforward:

1. If Christ was God, then there would be two Gods.
2. There is only one God.
3. Therefore, Christ was not God.

Arius and his supporters argued that a plain reading of the Gospels reveals that when Jesus was baptized, the voice of God declared him to be the Son. At the Transfiguration, God repeats that claim. Jesus prayed to God in the Garden of Gethsemane. While on the cross, Jesus called out to God in heaven. If this same Jesus had been God, then obviously that would mean that there were two Gods, one on heaven and one on earth. Because Christians are strict monotheists, the only reasonable theological conclusion to be drawn is that Christ was not God.

Arius was not trying to denigrate Jesus. Arius was himself a Christian; he accepted that Christ was the Word (or Logos) of God. The critical theological point upon which Arius insisted was that, like Wisdom, the Logos was *created*. "The Lord created me at the beginning of his work, the first of his acts long ago" (Prov 8:22). The slogan of the Arian cause was, therefore, "There was a time when he [i.e., the Son] was not." There was a moment, in other words, when the Father created the Son (just as all human sons and daughters are created in time). Arius could make very exalted claims about Christ, but stopped short of saying that the Logos was coeternal with God. Arius believed that taking that step would endanger the Christian commitment to monotheism.

Athanasius argued against him, saying that Christ's divinity is absolutely essential to the Gospel message of salvation. Athanasius's argument ran as follows:

1. Christ is our Savior.
2. Only God can save us.
3. Therefore, Christ was "of the same substance" as the Father.

Whereas Arius wanted to safeguard monotheism, Athanasius anchored his Christology in the Christian claims about salvation. If Christ was indeed the Savior of the world, and not merely a great prophet or an enlightened teacher, then Christ must have imparted eternal life. Only a divine being could give eternal life; therefore, Christ must have been divine. Athanasius's conclusion, however, needed to address Arius's point that the Gospels do in fact contain stories in which the heavenly voice speaks to Christ. He therefore employed a term not found in the New Testament: Christ was *homoousios*—"one in being with," or "of the same substance as," the Father.

The bishops at Nicaea declared Athanasius's position to be orthodox and produced a creed that included the term *homoousios* to describe the relationship of the Son to the Father. The creed, in part, stated:

> We believe in one God, the Father almighty, maker of all things, visible and invisible.
>
> And in one Lord Jesus Christ, the Son of God, the only-begotten generated from the Father, that is, Light from Light, true God from true God, begotten, not made, one in being *[homoousios]* with the Father, through whom all things were made, those in heaven and those on earth. For us men and for our salvation He came down, and became flesh, was made man, suffered, and rose again on the third day.[12]

The bishops added an appendix condemning those who believed that "there was a time when he was not." The official declaration had been made: Athanasius's position was correct; Arius's position was heretical. Some Christians refused to accept the creed. Even those who did soon found themselves deeply divided on the question of how Christ could at the same time be *fully* human and *fully* divine.

CHRISTOLOGY FROM NICAEA TO CHALCEDON

This period in Christian thought involved a clash of christo-logical perspectives between two of the leading intellectual centers in the ancient church. In many respects, the different approaches amounted to a different ordering of priorities. On the one side were the theologians in Antioch in Syria who wanted to affirm the humanity of Jesus. Once Christ's humanity was clear, then the

Antiochene theologians moved to the question of Christ's divinity. Their counterparts in Alexandria in Egypt took the opposite approach. They began with a strong affirmation of the divinity of Christ, and then speculated how Christ's divinity could could be joined to his humanity. Both Christologies employed the concept of the Word *(Logos)*. The Antiochene theologians spoke of the *Logos* and *anthropos*—the Word and the human person (body and soul).[13] Alexandrian theologians preferred to speak of the Logos and *sarx* (flesh)—the Word became flesh (see John 1:14). Critics of Antiochene theology charged that it too easily drifted into adoptionism. Critics of Alexandrian theology feared that it tended toward Docetism.

The figure who triggered the first major post-Nicene controversy was Apollinaris (or Apollinarius) (ca. 310 to ca. 390).[14] He supported his friend Athanasius and saw himself as a defender of the Nicene Creed. A proponent of the Logos-*sarx* Christology, he argued that the Logos replaced Jesus' soul. Underlying this controversy are two understandings of what it means to be a human being. The first conception divides the human person into two realities: body and soul, or flesh and spirit. The second conception divides the human person into body, soul, and spirit (see 1 Thess 5:23). As the theologian Donald J. Goergen noted,

> It appears as if Apollinaris held to the Platonic tripartite perspective; the human person is body, soul (the irrational or animal soul), and the spirit or mind (the human, rational soul). The third is the specifically human element. In Jesus Christ, for Apollinaris, there are the first two elements, body and irrational soul, but the third element is replaced by the Logos.[15]

Apollinaris wanted to safeguard the sinlessness of Jesus, and believed that replacing the human mind with the Logos would ensure that Jesus' thoughts were always divine thoughts. Apollinaris believed, according to the religious studies scholar Linwood Urban, that "whereas a human mind is 'fallible and enslaved to filthy thoughts,' the Logos is immune from fleshly passions. Moreover, Christ, having the Logos as his only mind, must be omniscient."[16]

This position secured Christ's divinity, but Antiochene thinkers believed it negated his humanity. Theodore of Mopsuestia (ca. 350–428) was one of the most vocal critics of Apollinaris. As Leland White explained,

> Whenever Alexandrians argued that the divine nature of the Word replaced the soul in Jesus, the Antiochene school suspected Apollinarianism. Theodore objected to the idea that Christ assumed "a body not a soul," saying "if the godhead had replaced the soul he would not have been hungry or thirsty, nor would he have tired or been in need of food."…As he explained, the body suffers because the soul is unable to satisfy all its needs, but an infinite Spirit within would have more than satisfied all needs. Thus, without a fully human soul, Christ would have had no human experience.[17]

Theodore and his fellow Antiochene thinkers wanted to safeguard the reality of the young Jesus growing in wisdom (Luke 2:52), the genuine temptation of Jesus in the desert, and his submission to the will of God in the Garden of Gethsemane. In order to do this, they spoke of the Word "indwelling" in Jesus' body, as the Spirit of God dwelt in the Temple in Jerusalem (see the comparison of Jesus' body to the Temple in John 2:21). The union of the human and divine was a union of wills, a moral union. Some Antiochenes even spoke of "two Sons"—the Son of God and the son of Mary. This terminology, argued the Alexandrians, revealed the inability of the Antiochene position to express adequately the *unity* of the divine and the human natures in Christ.

The position of Apollinaris was ultimately rejected because it violated a principle advanced by the one of the great Cappadocian thinkers, Gregory of Nazianzus: "What is not assumed is not healed; what is united with God is also saved."[18] According to this principle, if Christ did not assume, or possess, a genuinely human nature, or if there was a commingling of the divine and human natures that produced a third kind of nature unique to Christ, then Christ did not redeem human nature. Gregory's principle won wide acceptance and proved influential in subsequent christological debates.

The next round of the christological battles erupted when Nestorius, a student of Theodore of Mopsuestia and patriarch of Constantinople, declared that Mary should not be called *Theotokos*, "the Mother of God." As the patristics scholar J. N. D. Kelly explained,

> God cannot have a mother, [Nestorius] argued, and no creature could have engendered the Godhead; Mary bore a man, the vehicle of divinity but not God. The Godhead cannot have been carried for nine months in a woman's womb, or have been wrapped in baby-clothes, or have suffered, died, and been buried. Behind the description of Mary as Theotokos, [Nestorius] professed to detect the Arian tenet that the Son was a creature, or the Apollinarian idea that the manhood was incomplete.[19]

In keeping with the Antiochene tradition, Nestorius wanted to keep the two natures of Christ distinct. To the thinkers at Alexandria, especially the bishop Cyril, Nestorius's position suggested a split personality in Christ.

The final character in this complex chapter of church history was a monk in Constantinople by the name of Eutyches (ca. 378–454). His position was diametrically opposed to Nestorius's Christology. Eutyches stated, "I confess that before the union our Lord was of two natures, but after the union I confess one nature."[20] While other thinkers were seeking to strike the proper balance between Jesus' humanity and divinity, Eutyches threw the scales completely to the side of divinity. Christ possessed only a divine nature. For this reason, Eutyches's position was labeled monophysitism (from the Greek words *mono*, meaning "one," and *physis*, meaning "nature"). Christ's divinity overwhelmed his humanity, "like the sea receiving a drop of honey, for straightaway the drop, as it mixes with the sea's water, vanishes."[21]

The fourth ecumenical council was held in the city of Chalcedon not far from Constantinople in the year 451. The bishops declared that an orthodox Christology must affirm that Christ was one person with two natures. The bishops rejected what they took as the two extreme positions. First, against those who denied the unity of the divine and the human, the bishops insisted on the theological need to speak of "one person." Second, against the monophysite position, the bishops affirmed the two natures of Christ, without attempting to explain precisely *how* the human and divine natures of Christ were joined.

> We confess that one and the same Lord Jesus Christ, the only-begotten Son, must be acknowledged in two natures, without confusion or change, without division or separation. The distinction between the natures was never abolished by their union but rather the character proper to each of the two natures was preserved as they came together in one person...[22]

The theologian Roger Olson described the Chalcedonian definition as "an attempt to express and protect the mystery of the incarnation against distortions."[23] In this light, the period of time from the Council of Nicaea (325) to the Council of Chalcedon (451) can be understood as the church's extended, disciplined reflection on the Christian conviction that the Word became flesh and dwelt among us.

Soteriology in the New Testament and Early Church

The Christian tradition has always linked the question of Christology (the identity of Jesus) with soteriology (the work of Jesus). They are two sides of the same coin. For example, Athanasius's argument, which prevailed at Nicaea, was both christological and soteriological: Christ saved us from our sins; in order to be the Savior, Christ must be one in being with the Father. We turn our attention now to some of the leading soteriological concepts in the New Testament. We will focus our attention on three groups of writings: the Pauline corpus, including the letters of undisputed Pauline authorship (Romans, 1 and 2 Corinthians, Galatians, Philippians, 1 Thessalonians, and Philemon) and those of disputed Pauline authorship (2 Thessalonians, Colossians,

Ephesians, 1 and 2 Timothy, and Titus); second, the Catholic or General Epistles (James, 1 and 2 Peter, 1 John, 2 John, 3 John, and Jude); and third, Hebrews.

The Pauline writings do not contain a great deal of biographical information about Jesus, but they are filled with soteriological declarations about his death and resurrection. Paul insisted that Christ's death and resurrection had shattered his previously held belief in the need for strict adherence to the Law and the proper distinction between Jews and Gentiles. Three of Paul's favorite expressions for speaking about the work of Christ capture his conviction that these fundamental beliefs had been demolished. First of all, Paul speaks of Christ's "justification" of sinners. Paul borrowed the language of justification from the law courts. As the scripture scholar Joseph A. Fitzmyer explained in his commentary on Romans,

> When, then, Paul in Romans says that Christ Jesus "justified" humans beings "by his blood" (3:25; cf. 5:29), he means that by what Christ suffered in his passion and death he has brought it about that sinful human beings can stand before God's tribunal acquitted or innocent, with the judgment not based on observance of the Mosaic law. Thus "God's uprightness" is now manifested toward human beings in a just judgment, one of acquittal, because Jesus "our Lord...was handed over (to death) for our trespasses and raised for our "justification" (4:25).[24]

Paul also describes the effect of Christ's death as reconciliation, a term drawn from the battlefield. After hostilities have ceased, the warring factions are reconciled. "For if while we were enemies, we were reconciled to God through the death of his Son, much more surely, having been reconciled, will we be saved by his life" (Rom 5:10). Paul employs a third image of redemption. A slave was "redeemed," meaning that a price was paid and the slave was emancipated. When addressing the Corinthian church and his concerns about their behavior, Paul reminds them that they have been "bought with a price; therefore glorify God in your body" (1 Cor 6:20).

Paul did not develop a systematic soteriology, but his letters do contain many ideas that would serve as the framework for later soteriological theories. For instance, in Romans 5 (see also 1 Cor 15:21–22, 45–49), Paul contrasted Adam and Christ. With Adam, one man's disobedience brought sin and death into the world. With Christ, one man's obedience conquered the power of sin and death. In Philippians 2, Paul presented another model for understanding Christ's work in the world. In the course of his moral exhortation to the Philippian church, Paul cited what most scholars believe was a preexisting hymn. In this hymn, Christ "who, though he was in the form of God, / did not regard equality with God / as something to be exploited, / but emptied himself…" (Phil 2:6–7a). This "emptying" in Greek is a *kenosis*, hence this way of thinking about Christ is called a kenotic Christology. There is a descent-ascent pattern in the hymn. Christ "emptied himself" of his glory, suffered his death on the cross, and "God also highly exalted him / and gave him the name / that is above every other name" (Phil 2:9). A third model can be found in another hymn in Colossians 1:15–20. This hymn praises the cosmic effects of Christ's death and resurrection. "For in him all the fullness of God was pleased to dwell, and through him God was pleased to reconcile to himself all things, whether on earth or in heaven, by making peace through the blood of his cross" (Col 1:19–20).

Scattered in the Catholic or General Epistles are ideas regarding Christ's saving work that are also focused on the cross. In 1 Peter we find an intriguing passage that echoes the language of the Suffering Servant Songs in Isaiah. "He himself bore our sins in his body on the cross, so that, free from sins, we might live for righteousness; by his wounds, you have been healed" (1 Pet 2:24). The author of 1 John described Christ as "the atoning sacrifice for our sins, and not for ours only but also for the sins of the whole world" (1 John 2:2). God the Father initiated this process, according to 1 John, and did so out of love. "God's love was revealed among us in this way: God sent his only Son into the world so that we might live through him. In this is love, not that we loved God but that he loved us and sent his Son to be the atoning sacrifice for our sins" (1 John 4:9–10). Other passages in the New Testament emphasize the active participation and willingness of Christ: "Christ loved us and gave himself up for us" (Eph 5:2), and "I lay down my life in order to take it up again. No one takes it from me, but I lay it down of my own accord" (John 10:17b–18a).

The notion of sacrifice finds its most developed expression in Hebrews. In this intricate work, Christ is the "faithful high priest" (Heb 2:17) who offers "the sacrifice of himself" (Heb 9:26). Christ was tested in every way as all humans are, but he did not sin (cf. Heb 4:15). His death was an "expiation" (Heb 2:17; see also Heb 9:5 and Rom 3:25). Scholars debate the precise meaning of this expression, but most caution that this term should not be taken to mean that Christ's death somehow appeased a wrathful God. The background may be the Old Testament practice of the high priest sprinkling blood on the "mercy seat" in the sanctuary on the Day of Atonement (Lev 16). In any event, the Letter to the Hebrews presents Christ's death as the definitive and final sacrifice and "the source of eternal salvation for all who obey him" (Heb 5:9).

Soteriology in the Patristic Church

The New Testament writers did not attempt to construct an overarching theory of salvation. They presented rich images that captured some sense of the effect of Christ's life, death, and resurrection. In the early church, the soteriological themes were developed in various ways. There was no single dominant theme, but a number of trajectories can be detected in the literature of the early church. We will briefly focus our attention on four models: salvation as illumination, salvation as recapitulation, salvation as victory over the devil, and salvation as deification.

The concept of illumination relates primarily to the early church's view of Christ as the Teacher. In his classic study of early Christian soteriology, the patristics scholar H. E. W. Turner wrote, "The interpretation of the Redemption which Christ brought primarily in terms of knowledge, and of Christ first and foremost a Teacher, is especially characteristic of the Apostolic Fathers."[25] Clement of Rome (d. ca. 101) offered the following reflection: "Through him the eyes of our heart were opened. Through him our unintelligent and darkened mind shoots up into light. Through him the Master was pleased to let us taste the knowledge that never fades."[26] Thinkers in this particular tradition were cognizant of Paul's warning against the dangers of seeking knowledge (see 1 Cor 1) rather than faith or love, but they would insist that they were seeking to take on "the mind of Christ" (Phil 2:5) who is the truth (John 14:6). This soteriological metaphor of illumination also has the advantage of seeing Jesus' ministry—his sayings, parables, and miracles—as an essential element of Christ's saving work, and not just his crucifixion.

The second trajectory can be drawn from Paul's Letter to the Ephesians to the church thinker Irenaeus (ca. 130 to ca. 200). Its starting point is the opening chapter of Ephesians in which God's plan of salvation in Christ is described:

> In him we have redemption through his blood, the forgiveness of our trespasses, according to the riches of his grace that he lavished on us. With all wisdom and insight, he has made known to us the mystery of his will, according to his good pleasure that he set forth in Christ, as a plan for the fullness of time, to gather up all things in him, things in heaven and things on earth. (1:7–10)

This "gathering up" or "summing up" is known as recapitulation. J. N. D. Kelly offered the following summary of Irenaeus's interpretation of the work of Christ:

> "Because of His measureless love," [Irenaeus] writes, "He became what we are in order to enable us to become what He is." The method he outlines in the oft-repeated assertion that what we lost in Adam we recovered in Christ; its [premise] is the idea that, if we fell through our solidarity with the first man, we can be restored through our solidarity with Christ. The key-conception which Irenaeus employs to explain this is "recapitulation"…which he borrows from St. Paul's description of the divine purpose as being "to sum up all things in Christ." He understands the Pauline text as implying that the Redeemer gathers

together, includes or comprises the whole of reality in Himself, the human race being included.[27]

Irenaeus's theory offers a compelling vision of the solidarity of all humans across the ages, a Christ-centered view of history, and a theology that joins creation with redemption.

The third model, the victory of Christ over the power of evil, was dubbed "the classic Christian idea of the Atonement" by the Swedish theologian Gustaf Aulén in *Christus Victor*, one of the most influential works on soteriology to be written in the twentieth century. "Its central theme is the idea of the Atonement as a Divine conflict and victory; Christ—*Christus Victor*—fights against and triumphs over the evil powers of the world, the 'tyrants' under which mankind is in bondage and suffering, and in Him God reconciles the world to Himself."[28] In his temptations in the desert, in his exorcisms, and preeminently in his death and resurrection, Christ defeated the power of Satan. The Christian life is a sharing in that victory.

Continuing with this model a bit longer, two vivid images were used in the ancient church to describe Christ's victory over Satan. The first, that of a fishing hook, came from Gregory of Nyssa. "The Deity was hidden under the veil of our nature, that, as is done by greedy fish, the hook of the Deity might be gulped down along with the bait of the flesh and thus life being introduced into the house of death and light shining in the darkness..."[29] The second image was that of a ransom payment, based on the verse, "For the Son of Man came not to be served but to serve, and to give his life [as] a ransom for many" (Mark 10:45). The early church thinkers commonly employed this image. It conveyed the sense of liberation from the ultimate power of sin and death, which was won by Christ's death. However, when pushed too far, the metaphor presented a problem: to whom was the ransom paid? The two most likely candidates were either God or Satan. The Father using the Son as a ransom payment was clearly objectionable. However, the Son living his life as a ransom to the devil was no less troubling. Because of this problem, the ransom theory did not gain universal acceptance in the church.

The fourth soteriological model in the ancient church was deification—the process of becoming like God. In this model, Christ's gift of eternal life and his imparting of the divine life to his followers is central. Athanasius gave the classic expression of the principle: "The Word was made man in order that we might be made divine."[30] Although the concept of deification sounds odd to many Western Christians, the Orthodox Church in the East has assigned the concept a central role in its theology and spirituality. Scripture speaks in various ways about the mystery of deification. We are called to "share in the divine nature"(2 Pet 1:4) and become "children of God" (Gal 3:26). "See what love the Father has bestowed on us that we may be called the children of God. Yet so we are" (1 John 3:1). This intimate relationship with God is made possible when we are "united with Christ" (see Rom 6:5). Whereas Christ was God's Son by nature, we are sons and daughters of God by adoption (see Gal 4:4–7). In John's Gospel, Jesus prays that his followers "may all be one, as you, Father, are in me and I in you, that they may also be in us" (John 17:21).

These four models were not mutually exclusive. Two or three of them may appear in the work of a single author. They were all attempts at articulating the meaning of Christ for the life of each human being and for the world. The questions of Christ's identity and the significance of his life, death, and resurrection were asked anew in each succeeding generation of Christians, and so we will next examine some of the leading responses to these questions proposed by thinkers from the Middle Ages to the present.

Discussion Questions

1. Offer a one-sentence summary of your own Christology.
2. Which gospel story best captures your sense of who Jesus was?
3. Was Athanasius or Arius right? Why? Anticipate objections and respond to them.
4. What is the theological significance of the ancient principle, "What is not assumed is not healed; what is united with God is also saved"?

5. Do you accept that Jesus was one person in two natures? Offer a restatement of this idea in contemporary language.
6. What was the chief effect of the life, death, and resurrection of Jesus Christ?
7. Do any of the four soteriological theories that were prominent in the early church appeal to you? Why? Why not?

Suggested Readings

For a study of New Testament christology, see Frank J. Matera, *New Testament Christology* (Louisville, KY: Westminster John Knox Press, 1999); Paula Fredriksen, *From Jesus to Christ*, sec. ed. (New Haven: Yale University Press, 2000); and Part One of Veli-Matti Karkkainen, *Christology* (Grand Rapids: Baker Academic, 2003). For patristic Christology, see Richard A. Norris, Jr., "Introduction," in *The Christological Controversy*, edited by Norris (Philadelphia: Fortress Press, 1980); chapter eight of William L. Portier, *Tradition and Incarnation* (Mahwah, NJ: Paulist Press, 1994); and Donald J. Goergen, *The Jesus of Christian History* (Collegeville, MN: The Liturgical Press, 1992). For patristic soteriology, see chapter five of Donald K. McKim, *Theological Turning Points* (Atlanta: John Knox Press, 1988). For a contemporary survey of Christology and soteriology, see Thomas P. Rausch, *Who Is Jesus?* (Collegeville, MN: Liturgical Press, 2003); Gerald O'Collins, *Interpreting Jesus* (Ramsey, NJ: Paulist Press, 1983); and William M. Thompson, *The Jesus Debate* (Mahwah, NJ: Paulist Press, 1985).

Notes

1. D. E. Nineham, *The Gospel of St. Mark* in The Pelican Gospel Commentaries (New York: Seabury Press, 1963), 224–25.
2. Keith Nickle, *The Synoptic Gospels: An Introduction* (Atlanta: John Knox Press, 1980), 94.
3. Norman Perrin, *Rediscovering the Teaching of Jesus* (New York: Harper and Row, 1976), 74.

4. Richard B. Hays, *The Moral Vision of the New Testament* (San Francisco: HarperSanFrancisco, 1996), 119.

5. Veli-Matti Karkkainen, *Christology: A Global Introduction* (Grand Rapids: Baker Academic, 2003), 39.

6. Raymond E. Brown, *The Gospel According to John I–XII* in the Anchor Bible (Garden City, NY: Doubleday and Company, 1966), 32–33.

7. Donald K. McKim, *Theological Turning Points* (Atlanta: John Knox Press, 1988), 26.

8. Gerald O'Collins, *Christology* (New York: Oxford University Press, 1995), 170.

9. Richard A. Norris, Jr., "Introduction," in *The Christological Controversy*, Richard A. Norris, Jr., ed. (Philadelphia: Fortress Press, 1980), 14.

10. Leland J. White, *Christ and the Christian Movement* (New York: Alba House,1985), 96.

11. Roger Haight, *Jesus: Symbol of God* (Maryknoll, NY: Orbis Books, 1999), 247.

12. J. Neuner and J. Dupuis, eds., *The Christian Faith* (New York: Alba House, 1982), 6.

13. Donald J. Goergen, *The Jesus of Christian History* (Collegeville, MN: The Liturgical Press, 1992), 73n22.

14. Ibid., 78.

15. Ibid., 79.

16. Linwood Urban, *A Short History of Christian Thought* (New York: Oxford University Press, 1986), 83.

17. White, *Christ and the Christian Movement*, 154.

18. Quoted in Walter Kasper, *Jesus the Christ* (New York: Paulist Press, 1976), 212.

19. J. N. D. Kelly, *Early Christian Doctrines*, rev. ed. (San Francisco: Harper and Row, 1978), 311.

20. Quoted in Urban, *A Short History of Christian Thought*, 86.

21. Ibid., 87.

22. Neuner and Dupuis, *The Christian Faith*, 154–55.

23. Roger E. Olson, *The Story of Christian Theology* (Downers Grove, IL: InterVarsity Press, 1999), 233.

24. Joseph A. Fitzmyer, *Romans* in the Anchor Bible (New York : Doubleday, 1993), 117.

25. H. E. W. Turner, *The Patristic Doctrine of Redemption* (London: A. R. Mowbray and Co., 1952), 33.

26. Quoted in Jaroslav Pelikan, *The Christian Tradition,* Volume One: *The Emergence of the Catholic Tradition 100–600* (Chicago: University of Chicago Press, 1971), 152.

27. Kelly, *Early Christian Doctrines,* 172.

28. Gustaf Aulén, *Christus Victor* (New York: Macmillan, 1961), 4.

29. Quoted in Joseph F. Mitros, "Patristic Views of Christ's Salvific Work," in *Thought* 42 (1967): 425.

30. Quoted in McKim, *Theological Turning Points,* 84.

8

CHRIST AND SALVATION
IN THE MIDDLE AGES,
REFORMATION, AND MODERNITY

"Jesus Christ is the same yesterday and today and forever" (Heb 13:8). While this proclamation is undoubtedly true, it is also the case that each generation of Christians confronts anew Christ's question to Peter on the road to Caesarea Philippi: "But who do you say that I am?" (Mark 8:27). Over the course of time, as Christians continued to reflect on scripture and to study the early christological controversies, theologians brought the wisdom of the past to bear on their own particular questions about the person and work of Christ. In this chapter we will examine the theological positions in the areas of Christology and soteriology that dominated discussions during the medieval era, the Protestant Reformation, and the modern age.

Medieval Theology

The Scholastic theologians applied their powers of reason to the articles of faith and systematically presented the results of their inquiry. One of earliest representatives of this movement was St. Anselm (ca. 1033–1109) who became archbishop of Canterbury in 1093. In this prominent position Anselm came into repeated conflict with the English monarchy over the question of lay investiture (the appointment of bishops, abbots, etc., by a king or other layperson). As a result, Anselm's career was marked by several exiles. It was during one of these exiles in 1098 that Anselm completed *Cur Deus Homo* (Why God Became Man).

Cur Deus Homo takes the form of a dialogue between Anselm and one of his fellow monks named Boso. Anselm proposes the following question as the topic of their conversation: "For what reason or necessity did God become man and, as we believe and confess, by death restore life to the world, when he could have done this through another person (angelic or human), or even a sheer act of will?"[1] Anselm asks Boso to join him in a rational investigation of the logic behind the incarnation and to speculate as to the reason why the incarnation was the divinely chosen means of redemption.

Anselm first tackles the issue of sin. Anselm defines sin as a failure to render to God what God is due. Boso then asks Anselm to state precisely what humans owe to God. Anselm replies, "Every inclination of the rational creature ought to be subject to the will of God."[2] This is the honor humans owe to God. Anselm continued:

> This is the debt which angels and men owe to God. No one who pays it sins; everyone who does not pay it sins. This is the justice or rectitude of the will, which makes men just or upright in heart, that is, in will. This is the sole and entire honor which we owe to God, and God requires from us.[3]

Sin, then, is the human failure to show honor to God. "One who does not render this honor to God takes away from God what belongs to him, and dishonors God, and to do this is to sin."[4]

How, then, can things be made right? Anselm believed that it is fitting that proper "satisfaction" be made to the offended party, God.

> For it is not enough for someone who has injured another's health to restore his health without making some recompense for the pain and injury suffered, and similarly, it is not enough for someone who violates another's honor to restore the honor, unless he makes some kind of restitution that will please him who was dishonored, according to the extent of the injury and dishonor. We should also note that, when someone pays back what he unjustly took away, he ought to give something

that could not be required of him if he had not stolen another's property. So, then, everyone who sins must repay to God the honor that he has taken away, and this is the satisfaction that every sinner ought to make to God.[5]

The background of the concept of satisfaction continues to be a matter of some scholarly debate. For example, two respected commentators on Anselm's work, Jaroslav Pelikan and G. R. Evans, locate the origin of the term *satisfaction* in two different areas. According to Pelikan, "The term *satisfaction* as a description of the act that had taken place on the cross came from the penitential practice and canon law of the church: a sinner who was truly contrite for his sin, and who confessed that sin and was absolved, nevertheless had to make restitution of what the sin had taken away."[6] Evans argues that when Anselm speaks in terms of honor and satisfaction, he "is unconsciously adopting a feudal frame of reference, in which the notion of honour due to a lord is mixed in with the Biblical concept of God as Lord."[7] Despite their differences regarding the origin of the concept of satisfaction, both Pelikan and Evans agree that Anselm's use of the term expresses his fundamental conviction that there is a "moral order" to the universe.[8]

This sense of the moral order of the universe accounts for Anselm's next point. Why didn't God simply forgive the sin of humans? This seems like a fairly simple and theologically sound resolution to the problem, but Anselm believes that such a solution offends the moral order of the universe. "Therefore, if it is not fitting for God to do anything unjustly or without due order, it does not belong to his freedom or kindness or will to forgive unpunished the sinner who does not repay to God what he took."[9] With this possible solution set aside, Anselm moves to the heart of his argument.

In order for a proper satisfaction to be made, three conditions need to be met. First, the satisfaction must be proportionate to the offense. Second, the satisfaction must be offered by the offending party. Third, the satisfaction must be offered by someone who is able to do so. The historian R. W. Southern summarized these requirements as follows:

1. To restore the lost harmony and blessedness, an offering of obedience must be made equal to or greater than all that has been lacking in the past.
2. Only Man, as the offender, *ought* to make this offering; but no man can do this, because he already owes to God all and more than all he has to offer.
3. Only God *can* make an offering which transcends the whole unpaid debt of past offenses; but God ought not to make it because the debt is Man's.[10]

Because humans are the offending party, they must offer the satisfaction. But because humans already owe everything to God, they are unable to do so. Only God is able to offer the satisfaction. Therefore, concludes Anselm, "it is necessary for a God-Man to make it."[11]

Anselm's satisfaction theory has been highly influential in Christian thought. Its chief strength lies in its ability to join Christology and soteriology together in a single theory. Christ as "one person with two natures" (Christology) is the very same person who is uniquely qualified to offer satisfaction (soteriology). The nature of Christ and the work of Christ are two sides of the same coin for Anselm, although he does focus his attention on Christ's death. Christ was sinless and completely obedient to God, and therefore did not deserve death, so laying down his life had infinite value for sinners. But Anselm says little about the saving effect of Jesus' ministry. According to the modern theologian Gerald O'Collins, "Anselm turned Christ's life into a mere prelude to death."[12] The most powerful critique of Anselm's theory in the Middle Ages, however, came from a brilliant and brash theologian named Peter Abelard (1079–1142).

Abelard's chief objection to Anselm's theory appeared in his commentary on Paul's Letter to the Romans. Abelard objected to the very logic of the satisfaction theory. "Indeed, how cruel and wicked it seems that anyone should demand the blood of an innocent person as the price for anything, or that it should in any way please him that an innocent man should be slain—still less that God should consider the death of his Son so agreeable that by it he should be reconciled to the whole world!"[13] Whereas Anselm found it fitting that the God-man offer satisfaction for the sin of humankind, Abelard finds such a position simply incompatible with God's love and justice. What, then, is the effect of Christ's death on the cross? Abelard offered the following answer:

> Yet everyone becomes more righteous—by which we mean a greater lover of the Lord—after the Passion of Christ than before, since a realized gift inspires love [more] than one which is only hoped for. Wherefore, our redemption through Christ's suffering is that deeper affection in us which not only frees us from slavery to sin, but also wins for us the true liberty of sons of God, so that we do all things out of love rather than fear—love to him who has shown us such grace that no greater can be found, as he himself asserts, saying, "Greater love than this no man hath, that a man lay down his life for his friends."[14]

For Abelard, the cross demonstrates the love of Christ for us, and prompts us in turn to love our neighbors. The saving power of the cross rests in the interior transformation that it produces in all who look upon it.

Anselm's and Abelard's theories are often described respectively as objective and subjective accounts of salvation. As the theologian Roger E. Olson explained,

> Christian theories of atonement have been divided into at least two categories by scholars who study historical theology: *objective* and *subjective*. In fact, however, that is a somewhat artificial and misleading dualism. All of the Christian theories of atonement developed by constructive theologians attempt to be both objective and subjective. *Objective* here means that in the cross event something is actually achieved on behalf of humanity by God in Christ; atonement itself happens outside of the individual human subject even if it remains to be realized and appropriated by him or her. Any view that regards Christ's death on the cross as a payment of a required

penalty by Jesus Christ to God on behalf of humanity is objective. *Subjective* here means that the cross makes possible or enables a necessary response within the human person needing salvation and that the actual benefit of Christ's death is in that response. Any view that regards Christ's death on the cross as an example or a transforming influence on humanity is subjective.[15]

The theologian F. W. Dillistone argued that the difference between Anselm's theory and Abelard's theory can be better understood as a difference in perspective. "In reality Abelard marks the transition from an outlook which saw God dealing with humanity *as a whole*, either through a legal transaction or through a mystical transfusion, to one in which the ethical and psychological qualities of *the individual within the community* began to receive fuller recognition."[16]

Throughout the medieval period, Anselm's position enjoyed greater prominence than that advanced by Abelard, though its logical force depended on two important ideas: the unity of all humans beings throughout time and Christ's unity with all Christians. Both of these ideas figured prominently in the theological synthesis of the preeminent Scholastic thinker, Thomas Aquinas. The Dominican scholar Brian Davies summarized Aquinas's view in this way: "Like St. Paul (on whose teaching he is clearly drawing at this point), Aquinas teaches that, just as all people can be said to be 'in Adam,' so members of Christ's Church can be said to be 'in Christ.'"[17] Echoing the belief that all humans are "in Adam," the twentieth-century Catholic theologian Karl Adam wrote, "This much is certain, that we men do not stand in God's scheme of redemption as isolated, individual beings, but in essential solidarity with the entire human race; or rather, that it is in this essential unity of the race that God sees us, and in which he leads and directs us, rewards us and punishes us."[18] In terms of the question of how Christ is united to all Christians, the Dominican theologian Aidan Nichols offered the following question and answer: "For the question also arises, How are we to be united to the saving causality of the mysteries of the life of Christ? And Thomas's answer to *this* is, By faith and the sacraments of faith, a frequently encountered formula in his work."[19] The leaders of the Protestant Reformation in our next period of Christian thought will shift, to borrow Dillistone's concepts, from viewing the problem of sin for humanity as a whole to the problem of sin for the individual within the community.

Luther and Calvin and Trent

Luther accepted the classic "one person with two natures" Christology of Chalcedon. Luther relished paradox, and the Chalcedonian formula expressed a fundamental paradoxical truth of Christianity: namely, in a manger in Bethlehem, the Incarnate Son of God was born. In his survey of the history of Christology, the scripture scholar Dennis C. Duling offered the following observation about Luther's Christology:

> Luther's conception is well expressed in the German term *Ausbund,* a mercantile expression for "the faultless sample bound to the outside of a bolt of cloth to indicate the quality of the merchandise within." Jesus Christ is a visible, tangible manifestation of the God who is hidden from sight. He expresses the Father's will and heart; he is God's seal, standard, ensign, pledge, and especially beloved Son.[20]

While never compromising the divinity of Christ, Luther emphasized the genuine human experience of Jesus. "He ate, drank, slept, awoke, was tired. He was sad and happy. He wept and he laughed; He hungered and thirsted, froze, and perspired. He chatted and worked and prayed."[21] As Luther continually asserted, the central paradoxical truth of the gospel message is that Christ's horrifying death on the cross brought salvation to the world.

For Luther, Christology and soteriology were two sides of the same coin. To know Christ necessarily involved what Luther's colleague Philip Melanchthon called "the benefits" brought by faith. Personal experience of Christ's benefits, not mere intellectual comprehension of christological doctrines, comprised genuine knowledge of Christ according to Luther.

We find many people who say, "Christ is a man, Son of God, born of a pure virgin, has become man, dies, and is risen again from the dead, etc."—that is all nothing. The fact that he is Christ means that he was given for us without any of our works. He gained the Holy Spirit of God for us and made us children of God without our merits, so that we might have a gracious God, become lord with him over everything that is in heaven and earth, and in addition have eternal life through him. That is faith and that is what it means to really know Christ.[22]

Knowledge of Christ is always knowledge of what Christ has done "for us" or "for me." According to the theologian Paul Althaus, "Christ is known only in his works and I know his work only when I know it has taken place for me. Thus according to Luther, the doctrine of the person of Christ and the doctrine of his work cannot be separated from each other; they are one in such a way that I can grasp the meaning of Christ's work only in its significance for me."[23]

We can now see more clearly how Aquinas and Luther differ on the question of how believers share in the salvation won by Christ's death on the cross. For Aquinas, participation in the ongoing sacramental life of the church allows believers to share in Christ's ministry of salvation. For Luther, it is the individual's personal faith in Christ's saving work that brings about justification, or acquittal before God's tribunal. As the Evangelical theologian Clark Pinnock noted, for Luther, the innocent Christ took the place of a sinful humanity and endured God's punishment for our sins. Luther described the individual's act of faith as a marriage of the soul with Christ. The two become one. Althaus explained,

> Faith, however, is the way in which a man allows this "wonderful exchange" to take place in him; through faith he holds himself to and risks his life upon it. Christ says to the man, "Your sin is mine and my innocence is yours." Faith says to Christ, "My sin lies on you and your innocence and righteousness now belong to me." Thus the blessed exchange take place only through faith. Faith

is the wedding ring through which Christ's marriage with the soul and therewith the "wonderful exchange" takes place.[24]

In the patristic era, the concept of the happy exchange typically referred to the idea that "the Word of God, Jesus Christ our Lord...because of his overflowing love, became what we are so that he may make us what he himself is."[25] In Luther's thought, and to a greater degree in Calvin's thought, the concept acquired a sense of Christ taking our place and paying the price for our sins.

John Calvin subscribed to the "substitution theory" of the atonement. In his suffering on the cross, Christ bore the penalty for our sins. Christ took our place. Christ, who is innocent, suffered the punishment for the guilty. "He himself bore our sins in his body on the cross, so that, free from sins, we might live for righteousness; by his wounds, you have been healed" (1 Pet 2:24). The theologian Robert Letham offered the following description: "Christ himself willingly submitted to the just penalty which we deserved, receiving it on our behalf and in our place so that we will not have to bear it ourselves, just as a substitute in a football match comes onto the field and relieves a team-mate of the responsibility of continuing to play."[26]

Calvin situated the concept of substitution within his broader discussion of Christ's role in the plan of salvation in terms of the three "offices" in the Old Testament: priest, prophet, and king. All three served as mediators of God's will to the people, but each exercised that function in a different fashion. The priest had a cultic function, offering sacrifices on behalf of the people. The prophet played an ethical role, reminding the people of the demands of their covenant with God. The king ruled over the people, dispensing justice throughout the land, and protecting the people from enemy attacks.

As priest, Christ offered the perfect sacrifice. The Old Testament priesthood represented in Calvin's view a prefigurement of sacrifice offered by Christ on the cross. Calvin wrote, "In short, the old figures well teach us the force and power of Christ's death. And in the Letter to the Hebrews the apostle skillfully using this principle explains this point: 'Without the shedding of blood there is no forgiveness of sins' [Heb. 9:22]. Again, 'Christ was offered...to bear the sins of many' [Heb. 9:28]."[27] Because Christ himself was innocent of sin, the sacrifice was not for himself, but for us. Calvin argued, "The burden of condemnation, from which we were freed, was laid upon Christ"[28] Christ bore our sins; Christ died for us. "This is our acquittal: the guilt that held us liable for punishment has been transferred to the head of the Son of God [Isa. 53:12]. We must, above all, remember this substitution, lest we tremble and remain anxious throughout life—as if God's righteous vengeance, which the Son of God has taken upon himself, still hung over us."[29]

The bishops at Trent shared Luther and Calvin's belief that Christ "merited justification for us by his most holy passion on the wood of the cross, and made satisfaction to God the Father on our behalf."[30] The bishops, however, differed with Luther and Calvin on several key points. First, the bishops strongly reaffirmed their belief in free will and its essential role in salvation. It would be a serious error, assert the bishops, to say "that, after the sin of Adam, human free will was lost and blotted out, or that its existence is purely nominal, a name without substance, indeed a fiction intro-duced into the church by Satan."[31] Second, the bishops stressed that the saving work of Christ produces not just faith, but faith, hope, and love (or charity). For this reason, good works play an impor-tant role in a person's salvation. Third, with regard to predestina-tion, the bishops caution that "no one, so long as he remains in this present life, ought so to presume about the hidden mystery of divine predestination as to hold for certain that he is unquestion-ably of the number of the predestined."[32]

The Modern Age

In the seventeenth, eighteenth, and nineteenth centuries, much of the content and language of the traditional christological doctrine of the church was closely scrutinized by both the support-ers and detractors of Christianity. We will focus on three develop-ments in this time period: the promotion of Christ as "the teacher of common sense,"[33] the acceptance of the historical-critical method as a means of uncovering the identity of the historical Jesus, and the theological attempts to reformulate the classic "one person in two natures" Christology of the Council of Chalcedon.

JESUS AS THE TEACHER OF COMMON SENSE

The religious wars between Catholics and Protestants in the century following Calvin's death prompted many Christian thinkers to reassess the traditional Christian claims about the person and work of Jesus. Many political theorists, philosophers, and theologians identified certain tenets of Christian belief as the cause for the bloodshed. For too long, these thinkers claimed, Christians had stirred social unrest by asserting socially divisive claims that were not essential to Christianity. Chief among these beliefs were the claims that only those who believed in Christ or belonged to a specific denomination could be saved, that Christ was superior to the founders of every other religion in the world, and that God predestined some people to damnation. Christian thinkers in the early modern age often qualified, deemphasized, or eliminated these beliefs. They spoke instead of Christ as a teacher of moral principles who was willing to die for his cause, and they believed that the message Jesus imparted to his followers was similar in content to the essential teachings of the enlightened teachers of every culture (e.g., "Treat others the way you would like to be treated").

John Locke's 1695 work *The Reasonableness of Christianity* captured the tenor of the christological debate of the early modern period. First, Locke asserted the reliability of Christ's teachings based on the scriptural claims that Christ fulfilled prophecies and performed miracles. Second, Locke believed that the Christian Gospel boiled down to two essential elements: faith and repentance. "These two, faith and repentance, i.e. believing Jesus to be the Messiah, and a good life, are indispensable conditions of the new covenant, to be performed by all those who would obtain eternal life."[34] On these two requirements all humans will be judged on the last day. Third, Locke responded to the most commonly cited objections to his position. What about those who lived before the time of Christ? Locke didn't find much weight in this objection. "No body was, or can be, required to believe, what was never proposed to him to believe."[35] What about those who lived in a part of the world that never heard of Christianity? By the light of reason, Locke declared, these people could know the "eternal, immutable standard of right."[36]

At this point in his argument, Locke confronted the unavoidable consequence of his argument: If all people can know by the light of reason the "eternal, immutable standard of right," what need do we have for a revealer such as Jesus? Locke's reply was pragmatic in nature. The power of Jesus dispelled any lingering doubts in the ancient world about the truth of monotheism. Jesus may have assembled scattered teachings, presented them in a compelling way such as the parable of the Good Samaritan, but in the final analysis, Jesus did not teach us anything other than the precepts of the eternal moral law.

Locke was a transitional thinker in the field of Christology. On the one hand, he confidently asserted that Jesus performed miracles and fulfilled prophecy—two ideas that would be seriously questioned by later thinkers. On the other hand, he insisted on Christian belief being "reasonable." Christian claims about Christ were tailored to meet the demands of what Locke believed to be a universal standard of reasonableness. In this way, Christ was a teacher of *common* sense, of truths that in theory could be discerned by any thoughtful, reflective person. Lastly, Locke conceived of Jesus as a great moral teacher, and he regarded morality as the essence of religion. Locke, whether he realized it or not, had also assigned Jesus an ultimately dispensable role as a revealer of what all rational human beings would one day likely realize on their own.

About a hundred years after Locke's *The Reasonableness of Christianity* appeared, the philosopher Immanuel Kant published *Religion Within the Limits of Reason Alone*. Like Locke, Kant emphasized the rational nature of Christian belief, the universality of truth, and the moral character of religion. Kant also dealt with the tension of wanting to assign Christ a pivotal role in human history while also insisting that all rational human beings have access to universal principles of moral conduct. This tension arose, for example, when Kant dealt with the Christian concept of the atonement. Kant believed that radical evil existed in human nature, and moral wrongdoing is a "debt" that must be paid, but "this debt can never be discharged by another person, so far as we can judge according to the justice of our human reason."[37] Every individual is responsible for his or her own sins, and justice demands that each individual make amends for one's own sins. This responsibility cannot be justly transferred to a third party.

Kant's ideas are grounded in his conviction that all rational persons have an innate sense of moral duty or obligation. In our freedom, we can choose to act in ways contrary to the dictates of the universal moral law. However, if one individual were to always act according to the moral law, humanity would have what Kant called "a personified idea," or "archetype," of "a person morally well-pleasing to God." Kant described further the type of life this individual would live.

> This ideal of a humanity pleasing to God (hence of such moral perfection as is possible to an earthly being who is subject to wants and inclinations) we can represent to ourselves only as the idea of a person who would be willing not merely to discharge all human duties himself and to spread about him goodness as widely as possible by precept and example, but even, though tempted by the greatest allurements, to take upon himself every affliction, up to the most ignominious death, for the good of the world and even for his enemies.[38]

Christ is this archetype, the exemplar of moral perfection. This restatement of the traditional belief in the sinlessness of Christ, however, came with a proviso. Kant believed that such an ideal already existed in our mind. "We need, therefore, no empirical example to make the idea of a person morally well-pleasing to God our archetype; this idea as an archetype is already in our reason."[39]

Locke and Kant sought to offer a compelling Christology that was both faithful to scripture and compelling to Christians of their day. Their legacy consists of interesting christological positions, but more importantly, a set of questions that still concerns us. Was Christ primarily a teacher of moral principles? If so, did Jesus teach us anything new, or anything that we would not have discovered if Jesus had never existed? Did the founders of the major religious traditions of the world teach the same message?

THE QUEST FOR THE HISTORICAL JESUS

Our information about the lives of past historical figures always depends on the quality of our sources. This figure of Jesus of Nazareth is no exception. In Christian circles until the time of the modern age, a general consensus existed that the biblical writings in general, and the Gospels in particular, were divinely revealed, historically accurate documents. In the modern era, as this fundamental confidence in the historical accuracy of the Gospels was called into question, scholars began to differentiate between "the Jesus of history" and "the Christ of faith." The former referred to the Jesus of Nazareth who walked on the dusty roads of Galilee; the latter was the portrait of Jesus presented by the four evangelists. A survey of the origin and uses of this critical distinction between the Jesus of history and the Christ of faith provides a useful vantage point from which to survey the course of modern Christian thought. Scholars refer to this attempt to recover the actual Jesus of history from the pages of the Gospels as "the quest for the historical Jesus."

The first character in this modern story of biblical and christological investigation was a professor of languages at the University of Hamburg, Hermann S. Reimarus (1694–1768). According to the religious historian James C. Livingston, "At his death [Reimarus] left a four-thousand-page manuscript on which he had labored for twenty years. The work was so controversial that it remained unpublished until the philosopher G. E. Lessing obtained permission from Reimarus's daughter to issue it on the condition that the author's name not be divulged."[40] In its pages readers found a blazing attack on the historical accuracy of the Old Testament account of the exodus from Egypt and the New Testament accounts of Christ's resurrection. The overall thesis advanced through the work is that what the Bible says happened in history is often not what in fact did happen. This gap between what the Bible says and what actually happened is the starting point for the modern quest for the historical Jesus.

David Friedrich Strauss (1808–74) achieved instant notoriety with the publication of his *Life of Jesus* in 1835. In that work, Strauss argued that Christians had mistakenly approached the Bible in either one of two ways. Some Christians took a supernaturalist approach. They asserted the historical accuracy of every miracle story in the Bible. God had acted in dramatic ways by parting the Red Sea, providing manna to the Israelites, and raising Christ from the dead. A second group of Christian readers, whose numbers had grown since the beginning of the Enlightenment, supported a rationalistic approach to reading the Bible. They offered scientific explanations for the miracles. The parting of the Red Sea, for example, could have been caused by an earthquake or a quick change in the tides.

Strauss rejected both approaches, insisting instead that the biblical writings were mythical in character. By "myth," Strauss did not mean that the story lacked any basis in historical fact. Rather, as the theologian Robert King stated about Strauss,

> Myth, as he used the term, does not carry the connotation of false or invalid; rather, it signifies the poetic mode in which ideas characteristically come to expression within a religious community. Myth may have some historical basis, but that is not crucial. The meaning conveyed by the myth can be fully transported into conceptual terms and has validity independently of any historical occurrence.[41]

The contemporary biblical scholar Marcus Borg offered a helpful illustration of Strauss's mythical interpretation. The Gospels report that Jesus fed the crowd of five thousand by multiplying five loaves and two fish (Mark 6:30–44). Those who take a supernaturalist approach would picture Jesus creating a huge pile of food, or the crowd standing in amazement as food simply appeared in their hands. The rationalists would speculate that Jesus inspired the crowd to share the food they had with them, and consequently, all the people were fed. Borg continued,

> Having rejected both the rationalist and supernaturalist approaches, Strauss then argues for a mythical approach. Rather than reporting something that really happened (with either a rational or supernatural explanation), the

text has a different purpose. Namely, the text uses the imagery of the early church's inherited religious and literary tradition (the Hebrew Bible as a whole, and in this particular case, the story in Exod 16:13–36 of God feeding the people of Israel in the wilderness with manna) to make a statement about the spiritual significance of Jesus. That is, the point of the text is not to report what Jesus did on a particular day, but to make the claim that Jesus is "the bread of life" who feeds his followers with "spiritual food" even to this day.[42]

Strauss applied this mythical interpretation to the entire gospel story, including Jesus' birth, baptism, and resurrection. His *Life of Jesus* triggered a storm of controversy, but it also set the agenda for modern biblical studies and Christology.

Strauss's contention that the biblical writings were mythical in nature called into question the reliability of the Gospels as sources for reconstructing the life of Jesus. This raised the unsettling possibility that the Jesus of history could be lost. In response to this problem, late-nineteenth-century biblical scholars produced a number of "Lives of Jesus." Among these scholarly and popular works that offered reconstructions of the actual events in the life of Jesus, the most popular was Ernst Renan's *Life of Jesus* (1863). The widespread popularity of Renan's work prompted Strauss to end his twenty-year hiatus from theological writing and to publish his own life of Jesus in 1864. Renan's rich prose reconstructed Jesus' boyhood as he romped through green rolling hills of Galilee admiring the lilies of the field and the birds of sky. Renan offered the following colorful description of the impression these days had on the thoughts of Jesus:

> His preaching was gentle and pleasing, breathing Nature and the perfume of the fields. He loved the flowers, and took from them his most charming lessons. The birds of heaven, the sea, the mountains, and the games of children, furnished in turn the subject of his instructions.[43]

Renan seemed to get right inside the mind of Jesus, revealing his innermost thoughts and feelings.

Whereas Renan presented a Jesus spiritually moved by the natural beauty of the world, another important thinker, Adolf von Harnack (1851–1930) presented Jesus as a teacher of eternal ethical truths. In his popular work *What is Christianity?* (1900), Harnack wrote,

> If, however, we take a general view of Jesus' teaching, we shall see that it may be grouped under three heads. They are each of such a nature as to contain the whole, and hence it can be exhibited in its entirety under any one of them.
>
> *Firstly, the kingdom of God and its coming.*
>
> *Secondly, God the Father and the infinite value of the human soul.*
>
> *Thirdly, the higher righteousness and the commandment of love.*[44]

The kingdom about which Jesus taught is "the rule of the holy God in the hearts of individuals."[45] The infinite value of the soul teaches us to respect all people as children of God; and the higher righteousness is the humble love and service to our neighbors. Harnack believed that these truths were the "kernel" of Jesus' message; the incidental features of Jesus' ministry were the "husk." This strategy, which became a plank in the movement known as Liberal Protestantism, shielded to some degree the figure of Jesus from attacks on the historical accuracy of various gospel stories. The core message, Harnack argued, was eternally valid; whether Jesus delivered that message in a sermon on a mountain or on a plain was immaterial to the truth of the message.

The quest for the historical Jesus came to an abrupt end with the publication of *The Quest of the Historical Jesus* in 1906 by the missionary doctor and biblical scholar Albert Schweitzer (1875–1965). Schweitzer reviewed the leading works in the quest for the historical Jesus and concluded that they had minimized, if not overlooked entirely, the eschatological (end-time) character of Jesus' teachings. Jesus believed that the world as he knew it was coming to an end.

Schweitzer believed that the historical Jesus bore no resemblance to the romantic Jesus in Renan's work or the ethical Jesus in Harnack's study. In fact, according to the contemporary New Testament scholar, Mark Allan Powell, "Schweitzer's portrait of Jesus as a misguided eschatological prophet stripped him of relevance for the contemporary age."[46] Rather, as Schweitzer wrote, "The historical Jesus will be to our time a stranger and an enigma."[47] Schweitzer insisted that the past "Lives of Jesus" disclosed more about the author than they did about the historical Jesus. The authors, consciously or unconsciously, were finding the Jesus that they already had in their mind. Schweitzer's argument was so compelling that for nearly fifty years, no major biblical scholar produced a life of Jesus.

MODERN RESTATEMENTS OF CHALCEDON

While many biblical scholars in the modern age were attempting to uncover the historical Jesus buried under the layers of tradition, other theologians were reasserting the traditional christological claims of the Council of Chalcedon. Chalcedon declared the orthodox confession that Jesus was "one person with two natures." In the modern age, various theologians offered reformulations of the classic two-natures Christology using modern categories of thought. Two of the most noteworthy examples of this endeavor appeared in the works of the liberal Protestant theologian Friedrich Schleiermacher (1768–1834) and the philosopher G. W. F. Hegel (1779–1831). While critical of the language of Chalcedon, both thinkers believed that they were faithfully transposing the *meaning* of Chalcedon into a new modern key.

Schleiermacher was deeply influenced by both the Moravian Pietism instilled in him in his youth and the literary movement of Romanticism. Both traditions placed a great emphasis on experience. The Romantics spoke of a deeper sense of the unity between humans and the natural world. In our typical way of looking at the world, we see ourselves as separate and apart from the natural world, but in moments of intuitive insight, we sense our actual oneness with nature. In a similar fashion, Schleiermacher spoke of the human spirit's deeper unity with God, a unity obscured in our normal way of looking at the world. But, on a deeper level, we sense our lives are part of a larger spiritual reality. Furthermore, we sense our dependence on this greater Being—this sense of "absolute dependence" is the core of religious experience according to Schleiermacher.

Schleiermacher built his Christology on this analysis of human experience. Speaking theologically, all humans have a "God-consciousness," but our hectic lives draw our attention away from that deeper consciousness. Christ, however, was different. According to the theologians Stanley Grenz and Roger Olsen,

> Schleiermacher rejected the traditional doctrine of the Incarnation and replaced it with a Christology based on the experience of God-consciousness. He criticized the classical doctrine of Jesus' two natures (human and divine) as illogical. Two "natures" cannot coincide in a single individual....Jesus Christ is completely like the rest of humanity except that "from the outset he has an absolutely potent God-consciousness." His God-consciousness was not a product of humanity alone; it was a product of God's activity in his life. However, it was a fully human God-consciousness. From birth on he lived in full awareness of his dependence on God.[48]

Christ's uniqueness rested in the fact that he had uninterrupted God-consciousness, whereas all other persons had limited God-consciousness. In other words, Christ differed from other humans in his *degree* of awareness of God.

Hegel taught with Schleiermacher at the University of Berlin, but strongly opposed the basic thesis of his colleague's work. Hegel reportedly once sniped that if absolute dependence were the essence of religion, then his dog was the most religious creature of all because he depended completely on Hegel for food. Hegel preferred instead to ground his thought in history. Hegel believed that the course of history would display a pattern of rationality and intelligence. One of the ideas that history reveals is the unity of the divine and the human spirit. The theologian Stephen D. Crites explained,

Hegel's principle of the implicit unity of the divine and human natures, however, is not a statement about man's actual state of existence in history. Man has not been actually or intentionally, consciously or unconsciously, one with God. The principle that the divine and human natures are implicitly one is, in the first place, a statement about human destiny; in fact, the principle could be recognized only after the destiny has been fulfilled, after God and man have actually become one.[49]

The incarnation, therefore, disclosed this universal, eternal truth. The incarnation as a historical fact entered human consciousness and helped it move to a higher level of thought. Scholars still debate the role the incarnation played in Hegel's system. Did the life of Jesus offer a compelling example of a truth told in other ways, or did the life of Jesus introduce a radically unique new truth into human history?

The Twentieth Century

Of the many important developments in the field of Christology in the twentieth and early twenty-first centuries, we will limit our consideration to three: the new quest for the historical Jesus, the rise of liberation theology, and the encounter with the other world religions.

THE NEW QUEST FOR THE HISTORICAL JESUS

Schweitzer's devastating critique of the old quest for the historical Jesus left a lasting impression on the field of New Testament Christology. The confidence with which Renan and others had spoken about the historical Jesus vanished. One of the leading New Testament scholars of the twentieth century, Rudolf Bultmann, whose essay "New Testament and Mythology" we discussed in the opening chapter, was especially skeptical. "I do indeed think that we can know almost nothing concerning the life and personality of Jesus, since the early Christian sources show no interest in either, are moreover fragmentary and often legendary; and other sources about Jesus do not exist."[50]

In 1953 Ernst Kasemann, who had studied under Bultmann, launched what has become known as "the new quest" or "the second quest" for the historical Jesus. Kasemann differed with his former teacher on two essential points: the relevance of the Jesus of history for Christian faith, and the reliability of the historical findings produced by modern biblical scholarship. Bultmann had insisted that "it is the Christ of the kerygma [proclamation] and not the person of the historical Jesus who is the object of faith."[51] Bultmann had also warned that historical findings are subject to change. Schweitzer's work demonstrated that what one generation of scholars accepted as a reliable historical fact may very well be rejected by the next generation. Kasemann, however, insisted that the historical Jesus is an essential element in Christian faith, and that certain sayings or actions attributed to Jesus in the Gospels can be determined with high probability. Kasemann believed that while we can not speak with absolute *certainty* that a gospel verse came from the mouth of the historical Jesus, we can, by applying certain criteria to the gospel stories, determine the *probability* that it did.

The contemporary scripture scholar John P. Meier identified five primary criteria against which gospel stories can be measured to gauge their historical accuracy.

1. The first is the criterion of embarrassment. Meier explained, "The point of the criterion is that the early Church would hardly have gone out of its way to create material that only embarrassed its creator or weakened its position in arguments with opponents."[52] For example, Jesus delivers an apocalyptic discourse in Mark 13 detailing the events of the final days. Near the end of this discourse, however, Jesus says, "But about that day or hour no one knows, neither the angels in heaven, nor the Son, but only the Father" (13:32). Because it is extremely unlikely that the church would create a saying of Jesus that would cast doubt on his knowledge, it is highly probable that this verse goes back to Jesus himself. In other words, the higher the degree of embarrassment to the early church caused by a saying of Jesus, the higher the probability that the saying comes from Jesus.

2. The second is the criterion of discontinuity. "Closely allied to the criterion of embarrassment, the criterion of discontinuity (also labeled dissimilarity, originality, or dual irreducibility) focuses on words or deeds of Jesus that cannot be derived either from Judaism at the time of Jesus or from the early Church after him."[53] For example, Jews fasted and the early Christians fasted, but Jesus did not require his disciples to fast (see Mark 2:18–22). Meier cautions that the criterion of discontinuity alone would yield a distorted view of Jesus. "A more serious objection is that the criterion of discontinuity, instead of giving us an assured minimum about Jesus, winds up giving us a caricature by divorcing Jesus from the Judaism that influenced him and from the Church that he influenced."[54] The criterion of discontinuity isolates the unique features of Jesus' ministry, but overlooks the teachings or practices shared with his contemporaries.

3. The third criterion is multiple attestation. "The criterion of multiple attestation (or 'the cross section') focuses on those sayings or deeds of Jesus that are attested in more than one independent literary source (e.g., Mark, Q, Paul, John) and/or in more than one literary form or genre (e.g., parable, dispute story, miracle story, prophecy, aphorism)."[55] This approach parallels the strategy of a prosecutor building a case against a defendant. If two or three witnesses report seeing the same person committing a crime, and those three witnesses had no contact with each other, then it strengthens the prosecutor's contention that the defendant committed the crime. Both Paul's First Letter to the Corinthians and the Gospel of Mark, for example, contain a similar account of Jesus' words and deeds at the Last Supper (Mark 14:22–25 and 1 Cor 11:23–26). This increases the probability that on the occasion of the final Passover meal Jesus shared with his disciples, he spoke of the bread as his body and the wine as a covenant in his blood.

4. The fourth criterion, the criterion of coherence, "holds that other sayings and deeds of Jesus that fit well with the preliminary 'data base' established by using our first three criteria have a good chance of being historical (e.g., sayings concerning the coming of the kingdom of God or disputes with adversaries over legal observance)."[56] This criterion acts as a counterbalance to the criterion of discontinuity. It is highly probable that Jesus debated the "hot topics" of his day. For example, it is very likely that Jesus commented on

the payment of taxes to the Roman authorities, the issue of divorce, and the belief in the resurrection of the body.

5. The final standard is the criterion of rejection and execution. Which teachings or acts of Jesus can best account for the fact that he was crucified? Which powerful Roman or Jewish officials would have been offended by Jesus? As Meier reminded his readers, "A Jesus whose words and deeds would not alienate people, especially powerful people, is not the historical Jesus."[57]

Some scholars today speak of a "third quest" for the historical Jesus. Thomas P. Rausch noted that this third quest is marked by a heavy reliance on the social sciences (e.g., sociology, anthropology). Rausch observed,

> The use of social sciences has helped appreciate the social, cultural, and anthropological factors that effected first-century Palestinian Judaism and particularly, the social fabric of Galilean life. Thus, Third Quest scholarship investigates the structure of the Galilean family and social relationships, the position of women, the religious milieu, including the ways in which the tradition was passed on and communally expressed, the extent of Hellenistic Greek influence, the impact of Roman domination and its system of taxation.[58]

The most publicized group within the Third Quest is the Jesus Seminar, founded in 1985 by the biblical scholar Robert Funk. This group received great media attention and much scholarly reproach. During their first few years of existence, members of the Jesus Seminar would meet and debate the authenticity of the various sayings attributed to Jesus in the four Gospels and other ancient sources such as the Gospel of Thomas. Each member would then vote by casting a colored bead: red if the saying undoubtedly came from Jesus; pink if Jesus probably said it; gray if Jesus probably did not say it; and black if the saying most probably did not come from Jesus.[59]

The scholarly pursuit for the historical Jesus shows no signs of abating any time soon. At the same time, theologians in Latin America have raised concerns that such scholarly endeavors often do not address the social and political injustices that Jesus himself denounced.

LIBERATION THEOLOGY

Liberation theologians highlight the connection between theory and practice. The theologian Gonzalez Faus put the matter this way:

> In Europe the historical Jesus is an object of investigation, whereas in Latin America he is the criterion of discipleship. In Europe study of the historical Jesus seeks to establish the possibilities and the reasonableness of the act of believing or not believing. In Latin America the appeal to the historical Jesus seeks to confront people with the dilemma of being converted or not.[60]

The idea of Christ cannot be separated from the practice of living the Christian life. For example, in Luke's Gospel, Jesus returns to his hometown and celebrates Sabbath in the local synagogue. He is handed the scroll containing the book of the prophet Isaiah. Jesus unrolls the scroll and reads the following passage:

> "The Spirit of the Lord is upon me,
>   because he has anointed me
>   to bring good news to the poor.
> He has sent me to proclaim release to the captives
>   and recovery of sight to the blind,
>   to let the oppressed go free,
> to proclaim the year of the Lord's favor." (Luke 4:18–19)

Liberation theologians insist that when read by a small gathering of Christians living in the midst of political and economic oppression, this scene conveys a powerful Christology. Jesus proclaims good news to the poor, the outcasts, the ones shunned by society. Jesus reaches out to the sinners, the lepers, and tax collectors. Jesus challenges the political and religious authorities, who unjustly condemn him to a state-sanctioned execution.

The Christology presented by liberation theologians results in a different understanding of salvation. The dominant image of Jesus in the writings of liberation theologians is of one who offered emancipation from all forms of oppression. The liberation theologian Leonardo Boff wrote,

> The Christology that proclaims Jesus Christ as liberator seeks to commit itself to the economic, social, and political liberation of groups suffering oppression and domination. It endeavors to consolidate the theological dimension of the historical liberation of the vast masses of our continent....In this way it offers to articulate the contents of Christology and to create a style that highlights the liberative dimensions in the historical course of Jesus' life.[61]

Likewise, for liberation theologians, salvation consists of more than going to heaven after death. The salvation offered by Christ was not only religious, but also social, political, and economic in nature. At the Second General Conference of Latin American Bishops, held in Medellin, Columbia, in 1968, the bishops wrote,

> The Latin American Church has a message for all men on this continent who "hunger and thirst after justice." The very God who creates men in his image and likewise, creates the 'earth and all that is in it for the use of all men and all nations, in such a way that created goods can reach all in a more just manner,' and gives them power to transform and perfect the world in solidarity. It is the same God who, in the fullness of time, sends his Son in the flesh, so that He might come to liberate all men from the slavery to which sin has subjected them: hunger, misery, oppression and ignorance, in a word, that injustice and hatred which have their origin in human selfishness.[62]

Commenting on this passage, the liberation theologian Jon Sobrino noted the implications for salvation. "It states that Christ came to bring freedom from a *variety of evils*, moral, physical and social...rather than associating it with the later (reductive) universalization of salvation as redemption from sins."[63]

JESUS AND THE WORLD'S RELIGIONS

Just as liberation theologians are rethinking questions of Christology and soteriology in light of their political, economic, and social conditions, other theologians are asking new questions in light of their awareness of, and appreciation for, the various world religions. One of the leading thinkers pursuing this line of inquiry is the British philosopher and theologian John Hick. He contends that history is filled with the disastrous consequences of the church's traditional christological stance. He argued,

> In claiming that the life of Jesus was the one and only point in history at which God has been fully self-revealed, it implicitly sets Christians apart from the rest of humanity. In declaring that God has lived a human life on earth, so that here and here only men and women were able to meet God face to face, to hear God speak, and to respond to God in faith, Christianity declares that these fortunate few and their successors have a highly privileged access to the Creator....It follows that the Christian religion and it alone was personally founded by God. Must God not then wish all human beings to become part of the church, the body of the redeemed, the saved community? Is not Christianity thus singled out as the only religion that God has authorized, hence uniquely superior to all others? Christian history is indeed full of this assumption—and its practical outworkings in colonialism, anti-Semitism, the burning of "heretics," and the Western political and cultural superiority complex.[64]

In place of a Christology that sees God's presence exclusively revealed in the life of Jesus, Hick favors "an inspiration Christology." In this perspective, "we see in the life of Jesus a supreme instance of that fusion of divine grace/inspiration with creaturely freedom that occurs in all authentic human responses and obedience to God."[65] For Hick, Jesus was a supreme example of people who radiate the love and wisdom of the Supreme Reality to the world, but so too were Siddhartha Gautama, the founder of Buddhism, and Lao Tzu, the founder of Taoism.

Hick's theology raises some of the foundational questions in Christology. Was Jesus of Nazareth an inspired prophet, the Son of God, or the Second Person of the Trinity? Could he have been all three? If so, how can Christ be both fully human and fully divine? What does it mean to say that Jesus is the Savior of the World? These questions are as pertinent to today's discussions as they were to the thinkers in the early church. For this reason, a working knowledge of past christological and soteriological debates is critical for the discussion of our most urgent questions about Jesus of Nazareth.

Discussion Questions

1. What is your assessment of Anselm's satisfaction theory?
2. What is your assessment of Calvin's substitution theory of the atonement?
3. Did Jesus teach us anything that we would not have learned on our own?
4. Are the gospel stories mythical? What implications follow for how we should read the Bible?
5. Are core elements in Jesus' teachings eternally true?
6. How historically accurate are the gospel stories?
7. How important is the Jesus of history to Christian faith?
8. To what extent was Jesus a prophet for radical social change?
9. What is your evaluation of Hick's Christology?
10. Which question in Christology is the most important one in today's church?

Suggested Readings

For an overview of contemporary Christologies, see Veli-Matti Karkkainen, *Christology: A Global Introduction* (Grand Rapids: Baker Academic, 2003); William J. LaDue, *Jesus among the*

Theologians (Harrisburg, PA: Trinity Press International, 2001); and Scott Cowdell, *Is Jesus Unique?* (Mahwah, NJ: Paulist Press, 1996).

For current New Testament scholarship, see Thomas P. Rausch, *Who Is Jesus?* (Collegeville, MN: Liturgical Press, 2003); and Mark Allan Powell, *Jesus as a Figure in History* (Louisville, KY: Westminster John Knox Press, 1998).

For two contemporary systematic and more technical discussions of Christology, see Gerald O'Collins, *Christology* (New York: Oxford University Press, 1995); and Roch A. Kereszty, *Jesus Christ: Fundamentals of Christology*, Revised and Updated Edition (Staten Island, NY: Alba House, 2002).

For modern understandings of salvation, see Lee E. Snook, *The Anonymous Christ* (Minneapolis: Augsburg Publishing House, 1986).

Notes

1. Anselm, "Why God Became Man," in Eugene R. Fairweather, ed., *A Scholastic Miscellany: Anselm to Ockham* (Philadelphia: Westminster Press, 1956), 101. Hereafter *CDH (Cur Deus Homo)*.

2. Ibid., 119.

3. Ibid.

4. Ibid.

5. Ibid.

6. Jaroslav Pelikan, *Jesus Through the Centuries* (New Haven, CT: Yale University Press, 1985), 108. Italics his.

7. G. R. Evans, *Anselm* (Wilton, CT: Morehouse-Barlow, 1989), 76.

8. Pelikan uses this expression in *The Growth of Medieval Theology 600–1300* (Chicago: University of Chicago Press, 1978), 139. See also G. R. Evans, "Anselm of Canterbury," in *The Medieval Theologians*, G. R. Evans, ed. (Malden, MA: Blackwell, 2001), 99.

9. *CDH*, 121.

10. Quoted in J. Denny Weaver, *The Nonviolent Atonement* (Grand Rapids: Eerdmans, 2001), 190.

11. *CDH*, 151.

12. Gerald O'Collins, *Christology* (New York: Oxford University Press, 1995), 201.

13. Peter Abailard [Peter Abelard] "Exposition of the Epistle to the Romans," in Fairweather, *Scholastic Miscellany*, 283. I discovered this quotation in Philip L. Quinn's very helpful essay "Abelard on Atonement: 'Nothing Unintelligible, Arbitrary, Illogical, or Immoral about It,'" in Eleonore Stump, ed., *Reasoned Faith* (Ithaca, NY: Cornell University Press, 1993).

14. Abelard in Fairweather, *Scholastic Miscellany*, 284.

15. Roger E. Olson, *The Mosaic of Christian Belief* (Downers Grove, IL: InterVarsity Press, 2002), 256.

16. F. W. Dillistone, *The Christian Understanding of Atonement* (Philadelphia: Westminster Press, 1968), 325. Italics his.

17. Brian Davies, *The Thought of Thomas Aquinas* (Oxford: Clarendon Press, 1992), 334.

18. Karl Adam, *The Son of God* (Garden City, NY: Image Books, 1960), 217–18.

19. Aidan Nichols, *Discovering Aquinas* (Grand Rapids: Eerdmans, 2002), 122.

20. Dennis C. Duling, *Jesus Christ Through History* (New York: Harcourt, Brace, Jovanovich, 1979), 107.

21. Quoted in Duling, *Jesus Christ Through History*, 107.

22. Quoted in Paul Althaus, *The Theology of Martin Luther* (Philadelphia: Fortress Press, 1966), 192.

23. Althaus, *The Theology of Martin Luther*, 192.

24. Ibid., 213.

25. Irenaeus, *Against Heresies*, Preface, Book V, quoted in Roch A. Kereszty, *Jesus Christ: Fundamentals of Christology*, rev. ed. (Staten Island, NY: Alba House, 2002), 204.

26. Robert Letham, *The Work of Christ* (Downers Grove, IL: InterVarsity Press, 1993), 133.

27. John Calvin, *Institutes of the Christian Religion* (Philadelphia: Westminster Press, 1960), 531; brackets are in the original.

28. Ibid., 532.

29. Ibid., 510; brackets are in the original.

30. "Decree on Justification," Session Six of the Council of Trent in Norman P. Tanner, ed., *Decrees of the Ecumenical Councils,*

vol. 2 (London: Sheed and Ward; Washington, DC: Georgetown University Press, 1990), 673.

31. Ibid., 679.

32. Ibid., 676.

33. I borrowed this description of Jesus as the "Teacher of Common Sense" from Jaroslav Pelikan's splendid work, *Jesus Through the Centuries.*

34. John Locke, *The Reasonableness of Christianity* (Stanford, CA: Stanford University Press, 1958), 44–45.

35. Ibid., 52–53.

36. Ibid., 53.

37. Immanuel Kant, *Religion Within the Limits of Reason Alone* (New York: Harper and Row, 1960), 66.

38. Ibid., 55.

39. Ibid., 56.

40. James C. Livingston, *Modern Christian Thought*, sec. ed. (Upper Saddle River, NJ: Prentice Hall,1997), 30.

41. Robert H. King, "The Task of Systematic Theology," in Peter C. Hodgson and Robert H. King, eds., *Christian Theology* (Philadelphia: Fortress Press, 1982), 17.

42. Marcus Borg, "David Friedrich Strauss," at www. jesusseminar.com/Periodicals/4R_Articles/Strauss/strauss.html.

43. Quoted in Duling, *Jesus Christ Through History*, 195.

44. Adolf Harnack, *What is Christianity?* (Gloucester, MA: Peter Smith, 1978), 51. Italics his.

45. Ibid., 56.

46. Mark Allan Powell, *Jesus as a Figure in History* (Louisville, KY: Westminster John Knox Press, 1998), 18.

47. Quoted in Powell, *Jesus as a Figure in History*, 18.

48. Stanley J. Grenz and Roger E. Olson, *Twentieth-Century Theology* (Downers Grove, IL: InterVarsity Press, 1992), 49.

49. Stephen D. Crites, "The Gospel According to Hegel," *Journal of Religion* XLVI (April 1966): 250.

50. Rudolf Bultmann, *Jesus and the Word* (New York: Charles Scribner's Sons, 1958), 8. I discovered this quote in Meier's work discussed below.

51. Quoted in Leander E. Keck, *A Future for the Historical Jesus* (Nashville: Abingdon Press, 1971), 50.

52. John P. Meier, *A Marginal Jew* (New York: Doubleday, 1991), 168.

53. Ibid., 171.

54. Ibid., 172.

55. Ibid., 174.

56. Ibid., 176.

57. Ibid., 177.

58. Thomas P. Rausch, *Who Is Jesus?* (Collegeville, MN: Liturgical Press, 2003), 15.

59. For background on the Jesus Seminar, see chapter four of Mark Allan Powell, *Jesus as a Figure in History* (Louisville, KY: Westminster John Knox Press, 1998). For a strong criticism of the Jesus Seminar's work, see chapter one of Luke Timothy Johnson, *The Real Jesus* (San Francisco: HarperSanFrancisco, 1996).

60. Quoted in Jon Sobrino, *Jesus the Liberator* (Maryknoll, NY: Orbis Books, 1993), 50.

61. Quoted in Angelo Mato, "Christology V: In Perspective," in René Latourelle, ed., *Dictionary of Fundamental Theology* (New York: Crossroad, 1994), 135.

62. Jon Sobrino, "Justice," in the Medellin Documents, in Joseph Gremillion, ed., *The Gospel of Peace and Justice* (Maryknoll, NY: Orbis Books, 1976).

63. Sobrino, 18. Italics his.

64. John Hick, "An Inspiration Christology for a Religiously Plural World," in Stephen T. Davis, ed., *Encountering Jesus* (Atlanta: John Knox Press, 1988), 16.

65. Ibid., 21.

9

THE NATURE AND MISSION
OF THE CHURCH

"Christ has died, Christ has risen, Christ will come again."
This commonly used Memorial Acclamation at Mass illustrates
how theological reflection on the person and work of Christ
(Christology and soteriology) naturally leads to discussions about
the nature and mission of the church (ecclesiology). In the *past*,
Jesus of Nazareth lived in Galilee, taught in Jerusalem, and was also
crucified in Jerusalem under Pontius Pilate. The Gospel, however,
proclaims that Christ was raised from the dead and is now "seated
at the right hand of the Father." He is, at *present*, Lord over all. The
church celebrates his presence among us. Christians also believe
that human history will at some *future* point come to an end, and
that Christ will preside at the final judgement.

This historical framework that looks to the past when Jesus
lived among us, that celebrates Christ's ongoing presence, and that
hopes for a future destiny with Christ is the context for Christian
reflection on the church. In this context, countless questions arise.
Did Jesus intend to establish a church? If so, did he stipulate that
the church should have a particular system of governance? Did
Christ command his followers to uphold certain beliefs or perform
certain rituals? What role does the Holy Spirit play in the life of the
church? How is the church's faithfulness to the Gospel measured?
What is the hope the church proclaims? In what ways does that
future hope impact how we live in the present? These questions,
and many others like them, will eventually lead to discussions
regarding church authority, ministry, sacraments, spirituality, ethics,
and the afterlife. In this chapter, however, we focus our attention on
the general question of the nature and mission of the church,
though certainly other related topics will surface throughout our

investigation. As in past chapters, we will proceed historically. We begin with the images of the church in the New Testament, move to some of the important thinkers and debates in the patristic and medieval eras, continue through the Protestant and Catholic Reformations, and conclude with the modern age.

New Testament Images of the Church

The word *church* comes from the Greek word *ekklesia*, meaning "assembly" or "gathering." In the New Testament writings, we find a rich diversity of images for the church, various emphases on the function of the church, and different positions on the relationship of the church to the wider culture. This makes attempting to give a full explanation of the nature and mission of the church a daunting task. In many ways, the situation resembles what frequently takes place at a meeting or conference on the state of the family. The discussion often does not move beyond the first question: "What is a family?" How do we define the term? Is it based on biology or bonds of love? Is the traditional arrangement of a husband and wife living under the same roof with their biological children the ideal against which all other forms of family are measured, or is the traditional arrangement one of many possible instances of family that are all equally valid?

The different descriptions of the church in the New Testament arise from tensions built into the very fabric of Christian life. This is also true about present-day discussions of the church. The first tension is between the church's sanctity and its sinfulness. The church is the bearer of God's presence, the bride of Christ "without a spot or wrinkle or anything of the kind" (Eph 5:27), but it is comprised of humans who have all sinned and fallen short of the glory of God (Rom 3:23). In terms of church organization, the second tension may be described as "structure vs. spirit." The roots of the Roman Catholic and Orthodox hierarchical structure can be found in the Pastoral Epistles (1 Tim, 2 Tim, and Titus), but in John's Gospel, we are reminded that the Spirit is not confined or constrained in any way: "The wind blows where it chooses, and you hear the sound of it, but you do not know where it comes from or where it goes. So it is with everyone born of the Spirit" (John 3:8). The Spirit may very well be active in persons and movements not officially sanctioned by church authorities. The third tension deals with how the individual relates to the community. The Christian must develop his or her own relationship with God. This process is a very personal one that is unique to each individual, yet the Christian way of life is also communal. We are God's people (1 Pet 2:10). We live as a community of believers, and not simply as isolated individuals. The fourth tension is the church-world, or Christ-culture dynamic. Christians are commanded to "make disciples of all nations" (Matt 28:19), yet are also warned, "Do not be mismatched with unbelievers. For what partnership is there between righteousness and lawlessness? Or what fellowship is there between light and darkness?" (2 Cor 6:14). Because of these inherent tensions within the Christian life and the constantly shifting cultural landscape, conceptions of the church do not remain static.

The New Testament contains a wealth of images of the church. There are images drawn from family life (the church is "the household of God" [1 Tim 3:15]); from construction ("like living stones, let yourselves be built into a spiritual house" [1 Pet 2:5; see also 1 Cor 3:10–15]); and from Temple worship ("a dwelling place for God" [Eph 2:22]). A brief survey of the New Testament writings reveals the creative imagery the early Christians employed when speaking about the church.

Of the four gospels, Matthew's contains the most material directly related to the church. Matthew is the only Gospel in which we find the word *church* (*ekklesia*, Matt 16:18, 18:17). In both passages, the issue of authority is central. In Matthew 16:18–19 Jesus declares, "And I tell you, you are Peter, and on this rock I will build my church, and the gates of Hades will not prevail against it. I will give you the keys of the kingdom of heaven, and whatever you bind on earth will be bound in heaven, and whatever you loose on earth will be loosed in heaven." The second passage deals with the process of correction and forgiveness of a fellow Christian. The grieved party should see the offender privately. If the matter is not resolved, then two or three witnesses should be brought into the discussion. If the matter is again not resolved, "tell it to the church; and if the offender refuses to listen even to the church, let such a one be to you

as a Gentile or a tax collector" (Matt 18:17). Both of these important passages would figure prominently in later church discussions
regarding papal authority and the practice of excommunication.

While the other Gospels do not explicitly mention the
church, they do present images that influence later theological
reflection on the nature of the church. This is especially true of
John's Gospel in which we find the image of Jesus as the vine and
his followers as the branches (John 15), and Jesus as the Good
Shepherd (John 10) who guides his flock. The scripture scholar
Daniel J. Harrington offered the following comment on the relevance of John's Gospel for the church today.

> The farewell discourses in John 13–17 provide a checklist
> of ideal characteristics against which every Christian com-
> munity might examine and evaluate itself. These charac-
> teristics are acceptance of Jesus' saving work and imitation
> of his example of the humble service of others, love, faith,
> openness to the Holy Spirit, a vital relationship with Jesus,
> hope, mission, and unity. The instruction by the Johannine
> Jesus to his disciples remains the best advice for Christian
> communities in the twenty-first century.[1]

Lastly, the prominent role given to the Paraclete (Advocate, Holy
Spirit) in John's Gospel conveys the strong sense that the Christian
community is being instructed, guided, and comforted by the
Spirit. "But the Advocate, the Holy Spirit, whom the Father will
send in my name, will teach you everything, and remind you of all
that I have said to you" (John 14:26).

In the Gospel of Luke, and its companion volume, the Acts of
the Apostles, we find a plan of history in which the church plays an
integral role. In the Gospel, Luke places particular emphasis on Jesus'
outreach to the poor, sinners, lepers, and Samaritans. Luke records
not only Jesus' death and resurrection, but also his ascension. In a pattern reminiscent of the Elijah and Elisha story in the Old Testament,
Jesus ascends to heaven and promises to send down the Holy Spirit so
that his disciples can continue his ministry and be his witnesses in
"Jerusalem, in all Judea and Samaria, and to the ends of the earth"
(Acts 1:8). The universal scope of Jesus' ministry continues in Acts

when, after being empowered by the Holy Spirit at Pentecost, the apostles proclaim the Gospel to Jews and Gentiles alike. After receiving the approval of the church leaders at the Council of Jerusalem (Acts 15), Paul spearheads the mission to the Gentiles. As a result of his three successful missionary journeys, Paul establishes a network of churches throughout the Mediterranean world.

Not only was Paul actively involved in the practical work of founding churches, he also contributed to the theoretical discussions regarding the nature of the church. In 1 Corinthians 12 Paul speaks of the church as the "Body of Christ." This image serves Paul well as he works through its ecclesiological implications. Just as a body needs a soul in order to live, the body of believers needs the animating presence of Christ. Just as the various parts of the body perform different functions, so too the various members of the church have different roles to play in the life of the Christian community. Finally, just as the health of the human body requires the integration and proper functioning of all of its systems, the health of the church requires that all members of the Body of Christ work together for the common good.

In the Letters to the Colossians and Ephesians, Christ becomes identified with the head of the body (Col 1:18, Eph 1:22–23). But more significantly, the body image includes the entire universe. In this cosmic (*cosmos* means "universe") perspective, the church is comprised of more than just the living members on earth. As the scripture scholar Raymond Brown noted, "In Colossians/Ephesians 'the church' seems to be more than an earthly reality, for it affects the heavenly powers—a foreshadowing of the expansion in later theology to a church triumphant (in heaven) alongside a church militant (on earth), and, in Roman Catholicism, alongside a church suffering (in purgatory)."[2]

In the Pastoral Epistles (1 Tim, 2 Tim, Titus), we notice the emergence of specific "offices" in the church: bishops or overseers (1 Tim 3:1; see also Phil 1:1), presbyters or elders (1 Tim 5:17), and deacons (1 Tim 3:8; see also Acts 6). In the first century, these three offices were not clearly differentiated in terms of duties and responsibilities. However, the Pastoral Epistles do represent the point of origin of a trajectory that will lead to a formalized structure of church leadership by the third century.

First Peter provides the richest imagery for the church among the seven Catholic or General Epistles. It speaks of Christians as "a chosen race, a royal priesthood, a holy nation, God's own people" (1 Pet 2:9), yet acknowledges that "for a little while you have had to suffer various trials" (1 Pet 1:6). First Peter also describes Christians as "aliens and exiles" (1 Pet 2:11; see also 1:17) who must endure present persecution, but who have "an inheritance that is imperishable, undefiled, and unfading, kept in heaven" (1 Pet 1:4).

This otherworldly, future hope for the church finds its most elaborate expression in the New Testament in the Book of Revelation. Beginning in the second chapter, letters are sent out to the seven churches of Asia offering an account of their faithfulness or unfaithfulness. The church in Philadelphia is praised for having "kept my word of patient endurance" (Rev 3:10), while the church at Sardis is described as being at the point of death (Rev 3:2). The bulk of Revelation offers a symbolic foretelling of the events preceding the final battle between Christ and his armies against Satan and his forces. An important element of that drama, however, is the heavenly vision of "a great multitude that no one could count, from every nation, from all tribes and peoples and languages, standing before the throne and before the Lamb, robed in white, with palm branches in their hands" (Rev 7:9). This multitude is the assembly of believers who remained faithful to the Lamb (Christ) during persecution, and now enjoy their eternal reward. In the closing chapters of Revelation, a "new Jerusalem" descends from heaven. "And I saw the holy city, the new Jerusalem, coming down out of heaven from God, prepared as a bride adorned for her husband" (Rev 21:2). As the scripture scholar Frank J. Matera observed:

> The book of Revelation never explicitly identifies the Church as the bride of Christ, as does Ephesians. Indeed, all twenty references to *ekklesia* in Revelation are in the plural and refer to the seven churches of Asia. The narrative line of Revelation, however, suggests that the heavenly Jerusalem will be inhabited by those who have conquered with the Lamb. Thus, it is the destiny of the Church to be the bride of the Lamb.[3]

Between the present time and that future realization of the heavenly Jerusalem, the church continues on its pilgrim way, a fellowship of saints and sinners, striving to be faithful disciples of Jesus of Nazareth.

Patristic and Medieval Ecclesiology

CLEMENT OF ROME

One of the earliest sources we have outside of the New Testament for the organization of the church is a letter from Clement of Rome (ca. 96) to the church in Corinth. In Clement's words, "a few hot-headed and unruly individuals" had recently ousted legitimate presbyters from office in the Corinthian church.[4] Clement hoped that the Corinthians could settle this "odious and unholy breach of unity among you."[5] Clement argued for the reinstatement of the original presbyters, stating that,

> our Apostles knew, through our Lord Jesus Christ, that there would be dissensions over the title of bishop. In their full foreknowledge of this, therefore, they proceeded to appoint the ministers I spoke of, and they went on to add an instruction that if these should fall asleep, other accredited persons should succeed them in their office. In view of this, we cannot think it right for these men now to be ejected from their ministry, when, after being commissioned by the Apostles (or by other reputable persons at a later date) with the full consent of the Church, they have since been serving Christ's flock in a humble, peaceable and disinterested way, and earning everybody's approval over so long a period of time.[6]

Clement claimed that church unity is best safeguarded through what would later be called "apostolic succession," the transmission of authority from the apostles through a recognized chain of leaders.

Clement patterned church leadership on the authority structure of the Old Testament priesthood. In the view of scripture scholars

Raymond E. Brown and John P. Meier, "From the Jewish heritage, *I Clement* has drawn [upon] the symbolism of the levitical priesthood and adapted it to lend great support to the ecclesiastical structure that had developed in many churches by the end of the first century, i.e., a structure of presbyter-bishops and deacons."[7] Of greater importance for the history of ecclesiology, Clement also believed that "the ministers have to be respected as part of an order that God has approved and are not to be removed at whim."[8] In other words, the offices of presbyter-bishops (Clement used the terms interchangeably[9]), and deacons were not simply examples of effective corporate management, but were divinely willed institutions.

IRENAEUS

For Irenaeus of Lyons (ca. 130 to ca. 200), the bishops played the vital role of ensuring the continuity of the church's teachings with the message entrusted to the apostles. While the bishops were the final arbiters of theological controversies, the standard of orthodoxy for the whole church was conformity to the deposit of faith entrusted to the original apostles. Therefore, Christian churches around the world should agree on the essential matters of belief. Irenaeus claimed:

As I have already observed, the Church, having received this preaching and this faith, although scattered throughout the whole world, yet, as if occupying but one house, carefully preserves it. She also believes these points [of doctrine] just as if she had but one soul, and one and the same heart, and she proclaims them, and teaches them, and hands them down, with perfect harmony, as if she possessed only one mouth. For, although the languages of the world are dissimilar, yet the import of the tradition is one and the same. For the Churches which have been planted in Germany do not believe or hand down anything differently, nor do those in Spain, not those in Gaul, nor those in the East, nor those in Egypt, nor those in Libya, nor those which have been established in the central regions of the world. But as the

sun, that creature of God, is one and the same throughout the whole world, so also the preaching of the truth
shineth everywhere, and enlightens all men that are willing to come to a knowledge of the truth.[10]

Orthodox Christian belief, argued Irenaeus, can and should be distinguished from heterodox views. Orthodox beliefs are apostolic in
origin and universally recognized as true.

CYPRIAN OF CARTHAGE

One of the most important ecclesiologists in the early church
was a north-African nobleman named Cyprian who reluctantly
accepted the position of bishop of the city of Carthage in the
mid-third century. At the same time, the Roman Emperor Decius
unleashed a fierce wave of persecution. Decius also required
Christians to obtain a certificate to prove that they did indeed offer
the proper sacrifice to the Roman gods. There were three general
responses by the Christians. First, some Christians refused to comply
with Decius's edict. Of this number, some were killed. The church
declared them martyrs. Others in this category, however, were tortured, but not killed. Those who survived the torture without
renouncing their faith were known as the "confessors," and were held
in high esteem in the early church. A second group of Christians did
not offer the sacrifice, but bought certificates from other citizens. A
third group of Christians complied with the edict and offered the sacrifice. Many of these lapsed believers sought readmission to the
church after the persecution subsided with the death of Decius in 251.
This situation posed a serious pastoral challenge to Cyprian and the
other bishops of the church. At stake was the very self-understanding
of the church as a holy community. Could a holy community readmit
public sinners and still retain its holiness?

Cyprian himself fled Carthage during the persecution. Some
accused him of cowardice; others believed that his presence in the
city would have only increased persecution of the church in
Carthage. Upon his return, however, Cyprian faced a serious challenge. Many Christians believed that the only ones worthy to grant
readmission to the lapsed were those who had suffered the most, the

confessors. Cyprian, by contrast, argued that the bishop was the only one qualified to make that determination. In response to the problem, Cyprian convened a synod of bishops to discuss the matter. In advance, Cyprian outlined his policy. He took a middle course between those who favored a quick readmission of the lapsed and those who felt they should be permanently barred from the church. According to the historian Justo Gonzalez, Cyprian proposed that

> those who refuse to do penance should not be forgiven, even on their deathbeds. Those who purchased certificates should be admitted immediately; the fallen should do penance for the rest of their lives, and would be restored to the communion of the church on their deathbeds or when they proved the true nature of their repentance in another persecution; finally, the fallen clergy should be deposed.[11]

Cyprian's position was criticized from both sides. Some thought he was too lax; others thought he was too strict.

A similar crisis was taking place in the church at Rome. The newly elected bishop Cornelius adopted a policy toward the lapsed Christians that was quite similar to Cyprian's. A priest named Novatian objected to Cornelius's policy, believing it compromised the purity of the church. According to the patristics scholar J. Patout Burns, Jr., "Novatian's party, in contrast, not only rejected this lenient policy of reconciling the certified lapsed but refused to grant peace to penitents even at the time of death."[12] Novatian and his followers broke away from the church of Rome and formed a separate church with its own clergy.

Novatian's split from the church of Rome raised a difficult ecclesiological question. The theologian Donald McKim identified the crux of the problem:

> The Novationists argued that a church containing lapsed members could no longer be considered a church. To readmit the lapsed was to lose its holiness; to embrace the apostate was to forfeit its existence. The Novationists themselves were doctrinally orthodox; they accepted the

canon of faith and apostolic teachings. Thus the church could no longer claim that the basis of its unity was apostolic teaching alone. A new way had to be found for the church's unity to be expressed and guaranteed in history.[13]

Cyprian argued that the unity of the church depended not only on fidelity to the apostolic teaching, but also allegiance and obedience to the bishop: "You ought to know that the bishop is in the Church, and the Church in the bishop; and if anyone be not with the bishop, then he is not in the Church."[14] Because the Novatians did not have a legitimate bishop, Cyprian concluded, they did not have a legitimate church.

Cyprian's unwillingness to recognize the legitimacy of the Novatian church presented another pastoral problem. Should those baptized in a Novatian church be *re*baptized if they later sought admission to the catholic church? (The use here of the lowercased word *catholic* means the "universal church," rather than the small splinter groups that broke away. While *catholic* is still used to refer to all traditional Christian religions, the uppercased *Catholic* [or *Roman Catholic*] became the term for Christians in communion with Rome, as opposed to Orthodox and Protestant Christians.) Burns phrased the question of rebaptism presented by Cyprian in the following manner: "Should the bishops require that a person who had originally been baptized in one of these splinter communities submit to baptism again as a condition for admission to their universal communion?"[15] Cyprian believed that they *should* be rebaptized. The baptism of members of schismatic churches (i.e., those separated from the main Christian body) was performed by those who had no authority to do so. In this context, we can appreciate two of Cyprian's most quoted lines: "He cannot have God for his Father who does not have the Church for his mother,"[16] and "Outside the Church there is no salvation."[17] In other words, those outside the unity of the church cannot validly perform sacraments any more than foreign countries can print American dollar bills. Cyprian's stance on the issue of rebaptism was ultimately rejected by the church, but the question of the validity of sacraments would persist in the north-African church. It occupied the attention of the most influential theologian in the ancient church, Augustine of Hippo.

AUGUSTINE OF HIPPO

The circumstances surrounding Augustine's controversy with a group known as the Donatists bore a striking resemblance to Cyprian's earlier battle with the Novatians. The Novatians and the Donatists both wanted a pure church, and expelled from the church anyone who had betrayed the faith when confronted by imperial forces. The Novatians expelled those who had offered sacrifice to the Roman gods during the reign of Decius. Donatus and his followers believed that bishops who complied with the Emperor Diocletian's order to hand over the sacred books to the Roman authorities lost their ability to validly administer the sacraments. The bishops who handed over the books were known as traditores. The theologian Eric G. Jay explained the logic of the Donatists' position:

> A *traditor* is unholy, they argued, and cannot be a member of the holy Church. Those who have dealings with a *traditor* themselves lose sanctity and cease to be members of the Church. Those who are thus outside the Church cannot perform ecclesiastical functions. If they claim to have the sacraments the claim is false, for the validity of the sacraments depends on the worthiness of the minister.[18]

Just as the Novatians had insisted that lapsed Christians had forfeited their right to be members of the church, the Donatists insisted that bishops who were *traditores* forfeited their right to lead the church.

In order to respond theologically to the Donatists, Augustine needed to clarify the concept of the holiness of the church. The historian Peter Brown identified the crux of matter: "If the church was defined as 'pure,' if it was the only body in the world in which the Holy Spirit resided, how could its members fail to be 'pure'?"[19] Augustine responded to the Donatists by locating the holiness of the church not in its earthly representatives (since obviously all humans are sinners), but rather in Christ himself. The theologian Eugene TeSelle explained:

> Throughout his reply Augustine not only hammered at the internal weaknesses of the Donatist argument—the problem of the person who is baptized by someone who feigns righteousness, or the observable fact of differences in spiritual gifts between the baptizer and the baptized— but developed the alternative position that when the human minister baptizes externally with water it is Christ himself who baptizes inwardly with the Holy Spirit; and he supported this emphasis upon Christ rather than the human administrant by constantly quoting such biblical texts as "Cursed is he who trusts in man" (Jeremiah 17, 5) or "It is better to trust the Lord than to put confidence in man" (Psalm 118 [117], 8).[20]

Augustine prevailed over the Donatists on the question of the validity of baptism by *traditores*, but he also conceded that the Donatists were right when they stated that the earthly church had its fair share of sinners in its ranks.

Augustine began to distinguish between the visible and invisible church. The visible church comprised those who were officially welcomed into the church on earth. The invisible church consisted of a "fixed number of the elect"[21] known only to God. During the earthly pilgrimage of the church, members of both churches exist side by side. Only at the final judgement will God make the definitive separation between the two groups. As J. N. D. Kelly noted, Augustine never reconciled his contention, which he raised against the Donatists, that salvation is to be found only in the catholic (universal) church, with this idea that there is a "fixed number of the elect." If, as Kelly argued, heretics, schismatics, sinners, or unconverted pagans are predestined for salvation, then what need is there for church membership?[22]

Taking the writings of Clement of Rome, Irenaeus, Cyprian, and Augustine as a whole, we can see the rationale behind the ancient designation of "one, holy, catholic, and apostolic" as the four "marks" of the church. The true church is a united body, striving for greater holiness, upholding beliefs held "everywhere, always, by all,"[23] and rooted in the teachings of the apostles. Christian churches in the Eastern and Western Roman Empire, however, differed on how the church could best embody these four essential characteristics.

LEO THE GREAT

The first mark of the church is that it is one. Though it has many members, the church is the one Body of Christ. In what does this unity consist? How is it expressed? How is it preserved? The early church reached a consensus that the unity consisted primarily of a common set of beliefs, expressed in the common liturgical celebrations of baptism and Eucharist, preserved by the legitimate bishops. The unanswered question was whether the unity of the church was preserved by the people, by the entire body of bishops, or specifically by the bishop of Rome? To phrase the question in language that would not appear until later in church history: Did the bishop of Rome enjoy primacy of honor among the bishops or primacy of jurisdiction?[24]

Pope Leo I, or Leo the Great (d. 461) claimed a primacy of jurisdiction for the bishop of Rome in his famous *Tome*. The theologian T. Howland Sanks summarized the main points of Leo's position in this way:

1. Christ chose Peter and gave him precedence over the other apostles;
2. the Matthean text 16:18 ("upon this rock") refers to Peter himself and not his faith;
3. Peter was actually bishop of Rome and his authority is perpetuated in his successors;
4. the authority of the other apostles came through Peter, and that of the bishops is derived not immediately from Christ but through the bishop of Rome...and therefore
5. the bishop of Rome has a plenitude of power, *plenitudo potestatis*, over the whole church, whereas the other bishops only share in this responsibility...[25]

287

The concept of the primacy of Rome gained strong support in some quarters and met with equally strong resistance in other quarters. Two major developments in the millennium following the death of Leo that were directly related to the concept of the primacy of Rome were the split between the Eastern and Western churches, and the power struggles between the popes and secular rulers in the Middle Ages.

The bishops or patriarchs of Rome and Constantinople clashed over the centuries on various questions, but the issue that ultimately drove a wedge between the two, causing the first major division in the Christian church (1054), was papal primacy. The modern Orthodox bishop-theologian Timothy Ware stated that the Orthodox church

> does not deny to the Holy and Apostolic See of Rome a *primacy of honour*, together with the right (under certain conditions) to hear appeals from all parts of Christendom. Note that we have used the word "primacy," not "supremacy." Orthodox regard the Pope as the bishop "who presides in love," to adapt a phrase of Saint Ignatius: Rome's mistake—so Orthodox believe—has been to turn this primacy or "presidency of love" into a supremacy of external power and jurisdiction.[26]

The Orthodox would gladly refer to the pope as a "first among equals," but they would vest supreme authority in church councils, not in the bishop of Rome.

The medieval popes also used Leo's "plenitude of power" concept to assert their dominance over secular rulers. Among the claims contained in Pope Gregory VII's *Dictatus papae* ("Pronouncement of the Pope") in 1075 was "that it is licit for [the pope] to depose emperors."[27] In 1302 Pope Boniface VII made similar claims for papal authority in his *Unam sanctam*, including the claim that "in this Church and in her power are two swords, the spiritual and the temporal....Both are in the power of the Church, the spiritual and the material. But the latter is to be used for the Church, the former by her; the former by the priest, the latter by kings and captains but at the will and by the permission of the priest."[28]

The Protestant and Catholic Reformations

As we have seen, the early church placed increasing authority in the office of the bishop. By the time of Cyprian, the unity of the church was understood to be grounded in obedience to the local bishop. As Eric G. Jay pointed out,

> Here is a weakness in an ecclesiology such as Cyprian's. What is the Christian's duty if his bishop, properly elected and validly consecrated, lives a scandalous life which is tolerated by his brother bishops, and makes demands which are unreasonable and against conscience? In the course of the Church's existence many have felt that they must refuse obedience and form a separated Christian community.[29]

This flaw in Cyprian's ecclesiology exploded in the late Middle Ages and Reformation. John Wyclif (ca. 1328–84) in England and John Hus (ca. 1369–1415) in Bohemia both gained followers when they railed against the corruption they saw in the church. In 1309 the papal headquarters were moved from Rome to Avignon. In 1378 the so-called Great Schism began in which there were two claimants to the title of pope, one in Avignon and one in Rome. This embarrassing episode gave further credence to the calls for major reform.

When Pope Leo X authorized a massive campaign to sell indulgences in Germany, a young Augustinian monk named Martin Luther believed that he had to lodge a public protest against his church. The twentieth-century Catholic theologian Louis Bouyer identified four phases in Luther's thought on the church. In the first phase, Bouyer argued, Luther "never dreamed of founding a new church, or even substantially modifying the Catholic Church."[30] Initially, Luther sought to reform the church, not replace the church. In the second phase, Luther made a wholesale indictment against the Catholic Church. In his 1520 treatise "The Babylonian Captivity of the Church," Luther saw "the whole of traditional Catholicism as a radical corruption of the Gospel."[31] In this second phase, Luther retrieved Augustine's distinction between

the visible and the invisible church. Membership in the institutional church did not in any way guarantee inclusion in the true
assembly of God. The third phase, according to Bouyer, involved
Luther's appeal to the German princes. "Luther remained infused
with a notion of the Christian people identified, in principle, with
the Church as being built on earth....He turned to the Christian
prince in this danger, in a manner that was not basically different
from what many bishops had done before him, from Constantine
to Charlemagne."[32] In the final phase of Luther's ecclesiological
thought, Bouyer detected a shift toward a more traditional church
structure. "We thus reach a fourth and last Lutheran ecclesiology,
which in many respects is merely a reconstitution and destabiliza-
tion of elements of traditional ecclesiology."[33] In this regard,
Bouyer attached special significance to Luther's attendance at the
consecration of three Lutheran bishops in 1542 and 1544. Also in
this final phase, the official Lutheran statement of belief, known as
the Augsburg Confession (1530) appeared. In the Augsburg
Confession, the church is defined as the "assembly of all believers
among whom the Gospel is preached in its purity and the holy
sacraments are administered according to the Gospel."[34]

Calvin followed Luther in defining the church as the assembly in which the Gospel was rightly preached and the sacraments
rightly administered, but parted with Luther on the acceptance of
bishops. As the theologian Alister McGrath explained,

> Calvin referred to the "order by which the Lord willed
> his church to be governed," and developed a detailed
> theory of church government based on his exegesis of
> the New Testament, drawing extensively upon the ter-
> minology of the imperial Roman administration.
> Contrary to what the radicals asserted, Calvin insisted
> that a specific form of church structure and administra-
> tion is laid down by Scripture. Thus Calvin held that the
> ministerial government of the church is divinely
> ordained, as are the distinctions between "minister,"
> "elder," "deacon," and "people."[35]

Calvin also differed with Luther on the relationship between
church and state. For Calvin, church and state were distinct entities

with their separate responsibilities. As Calvin stated in his *Institutes*, "The church does not assume what is proper to the magistrate; nor can the magistrate execute what is carried out by the church."[36]

Another branch of the Protestant Reformation, the English Reformation, vacillated between a church that retained most elements of Catholic belief and practice, and a church structured along the lines of the Calvinist churches. The churches that sprang from the English Reformation are often described as the via media ("the middle way") between Catholicism and Calvinism. The fullest official expression of this ecclesiology came in 1563 with the promulgation of the Thirty-nine Articles. As theologians John Dillenberger and Claude Welch noted, Queen Elizabeth I rejected "the extremes of both Rome and the continental Reformation." They continue,

> Only in worship did uniformity appear essential, and that for the well-being of both church and state. Nevertheless, there was some demand for minimal doctrinal statements. The promulgation of the Thirty-nine Articles, which were accepted primarily as a guide rather than as a binding rule of faith, served this purpose. These are broadly Protestant in tenor, with stress at various points on the positive use of the tradition of the church.[37]

The Thirty-nine Articles rejected Catholic beliefs in transubstantiation, seven sacraments, and purgatory, yet like Rome asserted the church's authority to decide controversies of faith.

The twentieth-century Presbyterian theologian Benjamin Warfield once commented that "the Reformation, inwardly considered, was just the ultimate triumph of Augustine's doctrine of grace over Augustine's doctrine of the church."[38] Luther and Calvin especially were indebted to Augustine's work on justification and predestination. They both would embrace Augustine's understanding of the church as a fellowship of love, but neither would accept Augustine's declaration, "For my part, I should not believe the gospel except as moved by the authority of the catholic church."[39]

The Catholic Reformation took as its foundation the authority of the church, and the bishops at Trent used that authority to reform the church. Eric Plumer captured both of these aspects when he wrote that the Council of Trent

> reaffirmed traditional catholic teachings that had been repudiated by the Reformers: the hierarchical authority of the Church; the seven sacraments, including ordination; the necessity of receiving both Scripture and tradition "with equal reverence." Trent also instituted numerous reforms, including the establishment of seminaries to provide priests, who until then had not been given formal training, with both education and specific instruction in priestly ministry.[40]

In practice, the decrees of Trent placed the responsibility of church reform chiefly in the hands of the bishops. As one church historian observed, "More than any other figure, the bishop emerged from Trent as the major player in reinvigorating the sixteenth-century Catholic Church tested on so many fronts, inside and out."[41] In practice, this required the bishop to visit his diocese often and take a more active role in overseeing the liturgical life of the churches under his supervision, the selection and formation of priests under his jurisdiction, and the moral lives of those souls under his care.

The leading Roman Catholic ecclesiologist of the seventeenth century was the Jesuit Robert Bellarmine. Bellarmine defined "the one and true Church" as "the community of men brought together by the profession of the same Christian faith and conjoined in the communion of the same sacraments, under the government of legitimate pastors, and especially the one vicar of Christ on earth, the Roman pontiff."[42] This would remain the operative definition for the church found in the theological manuals used in Catholic seminaries well into the twentieth century. And the second half of the definition—that all members of the true church be "under the government of legitimate pastors, and especially the one vicar of Christ on earth, the Roman pontiff"—triggered two significant ecclesiological trends of the eighteenth and nineteenth centuries.

The Modern Age

Bellarmine's definition focuses on the visible, institutional aspects of church life: a community professing the same faith, celebrating the same sacraments, submitting to the governing authority of the community's leaders. In the nineteenth century, Johann Sebastian Drey (1777–1853) and Johann Adam Möhler (1796–1838), Catholic theologians at the University of Tübingen, presented more organic, less-institutional understandings of the church. As the contemporary ecclesiologist and cardinal Avery Dulles noted, "Reacting against the aridity of the institutional models, [Möhler and his associates at Tübingen] popularized the notion of the Church as a supernatural organism vivified by the Holy Spirit, a fellowship sustained by the outpouring of divine grace."[43] Möhler himself described the church as the "ongoing incarnation." "The visible church is the Son of God appearing within mankind in human form in a continuous fashion, constantly renewed, eternally rejuvenated, his ongoing incarnation, just as the faithful are also called in holy scripture the body of Christ."[44] Catholic theologians of the twentieth century would reap the benefits of Möhler's creative retrieval of the early church's ecclesiology.

Bellarmine's definition did not address the relationship between "the legitimate pastors" of the church and the "one vicar of Christ on earth, the Roman pontiff." Bellarmine compared the visibility of the true church with that of "the kingdom of France or the republic of Venice."[45] This analogy of the church to sovereign nations, however, when applied to the question of the relationship of a nation's bishops to the pope could yield varying interpretations. As the theologian Michael Himes explained:

> The cultural and political impact of the growth of nation-states in Western Europe provided a context in which one could respond in two ways: one might understand the Church as a highly centralized society with authority placed primarily in the papacy modeled on the absolute monarchies of the period, or one might cast the Church as itself determined by national boundaries and so emphasize the role of national hierarchies.[46]

293

Proponents on both sides of the debate clashed in the nineteenth century in France. Those who favored the former model, the church as a centralized society with authority placed primarily in the papacy, were known as the ultramontanes (literally, "beyond the mountains," i.e., over the Alps into Rome). Those who favored the latter model, the church as determined by national boundaries, were known as Gallicans (taking their name from the ancient name for France). This battle was to find its official resolution at the First Vatican Council (1869–70).

VATICAN I

Vatican I was a victory for ultramontanism. Not only did the bishops assert that the pope has "supreme power of jurisdiction over the whole church" and that, "as successor of Peter, the prince of the apostles," he possesses "apostolic primacy,"[47] they also declared the doctrine of papal infallibility. Many people assume that the doctrine of infallibility means that anything the pope says must be right. The doctrine, however, does not teach that. In order to understand what it does declare, we need to begin with the actual statement. At Vatican I, the bishops declared that

> we teach and define as a divinely revealed dogma that when the Roman pontiff speaks *ex cathedra*, that is when in the exercise of his office as shepherd and teacher of all Christians, in virtue of his supreme apostolic authority, he defines a doctrine concerning faith and morals to be held by the whole church, he possesses, by the divine assistance promised to him in blessed Peter, that infallibility which the divine Redeemer willed his church to enjoy in defining doctrine concerning faith or morals. Therefore, such definitions of the Roman pontiff are of themselves, and not by the consent of the church, irreformable.[48]

Because the teaching is stated in such technical language, five points of clarification might help bring the teaching into clearer focus.

First, the expression *ex cathedra* literally means "from the chair." This is the same root word for *cathedral*, which is literally the church where the bishop has his chair. In colleges and universities there are endowed chairs in the various academic departments. The chair (or seat) is, therefore, a symbol of authority.

Second, papal infallibility deals with the *office* of the papacy, not the characteristics of the *person* who holds the office. In other words, papal infallibility is not based on the holiness of the person occupying the papacy. For example, the president of the United States is the commander in chief of the armed forces. The president has the authority to send troops into war. Past presidents had that authority, but no longer do once they leave office. The candidate from the opposing party who lost the election, who may be a highly decorated veteran, does not have that authority. The ability to send troops into battle is not a function of the military valor of the president, but is a power given to the one who holds the office of the presidency.

Third, papal infallibility deals with "doctrine concerning faith and morals." The infallibility does not extend to far-flung areas such as the weather, politics, or sporting events. Papal infallibility deals with the competence of the successor of St. Peter to speak on matters that are integral to the life of the church.

Fourth, the definition refers to "the divine assistance promised to [the pope] in blessed Peter." The critical scriptural passage for this idea is Matthew 16:13–20. After Peter professes his belief that Jesus is the Messiah, Jesus replies:

> "Blessed are you, Simon son of Jonah! For flesh and blood has not revealed this to you, but my Father in heaven. And I tell you, you are Peter, and on this rock I will build my church, and the gates of Hades will not prevail against it. I will give you the keys of the kingdom of heaven, and whatever you bind on earth will be bound in heaven, and whatever you loose on earth will be loosed in heaven. (vv. 17–20)

Peter is the rock (*Petros* literally means "rock") upon which the church is built. The giving of the keys (see Isa 22:22) signifies the granting of authority. There has been much controversy regarding what exactly Peter is given authority to do: forgive sins, issue doctrine, or discipline members of the community. Pope Benedict XVI, as Joseph Cardinal Ratzinger the head of the Congregation for the Doctrine of the Faith, offered the following traditional interpretation:

> As the faithful steward of Jesus' message, Peter opens the door to the Kingdom of Heaven; his is the function of the doorkeeper, who has to judge concerning admission and rejection (cf. Rev 3:7). In this sense, the significance of the reference to the keys clearly approximates the meaning of binding and loosing. This latter expression is taken from rabbinic language, where it stands primarily for the authority to make doctrinal decisions and, on the other hand, denotes a further disciplinary power, that is, the right to impose or to lift the ban. The parallelism "on earth and in heaven" implies that Peter's decisions for the Church also have validity before God—an idea that also occurs in an analogous sense in Talmudic literature. If we bear in mind the parallel to the word of the risen Jesus transmitted in John 21:23, it becomes apparent that in its core the power to bind and to loose means the authority to forgive sins, an authority that in Peter is committed to the Church (cf. Mt. 18:15–18).[49]

The Catholic Church would thus insist that the claims made at Vatican I regarding the function and authority of the papacy are a logical outgrowth of the authority vested in Peter in the Gospel of Matthew.

Fifth, the definition states that the pope's infallible declarations are "irreformable." An infallible teaching is definitive. It cannot be revoked or amended by a later ecumenical council or a later pope.

The nineteenth-century convert to Catholicism, John Henry Newman, accepted the doctrine of papal infallibility, but did not favor its official promulgation. In his own writings, Newman stressed that "the sense of the faithful" (in Latin, *sensus fidelium*) was an essential element in the formulation of church doctrine. By this,

Newman meant that doctrines express the belief of the entire church, and that the laity need to be consulted on matters of faith. As Michael Himes observed,

> Newman's description may sound unobjectionable to us, but it was a source of bitter controversy in 1859. Let me quote to you a notorious letter of Msgr. George Talbot, the highest-ranking English-speaking member of the Roman curia at the time. Writing of Newman's preposterous idea that one might consult the laity on matters of faith, Talbot asked, "What is the province of the laity?" He answered his own question: "To hunt, to shoot, and to entertain. These matters they understand, but to meddle with ecclesiastical matters they have no right at all."[50]

Newman's insight into the nature of the church did not have much impact on the decrees of Vatican I, but it did profoundly influence the deliberations at Vatican II.

VATICAN II

In 1959 Pope John XXIII announced that he would convene an ecumenical council. From 1959 to 1962, preparations were made, proposals were solicited, and preliminary drafts of documents were composed. The first of the four sessions of Vatican II opened in October 1962. In his analysis of the first session, "the most dramatic and the most important" session, the theologian Joseph A. Komonchak identified four moments as being "particularly significant."

> The first was Pope John's opening address, in which he urged that the Council take a pastoral direction. It was not principally to be concerned with repeating what was already Catholic doctrine, nor to propose condemnations of errors....
>
> The second key moment came when, on the first working-session, the bishops refused to vote immediately on the membership of their own conciliar commissions.

This was seen at the time as an expression of a widespread disagreement with the tone and substance of many of the prepared drafts....

The third significant moment was the conciliar debate on the draft document on the liturgy, which revealed that a majority of the bishops would ratify the pope's call for renewal. The mind of the Council was further revealed when the debate on the draft "On the Sources of Revelation" began. This doctrinal text was very severely criticized by many of the bishops, and in a final vote on the text, over 60% of them asked that it be withdrawn. Although this was an insufficient number to remand the text, Pope John intervened and ordered that the text be thoroughly revised. This fourth dramatic moment illustrated the intention of the majority of the bishops to embark on a course which represented in several ways a departure from the attitudes and strategies which had characterized the Roman Catholicism of the previous 150 years.[51]

John XXIII died in June 1963, and his successor, Pope Paul VI, decreed that the Council would continue.

In the third session, the Dogmatic Constitution on the Church (*Lumen gentium*) was approved by a vote of 2151 to 5. *Lumen gentium* is the most complete, official statement of modern Catholic ecclesiology. In two significant ways, *Lumen gentium* complements the teachings regarding papal authority at Vatican I, and rediscovered a lost emphasis on the church as the people of God.

Lumen gentium reasserted the Vatican I teaching that the church is a hierarchical community with ultimate authority resting in the hands of the pope. However, the discussion of the bishops and the pope is situated within the broader context of the common bond shared by all the people of God. Here we have a retrieval of the ancient concept of the church as a *koinonia*, translated variously as "communion," or "community," or "fellowship." On this point of translation, the theologian Francis Schüssler Fiorenza stressed that *koinonia* conveys a sense "of participating and sharing in something."

The Church as koinonia does not consist simply, therefore, of those associating to confess their belief in Jesus as
Risen Lord, but rather they share in a communion and
participation with the Risen Lord that grounds their unity
with him. This unity is established in the baptism—also in
the Eucharist—of Christians.[53]

The laity and the clergy have different roles to play in the church,
but the common baptism they share—their common bond, or
koinonia—is fundamental to their membership in the people of
God. Seen in this light, laity are called to actively participate in the
life of the church. This is the basis, therefore, for the active lay participation in parishes since Vatican II. As the theologian Angel
Anton noted, "The concept of *communion* is without a doubt the
key concept for interpreting the ecclesiology of Vatican II and the
one that best summarizes its results in ecclesiological doctrine and
in the renewal of the church."[54]

Not only did *Lumen gentium* provide a fuller account of the role
of the laity in the church, it also had much to say about the relationship of the pope to the entire college of bishops. The theologian
Richard R. Gaillardetz wrote,

> One of the oft noted ironies of the last two ecumenical
> councils is that the ecclesiological framework of the
> *minority* bishops at Vatican I, those bishops operating out
> of a more collegial understanding of Church authority
> and a strong sense of the Church's fidelity to Scripture
> and tradition, became the framework of the *majority* bish-
> ops at Vatican II. From this point of view Newman was
> indeed prescient in predicting that a future council would
> "trim the boat," redressing the papocentric imbalance
> created by Vatican I. When Vatican II began its consider-
> ation of the Church, it became evident early on that the
> teaching of Vatican I on the papacy needed to be com-
> plemented by a much more developed understanding of
> the two other components in the teaching ministry of the
> Church, namely the college of bishops and the *sensus
> fidelium*.[55]

While the pope "has supreme and universal power over the whole Church, a power which he can always exercise unhindered" (*LG* 22), the college of bishops, acting in concert with the pope, also plays an essential role in guiding the church.

> The order of the bishops is the successor to the college of the apostles in their role as teachers and pastors, and in it the apostolic college is perpetuated. Together with their head, the Supreme Pontiff, and never apart from him, they have supreme and full authority over the universal Church; but this power cannot be exercised without the agreement of the Roman Pontiff. (*LG* 22)

The emphasis found at Vatican I on papal authority remains, but it is counterbalanced by a recognition of the full authority of the entire college of bishops.

This repositioning of both the laity and the college of bishops in the life of the people of God represented a significant shift in emphasis in the official thought regarding the church. Where *Lumen gentium* broke with the past was on the Catholic tradition of equating "the true church" with "the Roman Catholic Church." In his 1943 encyclical *Mystici corporis*, Pope Pius XII maintained that the Mystical Body of Christ was in fact the Catholic Church. As Dulles noted, "*Lumen gentium* does not assert that the Church of Christ or the Mystical Body is coterminous with the Roman Catholic Church."[56] Rather, *Lumen gentium* stated, "This Church, constituted and organized as a society in the present world, subsists in the Catholic Church, which is governed by the successor of Peter and by the bishops in communion with him. Nevertheless, many elements of sanctification and truth are found outside its visible confines" (*LG* 8). Commenting on this passage, Dulles observed,

> For ecumenical reasons the council distanced itself from the more controversial affirmations of *Mystici corporis*. Where Pius XII had said that the Mystical Body and the Roman Catholic Church were one and the same thing, Vatican II contented itself with saying that the Church of Christ "subsists in" the Roman Catholic Church—

an expression deliberately chosen to allow for the ecclesial reality of other Christian communities.[57]

Although this portion of *Lumen gentium* has been interpreted in various ways, it certainly presents a different understanding of the church than found in the writings of Cyprian, Bellarmine, or the decrees of Vatican I.

Conclusion

Just as there is a great diversity in terms of modern Christology, there is an equally diverse collection of contemporary reflections on the nature and mission of the church. Joseph F. Eagan has offered a sampling:

> Why the church? For what purpose did Christ establish the church? What task or mission did he give it? What should the church be doing today? Where should its emphasis be? Has the church gotten sidetracked from its main purpose?
>
> Various answers have been given by theologians: "To produce saints and make holiness possible" (Jean Danielou); "to offer worship to God for all humanity" (Jan Groot); "to be present in the world as a living witness to the love of the Trinity" (Robert Sears); "to proclaim the Gospel to the poor by word and deed" (Jon Sobrino); "to bring about the gospel values of Jesus Christ: freedom, peace, charity, compassion, reconciliation" (Richard McBrien); "to be the visible sign of the Lord's presence in the struggle for a more human and just society" (Gustavo Gutiérrez); "to be a leaven amid humanity" (Juan Segundo); "to set a new worldview before our eyes, to transform and Christianize the world," to be "salt of the earth, light of the world" (Walter Buhlmann).[58]

For those in the Catholic tradition, beliefs regarding Christ and the church find their most visible expression in the sacramental life of the church. Exploring the intimate relationship among these three aspects of Catholic thought and practice leads us more deeply into the particularly Catholic approach in Christian theology.

Discussion Questions

1. How would you define the term *church*?
2. What is the chief purpose of the church? How well is the church fulfilling its purpose?
3. Should we have a hierarchical structure in the church?
4. What authority should a local bishop have in the churches in the diocese?
5. How is unity in the church best preserved?
6. What should be the relationship between church and state?
7. Do you accept Möhler's description of the church as the ongoing incarnation? Why? Why not?
8. Do you accept the doctrine of papal infallibility? Why? Why not?
9. Do some ecclesiologies function better in different eras or different countries in the present time?
10. What type of ecclesiology would be most effective and least effective in the United States today?

Suggested Readings

For an excellent introduction to ecclesiology, see Peter C. Phan, ed., *The Gift of the Church* (Collegeville, MN: The Liturgical Press, 2000). Also see Richard P. McBrien, *Catholicism*, new ed. (San Francisco: HarperSanFrancisco, 1994): and Avery Dulles, *Models of the Church*, exp. ed. (Garden City, NY: Doubleday, 1987). For a history of ecclesiology, see Eric G. Jay, *The Church* (Atlanta: John Knox Press, 1980); and parts one and two of T. Howland Sanks, *Salt, Leaven, and Light* (New York: *Crossroad*, 1992). For a contemporary ecclesiology based on Vatican II, see Joseph F.

Eagan, *Restoration and Renewal* (Kansas City, MO: Sheed and Ward, 1995).

Notes

1. Daniel J. Harrington, *The Church According to the New Testament* (Franklin, WI: Sheed and Ward, 2001), 127.
2. Raymond E. Brown, *The Churches the Apostles Left Behind* (Mahwah, NJ: Paulist Press, 1984), 49.
3. Frank J. Matera, "Theologies of the Church in the New Testament," in Peter Phan, ed., *The Gift of the Church* (Collegeville, MN: The Liturgical Press, 2000), 19.
4. "The First Epistle of Clement to the Corinthians," #1 in Maxwell Staniforth, trans., *Early Christian Writings* (New York: Penguin Books, 1968), 23.
5. Ibid.
6. Ibid., 46.
7. Raymond E. Brown and John P. Meier, *Antioch and Rome* (Mahwah, NJ: Paulist Press, 1983), 179. Italics theirs. Chapter nine of this book provides a nice introduction to 1 Clement.
8. Ibid.
9. Matera, "Theologies of the Church in the New Testament," 24.
10. Irenaeus, *Against Heresies* I, X.2, in Alexander Roberts and James Donaldson, eds., *Ante-Nicene Fathers*, vol. 1 (Peabody, MA: Hendrickson Publishers, 1994; reprint Christian Literature Publishing Co., 1885), 331.
11. Justo Gonzalez, *A History of Christian Thought*, vol. 1 (Nashville: Abingdon, 1970), 246.
12. J. Patout Burns, Jr., *Cyprian the Bishop* (New York: Routledge, 2002), 7.
13. Donald McKim, *Theological Turning Points* (Atlanta: John Knox Press, 1988), 53.
14. Quoted in T. Howland Sanks, *Salt, Leaven, and Light* (New York: Crossroad, 1992), 58.
15. Burns, *Cyprian the Bishop*, 9.

16. Quoted in Eric Plumer, "The Development of Ecclesiology: Early Church to the Reformation," in Phan, *The Gift of the Church*, 29 n 20.

17. Ibid., 29.

18. Eric G. Jay, *The Church* (Atlanta: John Knox Press, 1980), 81.

19. Peter Brown, *Augustine of Hippo* (New York: Dorset Press, 1967), 221.

20. Eugene TeSelle, *Augustine the Theologian* (Eugene, OR: Wipf and Stock Publishers, 1970), 261.

21. J. N. D. Kelly, *Early Christian Doctrines*, rev. ed. (New York: Harper and Row, 1978), 416.

22. Ibid.

23. Jaroslav Pelikan, *The Christian Tradition*, vol. 1 (Chicago: University of Chicago Press, 1971), 333.

24. This distinction appears in the decrees of Vatican I (Session Four, chapter 1). See also Joseph F. Eagan, *Restoration and Renewal* (Kansas City, MO: Sheed and Ward, 1995), 198.

25. Sanks, *Salt, Leaven, and Light*, 67.

26. Timothy Ware, *The Orthodox Church* (New York: Penguin Books, 1964), 35. Italics his.

27. Richard P. McBrien, *Lives of the Popes* (San Francisco: HarperSanFrancisco, 1997), 186.

28. Quoted in McBrien, *Lives of the Popes*, 231.

29. Eric G. Jay, *The Church*, 72.

30. Bouyer, *The Church of God* (Chicago: Franciscan Herald Press, 1982), 47.

31. Ibid., 48.

32. Ibid., 50.

33. Ibid., 51.

34. Augsburg Confession, Article VII, in John H. Leith, ed., *Creeds of the Churches* (Atlanta: John Knox Press, 1982), 70.

35. Alister McGrath, *Christian Theology* (Cambridge, MA: Blackwell Publishers, 1994), 413.

36. John Calvin, *Institutes of the Christian Religion* (IV, 11.3). Quoted in Jay, The Church, 175.

37. John Dillenberger and Claude Welch, *Protestant Christianity* (New York: Charles Scribner's Sons, 1954), 70.

38. Quoted in J. Philip Wogaman, *Christian Ethics* (Louisville, KY: Westminster John Knox Press, 1993), 109.

39. Quoted in Pelikan, *The Christian Tradition*, vol. 1, 303.

40. Plumer, "The Development of Ecclesiology: Early Church to the Reformation," 41–42.

41. Christopher M. Bellitto, *The General Councils* (Mahwah, NJ: Paulist Press, 2002), 104.

42. Quoted in Avery Dulles, *Models of the Church* (Garden City, NY: Image Books, 1974), 20.

43. Ibid., 54.

44. Quoted in Dennis M. Doyle, *Communion Ecclesiology* (Maryknoll, NY: Orbis Books, 2000), 36. Doyle is using Michael Himes's translation.

45. Himes, "The Development of Ecclesiology: Modernity to the Twentieth Century" in Phan, *The Gift of the Church*, 48.

46. Ibid., 51.

47. Vatican I, Session Four, Chapter Three in Norman P. Tanner, ed., *Decrees of the Ecumenical Councils*, vol. 2 (London: Sheed and Ward; Washington, DC: Georgetown University Press, 1990), 814 and 815.

48. Ibid., 816.

49. Joseph Cardinal Ratzinger, *Called to Communion* (San Francisco: Ignatius Press, 1996), 63–64.

50. Michael Himes, "What Can We Learn from the Church in the Nineteenth Century," in Michael Himes, ed., *The Church in the Twenty-First Century* (Ligouri, MO: Ligouri, 2004), 73.

51. Joseph A. Komonchak, "Vatican Council II," in Joseph A. Komonchak, ed., *The New Dictionary of Theology* (Wilmington, DE: Michael Glazier, 1987), 1073.

52. Eagan, *Restoration and Renewal*, 29.

53. Francis Schüssler Fiorenza, *Foundational Theology* (New York: Crossroad, 1984), 131.

54. Angel Anton, "Postconciliar Ecclesiology," in René Latourelle, *Vatican II: Assessment and Perspectives*, vol. 1 (Mahwah, NJ: Paulist Press, 1988), 416.

55. Richard R. Gaillardetz, *Teaching with Authority* (Collegeville, MN: The Liturgical Press, 1997), 217.

56. Dulles, *Models of the Church*, 56.

57. Avery Dulles, "A Half Century of Ecclesiology," in *Theological Studies* 50 (1989): 430. See also Timothy G. McCarthy, *The Catholic Tradition* (Chicago: Loyola University Press, 1994), 189.

58. Eagan, *Restoration and Renewal*, 93–94.

10

THE SACRAMENTS OF INITIATION

We began our discussion of the church in the previous chapter by calling to mind the memorial acclamation "Christ has died, Christ has risen, Christ will come again." Reciting this liturgical expression reminds us that the church extends from the death, resurrection, and ascension of Christ to the end of time. Only in this historical context do the practices that are central to the life of the church make sense. The sacraments are memorials of what happened in the past ("Do this in remembrance of me," Luke 22:19); celebrations of the presence of Christ ("And remember, I am with you always, to the end of the age," Matt 28:20); and anticipations of the future realization of the kingdom of God ("For as often as you eat this bread and drink this cup, you proclaim the Lord's death until he comes," 1 Cor 11:26).

In this chapter we begin our exploration of the church's sacraments. After a brief discussion of the Old Testament and the Greco-Roman backgrounds to the Christian practice of sacraments, we will survey the development of Christian thought regarding the sacraments. We will then focus on what are commonly called the sacraments of initiation (baptism, confirmation, and Eucharist). In the following chapter we will explore the history and theology of the sacraments of healing (reconciliation and anointing of the sick) and the sacraments of commitment (marriage and holy orders).

Historical Background to the Sacraments

Christian sacramental practices sprang from the rich soil of Judaism. First of all, Jews maintained a strong sense of their identity as a covenant people who were bound to the Lord in a unique way. This uniqueness included both the blessings promised to Abraham, Isaac, and Jacob, and the demands to live a life of holiness as prescribed in the Law delivered to Moses on Mount Sinai. Second, the Jewish religious life was patterned on a sacred sense of time. There were yearly festivals and holy days, including Passover, Pentecost, New Year's, the Day of Atonement, and Booths (Lev 23). On a weekly basis, there were six days of work followed by the Sabbath. On these feast days and Sabbath observations, the Israelites recalled sacred events in Israel's past (Passover commemorated the exodus from Egypt), expressed gratitude to the Lord (Weeks was originally a harvest festival), or confessed their sins (the Day of Atonement is the highest holy day in the Jewish calendar). Third, the covenant relationship with God required the performance of certain rituals; for example, baby boys should be circumcised on the eighth day; Jews should gather for the annual celebration of the Seder meal at Passover, at which only unleavened bread should be eaten; and so on.

Popular religious movements in the Greco-Roman world also provide background for understanding early Christian sacramental practices. Among the various movements that enjoyed popularity in the ancient world, the one that bore the closest resemblance to Christianity was the "mystery religions," secret cults that provided initiates experiences deeper than what official religions offered. One of the more popular mystery religions was devoted to the god Mithras. The historian Sean Freyne described Mithras as

> the great god of light who slew a white cosmic bull, thus releasing creative energy into the world. Mithras had a very distinctive moral character, exemplified by such symbols as fire, water, honey and the repeated emphasis of the sect on light and brightness. Despite the affirmation of the present creation in the myth the religion had developed an elaborate system of seven stages of perfection through which the soul of the individual had to pass in its struggle with evil (probably paralleling the god's initial struggle with the bull). Thus there was particular emphasis on moral attributes accompanied by an initiatory rite suited to each stage.[1]

As Freyne noted, the mystery religions and early Christianity both grounded their practices in a myth or story about the divine force's interaction with the human race, offered initiation rituals by which those joining the mystery religion could come into contact with the chief deity, and celebrated ritual reenactments of the central event in the sacred story.[2] The Christians had their own distinctive account of their sacred person who came down from heaven; they welcomed new members through a rite of initiation they called baptism; those initiated into the community were required to live by a certain moral code; and the community of believers gathered weekly for a meal, often before dawn, that celebrated the death and resurrection of their founder.

The New Testament

The New Testament does not present a fully developed theory of the sacraments, but it clearly presumes the existence of certain sacramental practices within the early Christian communities. In some New Testament writings, Christ himself instructs his disciples to baptize (Matt 28:19) and to share the Eucharist (Luke 22:19). In other writings, the scriptural author offers a reflection on the meaning of baptism (Rom 6:3–11), Eucharist (1 Cor 10:17, 11:23–34), and marriage (Eph 6:21–33), or the author simply reports a practice that would eventually become a formalized ritual within the church (e.g., anointing of the sick in Jas 5:14).

The New Testament makes three assertions that would later become essential elements in Roman Catholic sacramental theology. First, Christ has been raised from the dead and has given the gift of the Holy Spirit to the church. This theme figures prominently in Luke-Acts, but is also essential to both the Pauline and Johannine writings. As Irenaeus wrote in the second century, "Where the church is, there is the Spirit of God; and where the Spirit of God is, there is the church and every kind of grace."[3] Second, Christians share in the life of the Spirit. To drive home this point, the New Testament speaks of believers as receiving the "seal" of the Holy Spirit. Christians "were marked with the seal of the promised Holy Spirit; this is the pledge of our inheritance toward redemption as God's own people, to the praise of his glory" (Eph 1:13–14). The concept of the seal might refer to the imprinted piece of wax that closed a scroll, a brand used to identify animals, or a tattoo to mark soldiers.[4] The theologian Joseph Martos explained,

> The fathers of the church then attempted to penetrate the meaning of the 'seal of the Spirit' by reading many biblical texts…in the light of one another, and searching for an understanding that would illumine them all. Eventually they came to the understanding that receiving the Holy Spirit meant somehow receiving the image of God on one's soul, or being impressed with his seal.[5]

This change, brought about by the work of the Spirit, is called "the effect" of the sacrament, and would continue to be a point of emphasis in Catholic sacramental theology. For example, the Council of Trent speaks of "a character, namely a spiritual and indelible mark" imprinted on the soul at baptism, confirmation, and orders (hence, these sacraments cannot be repeated).[6] Third, this sealing with the Spirit was the beginning of a process of sanctification. "But it is God who established us with you in Christ and has anointed us, by putting his seal on us and giving us his Spirit in our hearts as a first installment" (2 Cor 1:21–22). In Catholic thought, the process of spiritual growth would be intimately connected with ongoing participation in the sacramental life of the church.

Sacramental Theology in the Patristic and Medieval Eras

The early Greek-speaking Christian thinkers used the word *mysteries* rather than *sacraments*. The concept of mystery (*mysterion*, *mysteria*, in Greek) appears in the later writings in the Old Testament. In the book of Daniel, for example, the term refers to "what will happen at the end of days" (Dan 2:28; see also Wis 2:22).[7] In the Gospels, Jesus entrusts his disciples with the "secret of the kingdom of God" (Mark 4:14). In Colossians and Ephesians, the concept of mystery refers to "the mystery that has been hidden throughout the ages and generations" (Col 1:26; see also Eph 1:9). At the heart of this mysterious plan of God stands Christ (Col 1:27), who offers salvation to all humankind (Eph 3:1–6). The early Christian communities began to speak of those actions that enabled believers to enter into the mystery of Christ as "mysteries." The early bishop Ignatius of Antioch (d. 107) referred to deacons as those "who serve the mysteries of Jesus Christ."[8] The Orthodox Church has continued this ancient practice of speaking of mysteries rather than sacraments.

The understanding of sacraments as mysteries fit well with the outlook influenced by the Greek philosopher Plato. *Mystery* conveys a sense of something hidden from view. For Plato, beautiful objects in this world are copies, or shadows, of what he called "the Form" of Beauty—the eternal, unchanging, immaterial essence of Beauty. With regard to the sacraments, the visible outward action of pouring water on someone expresses a deeper invisible spiritual reality of cleansing from sin. The physical elements of the sacraments—water, oil, bread—are the outward signs of a greater reality. As the great Greek theologian John Chrysostom (d. 407) wrote, "A mystery is present when we realize that something exists beyond the things we are looking at."[9] The Christian life, therefore, is a continual entrance into the mystery of Christ through participation in the mysteries of the church. For this reason, the period of instruction immediately following baptism is known as mystagogy ("to instruct into the mysteries").[10]

The term *sacrament* entered the Christian vocabulary when the Latin-speaking theologian Tertullian (d. 225) used it to translate the Greek word *mystery*. As the theologian Donald McKim noted,

> Tertullian, the first Western theologian to write in Latin, was also the first to use the term *sacramentum* to indicate a Christian theological reality in the midst of Roman culture. In classical Latin *sacramentum* has two meanings. In military matters it refers to the oath of allegiance taken by a soldier, expressing his obligation to leader and to country. In this act the soldier dedicates himself to

obey authority....In the Roman legal proceedings *sacramentum* referred to the sum of money that plaintiffs in legal cases deposited with a priest as a sign of willingness to be humbled before the "divine judgement," since it was recognized that in some cases only an appeal to the gods could determine guilt or innocence.[11]

Taken in its military sense, the term *sacramentum* conveyed the sense of having a new allegiance, a new identity, a new mission in life. In this way, the term made obvious parallels with Christian initiation. The theologian German Martinez explained, "For Tertullian, who was a lawyer and the son of a Roman officer, baptism, and the Eucharist, as rites of Christian initiation, had the character of a consecration binding a person through a covenantal relationship to a new way of life in Christ."[12]

Augustine made a lasting contribution to sacramental theology by situating sacraments within the broader discussion of "signs." The theologian Emmanuel J. Cutrone insisted that

a full understanding of Augustine's theological reflections on sacraments must begin with his treatment of signs. Augustine operates within a Platonic worldview which understands the material, visible world to be a manifestation of a deeper inner reality. What is seen and experienced are reflections of a truer world, in such a way that material reality becomes a sign which both reveals and veils the inner world.[13]

Signs point us to other realities. Words, for example, signify the objects to which they refer. For Augustine, then, sacraments are sacred signs, or signs of sacred things.

Augustine produced much of his work on sacraments in response to the Donatists. As we discussed in the previous chapter, the Donatists believed that the validity of a sacrament depended upon the holiness of the one who administered it. Those bishops who handed over the sacred texts to the Roman authorities were not legitimate pastors of the church, and any sacraments they performed were not valid. Augustine responded by identifying Christ as the true minister of the sacrament. The holiness or sinfulness of the earthly minister was irrelevant. Against the Donatists, Augustine held that baptisms performed by schismatic groups or immoral bishops were, to use the language of later theology, "efficacious." In other words, the minister's unholiness did not prevent the sacramental act from having its spiritual effect.[14] In the centuries after Augustine, this idea would be expressed in the principle that sacraments are efficacious *ex opere operato* ("from the work done"), not from the one doing the work.

With the emergence of Scholastic theology in the early medieval period, theologians sought to define more precisely theological terms and propositions. In their efforts to clarify the meaning of the term *sacraments*, theologians differentiated sacraments from other holy rituals of the church, such as blessing with holy water, and receiving ashes on the forehead. The theologian Peter Lombard (ca. 1100–60) spoke of a sacrament as "the visible form of an invisible grace." He also insisted that a true sacrament *confers* God's grace.[15] The question of how a sacrament "causes" grace preoccupied medieval theologians. Martinez argued, "The question of the operation of the sacraments (the notion of cause versus the role of sign) dominated theological speculation so that there was an inevitable tendency to ask how a sacrament works rather than why a sacrament is given."[16]

Sacramental Theology in the Protestant and Catholic Reformations

In response to the Protestant Reformers, the Catholic Church defined the number of sacraments at the Council of Trent. Luther and the other Protestant Reformers believed that abuses and superstitions had corrupted the practices of the Catholic Church, so they called for a return to a church based solely on scriptural principles. Only those acts that were explicitly instituted by Christ can rightly be called sacraments. For Luther, this eventually meant that baptism and Eucharist were the only true sacraments.

Following from this emphasis on scripture, the Protestant Reformers rooted their theology in the Word of God contained in scripture, embodied by Jesus and communicated through preaching. Luther spoke of the sacraments as vital reminders of the promises found in the Word of God. "For the word can exist without the sacrament, but the sacrament cannot exist without the word. And in case of necessity, a man can be saved without the sacrament, but not without the word."[17] The contemporary Jesuit liturgical scholar Edward J. Kilmartin offered the following assessment:

> This [Reformation] theology of the word of God represents a justifiable reaction against the tendency of contemporary school theology to exaggerate the efficacy of the sacraments as objective means of grace....But while it may be said that there were good grounds for the Reformation reaction against the popular idea, often supported unwittingly by theologians, that the sacraments are a "cheap means of grace," the Reformation alternative was frequently weakened by a reduction of the theology of the Word of God to a theology of preaching.[18]

Generally speaking, the Protestant reformers assigned the sacraments secondary importance to the Word. They tended to regard the sacraments as a means to an end. The sacraments did not convey grace themselves, but rather pointed us toward grace.

The other contributing factor in the Protestant Reformers' deemphasis on sacraments was their commitment to the principle of justification by faith, and not by works. In his 1520 treatise, "The Babylonian Captivity of the Church," Luther argued,

> If the mass is a promise, as has been said, then access to it is to be gained, not with any works, or powers, or merits of one's own, but by faith alone. For where there is the Word of the promising God, there must necessarily be the faith of the accepting man. It is plain, therefore, that the beginning of our salvation is a faith which clings to the Word of the promising God, who, without any effort on our part, in free and unmerited mercy takes the initiative and offers us the word of his promise.[19]

Calvin was equally adamant in asserting that faith was the essential element in the sacraments. The sacraments "avail and profit nothing unless received in faith. As with wine or oil or some other liquid, no matter how much you pour out, it will flow away and disappear unless the mouth of the vessel to receive it is open; moreover, the vessel will be splashed over on the outside, but still remain void and empty."[20]

The official Catholic response to the Protestant Reformers came during the seventh session of the Council of Trent in 1547. In a series of canons the bishops declared beliefs regarding the sacraments that distinguished the Catholic from the Protestant positions.

> 1. If anyone says that the sacraments of the new law were not all instituted by our lord Jesus Christ; or that there are more or fewer than seven: namely, baptism, confirmation, eucharist, penance, last anointing, order, matrimony; or that one or other of these seven is not truly and in the full sense a sacrament: let him be anathema [meaning that the one espousing such a belief is considered excluded from the church].

> 4. If anyone says that the sacraments of the new law are not necessary for salvation but are superfluous, and that people obtain the grace of justification from God without them or a desire for them, by faith alone, though all [seven sacraments] are not necessary for each individual: let him be anathema.

> 5. If anyone says that these sacraments have been instituted only to nourish faith: let him be anathema.

> 8. If anyone says that grace is not conferred by the sacraments of the new law through the sacramental action, but that faith in the divine promise is by itself sufficient for obtaining the grace: let him be anathema.[21]

The bishops affirmed, in contradiction to Luther, that there are seven true sacraments, that participation in the sacraments is essential to the Christian life, that sacraments are not merely a means to express or confirm one's faith, and that sacraments are efficacious *ex opere operato*.

Sacramental Theology in the Nineteenth and Twentieth Centuries

In the nineteenth and twentieth centuries, various movements emerged within the Catholic Church that would have their impact on the Vatican II teachings on the sacraments. Perhaps the most important of all was the liturgical movement spearheaded by Benedictine monks whose historical scholarship yielded new insights into the history and dynamics of the sacraments. Special attention was given to the early church's liturgical thought and practice. At the beginning of the twentieth century, Pope Pius X publicly endorsed the aims of the liturgical movement, which increased academic and pastoral interest in liturgical renewal. Scholarly journals and academic institutes dedicated to the liturgy were founded. This scholarship would deeply impact the deliberations on the liturgy at the Second Vatican Council, most dramatically in its recommendations for liturgical renewal contained in chapter three of "The Constitution on the Sacred Liturgy."

Another significant development in twentieth-century theology was the incorporation of philosophical categories and terminology other than Thomism (the philosophy of Thomas Aquinas) into Catholic theology. Many scholars found the language and concerns of Thomism unresponsive to the questions posed by modern Catholics. As a result, they drew upon the work of modern philosophical movements of existentialism or personalism, modern psychological movements such as "depth psychology" or life-cycle development, anthropological studies on cultural rites of passage, and the field of linguistics and its theories regarding the meaning of words and the communication of ideas. This diversity of approaches resulted in a diversity of sacramental theologies in the post–Vatican II church.

A Survey of Contemporary Sacramental Theology

The present diversity of sacramental theologies provides a number of approaches for discussion: human experience, symbols, Christ, the Trinity, and the church.

The primary text for the religious instruction of many Catholics living before Vatican II was the *Baltimore Catechism*. Presented in a question-and-answer format, the *Baltimore Catechism* dealt with the central issues of the Catholic faith. To the question, "What is a sacrament?" the *Baltimore Catechism* gave the answer that was repeated throughout countless classrooms. "A sacrament is an outward sign instituted by Christ to give grace."[22]

In the years following the Council, many theologians and religious educators believed that sacraments could be better approached by situating them within the broader category of common human experience. The theologian Tad Guzie proposed the following alternative understanding of sacraments: "A sacrament is the festive action in which Christians assemble to celebrate their lived experience and to call to heart their common story."[23] There is an innate human drive to give expression to both the heights and depths of our personal and common experience. Sacraments, then, are examples of Christian festivity that celebrate and mourn our experiences, such as birth and death, as interpreted in light of the central story proclaimed in the Gospel.

In a second approach in contemporary sacramental theology, special attention is paid to the power of symbols. In describing the role of symbols, the twentieth-century Protestant theologian Paul Tillich stated that an essential characteristic of a symbol is "that it opens up levels of reality which otherwise are closed for us."[24] Symbols are physical objects or images, but they connect humans with cherished beliefs, profound loyalties, or spiritual truths. The waters of baptism, the bread brought to the eucharistic table, and the exchange of rings are therefore not "just symbols," but gateways into a deeper mystery that defies complete verbal expression. A symbol is not a dispensable element, but rather as Tillich noted, a symbol "participates in that to which it points: the flag participates in the power and dignity of the nation for which it stands."[25]

A third approach sees the sacraments as the present form of the very same ministry of Jesus two millennia ago. The French Dominican A.-M. Roguet once offered the following reflection on the sacraments:

> Just as of old Christ touched and cured the blind, the paralytics, the feverish, just as he blessed his disciples, breathed upon them, laid his hands upon them, broke bread for them, so in the sacraments we are absolved, healed and fed, hands are laid upon us and we are blessed in Christ's name. By the sacraments we are put into contact with the living Christ just as truly, although in another manner, as if we had escorted him on the paths of Galilee or in the streets of Jerusalem.[26]

As the eternal Word, the Son continues to do through the sacraments what he did while he walked on this earth. Based on Christ's assurance that "where two or three are gathered in my name, I am there among them" (Matt 18:20), Christians in any era can continue to experience his healing and sanctifying presence.

A fourth approach, represented by Edward Kilmartin, is Trinitarian. "What the sacraments manifest and realize is the Church in its deepest being, namely the communion of life between the Father and humankind in Christ through the gift of the Holy Spirit, which entails sharing the life of faith between those who participate in the mystery of the shared Trinitarian life."[27] In the same vein, Kilmartin speaks of the earthly liturgy as a foretaste of the heavenly liturgy, which he describes in Trinitarian language:

> In the heavenly liturgy there is the Father who sends, the Son who is sent and who sends, and the Spirit who is sent to be the bond of unity. There are the angels and blessed who enjoy the incorruptible life. The divine energy that vivifies the blessed comes from the thrones of the Father *and* the Son. The risen Lord is with the Father, the

source of all, to pour forth the "life-giving water," the Holy Spirit.[28]

Through the power of the Holy Spirit, our earthly liturgy joins with the heavenly liturgy. "The earthly liturgy is the enactment of the desire and hope for something that already exists elsewhere. But it is also a real participation in the heavenly liturgy."[29]

A fifth approach situates the seven sacraments within the context of the church itself as a sacrament; that is, a bearer of God's presence in the world. The Jesuit Karl Rahner was one of the theologians before the Second Vatican Council who proposed the concept that the church was the "fundamental sacrament." In this view, the seven sacraments are instances in the larger life of the church as the "the presence of saving grace in the world."[30] This idea was incorporated into statements at Vatican II and subsequently gained wider acceptance in post–Vatican II theology. The liturgist Kevin Irwin reported,

> A major revolution occurred in contemporary Roman Catholic sacramental theology when theologians capitalized on the seminal insights of Edward Schillebeeckx, Karl Rahner and Otto Semmelroth (among others) who focused attention on Jesus and the church as primordial sacraments. Spurred on by *Lumen gentium's* statement that the church is "a kind of sacrament or sign of intimate union with God, and of the unity of all humankind" much postconciliar writing on sacraments has referred to Christ and the church as "sacraments" and that these are the foundations for the celebration of all liturgy and the sacraments. Thus the ritual celebration of liturgy and sacraments has commonly been placed within a "foundational framework" that emphasized the role and action of Jesus and the church in the ritual celebration of sacraments.[31]

As Rahner insisted, the seven sacraments need to be situated theologically within the sacramentality of the church, which itself is derived from the sacramentality of Christ. "By the very fact of being in that way the enduring presence of Christ in the world, the

Church is truly the fundamental sacrament, the well-spring of the sacraments in the strict sense. From Christ the Church has an intrinsically sacramental structure"[32]

Early Rites of the Sacraments of Initiation

Now that we have reviewed some of the history and theology of the sacraments, let's turn to the early rites of the sacraments of initiation and then to the individual sacraments.

In the early church, baptism, confirmation, and the first reception of the Eucharist were three moments in a larger single act of initiation into the Christian community. We need to begin our examination of these three sacraments of initiation by putting them back into their original liturgical context. We will then examine the theology of each of the three sacraments individually.

The early church did not have a completely uniform manner of initiating Christians. The initiation rite in the East Syrian church, for example, differed in some ways from that in the Roman church. Despite these differences in local customs, however, we can discern a fairly common pattern. As a general rule, the three actions of baptizing, anointing, and receiving Eucharist for the first time were united in a single ceremony. The primary sources that we have for reconstructing the initiation ritual in the west are Justin Martyr's *First Apology* (ca. 150), Tertullian's treatise *On Baptism* (ca. 200), and *The Apostolic Tradition* (ca. 215) attributed to Hippolytus of Rome.[33]

In his study on early Christian initiation practice, the liturgist Aidan Kavanagh offered the following description of the pattern that developed in the Western church.

> The structure of initiation in this early Graeco-Latin context involves 1) stress on *instruction preparatory for baptism*; 2) an *anointing* with exorcized oil after Satan has been renounced; 3) the *water bath* by triple immersion in the Name of the Trinity; 4) an *anointing with chrism* (Tertullian) or *oil of thanksgiving* (Hippolytus): a *hand-laying* by the bishop with prayer invoking the Holy Spirit, joined in Hippolytus with a final anointing on the

forehead with consecrated oil as a "sealing"; 6) the *eucharist*.[34]

The first step in this sequence of events that comprised the process of initiation was the period of instruction preceding baptism known as the catechumenate. Those enrolled in the catechumenate were catechumens. The *Apostolic Tradition* recommended a three-year catechumenate. The next several steps in the sequence of events typically took place during the Easter Vigil. According to the *Apostolic Tradition*, the catechumens gathered on Holy Saturday and kept watch during the night. As the sun rose on Easter morning, those to be baptized removed their clothing. Children were baptized first, men second, and women last. The presbyter asked each catechumen to renounce Satan. The presbyter then anointed the person with "the oil of exorcism" and presented each person to the bishop for baptism. A deacon assisted each person into the water and immersed the person in the baptismal waters three times, each immersion following a profession of faith on the part of the one being baptized. The baptized person then came out of the water and was anointed with the oil of thanksgiving. The bishop laid hands on each of the newly baptized and prayed over them. The newly welcomed members of the church then received Eucharist with the community. *The Apostolic Tradition* reports the custom of sharing milk mixed with honey, a symbolic representation of entering the spiritual promised land, a land filled with milk and honey (Exod 3:8).

The rite of initiation found in the *Apostolic Tradition* eventually became divided into the three distinct sacraments of baptism, confirmation, and Eucharist. One reason for this change was the decision in Western churches not to permit priests to perform the postbaptismal anointing, thus separating baptism from confirmation and restricting confirmation to the bishops. In a letter to one of his bishops, Pope Innocent I (d. 417) offered the following instruction:

> Concerning the consignation [anointing in the sign of the cross] of infants, it is clear that this should not be done by any but the bishop. For presbyters, although they are priests, have not attained the highest rank of the pontificate. The right of bishops alone to seal (sign) and to

deliver the Spirit the Paraclete is proved not only by the custom of the Church, but also by that reading in the Acts of the Apostles [Acts 8:14–17] which tells how Peter and John were directed to deliver the Holy Spirit to people who were already baptized. For it is permissible for presbyters, either in the absence of the bishop, or when they baptize in his presence to anoint the baptized with chrism [oil mixed with perfume], but only with such as has been consecrated by the bishop: and even then they are not to sign the brow with that oil, for this is reserved to bishops alone when they deliver the Holy Spirit.[35]

Following the Second Vatican Council, however, the church sought to reinstitute the ancient pattern of initiation, beginning with the acceptance into the catechumenate and culminating in the baptism, anointing, and reception of the Eucharist at the Easter Vigil celebration. The result was the establishment of the Rite of Christian Initiation of Adults (RCIA), which has now become the typical manner in which adult converts are welcomed into the church. In this situation (and sometimes other circumstances where a bishop is not available), a priest can confirm.

Baptism

The New Testament writings regarding baptism fall into three categories: Jesus' own baptism by John the Baptist, the teachings of Jesus dealing with baptism or water, and reflections on the meaning of baptism by various authors in the New Testament beyond the Gospels. We will focus our attention on the third category of writings, but first we need to say a word about the first two.

The Synoptic Gospels record Jesus' baptism by John in the Jordan River (Mark 1:9–11; Matt 3:13–17; Luke 3:21–22). The details of the baptism story vary among the three Gospels, but in all three Jesus is baptized and the Spirit descends on him "in bodily form like a dove." The heavenly voice proclaims Jesus as the Son with whom God is well pleased. In the Synoptic Gospels Jesus rarely uses the term *baptism*. On one occasion, he asks James and

John, "Are you able to drink the cup that I drink, or be baptized with the baptism that I am baptized with?" (Mark 10:38). In John's Gospel, with its rich imagery and symbolic meanings, Jesus' teachings on water and washing may carry baptismal connotations. In his discussion with Nicodemus, Jesus declares, "Very truly, I tell you, no one can enter the kingdom of God without being born of water and Spirit" (John 3:5). Many ancient commentators detected baptismal overtunes in the scene of Jesus washing the feet of the disciples in which Jesus tells Peter, "Unless I wash you, you have no share with me" (John 13:8).

New Testament passages that fall into the third category can be found in Acts, 1 Peter, and Paul's Letter to the Romans. In each of these three writings, we find early Christian understandings of baptism. In Acts, baptism is associated with forgiveness of sins and entrance into the Christian way of life. While baptism is associated with the reception of the Holy Spirit, Acts does not speak uniformly of the sequence of events. In Peter's speech in Acts 2, baptism precedes the reception of the Holy Spirit. "Peter said to them, 'Repent, and be baptized every one of you in the name of Jesus Christ so that your sins may be forgiven; and you will receive the gift of the Holy Spirit'" (Acts 2:38). In Acts 10, however, as Peter is preaching, the Holy Spirit descends on the Gentile Cornelius, so Peter orders that Cornelius and the others be baptized (Acts 10:44–48).

First Peter contains a number of baptismal references. Many scholars believe that the opening section (1 Pet 1:3—2:10) is an early Christian reflection on the meaning of baptism. In the third chapter of 1 Peter we find an example of Christian typological interpretation of the Old Testament in which the Noah story prefigured Christian baptism:

> God waited patiently in the days of Noah, during the building of the ark, in which a few, that is, eight persons, were saved through water. And baptism, which this prefigured, now saves you—not as a removal of dirt from the body, but as an appeal to God for a good conscience, through the resurrection of Jesus Christ...(1 Pet 3:20–21)

We find similar typological interpretation in the early mystagogical literature. For example, Ambrose (d. 397), the bishop of Milan, believed the curing of Naaman the leper in the waters of the Jordan River (2 Kgs 5) to be a prefigurement of Christian baptism (*The Mysteries*, 3.16–18).

In his Letter to the Romans, Paul describes baptism as a sharing in the death and resurrection of Christ. The symbolism works best in the case of adults who are totally immersed in a river or some other body of water. As their heads are immersed under water, they are incorporated into Christ's death. The first breath they take after they emerge from the waters symbolizes their sharing in the resurrection of Christ.

> Do you not know that all of us who have been baptized into Christ Jesus were baptized into his death? Therefore we have been buried with him by baptism into death, so that, just as Christ was raised from the dead by the glory of the Father, so we too might walk in newness of life. For if we have been united with him in a death like his, we will certainly be united with him in a resurrection like his (Rom 6:3–5).

This theology of baptism as a symbolic reenactment of, and participation in, the death and resurrection of Christ permeates Paul's understanding of the Christian life: "For through the law I died to the law, so that I might live for God. I have been crucified with Christ; and it is no longer I who live, but it is Christ who lives in me" (Gal 2:19–20). Just as the newly baptized were wrapped in white linen garments, those who were "baptized into Christ have clothed yourselves with Christ" (Gal 3:27).

The understanding of baptism as the sign of a person's acceptance of Christ and the renunciation of his or her former way of living made sense in the case of an adult convert, but a question naturally arose in the early church: Is it appropriate to baptize infants? The *Apostolic Tradition* mentioned the baptism of infants, and Tertullian acknowledged the practice, though he had reservations about the wisdom of infant baptism. The practice of infant baptism, however, was at the heart of the battle between Augustine and a group known as the Pelagians. Although we do not know exactly what Pelagius himself taught, Pelagianism has come to refer to a set of beliefs about sin. Pelagians held that sin is a matter of human choice and that humans, apart from God's grace, have the ability to avoid sin. This seemed to the Pelagians the only way to preserve the concept of human responsibility.

Augustine believed that the Pelagians were minimizing the corruption of the human will and overlooking the need for God's grace to move the person to choose the morally correct act. Augustine's response to the Pelagians led him to discuss the concept of "original sin." The theologian John H. McKenna offered the following account of the progression of Augustine's thought on the question of "original sin."

> It was Augustine, however, who was to set the tone for our Western tradition on original sin. He seems to have moved through several stages in his thinking. At first, he passed over the question of infant baptism, noting that it was an obscure question but that someday reason would find an answer. He then moved, in his anti-Donatist writings, to a position that somehow the parents and the Church will supply the necessary faith for the infant. And again, arguing against the Pelagians that the forces of evil are strong and that salvation comes only from God in Jesus Christ, Augustine addresses the issue of infant baptism. The reasoning, which also appears in the provincial synod in Carthage in 418, goes like this: the Church has a tradition of baptizing infants. There must be a reason for this practice. The creeds and Acts 2:38 speak of "baptism for the forgiveness of sins." There must be, therefore, some sin on the infant's soul. So there must be a sin which is somehow inherited. Augustine was to name this sin "original sin."[36]

Augustine based this theory of original sin on the Latin translation of Romans 5:12 that stated that, just "as sin came into the world through one man and death through sin,…so death spread to all in whom all sinned."[37] The Latin text read "in whom all sinned" rather than "because all sinned," suggesting that all humanity shared in some way in the sin of Adam. It is also important to note that Augustine moved from the practice of infant baptism to the concept of original sin, and not the other way around. Augustine's argument gained wide acceptance. In the centuries following Augustine it became common to speak of the purpose of baptism as the "washing away of original sin."

In the Protestant Reformation, Luther accepted Augustine's theology supporting infant baptism, but other Protestant thinkers rejected the practice. The Anabaptists believed that Christianity required a conscious, voluntary decision; therefore, only adults should be baptized. The Anabaptists consequently rebaptized those members of the church who had been baptized as infants because those infant baptisms were considered invalid. Another group known as the Spiritualists assigned little importance to external rituals, believing that faith and spiritual enlightenment had nothing to do with water, bread, or oil. These elements might express a spiritual state of being, but they do not bring this spiritual state of being into existence. The Roman Catholic Church acknowledges "one baptism for the forgiveness of sins" and so those who were baptized in Protestant churches are received into the Catholic Church without being rebaptized.

Confirmation

As with infant baptism, the practice of confirmation was also called into question by many Protestant Reformers. The positions ranged from the immediate decision on the part of the Church of England to retain it as a sacrament to doing away with it entirely. Luther and Calvin fell somewhere in between the two. Martinez noted,

> The reformers refuted the sacramentality of confirmation because it had not been explicitly instituted by Christ. It also appeared to devalue the role and content of baptism. They reduced confirmation to a non-sacramental rite of public witnessing to one's faith and commitment. It was celebrated as part of a maturing process, before the coming of adulthood.[38]

Some contemporary Catholic thinkers have expressed support for Luther and Calvin's reservations about confirmation as a separate sacrament.

There are, in short, three general stances toward confirmation in contemporary Catholic theology. Some support the traditional Catholic position expressed in the decrees of Trent. Others call for a change in the practice of having confirmation as a separate sacrament. Those in the third school of thought believe that confirmation should be a separate sacrament, but offer a different rationale for its existence than the one expounded at Trent.

Trent did not devote a great deal of time to the question of confirmation. The bishops did, however, declare: "If anyone says that confirmation of the baptised is an empty ceremony, and not rather a true and proper sacrament; or that at one time it was nothing but a form of religious instruction in which those approaching adolescence presented an account of their faith publicly to the church: let him be anathema."[39] The traditional theological account of confirmation that developed after Trent described confirmation as a sacrament in which the Holy Spirit was bestowed on the person being confirmed in order to spiritually strengthen the person.[40] In language born in the days of chivalry, those who were confirmed became "soldiers of Christ."

Those in the second school of thought insist that confirmation as it is currently practiced lacks a credible theological basis. In the RCIA program, the anointing is one aspect of the entire process of initiation, and in this context the practice makes sense. In the majority of cases, however, confirmation is received years after baptism. If baptism is the moment of reception in the church and involves the reception of the Holy Spirit, then a separate sacrament of confirmation that also imparts the Spirit diminishes the importance of baptism. Either people are welcomed into the church and receive the Holy Spirit at baptism, or they do not. If baptism is the sacrament in which both events occur, then confirmation has no place.

Those in the third school of thought maintain that confirmation is a fitting and appropriate sacrament, but often explain the purpose of the sacrament in ways that have less to do with spiritual strengthening and more to do with faith development. In their study of the various current understandings of confirmation, many religious-education scholars Robert L. Browning and Roy A. Reed identified many different approaches, including the following as a typical alternative explanation for confirmation.

> 3. *The ratification of a person's baptism.* After a rigorous period of religious instruction, and after careful examination of the individual's knowledge of the faith, the candidate makes an autonomous decision to be personally committed to it and is admitted in a public ceremony to full rights in the church.[41]

Browning and Reed cited the research of the liturgist Paul Turner who examined confirmation programs in several dioceses and archdioceses throughout the country and "observed more emphasis being placed upon mature, personal, free response and affirmation of the baptismal faith than upon the gift of the Holy Spirit."[42] This approach to confirmation stresses the need for a public confirmation of the faith that the individual received at baptism. This public declaration of faith would occur around the age when Jewish boys celebrate their bar mitzvah and Jewish girls their bat mitzvah. In the early church, this anointing followed baptism and preceded the first sharing in the Eucharist, which is what usually happens today in RCIA programs. Today for young people confirmation is typically received in the mid-teens after both baptism at infancy and first communion around second or third grade.

Eucharist

In order to understand the importance of receiving first communion and the centrality of the Eucharist to Catholic life, we need to investigate the origin, history, and theology of the Eucharist.

There are four accounts of the institution of the eucharist found in the New Testament (1 Cor 11:23–26; Mark 14:22–25; Matt 26:26–29; Luke 22:14–20). There are differences in wording, sequence of events, and emphasis. For example, Jesus' command to continue the practice of breaking bread in memory of him appears in 1 Corinthians and Luke, but not Matthew and Mark. We begin with a few background comments on the various accounts.

The earliest of the four accounts is found in 1 Corinthians.

> For I received from the Lord what I also handed on to you, that the Lord Jesus on the night when he was betrayed took a loaf of bread, and when he had given thanks, he broke it and said, "This is my body that is for you. Do this in remembrance of me." In the same way he took the cup also, after supper, saying, "This cup is the new covenant in my blood. Do this, as often as you drink it, in remembrance of me." (1 Cor 11:23–25)

Paul uses the term *body* in reference to both the Eucharist and the church, so the Eucharist always has an ecclesiological connotation. Paul also describes Eucharist as a meal celebrated in anticipation of the return of Christ. "For as often as you eat the bread and drink the cup, you proclaim the Lord's death until he comes" (1 Cor 11:26). Paul records Jesus as describing the cup as a "new covenant in my blood." This expression recalls Moses ratifying the Sinai covenant with the Israelites by sprinkling the people with blood from the bulls offered in sacrifice. Jeremiah 31:31 speaks of a time when the Lord will make a "new covenant" with the house of Israel and the house of Judah.

In the Synoptic Gospels, Mark's and Matthew's versions are very similar. In Mark, Jesus says, "This is my blood of the covenant, which is poured out for many" (Mark 14:24). In Matthew, the parallel verse includes a reference to the forgiveness of sins: "Drink from it, all of you; for this is my blood of the covenant, which is poured out for many for forgiveness of sins" (Matt 26:27b–28). Luke's account shares many similarities with Paul's account. Luke explicitly mentions that the Last Supper is a Passover meal (Luke 22:15), though that fact is strongly implied in Mark and Matthew. Paul speaks of Christ as a Passover lamb. "For our paschal lamb, Christ, has been sacrificed" (1 Cor 5:7). At the Passover meal, unleavened bread was eaten. The Passover commemorates the exodus from Egypt and the sparing of the Israelites' life after the blood of the lamb was placed on the doorposts.

John's Gospel does not have an account of the institution of the Eucharist. During the Last Supper, which is not a Passover meal in John, Jesus washes the feet of the disciples. John's Gospel, however, does contain a very important passage regarding the Eucharist. In John's Gospel, a miracle (or sign) is often followed by a discourse by Jesus. As Passover nears, Jesus performs the miracle of the multiplication of loaves and fish. (This miracle is the only one recorded in all four of the Gospels.) Just as he does at the Last Supper in the Synoptics, Jesus takes the loaves into his hands, gives thanks, and distributes them. After the multiplication of the loaves, Jesus delivers the "Bread of Life" discourse in which he offers a typological interpretation of the Old Testament story of manna, or bread, coming from heaven (Exod 16). Just as the manna came down from heaven during the Israelites' time in the desert and provided food for their survival, Christ is the Bread of Life who has come down from heaven so that we may eat and have eternal life.

> "I am the bread of life. Your ancestors ate the manna in the wilderness, and they died. This is the bread that comes down from heaven, so that one may eat of it and not die. I am the living bread that came down from heaven. Whoever eats of this bread will live forever; and the bread that I will give for this life of the world is my flesh."
>
> The Jews then disputed among themselves, saying, "How can this man give us his flesh to eat?" So Jesus said to them. "Very truly, I tell you, unless you eat the flesh of the Son of Man and drink his blood, you have no life in you. Those who eat my flesh and drink my blood have eternal life, and I will raise them up on the last day; for my flesh is true food and my blood is true drink." (John 6:48–55)

It is also important to note that drinking blood would have been a repulsive act for first-century Jews. The Torah forbade the eating of meat with the blood still in it (Gen 9:4; Lev 17:10–14).

EUCHARIST IN THE EARLY CHURCH

The early Christian eucharistic celebrations were modeled on the synagogue service which, according to the historian Thomas Bokenkotter, "began with a greeting and reflection, followed by a reading from Torah (the Law), a hymn and reflection. A second reading was taken from the Prophets. A sermon came next to relate the readings to present concerns, and the service concluded with a prayer, blessing and dismissal."[43] To this earlier service devoted to the scriptures, Christians added the eucharistic meal (celebrated in a person's house, called house-churches; see 1 Cor 11:20–22). This basic structure underlies the Emmaus story in Luke 24. Luke employs an interesting literary device. Two disciples leaving Jerusalem are met by the Risen Lord, but they do not recognize him. After discussing the scriptures, they are intrigued by this man who has journeyed with them and they ask him to stay with them. "When he was at table with them, he took bread, blessed and broke it, and gave it to them. Then their eyes were opened, and they recognized him; and he vanished from their sight" (Luke 24:30–31). First came the reflection on scripture; then Jesus was made known to them in the breaking of the bread (Luke 24:35). This two-part structure can still be detected in today's Mass, with its division into the Liturgy of the Word and the Liturgy of the Eucharist.

Fragments of these early Christian liturgies are found in the letters of Ignatius of Antioch, *1 Clement*, and the *Didache*, but in the view of the theologian K. W. Noakes, the "earliest reasonably detailed account of the Eucharist is given by Justin [Martyr] (mid-second century), who describes two celebrations, one following baptism, and the other an ordinary Sunday service."[44] In his *First Apology*, Justin Martyr gave the following description of the Sunday liturgy:

> On the day which is called Sunday we have a common assembly of all who live in the cities or in the outlying districts, and the memoirs of the Apostles or the writings of the Prophets are read, as long as there is time. Then, when the reader has finished, the president of the assembly verbally admonishes and invites all to imitate such examples of virtue. Then we all stand up together and offer up our

prayers, and, as we said before, after we finish our prayers, bread and wine and water are presented. He who presides likewise offers up prayers and thanksgivings, to the best of his ability, and the people express their approval by saying "Amen." The Eucharistic elements are distributed and consumed by those present, and to those who are absent they are sent through the deacons. The wealthy, if they wish, contribute whatever they desire, and the collection is placed in the custody of the president.[45]

Earlier in the *Apology*, Justin described the Eucharist in language that would anticipate many later eucharistic controversies in the Western church.

Not as ordinary bread or ordinary drink do we partake of them, but just as, through the word of God, our Savior Jesus Christ became Incarnate and took upon himself flesh and blood for our salvation, so, we have been taught, the food which has been made the Eucharist by the prayer of His word, and which nourishes our flesh and blood by assimilation, is *both the flesh and blood of that Jesus* who was made flesh.[46]

Justin's theology reflected the deep influence of the Bread of Life theology of John's Gospel.

TRANSUBSTANTIATION

The "real presence," meaning the actual presence, of Christ at the eucharistic celebration, and more specifically within the consecrated bread and wine, generated a series of theological debates beginning in the eleventh century. The French theologian Berengar of Tours (d. 1088) created a stir by denying the physical presence of Christ in the Eucharist. Martos outlined the logic of Berengar's position:

To Berengar it seemed natural to assume that things were what they appeared to be, and since the bread and wine did not change their appearance after the words of consecration were spoken, he reasoned that they must still be bread and wine. Christ's presence in the eucharist therefore had to be a spiritual, not a physical presence, and Berengar used Augustine's definition of a sacrament as "a sign of a sacred reality" to support his position. If the eucharistic bread and wine were a sacrament, he argued, they had to be a sign of Christ's body and blood, not identical with it. Besides, if the pieces of bread were really Christ's body, then logically speaking the body of Christ was in pieces, and if the wine were really his blood then his blood was not in his body.[47]

In his study of the history of eucharistic theology, the theologian Gary Macy argued that Berengar and his opponents shared a similar problem: "How could one affirm that the presence of the Lord in the eucharist was a saving presence (i.e., *real*) and yet also admit the obvious fact that the Lord was not present to the senses?"[48] The solution to this problem that gained the widest acceptance was the doctrine known as transubstantiation.

Transubstantiation affirms the real presence of Christ in the Eucharist. One of the most common objections to the concept of Christ's real presence was that Christ was now seated at the right hand of the Father, so how can Christ be present on an altar? The contemporary theologian George Hunsinger offered the following summary of Thomas Aquinas's response to this objection.

> Real presence, Aquinas continued, must be kept logically distinct from local presence. "The body of Christ is not in this sacrament in the way a body is located in a place. The dimensions of a body in a place correspond with the dimensions of the place that contains it. Christ's body is here in a special way that is proper to this sacrament" (*ST*, 3a. 75,1). Or again, Christ's body is in the sacrament "[not] as if it were present in the way that is natural for a body to be present, that is, visibly in its normal appearance...[but] a spiritual, non-visible presence, in the way of a spirit and by the power of the Spirit" (*ST*, 3a. 75,1).

Christ's bodily presence, Aquinas affirmed, is spiritual, and it comes about only by the power of the Holy Spirit. Nevertheless, although lacking in spatial dimensions, it is also substantial.[49]

For Aquinas, the presence of Christ at the Eucharist is not a physical presence in the sense of taking up space, or being visible to our eyes, as a material object would. Nevertheless, the presence of Christ is "substantial."

Transubstantiation also proposes a way of speaking about the change within the bread and wine themselves. The language of the crucial distinction is borrowed from Aristotle. If you visit certain relatives only each summer, you may be struck by how much a teenage cousin has grown in a year's time. Your cousin has a different physical appearance, but he or she is still the same person. Aristotle called that which remains unchanged "substance" and those things that do change he called "accidents." Employing Aristotle's distinction, Aquinas spoke of the Eucharist as a change in the substance of, but not the accidents of, the bread and wine; that is, their appearance, taste, texture. The bread actually becomes the Body of Christ and the wine actually becomes the Blood of Christ, but the bread retains all the physical appearances of bread, and likewise, the wine retain all the physical characteristics of wine. This teaching first received official approval at the Fourth Lateran Council (1215) and was reaffirmed at the Council of Trent and the Second Vatican Council.

So far we have considered the baptismal union with Christ, the anointing with chrism, and Christ's presence in the breaking of the bread. The Catholic community also celebrates the healing power of Christ in the anointing of the sick and in reconciliation, as well as in the covenant of love between a husband and a wife, and in the ministry of holy orders. We turn attention in the next chapter to the sacraments of healing (reconciliation, anointing of the sick) and the sacraments of commitment (marriage, orders).

Discussion Questions

1. How would you define the term *sacrament*?
2. Does it make sense to define a sacrament as "the visible form of an invisible grace"?
3. Should we baptize infants? Why? Why not?
4. Should baptism, confirmation, and Eucharist be celebrated in a single ceremony?
5. Do you believe that we are born with original sin? What implications follow for your understanding of baptism?
6. How do you interpret Jesus' words at the Last Supper regarding the bread and wine?
7. How do you interpret the Bread of Life discourse in John's Gospel?
8. What is transubstantiation? Is the concept intelligible? Is it meaningful?
9. In what ways would you describe the real presence of Christ in the Eucharist?
10. Suppose you were teaching a CCD class for second-grade students. How would you describe the eucharist to them?

Suggested Readings

For a very helpful introduction to the sacraments see German Martinez, *Signs of Freedom* (Mahwah, NJ: Paulist Press, 2003); Francis Schüssler Fiorenza and John P. Galvin, eds. *Systematic Theology*, Volume Two (Minneapolis: Fortress Press, 1991); and part five of Richard P. McBrien's *Catholicism*, New Edition (San Francisco: HarperCollins, 1994). For a history of the sacraments, see Joseph Martos, *Doors to the Sacred*, Revised and Updated Edition (Liguori, MO: Liguori, 2001). For the sacraments of initiation, see Kenan B. Osborne, *The Christian Sacraments of Initiation* (Mahwah, NJ: Paulist Press, 1987). For a history of Christian initiation, see Maxwell E. Johnson, *The Rites of Christian Initiation* (Collegeville, MN: The Liturgical Press, 1999). For a detailed history of eucharistic theology and practice, see David N. Power, *The Eucharistic Mystery* (New York: Crossroad, 1992).

Notes

1. Sean Freyne, *The World of the New Testament* (Wilmington, DE: Michael Glazier, 1980), 38–39.

2. Ibid., 40–41.

3. Quoted in Jaroslav Pelikan, *The Christian Tradition*, vol. 1 (Chicago: University of Chicago Press, 1971), 156.

4. Joseph Martos, *Doors to the Sacred* (Garden City, NY: Doubleday and Co., 1981), 45–51.

5. Ibid., 49.

6. Council of Trent, Session Seven, in Norman P. Tanner, ed., *Decrees of the Ecumenical Councils*, vol. 2 (London: Sheed and Ward; Washington, DC: Georgetown University Press, 1990), 685.

7. Alexander Ganoczy, *An Introduction to Catholic Sacramental Theology* (New York: Paulist Press, 1984), 12.

8. Ignatius of Antioch, "The Epistle to the Trallians," 2, in Maxwell Staniforth, trans., *Early Christian Writings* (New York: Penguin Books, 1968), 95. See also Johann Auer, *A General Doctrine of the Sacraments and the Mystery of the Eucharist* (Washington, DC: The Catholic University of America Press, 1995), 10.

9. Quoted in Martos, *Doors to the Sacred*, 41.

10. "Mystagogy," in Richard P. McBrien, ed., *The HarperCollins Encyclopedia of Catholicism* (San Francisco: HarperCollins, 1995), 898.

11. Donald K. McKim, *Theological Turning Points* (Atlanta: John Knox Press, 1988), 117.

12. German Martinez, *Signs of Freedom* (Mahwah, NJ: Paulist Press, 2003), 32.

13. Emmanuel J. Cutrone, "Sacraments," in Allan D. Fitzgerald, ed., *Augustine Through the Ages* (Grand Rapids: William B. Eerdmans, 1999), 741.

14. Augustine further distinguished between the validity and the "fruitfulness" of a sacrament. A validly performed sacrament may not always produce a change in the person's behavior. See Martos, *Doors*, 58; and Maxwell E. Johnson, *The Rites of Christian Initiation* (Collegeville, MN: The Liturgical Press, 1999), 151–53.

15. Peter Lombard, *Sentences*, Book IV, in Eugene R. Fairweather, ed., *A Scholastic Miscellany: Anselm to Ockham* (Philadelphia: Westminster Press, 1956), 338–39.

16. Martinez, *Signs of Freedom*, 35. Martinez quotes from Regis Duffy, "Sacraments in General," in *Systematic Theology*, F. Schüssler Fiorenza and J. Galvin, eds. (Minneapolis: Fortress Press, 1991), 195.

17. Quoted in McKim, *Theological Turning Points*, 122.

18. Edward J. Kilmartin, *Christian Liturgy: Theology and Practice* I (Kansas City, MO: Sheed and Ward, 1988), 294.

19. Martin Luther, "The Babylonian Captivity of the Church," in *Three Treatises* (Philadelphia: Fortress Press, 1970), 156.

20. John Calvin, *Institutes of the Christian Religion*, IV.14.17 (Philadelphia: Westminster Press, 1960), 1292.

21. Council of Trent, Session Seven, in Norman P. Tanner, ed., *Decrees of the Ecumenical Councils* Volume Two, 684–85.

22. *The New St. Joseph Baltimore Catechism*, rev. ed. (New York: Catholic Book Publishing Co., 1969), 113.

23. Tad Guzie, *The Book of Sacramental Basics* (New York: Paulist Press, 1981), 53.

24. Paul Tillich, *Dynamics of Faith* (New York: Harper and Brothers, 1957), 42.

25. Ibid.

26. A.-M. Roguet, *Christ Acts through Sacraments* (Collegeville, MN: The Liturgical Press, 1954), 36.

27. Edward J. Kilmartin, "Sacraments as Liturgy of the Church," *Theological Studies* 50 (1989): 527.

28. Ibid., 189.

29. Ibid., 190.

30. Karl Rahner, "The Fundamental Sacrament and the Sacraments," in Gerald A. McCool, ed., *A Rahner Reader* (New York: Crossroad, 1975), 280.

31. Kevin W. Irwin, "A Sacramental World—Sacramentality as the Primary Language for Sacraments," *Worship* 76 (2002): 200.

32. Karl Rahner, *The Church and the Sacraments* (New York: Herder and Herder, 1963), 18. I discovered this quotation in Kenan B. Osborne, *Sacramental Theology* (Mahwah, NJ: Paulist Press, 1988), 91.

33. For the historical background, I am relying upon chapter two of Aidan Kavanagh, *The Shape of Baptism: The Rite of Christian Initiation* (Collegeville, MN: The Liturgical Press, 1991); and chapter two of Maxwell Johnson, *The Rites of Christian Initiation.* Maxwell argues that Justin's theology reflects the East Syrian practice. Justin taught in Rome and that is why he is included in this chapter with other Western sources. There is also much scholarly debate about the authorship and sources of *The Apostolic Tradition.* For a current evaluation, see John F. Baldovin, "Hippolytus and the *Apostolic Tradition:* Recent Research and Commentary," in *Theological Studies* 64, no. 3 (2003): 520–42.

34. Kavanagh, *The Shape of Baptism,* 46. Italics his.

35. Quoted in Massey H. Shepherd, Jr., "Confirmation: The Early Church," in *Worship* 46 (1972): 17–18. The parenthesis is in the original; the brackets are mine.

36. John H. McKenna, "Infant Baptism: Theological Reflections," *Worship* 70 (1996), 196–97.

37. I am using the translation of Johnson, *Rites,* 155. See also Carter Lindberg, *The European Reformations* (Cambridge, MA: Blackwell Publishers, 1996), 205–6.

38. Martinez, *Signs of Freedom,* 131–32.

39. Trent, Session Seven in Tanner, *Decrees,* vol. 2, 686.

40. Richard P. McBrien, *Catholicism,* new ed. (San Francisco: HarperCollins, 1994), 817.

41. Robert L. Browning and Roy A. Reed, *Models of Confirmation and Baptismal Affirmation* (Birmingham, AL: Religious Education Press, 1995), 12. Italics theirs.

42. Ibid., 18–19.

43. Thomas Bokenkotter, *Essential Catholicism* (Garden City, NY: Doubleday, 1985), 206–7.

44. K. W. Noakes, "From the Apostolic Fathers to Irenaeus," in Cheslyn Jones et al., eds., *The Study of Liturgy,* rev. ed. (New York: Oxford University Press, 1992), 211.

45. Justin Martyr, *First Apology,* 67, in *Fathers of the Church,* vol. 6 (New York: Christian Heritage, 1948), 106–7.

46. Justin Martyr, *First Apology,* 66, 105–6. Italics mine.

47. Martos, *Doors,* 266.

48. Gary Macy, *The Banquet's Wisdom* (Mahwah, NJ: Paulist Press, 1992), 79. Italics his.

49. George Hunsinger, "The Bread That We Break: Toward a Chalcedonian Resolution of the Eucharistic Controversies," *The Princeton Seminary Bulletin* XXIV, no. 2 (2003): 243.

11

THE SACRAMENTS OF HEALING AND THE SACRAMENTS OF COMMITMENT

In our examination of the sacraments of initiation we entered into the mystery of our participation in the life, death, and resurrection of Christ (baptism); the strength provided by the Holy Spirit (confirmation); and the presence of Christ (Eucharist). We now delve into the mysteries of sin, sickness, and vocation as we focus on the sacraments of healing (reconciliation and the anointing of the sick) and the sacraments of commitment (orders and marriage). We will trace the historical development of each of these four sacraments as well as identify some of the theological questions associated with each of them.

The Sacraments of Healing: Reconciliation and Anointing of the Sick

What is the heart of Christianity? If we had to summarize the good news proclaimed by Jesus, what would we say? It might be Jesus' teaching about the need to love our neighbor as we love ourselves, his assurance of God's love, or his promise of eternal life. If we take Paul's lead in 2 Corinthians, we could also say that it is ultimately about reconciliation. "All this is from God, who reconciled us to himself through Christ, and has given us the ministry of reconciliation; that is, in Christ, God was reconciling the world to himself, not counting their trespasses against them, and entrusting the message of reconciliation to us" (2 Cor 5:18–19). Here Paul identifies reconciliation as one of God's chief intentions for the world, a key element of Christ's ministry, and a chief characteristic of the Christian life.

The Gospels have as one of their common themes the forgiveness of sins offered by Jesus. In Mark, Jesus offends the religious authorities when he forgives the sins of the paralytic (Mark 2:5–7). In Matthew, Peter asks Jesus, "Lord, if another member of the church sins against me, how often should I forgive? As many as seven times?" Jesus replies to Peter, "Not seven times, but, I tell you, seventy-seven times" (Matt 18:21–22). In some translations, Jesus' response is "seven times seventy times." Jesus then tells the parable of the unforgiving servant (Matt 18:23–35). In Luke we find the classic parable of the prodigal son (Luke 15:11–32). John's Gospel presents the story of the woman caught in the act of adultery (John 8:1–11). All four of these stories convey a powerful message of God's love, the forgiveness of sinners, and the need for humans to be reconciled with both God and neighbor.

While reconciliation stands at the heart of the ministry of Jesus and the life of the church, the practice of reconciliation raised a number of difficult questions for the church. Three in particular deserve mention. First, are certain sins unforgivable? Second, did Christ empower church leaders to forgive sins? Third, does the person whose sin has been forgiven need to perform some form of penance? These three questions would play prominent roles in the debates in the development of the sacrament of reconciliation.

HISTORICAL OVERVIEW
OF THE SACRAMENT OF RECONCILIATION

The dilemma that eventually gave rise to the sacrament of reconciliation was how to square the baptismal theology of the church with the reality of human sinfulness. In the waters of baptism we die to our old selves and are raised up to our new life in Christ. We become new creations (2 Cor 5:17) and Christ lives within us (Gal 2:20). Given this theology of baptism and the resulting understanding of the Christian life, the church struggled with those cases in which a baptized Christian committed a very serious sin. How can someone be a new creation in Christ, yet also be an adulterer, a murderer, or an apostate—one who renounces the Christian faith? During times of persecution, some Christians renounced their faith rather than suffer torture, exile, or execution.

Others, as we have discussed earlier, continued to profess the faith and suffered martyrdom. What should the church do if an apostate later sought readmission to the church? Out of the church's struggle with this pastoral and theological problem, the sacrament of reconciliation would eventually arise.

Because some of the most well-known and beloved gospel stories convey a powerful sense of forgiveness—the parable of the prodigal son, the woman caught in the act of adultery, and the Risen Lord's forgiveness of Peter—it might seem that any appeal to the writings that would become the New Testament would quickly settle the issue of readmitting apostates. This, however, was not the case. Two New Testament passages seemed to bolster the case of those who believed that apostates should be denied readmission to the Christian community. The first of these dealt with Jesus' mysterious teaching about the "unforgivable sin": "Truly I tell you, people will be forgiven for theirs sins and whatever blasphemies they utter; but whoever blasphemies against the Holy Spirit can never have forgiveness, but is guilty of an eternal sin" (Mark 3:28–29). The second came from the Letter to the Hebrews: "For it is impossible to restore again to repentance those who have once been enlightened, and have tasted the heavenly gift, and have shared in the Holy Spirit, and have tasted the goodness of the word of God and the powers of the age to come, and then have fallen away, since on their own they are crucifying again the Son of God and are holding him up to contempt" (Heb 6:4–6).

The church arrived at a consensus, one that was certainly challenged from time to time by various local churches, that one opportunity for repentance would be granted to those who had committed a serious sin. The second-century work *The Shepherd of Hermas* articulated a policy that would eventually become adopted by the entire church. According to Joseph Martos, "In *[The Shepherd,]* Hermas recounted a revelation given to him by an angel who told him that God in his mercy had provided that sinners who turned from their evil ways should be received back into the community, 'but not repeatedly, for there is only one repentance for the servants of God' (*The Shepherd*, Mandate 4.1)."[1] This second chance required that the sinner undergo another period of instruction and perform public displays of remorse. The instruction would be similar to the type received by the catechumens. The persons who were enrolled in the "order of the penitents" were excluded from Eucharist as were those in the "order of the catechumenate." There was no one prescribed form of public penance; such matters were determined by the local bishop. When the bishop determined that the person had reformed, the sinner was welcomed back into the church and could once again celebrate the Eucharist with the community.

The bishops played a crucial role in this process of canonical penance. They determined the form and duration of the penance. They also determined when a sinner should be readmitted to the Eucharist. One of the important scriptural passages that under-girded the authority of the bishops to act in this capacity was the "Doubting Thomas" story in John's Gospel. The Risen Lord appeared to the disciples when Thomas was absent.

> Jesus said to them again, "Peace be with you. As the Father has sent me, so I send you." When he had said this, he breathed on them and said to them, "Receive the Holy Spirit. If you forgive the sins of any, they are forgiven them; if you retain the sins of any, they are retained." (John 20:21–23)

This passage was taken to mean that Christ empowered the leaders of the church to act in his name and forgive sins. Some thinkers believed that only God can forgive sins, so the bishops did not bring about the forgiveness of sins, but acted as the official representative who celebrated the forgiveness of sins that the truly contrite had already received from God.

After Constantine ended the persecution of Christians, the challenge of dealing with those who had renounced the faith lessened considerably. By the end of the fourth century, the practice of public penance had declined. The rigors of the penance itself, along with the human reluctance to publicly confess sins, contributed to the growing infrequency with which public penance was practiced. A shift in the understanding of the relationship between reconciliation and Eucharist also took place. As Martinez observed, "Christians saw forgiveness not so much as *preparation* for eucharistic communion, but rather hoped for forgiveness as a *result* of eucharistic celebration."[2] In other words, the pre-Constantinian pattern was to seek reconciliation in order to rejoin the church's eucharistic celebration. After Constantine, in a time when martyrdom was far less prevalent, the Eucharist became seen as a means of forgiveness, especially for lesser sins. With the mass conversions of peoples, the catechumenate also fell into disuse. In its place Lent became a penitential season in which Christians were to closely examine how well they were living out the Gospel.

These shifts in thought, as well as changing social conditions in the West following the fall of the Roman Empire in the fifth century, created the conditions for the emergence of a new form of reconciliation. In Eastern monasteries the practice had developed in which the monks would privately confess their sins to a fellow monk. In the West, the Irish monks extended this practice beyond the monastery. As Martos explained,

> There were no cities on the island and so Christian life centered around the monasteries. From them, the monks traveled out to the countryside bringing baptism and the mass and preaching the forgiveness of sins….To make matters worse, the monasteries were few and far between, and the itinerant preachers could not always be on hand to bring them the church's assurance of forgiveness on their deathbed. To remedy the situation the monks prescribed the same means that they themselves used to overcome their sins and make satisfaction for them during their lifetime: private, repeated confession and continuous works of penitence. On one trip they would hear the confessions of those who had seriously violated God's or the church's commandments, and assign them their penance. On the next trip, or whenever the penance was completed, they would pray with the penitents, asking for God's merciful pardon.[3]

Reconciliation changed from a public, singular event to a private, repeatable practice.

In order to help their confreres, monks began to catalogue various types of sins and list the appropriate penances. Known as penitentials, these manuals provide an interesting glimpse into the life and thought of Christians living in "the Dark Ages" of Western history. Not only were sections devoted to sins such as homicide, theft, and lies; one eighth-century penitential specified the penance for the use of magic:

> 31. If one by his magic causes the death of anyone, he shall do penance for seven years, three years on bread and water.

> 32. If anyone acts as a magician for the sake of love but does not cause anybody's death, if he is a layman he shall do penance for a half a year; if a cleric, he shall do penance for a year on bread and water; if a deacon, for three years, one year on bread and water; if a priest, for five years, two on bread and water...

> 33. If anyone is a conjurer-up of storms he shall do penance for seven years, three years on bread and water.[4]

The earlier practice of reconciliation took a juridical value. The theologian Regis Duffy described the shift as one in which "the role of the minister of reconciliation is transformed from the patristic notion of *'medicus'* (doctor/healer) to that of *'judex'* (judge)."[5]

As reconciliation assumed this juridical quality, features of the Irish legal system also made their way into the church's practices. The theologian James Dallen noted some of the ways Irish culture impacted the practice of reconciliation.

> Satisfaction, regulated by tariffs (taxes or fines) and commutations (lesser, substitute penalties), had to be made for crimes, and this led to the human relationship with God being seen largely in legal and commercial terms....
>
> Secular law also provided for composition, a money payment or fine to satisfy for crime. The monastic penitentials (guides for confessors, containing lists of sins and appropriate penances) only rarely allowed a money payment or the hiring of a proxy to do one's penances. They did, however, provide for commutations of sentences.

These were substitute penalties, generally easier and more lenient, that took age, health, and occupation into account: shorter but more intense fasts, repeated prayers, kneeling on stones, keeping arms outstretched during prayer, genuflecting repeatedly, and the like. Commutations became more common in the later penitentials to temper excess severity. Their use (and abuse) helped provoke the ninth-century continental reaction to the penitentials. They are also the origin of indulgences.[6]

Not all church officials approved of the practice of private confession. The practice violated the long-standing tradition of having only one reconciliation after baptism.

Not only did the notion of "doing penance" for one's sins became an established feature of personal piety, it also became an integral part of the social and religious landscape. The historian R. W. Southern described the role monasteries played in the social and religious life of the early medieval period.

> The penitential system of the early Middle Ages provided a special reason for relying on the disciplined work of the monks. For serious sins penances were extremely heavy, and even for sins almost inseparable from any form of secular life, the penances were sufficient to make ordinary activity impossible. For instance, the Frankish bishops in 923 imposed three years' penance on everyone who had been present at the battle of Soissons between Charles the Simple and Robert of Lorraine. This penance entailed fasting on bread, salt, and water for three periods of forty days in each year—not an impossible undertaking, but sufficient to put a large part of the nobility of northern France out of action for many months.[7]

Confronted with this urgent necessity to do penance, a noble family could entrust the task to a monastic community. In an expression of gratitude, the family might endow the monastery with a sum of money to ensure the monastery's long-term survival.

The concept of indulgences grew out of this medieval sense that an individual can perform penitential practices on behalf of someone else. Those in purgatory benefitted from the prayers and good works done on their behalf by their loved ones. Luther sparked the Protestant Reformation by condemning the sale of indulgences in his Ninety-five Theses. Luther's first thesis stated, "When our Lord and Master, Jesus Christ, said 'Repent,' He called for the entire life of believers to be one of penitence."[8] For Luther, God's forgiveness of sins is truly the heart of the Gospel, but this forgiveness is unmerited. The theologian Herbert Vorgrimler summarized Luther's position in the following way:

> Martin Luther's concentration on the justification of sinners by faith alone led him to emphasize the internal penitential disposition that should mark the whole life of believers, since God's grace accomplishes nothing for those who do not acknowledge their sins. Closely united with this is believers' mutual forgiveness. Luther found that the Church teachings and practices concerning complete contrition, satisfaction, absolution (and purgatory) conflicted with the gospel's teachings on sinners being forgiven by God alone; consequently, he rejected them from the start.[9]

Luther believed that confession of sin and mutual forgiveness were essential to the Christian life, but insisted that God's forgiveness was not dependent upon human acts of penance or absolution. Luther personally continued the practice of personal confession as an element of his own spirituality, but theologically did not regard reconciliation as a sacrament as much as a constant "return to baptism."[10]

Trent accepted reconciliation as a sacrament. In their sixth session (1547) the bishops declared,

> Those who through sin have forfeited the grace of justification they had received, can be justified again, when, awakened by God, they make the effort to regain through the sacrament of penance and by the merits of Christ the grace they have lost. This manner of justification is the restoration of the sinner which the holy

Fathers aptly called "the second plank after the ship-wreck of the loss of grace."[11]

After the close of the Council of Trent, the popes began a process of liturgical reform. The Tridentine (i.e., derived from Trent) rite of confession was issued in 1614.[12] The liturgist Antonio Santantoni commented,

> When one speaks of the Tridentine ritual [of confession], one speaks of that ritual that was still in force until the end of the 1960s.
>
> Of all the sacramental celebrations, this has been the most private, even if there have been exhortations, especially in recent decades, to leave behind the purely private nature of the celebration. The introduction of a place for confession that is closed off and separated from the rest of the assembly, and the use of a grill between the confessor and penitent (which dates from 1614), have imposed both a style of celebration on the sacrament as well as an understanding of what it means.[13]

This experience of "going to confession" by entering a darkened confessional and recounting the nature and frequency of one's sins to the priest, who would then assign a penance and offer absolution, was a central feature of Catholic spiritual and moral discipline well into the twentieth century.

Just as Trent prompted a series of liturgical reform, Vatican II called for reforms of the sacramental celebrations, including reconciliation. The Vatican approved a new ritual for the celebration of reconciliation in 1973, and it appeared in print in 1974. The 1974 Rite of Penance proposed three forms of reconciliation, which the liturgist P. M. Gy identified as "the individual rite; the communal rite with individual confession and absolution; and the communal rite 'with general confession and absolution.'"[14] Dallen offered his assessment of the three forms.

> The individual rite emphasizes the personal character of the conversion, individual responsibility, and the

deepening of spiritual life through dialogue with the confessor. The second rite assists formation of conscience in community, allows reconciliation with others to be experienced as the condition of reconciliation with God, and attempts to balance the personal and communal elements. The third rite permits a more frequent celebration than would otherwise be possible and, most important, shows the need of true conversion as a permanent dimension of the Christian life by making repentance superior to self-accusation.[15]

The sacramental form of reconciliation has changed over the past two millennia, but the challenge of acknowledging our sins before God and forgiving those who have wronged us has remained a personal and communal experience in the sacramental life of the church.

HISTORICAL OVERVIEW OF THE ANOINTING OF THE SICK

In Buddhism, a story is told about Siddhartha Gautama, the Buddha. His father had been told that his son would either be a great ruler or a great spiritual teacher. Wanting his son to succeed him as king, the father provided Siddhartha with luxuries so that he would not be drawn to spiritual pursuits. At age twenty-nine, Siddhartha went out in his chariot and witnessed the "Four Sights": an elderly and infirm person, a sick person, a dead person, and a monk. The first three sights convinced him that things in this world are transitory, so he sought to undertake the monastic way of life. He renounced his wealth and began a journey that would end in his becoming one of the great spiritual teachers in human history.[16]

The sacrament of the anointing of the sick focuses our attention on those aspects of the human condition that Siddhartha experienced in the first three sights: infirmity, illness, and death. During Jesus' ministry, he not only forgave sins, he also restored sight to the blind, cleansed lepers, expelled demons, and cured those who were paralyzed. He cured the physical and psychological ailments of the people with whom he came into contact. In Mark's Gospel, Jesus sent out the Twelve and they "cast out many demons, and anointed with oil many who were sick and cured them" (Mark 6:13).

This concern on the part of Jesus for the physical and psychological well-being of his followers carried over into the practices of the early Christians as they cared for the sick and dying in their communities. The most important New Testament passage in this regard is found in the letter of James.

> Are any among you suffering? They should pray. Are any cheerful? They should sing songs of praise. Are any among you sick? They should call for the elders of the church and have them pray over them, anointing them with oil in the name of the Lord. The prayer of faith will save the sick, and the Lord will raise them up; and anyone who has committed sins will be forgiven (Jas 5:13–15)

As indicated in this passage from James, the early church continued the long biblical tradition of using oil in religious rituals. Jacob marked the site where he witnessed a ladder reaching to heaven by pouring oil on a stone pillar (Gen 28:18); priests invested kings with the authority to rule by anointing them (1 Kgs 1:39); and oil was used to heal wounds, as we find in the parable of the Good Samaritan (Luke 10:34).

We possess little information on how anointing the sick was actually practiced in the early church. The references to second-century practices are scant and inexact. The third-century *Apostolic Tradition* of Hippolytus includes a blessing of oil to be pronounced by the bishop at the eucharistic celebration. "Lord, just as by sanctifying this oil, with which you anointed kings, priests and prophets, you give holiness to those who are anointed with it and receive it, so let it bring comfort to those who taste of it and health to those who use it."[17] The number of historical sources about anointing increases in the fifth century. The liturgist Philippe Rouilland summarized the fifth-century evidence in the following way:

> As early as the fifth century, we find that the information is rather abundant: the oil destined for the anointing of the sick is blessed by the bishop, and sometimes by a priest, but anointing itself can be done by a priest, a family member, or by the sick person himself or herself. In a letter

addressed in 416 to Decentius, bishop of Gubbio, Pope Innocent I wrote that it belongs to the bishop to bless the holy oil, but that all Christians, and not only priests, can use it in case of illness to anoint themselves or their relatives. Thereafter, this letter became part of almost all the Western canonical collections until the end of the eighth century.[18]

Until the ninth century, the ritual of the anointing of the sick took various forms, but the emperor Charlemagne would prove a pivotal figure in the establishment of a uniform ritual.

In the eighth and ninth centuries a number of political, social, and religious changes produced a significant shift in the theology underlying the anointing of the sick. First, according to Martos, Charlemagne began "a period of organizational reform...and under its impetus bishops began to meet in councils and issue regulations for more uniform church practices."[19] Second, lay people were forbidden in many dioceses from performing the anointing. The practice of anointing increasingly was reserved to the priests. Third, the focus of the sacrament shifted from physical and psychological healing to a preparation for death. Earlier in church history, the final sacramental act was viaticum ("food for the journey"), which is reception of the Eucharist before death. Gradually the final sacramental act became the anointing, which was now called last rites, or "extreme unction."

The bishops at Vatican II sought to restore the early church practice of anointing the sick and thus break the centuries-old association of anointing the sick with imminent death. In their Constitution on the Sacred Liturgy, the bishops declared, "'Extreme Unction,' which may also and more fittingly be called 'Anointing of the Sick,' is not a sacrament for those only who are at the point of death. Hence, as soon as anyone of the faithful begins to be in danger of death from sickness or old age, the fitting time for him to receive this sacrament has certainly already arrived."[20] In regard to both sacraments of healing—reconciliation and the anointing of the sick—the bishops at Vatican II retrieved many of the church's ancient practices, believing that those earlier practices responded more effectively to the needs of modern Christians struggling with sin, sickness, and death.

The Sacraments of Commitment:
Holy Orders and Marriage

The image of the blinded Paul knocked to the ground staring up at the sky on the road to Damascus has been seared into the Christian imagination. While the experience was exceptional, the underlying concept has resonated with Christians from the time of Paul to the present day. Paul regained his sight after he received a blessing by a disciple in Damascus named Ananias, who did so at the command of God. Given Paul's well earned reputation as a persecutor of Christians, Ananias was perplexed by the divine command. "But the Lord said to him, 'Go, for [Paul] is an instrument whom I have chosen to bring my name before Gentiles and kings and before the people of Israel…'" (Acts 9:15). Not only is the story of Paul a classic account of Christian conversion, it also vividly illustrates the concept of vocation—a calling from God. The concept of vocation revolves around the belief that God has given each individual certain gifts. Each person must discern what those gifts are and consider how to best put them to use in a manner pleasing to God. Two of these vocations are celebrated as sacraments in the Catholic tradition: holy orders and marriage. Because of their lifelong nature and role in the community, they are considered together as sacraments of commitment, sacraments of vocation, or—as the Catechism of the Catholic Church puts it (Pt. 2, sec. 2, ch. 3)—sacraments at the service of communion.

HISTORICAL OVERVIEW OF HOLY ORDERS

Questions of church leadership (Should we have bishops?) are inextricably bound with questions of the nature of the church (What do we mean when we say that the church is "the Body of Christ?"). We cannot decide the appropriate church structure and forms of ministry without also asking what the nature and mission of the church is. Catholic tradition has long held that the church should be episcopal in structure; that is, authority should rest with the bishops. The role of the bishops was to oversee the liturgical, moral, and doctrinal life of the church so that the Body of Christ would remain healthy. The term *orders* was eventually used to speak of the ranks of those charged with leadership of the community. As the liturgist Pierre Jounel has observed, the term *ordo* was drawn from Roman civic life when it "signified a well-defined social body that was distinct from the people."[21] Just as there was a senatorial order that governed the state, there was an ecclesiastical order that governed the church.[22] Finally, over time, the church hierarchy was further divided into three orders: bishops, priests, and deacons.

The development of the three orders of bishops, priests, and deacons parallels the development of ecclesiology. In general terms, the New Testament preserves two strains of thought regarding the organization of the Christian community. The first, the charismatic approach, emphasizes that the Spirit gives different gifts to each person (1 Cor 12). Church bureaucracy should be kept minimal to prevent the Spirit from being stifled. The second, the hierarchical approach, emphasizes the need for stable, authoritative succession of leaders who are charged with maintaining continuity with the apostolic teachings. The public sign of this succession is the act of laying hands upon the one who is to become a bishop, priest, or deacon (see 1 Tim 4:14, 5:22).

The *Apostolic Tradition* of Hippolytus provides us with an account of the ordination of a bishop as it was practiced in the early church. The entire body of the faithful select the bishop. On Sunday, the people gather along with the presbyters and bishops from the nearby area. The bishops lay hands on the candidate and silently pray over him. Then one of the bishops offers a blessing that includes a recitation of the responsibilities of a bishop. The newly ordained bishop then receives the kiss of peace. At this point, the deacons present the bread and wine to him, and along with the presbyters, he offers the Eucharistic prayer.[23]

Many commentators describe the ancient and medieval ages as ones in which the people viewed the world in hierarchical terms. The theologian Thomas O'Meara wrote, "The Roman world was marked by organization and arrangement of rights, duties and services ordered by law. The church could not help but be modified in its self-understanding by the powerful and useful thought-forms and political institutions of the Roman world bestowing fixed positions and subordinate arrangement."[24] One frequently cited writer

who captured the hierarchical perspective of that age was the fifth-
or sixth-century author known to us today as Pseudo-Dionysius,
Dionysius the Areopagite, or Denys the Areopagite. His work
"The Celestial Hierarchy" offers his description of the heavenly
reality called the "divine hierarchies," or "the sacred order."[25] This
heavenly hierarchical structure is then reflected in the earthly
ecclesiastical hierarchy. A hierarchically structured church is therefore fitting and proper.

In this hierarchical perspective, it was natural to refer to a
vocation to the priesthood as a "higher calling." Many Christians
regarded the renunciation of desire, including sexual desire and the
desire for a family, as a spiritual challenge that only a few could
accept. Jesus' teaching on divorce in the Gospel of Matthew, in the
view of many interpreters, supported this contention.

> His disciples said to him, "If such is the case of a man
> with his wife, it is better not to marry." But he said to
> them, "Not everyone can accept this teaching, but only
> those to whom it is given. For there are eunuchs who
> have been so from birth, and there are eunuchs who have
> been made eunuchs by others, and there are eunuchs
> who have made themselves eunuchs for the sake of the
> kingdom of heaven. Let anyone accept this who can."
> (Matt 19:10–12)

Also in 1 Corinthians, Paul advised the unmarried and the widows
to remain unmarried as Paul himself was (1 Cor 7:8).

The question of priestly celibacy was handled differently by
the Eastern and Western churches. The Eastern church adopted a
policy that deacons and priests may be married, but they must
marry before entering into orders. Only celibate priests are permitted to become bishops. The universal requirement of priestly
celibacy emerged slowly in the Western church. The theologian
Thomas Rausch reported, "The first legislation requiring sexual
abstinence for married priests appeared at Rome toward the end of
the fourth century. However the law of celibacy was not made
mandatory for the entire western church until the Second Lateran
Council in 1139."[26] There was a practical dimension involved in

this discipline as well. Bishops and priests could no longer deed church property to their children.

Luther rejected both the concept of a ministerial priesthood (i.e., priesthood received through ordination) and the requirement of celibacy. In contrast, Luther emphasized "the priesthood of all believers," or "the universal priesthood." Luther insisted that all Christians participate in the royal priesthood (1 Pet 2:9) and therefore no mediators between Christians and God are necessary. Likewise, the clergy should not be restricted to the celibate. Luther himself married Katherine von Bora in 1525. In response to Luther, Trent reaffirmed both the ministerial priesthood and the requirement of priestly celibacy.

> When anyone claims that all Christians are in the same manner priests of the new covenant, or that all, without exception, are given the same spiritual authority, then this is nothing other than bringing confusion into the hierarchy of the Church which is like a "disciplined army" (Song of Songs 6:4), just as if all were apostles, all were prophets, all were evangelists, all were shepherds, all were teachers contrary to the teaching of St. Paul (cf. 1 Cor 12:29).[27]

Like Trent, Vatican II stressed the legitimacy of the ministerial priesthood. Greater attention, however, was given to the universal priesthood. The theologian Frederick J. Cwiekowski noted the shift in emphasis at Vatican II:

> By Baptism all the faithful are called to be a priestly people who, by the Spirit of Christ, continue the threefold mission of Christ as prophet, priest, and servant of the kingdom of God (Dogmatic Constitution on the Church, chap. 1). All the faithful have a share in the mission of the Church and in the worship of the Church. The notion of the priesthood of the faithful is invoked specifically as the basis for the faithful's participation in the offering of the Eucharist (n. 10). The reassertion of the priesthood of all believers is a major element in conciliar teaching on the sacrament of Holy Orders.[28]

By virtue of baptism, all members of the church share in the priesthood of Christ, but some are "consecrated by God through the ministry of the bishops…[so that] they should be made sharers in a special way in Christ's priesthood and, by carrying out sacred functions, act as his ministers who through his Spirit continually exercises his priestly function for our benefit in the liturgy" (Decree on the Ministry and Life of Priests, n. 5).

While this Vatican II teaching accented the concept of the universal priesthood, the Roman Catholic Church still confronts two controversial questions regarding those who should be deemed qualified for admittance to priestly orders: Should married men be ordained? Should women be ordained? Many Catholics believe that one or both of these options needs to be pursued if the American church is to have enough priests to adequately serve the number of Catholics in the country.

The historian Chester Gillis offered the following summary of the crisis in the declining number of diocesan priests in the United States. "Diocesan priests" or "secular priests" have promised obedience to a local bishop; a priest in a religious order (e.g., a Jesuit) has vowed obedience to the superior in the religious order.

> In 1996, 35,070 diocesan priests were active; sociologists Schoennherr and Young predict that by the year 2005 there will be 21,030, a 40 percent loss. Church membership in 1965 was 44,790,000. They predict it will reach 74,109,000 in 2005. The ratio of priests to parishioners in 1975 was 1:1,100; in 1990 it was 1: 2,200; by the year 2005 it will be 1: 3,100. More than 40 percent of the dioceses in the United States have at least one parish headed by a non-priest, and many dioceses have multiple parishes without clerical leadership.[29]

Many Catholics argue that a married man could serve the church just as effectively as a celibate man, and he would be in a better position to counsel those experiencing marital difficulties. Other Catholics believe the current practice should be continued. The theologian and Holy Cross priest Edward O'Connor argued, "Celibacy permits [priests] to be at the service of their flock far more than is possible for a man with wife and children to care for. Even more profoundly and intimately, because of his calling to be 'another Christ,' the priest needs to have a heart given over totally to the Lord."[30]

In 1994, Pope John Paul II issued an apostolic letter *(Ordinatio Sacerdotalis)* that restated the official church policy reserving priestly ordination to men. Pope John Paul II concluded (n. 4) by reiterating the teaching in strong language.

> Although the teaching that priestly ordination is to be reserved to men alone has been preserved by the constant and universal Tradition of the Church and firmly taught by the Magisterium [the teaching office of the church] in its more recent documents, at the present .time in some places it is nonetheless considered open to debate, or the Church's judgment that women are not to be admitted to ordination is considered to have a merely disciplinary force.
>
> Wherefore, in order that all doubt may be removed regarding a matter of great importance, a matter which pertains to the Church's divine constitution itself, in virtue of my ministry of confirming the brethren (cf. Lk 22:32) I declare that the Church has no authority whatsoever to confer priestly ordination on women and that this judgment is to be definitively held by all the Church's faithful.

Earlier in his letter (n. 2), the pope stated that "the Church has always acknowledged as a perennial norm her Lord's way of acting in choosing the twelve men whom he made the foundation of his Church (cf. Rev 21:14)." Christ did not choose any women to be part of the Twelve and the long-standing tradition of the church has been to similarly reserve ordination to men. Critics would cite Paul's teaching, "There is no longer Jew or Greek, there is no longer slave or free, there is no longer male and female; for all of you are one in Christ Jesus" (Gal 3:28). They would also suggest that the choice of twelve men may have been a reflection of the first-century culture rather than an eternal divine decree. Lastly, critics would insist that the key factor in the incarnation is not that the Word took on a specific gender, but that the Word took on a human nature.

The shortage of priests has created an increasing number of priestless parishes in the United States. In response to this growing pastoral problem, the National Conference of Catholic Bishops issued guidelines for Sunday celebrations in the absence of a priest.

> On other grounds today, namely, the scarcity of priests, in many places not every parish can have its own eucharistic celebration each Sunday. Further, for various social and economic reasons some parishes have many fewer members. As a consequence many priests are assigned to celebrate Mass several times on Sunday in many, widely scattered churches. But this practice is regarded as not always satisfactory either to the parishes lacking their own parish priest (pastor) or to the priests involved.[31]

In many priestless parishes, a priest may only be able to celebrate Mass at that parish once a month. During that Mass, the priest will consecrate a large quantity of hosts and lay persons will lead eucharistic prayer services on the other three Sundays of the month.

One of the most significant changes in the area of church ministry approved at Vatican II was the restoration of the permanent diaconate (the order of deacons). As we have discussed, deacons played an integral role in the life of the early church, but by the Middle Ages, the diaconate had been reduced to a stepping-stone toward priestly ordination. A seminarian in his final year who becomes a deacon is obviously planning to enter the priesthood, so he is referred to as a "transitional deacon." Vatican II called for "permanent deacons": men who are not pursuing ordination, but feel called to the diaconate. Permanent deacons may be either married or single. If they are married, they are not free to remarry if their wives should die. If they are single at the time they become deacons, they must remain single. Deacons can deliver homilies, baptize members into the church, and witness church marriages.

So far, we have discussed the vocation of orders. A Catholic may also be called to vowed life in a religious order. Sisters and brothers in religious orders take vows of poverty, chastity, and obedience. There are active and contemplative religious orders. Active religious orders perform works of charity. They typically focus on one type of ministry; for example, doing missionary work, staffing hospitals, or running schools. Contemplative religious orders are devoted to a life of prayer. Those in the religious life are not ordained and therefore do not have clerical responsibilities, but they have also taken vows of chastity and obedience, so they do not marry. Instead they live "the common life" with their fellow brothers or sisters in the religious order.

HISTORICAL OVERVIEW OF MARRIAGE

The first official church declaration that marriage is a true sacrament was made in 1184 at the Council of Verona.[32] However, before 1184's declaration, church officials and theologians only gradually realized what Christian married couples had known for a millennium; namely, that God's grace is sacramentally present in the joys and struggles of married life, that children are gifts from God, and that in the love between husband and wife we watch a glimpse of Christ's love for the church.

The Old Testament contains some of the most edifying passages regarding marriage. The author of the second creation story suggests that marriage is as old as humanity itself. "It is not good that the man should be alone; I will make him a helper as his partner" (Gen 2:18). The critical verse that will later be cited by Jesus and the author of Ephesians comes from this story. God creates Eve from the rib of Adam. "Then the man said, 'This at last is bone of my bones and flesh of my flesh; this one shall be called Woman, for out of Man this one was taken.' Therefore a man leaves his father and his mother and clings to his wife, and they become one flesh" (Gen 2:23–24). In the estimation of the twentieth-century Old Testament scholar Gerhard von Rad, the author of the second creation story accords "the relationship between man and woman the dignity of being the greatest miracle and mystery of Creation."[33] God built marriage into the very fabric of creation. Out of the sexual union of husband and wife, new life is created. The human ability to bring new life into the world mirrors in some small way God's power of creation. This passage conveys a powerful sense of the beauty of marriage and childbearing.

The Old Testament also contains some of the most challenging passages regarding marriage. First, polygamy was practiced in the ancient world. First Kings puts the number of Solomon's wives at seven hundred, along with three hundred concubines (1 Kgs 11:3). The Bible does not morally condemn the polygamy of Jacob, David, or Solomon. It simply seems to be accepted as part of the cultural landscape of the ancient world. Second, the Old Testament sanctions divorce (see Deut 24:1–4). A man was permitted to divorce his wife, but the reverse was not accepted. Even in Jesus' day, rabbis debated what grounds would be sufficient for a man to divorce his wife. By accepting both polygamy and divorce, the Old Testament presents a challenge to the Catholic view of marriage as a monogamous, indissoluble union of man and woman.

While the Gospels record no discussion by Jesus regarding the polygamy found in the Old Testament, Jesus does address the question of divorce. When asked by the Pharisees to comment on the Mosaic provision for divorce, Jesus replies that divorce was not the original intent of God.

> Some Pharisees came, and to test him they asked, "Is it lawful for a man to divorce his wife?" He answered them, "What did Moses command you?" They said, "Moses allowed a man to write a certificate of dismissal and to divorce her." But Jesus said to them, "Because of your hardness of heart he wrote this commandment for you. But from the beginning of creation, 'God made them male and female.' 'For this reason a man shall leave his father and mother and be joined to his wife, and the two shall become one flesh.' So they are no longer two, but one flesh. Therefore what God has joined together, let no one separate." (Mark 10:2–9)

In 1 Corinthians, Paul repeats this teaching: "To the married I give this command—not I but the Lord—that the wife should not separate from her husband (but if she does separate, let her remain unmarried or else be reconciled to her husband), and that the husband should not divorce his wife" (1 Cor 7:10–11).

In the letter to the Ephesians, the passage from Genesis 2 regarding marriage is used to describe Christ's love for the church. "'For this reason a man will leave his father and mother and be joined to his wife, and the two will become one flesh.' This is a great mystery, and I am applying it to Christ and the church" (Eph 5:31–32). In addition to its original role in the creation story, this Genesis passage has appeared both in Mark's Gospel with regard to the question of divorce and in Ephesians as a foreshadowing of Christ's love for the church. The eternal love of Christ for the church becomes a model for the love shared by husband and wife. In this way, both the relationship of Christ to the church and the husband to the wife would later come to be viewed as binding covenants.

The theologians in the early church did not always hold marriage in high esteem as a state of life that fostered spiritual growth. Ancient philosophical and religious traditions often categorized the creation along dualistic lines: matter/spirit or body/soul. Paul speaks in these terms in his letter to the Galatians: "For what the flesh desires is opposed to the flesh; for these are opposed to each other, to prevent you from doing what you want" (Gal 5:17). Thinkers often viewed marital sexual relations as an attachment to the physical, and therefore as a hindrance to the spiritual. Stoicism also made an impact on early Christian thought and contributed to the negative assessment of marriage. In this philosophy, passions and desires, including sexual drives, disrupted the soul. Contentment, therefore, consisted in achieving a detachment from the pleasure and pains of this world. Stoic Christians consequently regarded celibacy as a higher spiritual state than marriage.

The theologian Waldemar Molinski characterized the early church's attitude towards marriage as ambivalent. No theologian illustrates this ambivalence better than Augustine. On the one hand, Augustine had positive things to say about marriage. As Molinski noted, "Given the testimony of Scripture and the tradition that has been built upon it, Augustine will not deny—is not tempted to deny—that marriage is an honourable state, in some sense a sanctifying one; but this in his view, is precisely because of the 'goods' that excuse it, and especially the spiritual love between husband and wife."[34] The goods or values that "excused" marriage were children, the faithfulness of the spouses, and marriage's sacramental sign foreshadowing the future unity of humanity to be enjoyed in heaven.[35] On the other hand, Augustine held that sexual desire (concupiscence) was a result of the Fall of Adam and Eve. As the moral theologian Julie Hanlon Rubio noted,

> No doubt Augustine and others were limited in their writing by a sense, widely shared in their time, that everything bodily was inferior to everything spiritual. These writers simply could not see anything related to sex as truly good. However, the fathers do not see sex as the only problem in marriage; they also think of the distraction of spouses and children as weights on the Christian striving for a godly life.[36]

Augustine's ambivalence toward marriage and procreation had a profound and long-lasting effect on Catholic theology.

For the first millennium of Christian history, marriage laws were generally affairs of the state, not the church. However, as theologians began to accept marriage as one of the seven sacraments, the church became more involved in the legal dimensions of marriage. One of the most important legal questions concerned the point at which a couple was in fact legally married. The theologian Michael Lawler described the theological challenge in the following way.

> In a community of believers who hold that marriage is a sacrament, that it symbolizes the union of Christ and his Church, confers grace on those who receive it worthily, and is indissoluble, a crucial question needs to be settled. It is an apparently simple, but in reality a very complex, question: when is there a sacramental marriage? At what precise moment in time are two persons sacramentally and indissolubly married?[37]

Some theologians believed a valid marriage existed when two parties freely and without reservation exchanged vows; other theologians believed that sexual relations after the exchange of vows marked the beginning of a sacramental marriage. This debate would most likely seem strange to modern Christians, but the legal points had practical consequences in terms of determining royal lines of succession and inheritance.

These ancient and medieval theological debates concerning the point at which a marriage becomes binding have relevance for the contemporary church's practice of granting annulments. This is the crucial distinction that needs to be explained, *The church does not recognize divorce, but the church does grant annulments.* In order to be married in a Catholic church in the United States, the couple needs to secure a marriage license issued by the state, and to arrange for a priest or deacon to witnesses the marriage on behalf of the church. At the church wedding, the couple is married in accordance with both state law and church law. According to the laws of the state, the couple can at some later date seek a divorce. When the divorce is granted by a judge, they are no longer legally married, and both parties are free to enter into other marriages if they choose. However, based on Jesus' teaching on marriage in Mark 10 (see also Matt 19, especially the debate over the meaning of v. 9), the church does not allow divorce. In the eyes of the church, a divorced couple is still married. By contrast, an annulment is a decision rendered by a church court (a tribunal) that according to the law of the church (canon law), a valid (i.e., binding) marriage never really existed. For example, if the man knew that he was physically unable to have children and deliberately withheld that information from his fiancée and, in a pre-wedding interview with the priest or deacon, did not answer truthfully any question about having children the woman would have grounds for seeking an annulment. If an annulment is granted, both parties are free to remarry in the Catholic Church. If the annulment is not granted, then in the eyes of the church, the couple is still married. They could not validly enter into second marriages in the church.

These technical discussions regarding the validity of marriage should not obscure the fact that many of the official statements in both Vatican II and the pronouncements of John Paul II speak of marriage in very positive tones. The theologian David Thomas offered the following assessment: "What occurred at Vatican II was the development of the new basic paradigm or model for describing

Christian marriage. This shift can be summarized as one which moved from viewing marriage primarily as a biological and juridical union to one which is more interpersonal, spiritual, and existential."[38] In "The Pastoral Constitution on the Church in the Modern World" *(Gaudium et spes)*, sections 47–52, the bishops devote their attention to the question of marriage and family. In the closing paragraph of that section, the bishops emphasized marriage as a sacrament of vocation or calling.

> Let married people themselves, who are created in the image of the living God and constituted in an act of authentic personal dignity, be united together in mutual affection, agreement of mind, and mutual holiness. Thus, in the footsteps of Christ, the principle of life, they will bear witness by their faithful love in the joys and sacrifices of their calling, to that mystery of love which the Lord revealed to the world by his death and resurrection.[39]

In his 1981 apostolic exhortation *Familiaris Consortio*, Pope John Paul II offered similarly positive reflections on marriage as a sacrament of vocation. "Christian marriage, like the other sacraments, 'whose purpose is to sanctify people, to build up the body of Christ, and finally, to give worship to God,' is itself a liturgical action glorifying God in Jesus Christ and in the Church. By celebrating it, Christian spouses profess their gratitude to God for the sublime gift bestowed on them of being able to live in their married and family lives the very love of God for people and that of the Lord Jesus for the Church, His bride."[40]

The sacraments of healing (reconciliation and anointing of the sick) and of commitment or vocation (orders and marriage) find their place in the deep conviction that the quest for holiness is an ongoing process within the Christian life. The times in which we acknowledge our sins, experience sickness, or celebrate a momentous decision to pursue a life of ordained ministry or Christian marriage are all moments of greater possibility for coming to a deeper knowledge and love of God in our lives.

Discussion Questions

1. Should the early church have readmitted apostates? Why? Why Not?
2. Did Christ empower the apostles and their successors to forgive sins?
3. Was the the rise of private confession a positive or negative development?
4. Is the performance of some form of penance an essential element in the process of reconciliation?
5. Do Catholics have to confess their sins to a priest? Why? Why not?
6. Is the anointing of the sick an extension of Jesus' ministry of healing?
7. In what sense are all Christians priests? In what was does the ministerial priesthood differ from the universal priesthood?
8. Should married men be ordained to the priesthood?
9. Should women be ordained to the priesthood?
10. Should divorce and remarriage be permitted by the church?

Suggested Readings

For an introduction to the sacraments of healing and commitment, see sections three and four in German Martinez, *Signs of Freedom* (Mahwah, NJ: Paulist Press, 2003); the relevant sections of chapter nine in Francis Schüssler Fiorenza and John P. Galvin, eds., *Systematic Theology*, vol. 1, (Minneapolis, MN: Fortress Press, 1991); chapters 23 and 24 of Richard P. McBrien *Catholicism*, new ed. (San Francisco: HarperCollins, 1994), and the relevant chapters in Joseph Martos, *Doors to the Sacred*, rev. and updated ed. (Liguori, MO: Liguori, 2001).

For a detailed study of reconciliation, see James Dallen, *The Reconciling Community* (Collegeville, MN: The Liturgical Press, 1991).

For studies on holy orders, see the suggested readings in Fiorenza and Galvin, 303–4.

For an overview of marriage, see Michael G. Lawler, *Marriage and Sacrament: A Theology of Christian Marriage* (Collegeville, MN: The Liturgical Press, 1993).

Notes

1. Joseph Martos, *Doors to the Sacred* (Garden City, NY: Doubleday and Co., 1981), 315.

2. German Martinez, *Signs of Freedom* (Mahwah, NJ: Paulist Press, 2003), 204. Italics his.

3. Martos, Doors, 329–30.

4. "The So-Called Roman Penitential of Halitgar," in John T. McNeil and Helena M. Gamer, eds., *Medieval Handbooks of Penance* (New York: Columbia University Press, 1938), 305.

5. Regis A. Duffy, "Reconciliation," in Joseph A. Komonchak, ed., *The New Dictionary of Theology* (Wilmington, DE: Michael Glazier, 1987), 834.

6. James Dallen, *The Reconciling Community* (Collegeville, MN: The Liturgical Press, 1991), 106–7.

7. R. W. Southern, *Western Society and the Church in the Middle Ages* (New York: Penguin Books, 1970), 225–26.

8. Martin Luther, "Ninety-Five Theses," in John Dillenberger, ed., *Martin Luther* (Chicago: Quadrangle Books, 1961), 490.

9. Herbert Vorgrimler, *Sacramental Theology* (Collegeville, MN: The Liturgical Press, 1992), 211–12.

10. Alexandre Ganoczy, *An Introduction to Catholic Sacramental Theology* (New York: Paulist Press, 1984), 114.

11. Ibid., 212–13.

12. Dallen, *The Reconciling Community*, 172.

13. Antonio Santantoni, "Reconciliation in the West," in Anscar J. Chupungco, ed., *Handbook for Liturgical Studies*, vol. 4 (Collegeville, MN: The Liturgical Press, 2000), 146.

14. P. M. Gy, "Penance and Reconciliation," in A. G. Martimort, ed., *The Church at Prayer*, new ed., vol. 3 (Collegeville, MN: The Liturgical Press, 1988), 114.

15. Dallen, *The Reconciling Community*, 231–32.

16. Niels C. Nielsen, Jr., et al., *Religions of the World*, 2nd ed. (New York: St. Martin's Press, 1988), 205; and Mary Pat Fisher, *Living Religions*, 4th ed. (Upper Saddle River, NJ: Prentice-Hall, 1999), 139.

17. Quoted in Martinez, *Signs of Freedom*, 226.

18. Philippe Rouillard, "The Anointing of the Sick in the West," in Chupungco, *Handbook*, 171–72.

19. Martos, *Doors*, 377.

20. "The Sacred Constitution on the Sacred Liturgy," n. 73, in Austin P. Flannery, ed., *Documents of Vatican II* (Grand Rapids: Eerdmans,1975), 22.

21. Pierre Jounel, "Ordinations" in Martimort, ed. *The Church at Prayer*, 139.

22. Jounel, "Ordinations," in Martimort, ed., *The Church at Prayer*, 139.

23. Ibid.

24. Thomas O'Meara, "Orders and Ordination," in Joseph A. Komonchak, ed., *The New Dictionary of Theology*, 724–25.

25. "The Celestial Hierarchy," in *Pseudo-Dionysius: The Complete Works*, Colm Luibheid, trans. (Mahwah, NJ: Paulist Press, 1987), 147 and 153.

26. Thomas P. Rausch, *The Roots of the Catholic Tradition* (Wilmington, DE: Michael Glazier, 1986), 203–4.

27. Quoted in Ganoczy, *An Introduction to Catholic Sacramental Theology*, 127–28.

28. Frederick J. Cwiekowski, "Holy Orders," in Richard P. McBrien, ed., *The HarperCollins Encyclopedia of Catholicism* (San Francisco: HarperCollins, 1995), 623–24.

29. Chester Gillis, *Roman Catholicism* (New York: Columbia University Press, 1999), 245–46.

30. Edward D. OConnor, *The Catholic Vision* (Huntington, IN: Our Sunday Visitor Publishing Division, 1992), 409–10.

31. "Directory for Sunday Celebrations in the Absence of a Priest," n. 5, in *Sunday Celebrations in the Absence of a Priest*, Liturgy Document Series 10 (Washington, DC: United States Catholic Conference, 1996), 4.

32. Martinez, *Signs of Freedom*, 272.

33. Gerhard von Rad, *Old Testament Theology*, vol. 1 (New York: Harper and Row, 1962), 150.

34. Waldemar Molinski, "Marriage," in Karl Rahner, ed., *Encyclopedia of Theology* (New York: Crossroad, 1975), 909–10.

35. Richard P. McBrien, *Catholicism*, new ed. (San Francisco: HarperCollins, 1994), 855; and Francis Schüssler Fiorenza, "Marriage," in Francis Schüssler Fiorenza and John P. Galvin, eds., *Systematic Theology*, vol. 2 (Minneapolis, MN: Fortress Press, 1991), 317–19.

36. Julie Hanlon Rubio, *A Christian Theology of Marriage and Family* (Mahwah, NJ: Paulist Press, 2003), 72.

37. Michael G. Lawler, *Marriage and Sacrament: A Theology of Christian Marriage* (Collegeville, MN: The Liturgical Press, 1993), 63.

38. David M. Thomas, "Marriage," in Joseph A. Komonchak, ed., *The New Dictionary of Theology*, 624.

39. Gaudium et spes, n. 52, in Austin P. Flannery, ed., *Documents of Vatican II*, 957.

40. *Familiaris Consortio* at the Vatican website, www. vatican.va.

12

MORAL THEOLOGY

Christians have long recognized that their claims about God, Christ, and the sacraments require that they live in a way that often put them at odds with the wider culture. They could not worship the Roman gods and preserve their commitment to monotheism. They could not ignore the poor and claim to be faithful disciples of Jesus. They could not celebrate their new life in Christ through baptism and continue to earn a living as gladiators, pickpockets, or prostitutes. In this chapter we will trace the historical development of the branch of theology concerned with the proper conduct for Christians; this is known as moral theology, or Christian ethics. We will identify some of the major thinkers, popular moral theories, and specific moral issues that occupied the church in the ancient and medieval periods, as well as in the Reformation and modern eras.

The Biblical Roots of Moral Theology

Jews and Christians share the conviction that religious observance has as one of its essential elements adherence to a divinely willed moral code. For Jews, the content of this moral code appears in the revelation of the Decalogue (Ten Commandments) in the Torah, the cries for justice found in the prophets, and in the wise insights contained in the Wisdom books. In addition to these scriptural sources of ethical insight, Christians look to the proclamation of Jesus contained in the four Gospels, and the ethical injunctions and virtues scattered throughout the other writings of the New Testament.

A sampling of New Testament writings reveals the range of ethical concerns in both Jesus' teaching and the preaching of the early church. Our sampling will be confined to the Synoptic Gospels, the Pauline correspondence, and the Catholic, or General, Epistles.

The Synoptic Gospels unanimously report that Jesus' preaching centered on the concept of the kingdom of God. The precise meaning Jesus attached to this concept has been a source of debate throughout Christian history, but some general observations about the ethical implications of this concept can be made. First, in order to accept or enter into the kingdom, one must repent. Following in the tradition of the Old Testament prophets, Jesus preached a message of conversion. Second, this conversion required a reversal in one's outlook, attitudes, and values. For example, Jesus instructed the rich young man to sell all that he owned and give the money to the poor, and only then to come and follow him (Mark 10:21). Third, the synoptic writers invite their readers to believe that in the ministry of Jesus, God's kingdom had drawn near; that is, in the life, death, and resurrection of Jesus, the power and promise of the kingdom of God was definitively revealed. This revelation, however, should not be mistaken for a complete realization of God's desired state of existence for humanity. The full realization of the kingdom of God remains in Jesus' preaching a future event—a reality that will be made manifest at the end of time. In this final age, the gospel writers assure us, the truth of Jesus' message regarding the kingdom will be clearly displayed.

While the concept of the kingdom of God appears in Paul's letters (e.g., Rom 14:17), it does not figure prominently in his ethical teachings. Instead, the presence of the Holy Spirit (1 Cor 12:7), the new life in Christ (Rom 6:4), and the certain hope of the age to come (1 Cor 15:24) underlie his ethical admonitions. These core beliefs help Paul both address specific pastoral and ethical questions of his day and offer more general descriptions of the Christian life. In 1 Corinthians Paul tackles the specific questions raised by the Corinthian church regarding issues such as the eating of meat that has been offered to pagan idols, lawsuits among Christians, and sexual morality. In Romans 13 Paul addresses the question of the Christian's obligations to the ruling political authorities. At other times, Paul speaks of the virtues that need to be cultivated in order to live according to the Spirit. Chief among them are faith, hope, and love (1 Cor 13), what moral theologians will later call the three theological virtues. Also included are joy, peace, patience, kindness, generosity, faithfulness, gentleness, and self-control (Gal 5:22).

The Catholic, or General, Epistles are the seven letters that appear in the New Testament between Hebrews and Revelation. The authors of these later writings of the New Testament constantly urge their audiences to unite belief and action. In the three Letters of John, the theme of love dominates. "Those who say, 'I love God,' but hate their brothers or sisters, are liars; for those who do not love a brother or sister whom they have seen cannot love God whom they have not seen. The commandment we have from him is this: those who love God must love their brothers and sisters also" (1 John 4:20–21). The theme of uniting faith and good works dominates The letter of James.

> What good is it, my brothers and sisters, if you have faith but do not have works? Can faith save you? If a brother or a sister is naked and lacks daily food, and one of you says to them, "Go in peace; keep warm and eat your fill," and yet you do not supply their bodily needs, what is the good of that? So faith by itself, if it has no works, is dead. (Jas 2:14–17)

The precise relationship between faith and works has been a source of theological contention, especially in the Reformation period, but no serious Christian theologian ever denied the love of neighbor as an essential element of the Christian life.

Moral Theology in the Early Church

The early Christian authors often describe the moral life as a choice between two paths in life. The Epistle of Barnabas contrasts the way of light and the way of darkness. The *Didache*, an early handbook of church teachings, takes a similar approach. "There are two Ways: a Way of Life and a Way of Death, and the difference between these two Ways is great."[1] The Way of Life consists of loving God and neighbor and observing the Golden Rule. The Way of Death pursues falsehood and wickedness. Understanding the Christian life as the way of light or the way of life dovetails with the belief that baptism calls us to a new way of life in Christ. Old ways—the ways of darkness and death—are left behind, and a new path in life is taken. For this reason, many scholars believe this early form of Christian moral thought was common in the instruction preceding and following baptism.

While church leaders were crafting ways to describe the Christian way of life to the recently baptized, the apologists of the church took up the task of defending Christian morality against charges from pagan critics. One of those early second-century pagan critics was Lucian of Samosata, who offered the following description of the Christians:

> These gullible people believe that they are immortal and will go on living. Therefore, they do not fear dying, and many of them are willing to give themselves up to the authorities. In addition, their first leader persuaded them that they become brothers and sisters when they give up their Greek gods and worship him....They have no concern for possessions and treat them as common property....Any impostor could easily join them and become wealthy by capitalizing on their naiveté.[2]

Rumors concerning Christians abounded. Given their practice of calling each other brother and sister, Christians were accused of incest. Given their custom of meeting secretly to eat the Body of Christ, they were suspected of being cannibals. Given their refusal to worship the gods, the Christians were deemed a threat to the welfare of the state. In response to these allegations, apologists such as Justin Martyr (d. ca. 165) argued for the rationality and moral superiority of Christianity. Christ taught a message of moral purity based on love. Such a way of life in no way undermines the stability of the state, insisted Justin. On the contrary, Christians contribute to the moral well-being of the community.

While Justin battled with his pagan contemporaries, Irenaeus (d. ca. 200) and others confronted the Gnostics within the church. Earlier we discussed Marcion's repudiation of the Old Testament and the impact it had on the development of the canon. Marcion sharply differentiated between the God of the Old Testament and the God of the New Testament. The former was a stern judge who created the material world; the latter was a loving God who sent the Spirit. This dualistic thinking had implications for the moral life as well. The most significant consequence came in the understanding of the material world, especially the human body. The Gnostics regarded the body as a prison of the soul from which we should seek liberation, not a part of God's good creation. In the view of the patristics scholar Maurice Wiles, the Gnostic disdain for the world has never been fully eradicated from Christian thought.

> The early Church firmly repudiated the dualism of the Gnostics which regarded the natural world as evil. Yet she never really accepted that God can be as fully served within the affairs of the world as in seclusion from them. The reasons for her doubts and her hesitations are obvious. But they have to be overcome. To work out in practice the implications of that conviction that life in the world can be Christian in just as full a sense as the life of monastic seclusion is the unceasing task of the Church in every age.[3]

The rejection of Gnostic dualism is at the same time an affirmation of the beauty of the created order, the dignity of marriage, and spiritual blessing of children.

Gnostic thinkers typically interpreted the story of the Fall in cosmic terms. In this version of the Fall, the spiritual powers of the universe fell into the material realm. Some fell farther than others, resulting in a variety of spiritual powers, described in scripture as "the rulers and authorities in heavenly places" (Eph 3:10) or "elemental spirits" (Col 2:8). The Gnostics pictured the universe as a multitiered unit inhabited at the various levels with angelic beings, demonic powers, and other supernatural forces. The human race is similarly mixed. Some persons possessed a purer spiritual nature. Others, however, possessed souls more attached to the material world. The spiritual forces at work in the universe and the given nature of the individual's soul exerted tremendous influence over the human will. As Jaroslav Pelikan noted, "In one way or another, the various schools of Gnosticism depicted man as the victim and slave of forces over which he had no control, and therefore they diagnosed sin as inevitable."[4] The opponents of Gnosticism argued that such a view undermined the moral life. Without freedom, humans are incapable of voluntary conversion from sin, and have no responsibility for their actions.

Clement of Alexandria (ca. 215), a philosopher, theologian, and head of the catechetical school at Alexandria, disputed the moral claims of the Gnostics. First, he argued strenuously against the Gnostic claim that the human will was enslaved by forces beyond its control. In his classic study of the history of Christian thought, Arthur C. McGiffert wrote,

> [Clement's] estimate of human nature was high. Man was made in the divine image by the Logos and is himself in possession of logos or reason. The image of God Clement found in man's rational nature. Because he is a rational being man is like God. As a rational being he is also free, for freedom and rationality go together....Clement laid the greatest emphasis on the freedom of the will. Man would be subject neither to praise nor blame were he not free and were his beliefs and his conduct not always completely within his own power.[5]

Second, Clement held the material things of this world in higher regard. McGiffert commented, "The dualistic notion of the essential evil of matter was widespread...and its natural consequence was asceticism. But Clement did not share this dualism and for all his insistence on self-restraint and superiority to worldly desires he was far from being an ascetic."[6] Clement's call for moderation can be seen in his most famous sermon based on Mark 10:17–27, "Who Is the Rich Man That Shall Be Saved?" According to the contemporary ethicist J. Philip Wogaman, Clement did not see the mere possession of wealth to be an obstacle to salvation, but rather the person's attitude towards his or her financial resources. "So, when Jesus says 'sell thy possessions,' the point is not to get rid of the property itself but to 'banish from his soul his notions about wealth, his excitement and morbid feeling about it, the anxieties, which are the thorns of existence, which choke the seed of life.'"[7]

In the fourth century, Ambrose of Milan (d. 397) composed the first systematic work of moral theology, entitled *The Duties of the Clergy*.[8] Like Clement, Ambrose incorporated non-Christian philosophy in his moral theology. In fact, Ambrose modeled *The Duties of the Clergy* on a work by Cicero. Ambrose also drew upon the Platonic and Stoic treatment of the four cardinal virtues of prudence, temperance, fortitude, and justice. The virtues—the skills that need to be cultivated in order to lead a moral life—would become an essential element of Christian moral theology.

The towering theological figure of the late fourth and early fifth century was Augustine (d. 430). While no one disputes the pervasive influence Augustine had on Western theology, many commentators regard this influence as a mixed blessing. For example, in his historical survey of Catholic moral theology, John Mahoney offered the following assessment of Augustine's moral theology:

> If one considers the whole sweep of Augustine's theological and philosophical output, no one can reasonably doubt both the profundity and the brilliance of his magisterial thought. But if one is concentrating precisely on his moral teachings, it is there that the darkness and the sombre pessimism are most in evidence and, it must be said, at their most dogmatic and devastating.[9]

The root of both Augustine's profundity and pessimism may well be found in his analysis of love. Jesus commanded his followers to love the Lord their God with all their heart, soul, and mind, and to love their neighbor as they loved themselves (Matt 22:37–40). Augustine possessed great rhetorical skills. In his sermons and his writings he beautifully expounded upon the theme of love. As he dealt with the various controversies over his career as bishop, however, Augustine seemed to grow increasingly aware of the gap that existed between the ideal of love and its actual expression in human relations.

Augustine arrived at the conclusion that the moral life requires that we love the right things in the right way. When we desire the wrong things, we turn away from God. However, we can also love the right things, but do so in the wrong way. In the *Confessions*, Augustine advised, "If the things of this world delight you, praise God for them but turn your love away from them and give it to their Maker."[10] The beautiful things of this world derive their beauty from God; therefore, we should praise the Creator, not cling to the created. The things of this world will perish. When we attach exaggerated importance to the things of this world, or believe that our happiness lies in possessing them, we love in the wrong way. To love things in this life properly, we should therefore love them in terms of their relation to the eternal God. Augustine believed so strongly in this idea that morality was based on loving the right things in the right way that he could confidently advise, "Love and do what you will."

This proper ordering of our loves formed the foundation for the church's theory of the just war. The prospect of going to war has always presented a moral challenge to Christians. Jesus' instructions to turn the other cheek and to offer no resistance to the one who is evil (Matt 5:39) seemed to categorically exclude Christian participation in a violent act. Augustine believed, however, that Christian love requires that we defend the innocent against the attack of an unjust aggressor. This raised the possibility that a Christian could in certain circumstances attack and, if necessary, kill soldiers attacking innocent civilians. The specific conditions that create a just war would later be developed, but the impetus for that position was Augustine's theology of love.

Moral Theology in the Medieval Period

Augustine died as the Vandals were attacking the city of Hippo in northern Africa. The Roman Empire was collapsing, and in less than fifty years the last of the Roman emperors would be deposed. The West would enjoy a political rejuvenation during the reign of Charlemagne, but only in the twelfth century did the West experience a sustained period of political, economic, and cultural revival. One of the most significant developments of this period was the emergence of universities. In these new centers of learning, theologians labored to assemble the various elements of Christian theology into one coherent and consistent system of thought. One of the towering figures of this period, called Scholasticism, was Thomas Aquinas, whose synthesis of scripture, patristic teachings, and Aristotelian philosophy would prove to have a determinative influence on Catholic moral theology to the present day.

Aquinas saw in Aristotle's work a perceptive account of the nature of the human person, the human quest for fulfillment, and the principles for a just society. Aquinas also believed that Aristotle's work had enormous potential as a vehicle for conveying Christian moral teachings. In his treatment of natural law, the virtues, and the common good, Aquinas blended the insights of the Christian tradition with Aristotle's philosophy. In doing so, Aquinas was able to unify the various elements of Christian moral theology and situate that topic within the broader context of beliefs about God, Christ, and the life to come.

Based on his observations, Aristotle concluded that different species of animals have different natures. For example, it is in the very nature of a golden retriever to fetch objects, just as it is in the very nature of geese to fly in a V formation. The philosopher Emmett Barcalow explained:

> In addition to such physical laws of nature [such as] water freezes at 32 degrees Fahrenheit and expands when it freezes, physical laws of nature pertaining to biological organisms specify what is "natural" for members of certain species. The physical "law" that birds eat worms is a law of that kind. According to this view, each kind of thing has its own inherent "nature." A thing's inherent nature is a system of capacities and ways of behaving that is "natural" for or characteristic of members of its species. For example, it is part of a cat's nature that it tends to stalk and kill birds and mice; it is part of a dog's nature that it tends to chase cats; it is part of a cow's nature that it grazes on grass; it is part of a lion's nature that it catches, kills, and eats other animals.[11]

Aristotle concluded that we could also speak of a "human nature," a set of inborn characteristics, inclinations, and needs common to all human beings.

An adequate description of this human nature, Aristotle reasoned, would have to note the similarities between humans and other animals, as well the characteristics that were unique to human beings. Aristotle began by noting that the most basic similarity shared by all living beings was that they take in nutrients and grow. Plants, dogs, and humans therefore possess a "nutritive" soul. Unlike plants, however, animals are aware of their environment. They collect and process data gathered by their senses. Aristotle believed that this capacity indicated that animals possessed a "sensitive" soul. Lastly, Aristotle held that humans were endowed with a rational capacity that set them apart from the other animals. This "rational" soul enabled humans to think abstractly, perform complex mental operations, and speculate about the future.[12]

Aristotle also observed that there is a discernible order to nature. Things in the natural world develop along predictable lines and serve specific functions. A fertilized egg passes through several stages on the way to becoming a newborn. Tadpoles naturally develop into frogs. The purpose of the lungs is to pick up oxygen and expel carbon dioxide. The tail feathers on a hawk help control its flight. Aristotle called this goal, purpose, or end *teleos*. What, then, are the goals that are built into human nature? In the most general terms possible, humans seek happiness or well-being (in Greek, *eudaimonia*). Humans naturally desire a life in which their basic human needs are met (food, shelter, clothing) so that they can pursue their personal fulfillment. Because humans are also "political animals," they wish to contribute to the well-being of society. In more specific terms, humans strive to acquire knowledge, live in an orderly society, and raise children.

Aristotle realized that human nature possesses the potential to achieve happiness, but to actually do so, certain skills must be cultivated. A college premed student has the potential to be a good doctor. But in order to be a good doctor, this student needs to learn a body of information, acquire the skills to diagnose patients, and develop a sensitive manner in dealing with the ill. In the Greek tradition the skills or habits that were needed in order to reach the desired goal, or *teleos*, were called virtues. The skills needed to be a good doctor may not be the same as those needed to be a good poet or a good cook. The skills varied with the end result the person was seeking.

However, the Greeks regarded four virtues, or skills, to be absolutely essential for all people and so which were called the cardinal virtues. The first was prudence, or practical judgment. Prudence consists of the ability to know how to apply principles to specific situations. For example, suppose two college sopho-mores, both first-time offenders, are caught by campus security violating a regulation of campus life. After the students plead guilty, they appear before the dean of student affairs. The dean must consider the severity of the offense, each student's account of the events, and each student's sense of remorse. Even if both students are placed on probation, the dean may adopt a more sympathetic tone with one student than the other. Prudence requires that we apply rules fairly, but that we do so in a way that is fitting to each individual case. The second of the cardinal virtues was temperance, or moderation. Temperance requires that we strike the proper balance between two extremes. Aristotle, for example, used the example of a soldier. A soldier who is a coward will not fight, but a soldier who has no fear at all will fight reck-lessly. The ideal soldier is one who knows the dangers, but is courageous enough to fight. Fortitude, the third cardinal virtue, is courage, the strength to do what is right. Finally, the fourth cardinal virtue is justice, giving or getting what one is due. One is justly due a fair wage for one's labor. One is also justly due pun-ishment when one commits a crime. In the Christian tradition, the four cardinal virtues were combined with the three theologi-cal virtues of faith, hope, and love.

These features of Aristotle's philosophy played a critical role in Aquinas's moral theology. First, Aquinas also believed that humans possessed a human nature. Humans were created in the image of God, and so the qualities that they possess are implanted by their Creator. Humans have a fallen nature, according to Aquinas, but the image of God is not destroyed. The spiritual goal, or *teleos*, toward which humans are directed is eternal life with God. The grace of God builds on human nature and brings us into greater friendship with God. Second, given the rational nature of humans, we know that we should do the good and avoid evil. Because human nature has not been thoroughly corrupted by the Fall, humans have the potential to become skilled at the moral life, but this requires the cultivation of the cardinal and theological virtues. To put the matter in modern terms, the human person is shaped by both nature and nurture. Third, through the use of human reason we can identify some of the drives inherent in human nature. What we know through reason is then supplemented and brought to completion by what we learn through revelation. For example, there is a natural drive to propagate the species. Through God's revelation, we learn that God established marriage for the realization of this natural inclination. Fourth, Aquinas believed that morality had both a personal and a social dimension. Aristotle believed that humans are social beings who by nature live in community. Just as individuals seek happiness or well-being for themselves, societies need to establish and enforce rules that promote the common good.

Moral Theology in the Protestant and Catholic Reformations

One might suspect that given Luther's unwavering insistence on justification by faith, and not by works, that he would have little to say about moral and immoral acts. This, however, is not the case. Luther never denied the role of good works in the Christian life. He insisted that faith manifests itself in good deeds, but these good deeds in themselves do not have any salvific value. Luther insisted that Christians should not love in the hope of gaining some reward. As the historian Jaroslav Pelikan explained, "Faith was not opposed to good works; on the contrary, it was only by the righteousness of faith that one could be set free from the anxiety of seeking to appease the wrath of God by works....The good works of faith were works for the benefit of 'the neighbor,' now that it was no longer necessary to perform them for one's own benefit or to gain the favor of God."[13]

In his social ethics, Luther saw the Christian living simultaneously in two kingdoms. The twentieth-century theologian Dietrich Bonhoeffer, who was executed for his role in a plot to kill Hitler, offered the following description of Luther's position:

There are two kingdoms which, so long as the world continues, must neither be mixed together nor yet be torn asunder. There is the kingdom of the preached word of God, and there is the kingdom of the sword. The kingdom of the Church, and the kingdom of the world. The realm of the spiritual office, and the realm of secular government. The sword can never bring about the unity of the Church and of the faith. Preaching can never govern nations. But the Lord of both kingdoms is the God who is made manifest in Jesus Christ.[14]

There are two consequences of this perspective that are worth noting. First, Luther's position affirmed the religious value of work in the secular world, the everyday tasks of making a living and raising a family. Second, Luther's stance did invest the government with the right to use the sword (Rom 13) in order to maintain social stability. This position also implied that Christians should obey the dictates of their ruler. Luther himself penned a sharply worded treatise encouraging the authorities to put down the peasants' rebellion in 1524–25. Twentieth-century Lutherans in Germany confronted the problem of obedience to the civil authorities head-on when Hitler rose to power.

Calvin shared many of Luther's views, but he also had his distinctive emphases. First, Calvin too believed that Christians needed to obey the civil authorities. The state had the right to tax people and to wage war. But as Wogaman noted, "Calvin goes further than Luther or most medieval political thought in justifying rebellion against unjust rulers."[15] In the *Institutes*, Calvin argued that while we need to be obedient to the political authorities, "we are always to make this exception…that such obedience is never to lead us away from obedience to [God]."[16] Second, Calvin shared Luther's sense of the dignity of work. In fact, the sociologist Max Weber argued that Calvin's theology created "the Protestant ethic" that one must work and be a productive member of society. Included in the Protestant ethic was the value of frugality and support for the legitimacy of private property. Weber's thesis was that this combination created the fertile soil in which Western capitalism could flourish.[17]

Calvin was concerned with social order. The Radical Reformers were far less theologically concerned with constructing and maintaining a stable society. They viewed the church as a community of believers called to live as a Christian witness to the world. The difference in perspective between Calvin and the Radical Reformers can be illustrated by their views on money. The historian William J. Bouwsma described Calvin's position:

> Calvin thought private property fundamental to social order. "It pertains to the maintenance of human society," he argued, "that each person should possess what is his own; that some should acquire property by purchase, to others it should come by hereditary right, to others by title of gift; that each should increase his means by ingenuity or physical strength or other gifts. In short, political order requires that each should hold what is his own." The advocacy of communism by sectarian groups threatened, he believed, to "overthrow all order" and "turn all the world into a forest of brigands where, without reckoning or paying, each takes for himself what he can get." He thought Scripture so clearly opposed to communism "that no one can be ignorant on the subject." He denied that the apostolic church had practiced it.[18]

The late Mennonite theologian John Howard Yoder summarized the contrasting position of the Radical Reformers:

> In the New Testament "mammon" and "the sword" were clearly identified and renounced by the teachings and example of Jesus and the apostles. The church after Constantine reversed the New Testament attitude toward these matters and thereby changed the very nature of what it means to be church. The official reformation of Luther and Zwingli made significant changes, but did not fundamentally reverse the structural decisions of the age of Constantine. The radical reformers restored the New Testament standards as their goal. Wealth, they held, is to be dealt with by sharing and simplicity of life. The sword is to be avoided by believers and left, as in New Testament times, in the hands of pagan Caesars.[19]

For Calvin, preservation of the social order is essential, private property maintains social stability, and communism is neither socially desirable nor scripturally sound. For the Radical Reformers, the countercultural witness of the church is foremost, the early Christians shared their resources and practiced nonviolence, and the church after Constantine drifted from the New Testament teachings regarding wealth and violence.

Against the Protestant Reformers, the bishops at Trent insisted that the pope was the pastor and shepherd of the entire church. The bishops contended that the pope had the authority to decide doctrinal and moral questions for the universal church. According to Robert Bellarmine, the leading ecclesiologist of the Counter Reformation, this included the authority to decide moral issues that were doubtful. "For in doubtful matters the Church is obliged to agree with the judgement of the Supreme Pontiff and to do what he commands and not to do what he prohibits; and lest it should act against conscience, it is obliged to believe that good which he orders, and that bad which he prohibits."[20] As John Mahoney has observed, Bellarmine's comment deals with doubtful moral issues about which the pope has taken a stand, but it leaves unanswered the question of how a Catholic should resolve moral questions that are doubtful about which the pope has not stated a position. The natural question to arise, and the one that dominated the moral debates following Trent was, in the words of Mahoney, "What am I to do when I am not sure what to do?"[21]

Moral theologians held different positions regarding this question and many schools of thought developed. Disputes raged between groups such as the Jesuits, who allowed for greater individual discretion in doubtful moral matters, and the Jansenists, who feared that people too often labeled a moral issue "doubtful" in order to avoid doing the right thing. The moral theologian Timothy O'Connell summarized the general situation in the following way:

> At the one extreme, a Jansenist rigorism was proposed; at the other (and partly in reaction to Jansenism), a laxist preoccupation with freedom. And all these debates eventually led to the development of a variety of moral systems for the responsible resolution of ethical doubts. Of these

systems, perhaps the best known today is "probabilism," the system that held that when there is a genuine division of expert opinion on a specific moral issue—and therefore two probable (reasonable) opinions—one may feel free to follow the more lenient opinion. And this even if the lenient opinion is held only by a minority of the experts.[22]

An unfortunate consequence of these developments was the separation of moral theology from other areas of Catholic thought.[23] This made it more difficult to preserve the organic unity of belief, action, and worship that was so clearly evident in patristic theology.

Moral Theology in the Modern Age

With Catholics, Lutherans, Calvinists, and Radical Reformers divided over fundamental questions of morality, it is not surprising that the Enlightenment thinkers sought to establish a basis for morality that would be acceptable to all rational human beings. Immanuel Kant (1724–1804), one of the leading thinkers of the Enlightenment, believed he had discovered such a foundation in the universal human experience of moral obligation. Kant's moral theory focused on principles. In the nineteenth century, thinkers such as Jeremy Bentham (1748–1832) and John Stuart Mill (1806–73) shifted the focus away from principles to results. The competing moral theories advanced by Kant, and by Bentham and Mill, continue to mark the great divide in contemporary moral thought. The final decade of the nineteenth century also saw the beginning of modern Catholic social thought. In 1891 Pope Leo XIII issued an encyclical entitled *Rerum Novarum* that would address the plight of workers in the modern industrialized society. The popes of the twentieth century would continue to apply the basic insights of Leo XIII's encyclical to the changing global social, economic, and political realities.

Immanuel Kant's moral theory stemmed from his fundamental conviction that all rational human beings have a sense of moral duty or obligation. The goal, then, of the moral life is to do the right thing for the right reason. The person's intention was important for

Kant. Genuinely moral individuals do not act to win the praise of others or to avoid the scorn of others. Moral individuals choose the right thing because it is the right thing to do. For Kant, the right thing to do is to act in accordance with sound moral principles. This leads to the heart of Kant's moral theory. How can rational persons know that the moral principles upon which they are acting are sound? In response to this question, Kant proposed the categorical imperative: "Act only according to that maxim by which you can at the same time will that it should become a universal law."[24]

How would someone using the categorical imperative decide what to do? According to Kant, the litmus test for deciding whether an act is moral or immoral is to identify the principle upon which the person is acting. This person must then ask himself or herself, "Would I allow all people in all cases to act according to this principle?" If the person answers this question negatively, then as a rational human being, that person knows not to perform that act him or herself. If the person answers this question affirmatively, then he or she can be sure that the act is moral. For Kant and other like-minded thinkers, the categorical imperative yielded absolute moral prohibitions (e.g., never lie). Not all ethicists in the generation following Kant shared his belief that certain principles could never be violated.

Jeremy Bentham and John Stuart Mill developed an alternative moral theory based not on principles but on consequences. Known as utilitarianism, this theory proposed that the moral action is the one that produces the greatest good for the greatest number of people. According to the utilitarians, no moral principle could be held as absolutely inviolable: we should never say "never." Lying, stealing, and killing are, in the vast majority of cases, immoral acts, but in certain circumstances all of these can be morally justified according to the utilitarians.

The differences between the Kantians and the utilitarians are fundamental and irreconcilable. The crucial difference lies in their views toward the existence of intrinsic evils—acts that are always wrong to perform. This abstract point can be illustrated by a consideration of the claim that it is always wrong to directly kill the innocent. The test case for this would be the bombing of Hiroshima during World War II. Those who defend the dropping of the atomic bomb would argue that this act saved more lives in the long run because a land invasion of Japan would have resulted in a greater number of deaths. Those who oppose the bombing would insist that the action directly targeted innocent civilians and that this is always, in all cases, an immoral thing to do, regardless of the results. On the question of whether some acts are intrinsically evil, one hits a fork in the road. Kantians go one way and utilitarians go the other. The principle that we may never directly kill the innocent also underlies current discussions of the morality of abortion, euthanasia, and war.

While nuclear annihilation was the most horrific possibility brought about by modern technology, it was not the only area of concern. The Industrial Revolution created large factories for the large-scale production of textiles, steel, and other goods. This shift from a rural, agrarian economy to an urban, industrialized one produced tremendous social change. By the late nineteenth century the population in Europe was centered in the cities. According to the theologian Timothy McCarthy, "In 1891, approximately 77 percent of all Catholics lived in the industrialized world of the north and 23 percent in the countries now called the third world. Factory workers, many of them women and children, crowded into the cities where they either worked fifteen or more hours a day, seven days a week, at less than subsistence pay, or were unemployed."[25] The issues of a just wage, the right of workers to form unions, safe working conditions, and child labor garnered the greatest attention among social thinkers. On one side, some economists defended unbridled capitalism, insisting that it produced the best means for increasing the wealth of both owners and workers. On the other side, thinkers such as Karl Marx and Friedrich Engels denounced capitalism as a system that perpetuated the economic and social exploitation of workers. These were moral, and not just economic or political, issues.

It was in this highly charged environment that Leo XIII issued his encyclical *Rerum Novarum* in 1891. In the view of the theologian Donal Dorr, the power of Leo XIII's statement rested in its clear and unwavering defense of the rights of workers.

Though the content of Leo's encyclical was important and remains important, what was perhaps even more important was the character of the document as a cry of protest against the exploitation of poor workers. It is not so much the detail of what Leo had to say that was significant but the fact that he chose to speak out at that time, intervening in a most solemn way in a burning issue of the day. His intervention meant that the Church could not be taken to be indifferent to the injustices of the time. Rather, the Church was seen to be taking a stand on behalf of the poor.[26]

Dorr also emphasized the point that "the encyclical did not attempt to put the Church on the side of the working class *against* another class. What it was against was not a group or class but simply the fact of exploitation."[27] On this point, Leo rejected the Marxist contention that class struggle was inevitable and those in the struggle for social justice needed to "choose sides."

In terms of the specific teachings contained in *Rerum Novarum*, many commentators note that Leo attempted to steer a middle course between socialism and capitalism. This would become a feature of modern Catholic social thought. In terms of the proper role of the state, for example, the Catholic tradition would come to speak of the two competing principles of subsidiarity and socialization. The former, according to the ecclesiologist Richard P. McBrien, holds that the "state should intervene only when lesser bodies cannot fulfill a given task required by the common good. In broader terms, the principle of subsidiarity means that nothing should be done at a higher level that can be done as well or better at a lower level."[28] The latter principle holds that some problems cannot be adequately addressed by local bodies and that state involvement is necessary to secure the rights of all. McBrien added, "The two—subsidiarity and socialization—must be kept in creative tension."[29]

Rerum Novarum set the agenda for modern Catholic social thought. The concerns that Leo expressed and the principles he highlighted reappeared in each of the major social encyclicals of the twentieth century. A succession of encyclicals in the twentieth century celebrated the anniversary of *Rerum Novarum*: Pope Pius XI's *Quadragesimo Anno* (1931); John XXIII's *Mater et Magistra* (1961);

Paul VI's *Octagesima Adveniens* (1971); and John Paul II's *Centesimus Annus* (1991). In their own commemoration of *Rerum Novarum* the American National Conference of Catholic Bishops identified six essential themes in Catholic social thought: the life and dignity of the human person; the rights and responsibilities of the human person; the call to family, community, and participation; the dignity of work and the rights of workers; the option for the poor and the vulnerable; and solidarity of the human family.[30]

Three Post-Vatican II Papal Encyclicals

In this final section we will focus on three of the several encyclicals that have appeared since the close of Vatican II. The first is Paul VI's *Populorum Progressio* (1967), in which the pope related Catholic social thought to questions of international development. Second, *Humanae Vitae* (1968), also by Paul VI, dealt with the question of artificial contraception. Third, John Paul II's *Evangelium Vitae* (1995) expressed his deep reservations regarding "the culture of death."

When Leo XIII issued *Rerum Novarum* in 1891, he addressed the social and economic conditions wrought by capitalism and industrialization. The discussion at that time was framed in terms of the relationship between the owners and the workers. The owners determined the workers' wages, fixed the number of hours in a workday, and decided the date and duration of shutdowns in production. The power rested with the owners, and so Leo XIII affirmed the right of workers to unionize and insisted that the owners pay their workers a just wage. In the century following Leo XIII's encyclical, the labor movement in Europe and North America won widespread acceptance of collective bargaining, health and safety laws, and child-labor laws.

In 1967, when Paul VI issued *Populorum Progressio*, the burning question of social justice was not so much the relationship between owners and workers in the industrialized world as much as the relationship between the wealthier nations of the world and the developing nations. What moral obligation did those who live in prosperity with abundant food supplies, high-tech medical resources, and educational opportunities have to those in poorer countries who lacked food, medical resources, and decent housing? The theologian Joseph F. Eagan summarized Paul VI's application of the concerns and principles of *Rerum Novarum* to this global situation in *Populorum Progressio:*

> This, the first encyclical devoted to international development, is one of the most important and radical of all papal documents. Paul VI proposed a carefully thought out theology of development for the poor nations of the world. He coined the famous phrase "development is the new name for peace." For the root of world conflicts is poverty; the growing disparity between rich and poor nations tempts the poor to violence and revolution. Paul stated unambiguously that "the superfluous wealth of rich countries should be placed at the service of poor nations" (49). He condemned the type of capitalism that "considers profit as the key motive for economic progress, competition as the supreme law of economics, and private ownership of the means of production as an absolute right that has no limits and carries no corresponding social obligation" (26). He called for "basic reforms" and the establishment of "an international morality based on justice and equity" (81).[31]

As Paul VI described it, those in the developed nations were in a similar position to the owners during Leo XIII's time, and the poorer nations were akin to the workers. The living conditions of those in developing nations needed to be addressed with the same vigor that was applied to the plight of workers in nineteenth-century Europe and North America.

The teachings in *Populorum Progressio* inspired the bishops of Latin America. In the year following the appearance of *Populorum Progressio*, the Latin American bishops met in Medellin, Columbia, for their Second General Conference (1968). Drawing on Paul VI's encyclical, the bishops wrote, "If 'development is the new name for peace,' Latin American under-development with its own characteristics in the different countries is an unjust situation which promotes tensions that conspire against peace."³² In their Third General Conference held in Puebla, Mexico in 1979, the bishops spoke of the need for the church to have a "preferential option for the poor"—a phrase that captured the spirit of the burgeoning movement known as liberation theology pioneered by Latin and South American theologians.

In 1968 Paul VI issued the encyclical *Humanae Vitae* in which he expressed the magisterium's opposition to artificial contraception. Paul VI wrote that "the Church, calling men back to the observance of the norms of the natural law, as interpreted by their constant doctrine, teaches that each and every marriage act must remain open to the transmission of life" (#11). Paul VI's teaching was rooted in the natural law tradition, which looked to the goal or purpose of things. A natural and divinely willed consequence of sexual relations in marriage is procreation. Any deliberate act that breaks the connection between sexual relations and procreation is therefore immoral.

The reception of *Humanae Vitae* raised two important questions. First, was the traditional natural law approach employed by Paul VI an adequate methodology? Ethicist Andrew Varga noted that critics of the encyclical

> point out that man has a certain dominion over his body and that biological laws should not be identified with morality. Man is more than the sum total of biological processes. He is spirit in matter, a unique being, neither pure spirit nor pure matter. Through his reason he can appraise the importance of values that refer to his whole being and not just to his body. Human sexuality differs from animal sexuality, and the use of the generative faculties must take into consideration the good of the whole family, the parent and children together, and even the good of the larger social body. One may interfere with biological laws for the well-being of the person because man is a rational being and as such is under the guidance of his intellect and not of his instincts. By virtue of his rational nature, man is obliged to search for the good of his total being, to which biological laws are subordinated.³³

Were proponents of the natural law approach moving too quickly from biology to morality? Were other factors not being given their proper moral weight in their moral evaluation? Did advances in medical technology undercut the traditional confidence in defining what is a "natural" act? Could faithful Catholics dissent from an official church teaching? Soon after the publication of *Humanae Vitae*, a group of Catholic theologians released a statement in 1968 in which they concluded, "Therefore, as Roman Catholic theologians, conscious of our duty and our limitations, we conclude that spouses may responsibly decide according to their conscience that artificial contraception in some circumstances is permissible and indeed necessary to preserve and foster the values and sacredness of marriage."[34] But for the supporters of *Humanae Vitae*, artificial contraception was an intrinsically evil act that was never permitted.

The late Cardinal Joseph Bernardin of Chicago popularized a "seamless garment," or consistent ethic of life. Bernardin warned, "When human life is considered 'cheap' or expendable in one area, eventually nothing is held as sacred and all lives are in jeopardy."[35] Pope John Paul II echoed this idea in his 1995 encyclical *Evangelium Vitae*. John Paul II feared the spread of what he called "the culture of death."

> This situation, with its lights and shadows, ought to make us all fully aware that we are facing an enormous and dramatic clash between good and evil, death and life, the "culture of death" and "the culture of life." We find ourselves not only "faced with" but necessarily "in the midst of" this conflict: we are all involved and we all share in it, with the inescapable responsibility of *choosing to be unconditionally pro-life*. (#28, emphasis his)

Being pro-life in this sense means being opposed not only to abortion, but also to direct euthanasia and the death penalty. Being pro-life means that one is committed to fighting poverty, hunger, and illiteracy. This position raises the interesting question of moral consistency. Is it inconsistent to oppose abortion and support capital punishment? Some argue that there is a key difference between the two issues: abortion is the taking of an *innocent* person's life while capital punishment is the taking of a *guilty* person's life. Others believe that a consistent commitment to the gospel of life would protect all human life. This gospel of life is as much a spiritual vision of the unity of the human family as it is a unifying theme for Christian morality. It is to this spiritual vision offered by the gospel of life that we next turn our attention.

Discussion Questions

1. What was the ethical content of Jesus' teachings?
2. "Love, and do what you will"—is this advice, sound? How could it be easily misused and misunderstood?
3. Is there such a thing as human nature? If so, is it a sound basis for determining moral and immoral actions?
4. Which virtues are most characteristic of the Christian way of life?
5. What obligations do Christians have to the state? What things might the state demand that Christians should always refuse to do?
6. Was Kant's categorical imperative a sound basis for determining the right thing to do?
7. Should we always do the greatest good for the greatest number of people?
8. What obligations do wealthier nations have toward poorer nations?
9. In what sense do we live in a culture of death?
10. What are the three biggest moral issues we will be confronting in the next five to ten years?

Suggested Readings

For a very good historical survey of Christian ethics, see J. Philip Wogaman, *Christian Ethics* (Louisville, KY: Westminster/ John Knox Press, 1993). Also helpful is Denise Lardner Carmody and John Tully Carmody, *Christian Ethics* (Englewood Cliffs, NJ: Prentice-Hall, 1993). For a survey of moral issues, see Robin Gill, ed., *The Cambridge Companion to Christian Ethics* (New York: Cambridge University Press, 2001). For a nice introduction to Aquinas's moral theology, see Paul Wadell, *The Primacy of Love* (Mahwah, NJ: Paulist Press, 1992). For a brief introduction to post–Vatican II developments, see chapters ten and eleven of John A. Gallagher, *Time Past, Time Future* (New York: Paulist Press, 1990). For a short introduction to Catholic social thought, see Edward T. Mechmann, *God, Society and the Human Person* (New York: Alba House, 2000).

Notes

1. *The Didache*, 1, in Maxwell Staniforth, trans., *Early Christian Writings* (New York: Penguin Books, 1968), 227.

2. Lucian, *On the Death of Peregrinus*, 13. Quoted in Jan L. Womer, *Morality and Ethics in Early Christianity* (Philadelphia: Fortress Press, 1987), 16.

3. Maurice Wiles, *The Christian Fathers* (New York: Oxford University Press, 1966), 175.

4. Jaroslav Pelikan, *The Christian Tradition*, vol. 1 (Chicago: University of Chicago Press, 1971), 283.

5. Arthur C. McGiffert, *A History of Christian Thought* (New York: Charles Scribner's, 1932), 197.

6. Ibid., 187.

7. J. Philip Wogaman, *Christian Ethics: A Historical Introduction* (Louisville, KY: Westminster/John Knox Press, 1993), 39.

8. Elizabeth Willems, *Understanding Catholic Morality* (New York: Crossroad, 1997), 146.

9. John Mahoney, *The Making of Moral Theology* (Oxford: Clarendon Press, 1987), 45.

10. Augustine, *Confessions*, IV, 12, R. S. Pine-Coffin, trans. (New York: Penguin Books, 1961), 82. I am relying here on Gerald W. Schlabach's work on the *ordo amoris* in "Ethics," in Allen Fitzgerald, ed., *Augustine Through the Ages* (Grand Rapids: W. B. Eerdmans, 1999), 323.

11. Emmett Barcalow, *Moral Philosophy* (Belmont, CA: Wadsworth, 1994), 150.

12. Ibid., 70.

13. Pelikan, *The Christian Tradition*, vol. 4, 147.

14. Dietrich Bonhoeffer, *Ethics* (New York: Macmillan, 1955), 31–32.

15. Wogaman, *Christian Ethics*, 123.

16. John Calvin, *Institutes of the Christian Religion*, IV.20.32 (Philadelphia: Westminster Press, 1960), 1520.

17. Wogaman, *Christian Ethics*, 124–35.

18. William J. Bouwsma, *John Calvin* (New York: Oxford University Press, 1988), 197.

19. John Howard Yoder, *The Priestly Kingdom* (Notre Dame: University of Notre Dame Press, 1984), 107.

20. Quoted in Mahoney, *The Making of Moral Theology*, 134.

21. Ibid.

22. Timothy O'Connell, *Principles for a Catholic Morality*, rev. ed. (San Francisco: HarperCollins, 1990), 19.

23. Richard P. McBrien, *Catholicism*, new ed. (San Francisco: HarperCollins, 1994), 907; and Bernard Häring, *The Law of Christ*, vol. 1 (Paramus, NJ: The Newman Press, 1966), 20.

24. Quoted in Barcalow, *Moral Philosophy*, 137.

25. Timothy G. McCarthy, *The Catholic Tradition* (Chicago: Loyola University Press, 1994), 240–41.

26. Donal Dorr, *Option for the Poor* (Maryknoll, NY: Orbis Books, 1983), 11–12.

27. Ibid., 15.

28. Richard P. McBrien, *Catholicism*, new ed. (San Francisco: HarperCollins, 1994), 945.

29. Ibid., 946.

30. National Conference of Catholic Bishops, "A Century of Social Teaching," in *Contemporary Catholic Social Teaching* (Washington, DC: United States Catholic Conference, 1991), 4–5.

31. Joseph F. Eagan, *Restoration and Renewal* (Kansas City, MO: Sheed and Ward, 1995), 168–69.

32. "Peace," in the Medellin Documents, in Joseph Gremillion, *The Gospel of Peace and Justice* (Maryknoll, NY: Orbis Books, 1976), 455.

33. Andrew C. Varga, *The Main Issues in Bioethics*, rev. ed. (New York: Paulist Press, 1984), 41.

34. Statement by Catholic Theologians, Washington, DC, July 30, 1968, in Charles E. Curran and Richard A. McCormick, eds., *Readings in Moral Theology* #8 (Mahwah, NJ: Paulist Press, 1993), 136–37.

35. Cardinal Joseph Bernardin, "The Consistent Ethic: What Sort of Framework?" in Patricia Beattie Jung and Thomas A. Shannon, eds., *Abortion and Catholicism* (New York: Crossroad, 1988), 262.

13

CHRISTIAN SPIRITUALITY

The inquiry into the nature of Christian spirituality is in many key respects a continuation of our discussion in the previous chapter. "Those who say, 'I love God' and hate their brothers or sisters, are liars; for those who do not love a brother or sister whom they have seen, cannot love God whom they have not seen" (1 John 4:20). Our actions toward our neighbors function as a barometer of our love of God. In turn, our struggles to love God with all our heart, soul, strength, and mind, and our neighbor as ourselves (Luke 10:27), provide the insights that enable us to deepen our awareness of God's presence in our lives. Morality and spirituality, then, are linked in a reciprocal relationship. Both have their points of emphasis and special areas of concern, but they also share a common desire to live a life well-pleasing to God. In this chapter we will trace the historical development of Christian spirituality or Christian spiritual theology in the early church, the medieval period, the Reformation, and the modern age.

The Foundations of a Christian Spirituality

The theologian Michael Buckley has commented, "Every Christian spirituality is a statement about (1) God, about (2) what it means to be a human being, and about (3) the way or the means or the journey by which the human is united with the divine."[1] Buckley's observation sheds valuable light on the structure of positions regarding Christian spirituality. Considering Buckley's first two aspects, we can say that a Christian spirituality must correlate and coordinate underlying theological convictions about, among other things, God and the human person. For example, Calvin paired his belief in the total depravity of the human person with an emphasis on the majesty and power of God. Clement of Alexandria, however, held a very optimistic view of the human person and believed that wisdom about God could be found in the work of philosophers who knew nothing of Christ. When evaluating a spiritual theology, it is also instructive to identify the biblical texts that figure most prominently in the author's work. Of the many passages, images, and themes available in the biblical writings, which ones did the author highlight? Which aspect of God's nature does the image convey? Which dimensions of the human personality receive greatest attention?

For Christian theology, the third aspect of Buckley's observation necessarily involves Christology. In Christian self-understanding, Christ is "the way or the means or the journey by which the human is united with the divine," or as the fourteenth-century mystic Catherine of Siena described him, "the Bridge" between God and humanity. In the New Testament, we find two ways of describing the relationship between Christ and the believers who lived after the time of his resurrection. In the first way, Christians are to imitate Christ whose life serves as the supreme example of moral integrity and spiritual enlightenment. Paul advised the Corinthian church, "Be imitators of me, as I am of Christ" (1 Cor 11:1). In this approach, the emphasis is primarily ethical. We should act in ways similar to how Jesus himself acted and we should follow his teachings. The second way is mystical. Believers "participate" in Christ. Paul used this type of language when speaking about baptism. As the scripture scholar Bart Ehrman explained,

> For Paul the act [of baptism] was not simply significant as a symbolic statement that a person's sins had been cleansed or that he or she had entered into a new life; the act involved something that really happened. When people were baptized, they actually experienced a union with Christ and participated in the victory brought at his death.[2]

The four corners of the foundation upon which a Christian spirituality rests, therefore, are an understanding of the nature and activity of God, a description of what it means to be a human person, a selection of certain themes or images taken from scripture, and an understanding of the life, death, and resurrection of Jesus. Each of these four areas provides an avenue into the heart of a spiritual theology, as we will see as we turn our attention to the spiritual theology of some of the leading figures in the early church.

Christian Spirituality in the Early Church

The early church revered the martyrs. Martyrdom represented the ultimate imitation of Christ and the most complete expression of faithfulness. One of the most famous second-century martyrs was Polycarp, the bishop of Smyrna who was martyred at the age of eighty-six. Shortly after his death in AD 155, an account of his martyrdom began to circulate and became a widely read and very popular inspirational work in the early church.

The Martyrdom of Polycarp[3] builds on the theme of Christian martyrdom as the imitation of "the Martyrdom which we read of in the Gospel" (#1). Polycarp's final hours recall the events surrounding Christ's death. Just as with Judas, an informant "of his own household" (#6) provides the authorities with knowledge of Polycarp's whereabouts. Like Jesus in the Garden of Gethsemane, Polycarp does not flee, but resigns himself to God's will (#7). After his arrest, he rides into the city mounted on a donkey (#8) and appears before the governor (#9). When Polycarp refuses to recant, the governor orders that he be burned at the stake. Polycarp himself is "like a noble ram taken out of some great flock for sacrifice, a goodly burnt-offering all ready for God" (#14). Polycarp is bound to the stake and like Christ on the cross, "casts his eyes up to heaven" (#14) and prays. The flames surround Polycarp but do not touch his body. At this point those witnessing the event "became aware of a delicious fragrance, like the odour of incense or other precious gums" (#15), recalling the verse from Ephesians that "Christ loved us and gave himself up for us, a fragrant offering and sacrifice to God" (Eph 5:2). Finally, one of the guards stabs Polycarp with a dagger. "As he did so, there flew out a dove, together with such a copious rush of blood that the flames were extinguished" (#16).

At the conclusion of *The Martyrdom of Polycarp* we learn of a practice that was common among the early Christians. The author reports that after Polycarp's death,

> we did gather up his bones—more precious than jewels, and finer than pure gold—and we laid them to rest in a spot suitable for the purpose. There we shall assemble, as occasion allows, with glad rejoicings; and with the Lord's permission we shall celebrate the birthday of his martyrdom. It will serve both as a commemoration of all who have triumphed before, and a training and a preparation for any whose crown may be still to come. (#18)

Not only did the early church glorify the martyrs as the ideal Christians, they gathered their bones. The collection of these relics would become a common practice in the ancient world, as did the custom of gathering at the graves of the martyrs and celebrating their "birthdays"; that is, the date on which they entered into eternal life. According to the theologian Lawrence Cunningham, "in the ancient world, it was widely, if not universally, held that the martyrs were the source of sacred power. Their tombs, housing their relics, were places where intercessory prayer could provoke divine intervention by the showing forth of divine power."[4]

The Alexandrian theologian Origen (d. ca. 254) would have followed his own father's example and become a martyr himself at a young age if his mother had not hidden his clothes, forcing him to remain at home that day. In his work "An Exhortation to Martyrdom," Origen praised the martyrs for their imitation of Christ. "Jesus once endured the cross, despising the shame, and therefore is seated at the right hand of God (Heb 12:2, 8:1). And those who imitate Him by despising the shame will be seated with Him and will rule in heaven (cf. 2 Tim 2:12) with Him..."[5] In his history of Christian spirituality, Michael Cox noted that Origen also spoke of martyrdom in terms of the Pauline concept of the Christian's participation in Christ. "For Origen, martyrdom indicated the love of the whole soul for God. The martyr was, literally, a witness [....Origen said that] 'he who bears witness to someone, especially in a time of persecution and trial of faith, unites and joins himself to him to whom he bears witness.'"[6]

One of the most significant of Origen's several contributions to the development of Christian spiritual theology was his delineation of three stages in the spiritual life. In his *Commentary on the Song of Songs*, Origen suggests that the canonical order of the biblical books attributed to Solomon—Proverbs, Ecclesiastes, and Song of Songs—reveals a truth about the spiritual life. The Greeks had traditionally divided the sciences into three categories: the moral, the natural, and the contemplative. In a similar way, argued Origen, the three books of Solomon offer three types of knowledge of God:

> First, in the book of Proverbs, he taught morals and set out the rules for living a good life. Then he put the whole of physics into Ecclesiastes. The aim of physics is to bring out the causes of things and show what things really are, and thus to make it clear that men should forsake all this emptiness and hasten on to what is lasting and eternal. It teaches that everything we see is frail and fleeting. When anyone in pursuit of Wisdom comes to realize that, he will have nothing but scorn and disdain for those things. He will, so to say, renounce the whole world and turn to those invisible, eternal things the Song of Songs teaches us in figurative terms, with images taken from love-making. Thus, when the soul has been purified morally and has attained some proficiency in searching into the things of nature, she is fit to pass on to the things that form the object of contemplation and mysticism; her love is pure and spiritual and will raise her to the contemplation of the Godhead.[7]

Over the course of Christian history, these three stages would become labeled the purgative, the illuminative, and the unitive ways. "The three ways" would become the standard framework in Western thought for presenting the Christian spiritual journey.

In the early fourth century another great mind from Alexandria impacted the course of Christian thought about the spiritual life. Athanasius (d. 373), the early proponent and constant

defender of the Christology of the Nicene Creed, offered two valuable contributions to the development of spiritual theology. First, in
his early work *On the Incarnation* (ca. 318), Athanasius enunciated
the christological principle that underlay Christian spiritual theology in the East: "He became human that we might become divine."[8]
This widely cited principle that God became human so that humans
could become God generated an understanding of the Christian
spiritual life as one of deification (also known as divinization, or
theosis). The key to this conception of the Christian life is
Christology—in Christ, human nature was united with divine
nature. Christ repaired the fractured human nature that resulted
from the Fall. By participation in Christ through the action of the
Holy Spirit, Christians grow into unity with God. The orthodox
scholar Christoforos Stavropoulos explained divinization this way:

> As human beings we each have this one, unique calling,
> to achieve theosis. In other words, we are each destined
> to become a god, to be like God himself, to be united
> with him. The apostle Peter describes with total clarity
> the purpose of life: we are to become partakers of divine
> nature (2 Peter 1:4). This is the purpose of life: that we
> be participants, sharers in the nature of God and in the
> life of Christ, communicants of divine grace and
> energy—to become just like God, true gods.[9]

This idea of humans participating in the divine nature is foreign
to most Catholics and Protestants. In general, Christian theologians
in the Western world have been uneasy with language of deification,
preferring to emphasize the separation between God and humanity.
Similar concerns can be found in the Orthodox tradition, but this did
not diminish the prominence of deification in Eastern thought. The
Orthodox theologian Gregory Palamas (ca. 1296–1359), for example,
sought to craft a formulation that would, in the words of the historian
Jaroslav Pelikan, "preserve the reality of salvation as deification without implying the absurd and blasphemous idea that those who were
deified became 'God by nature.'"[10]

Athanasius's second valuable contribution was to pen a biography of one of his contemporaries—Anthony (or Antony), who

had gone into the Egyptian desert to seek spiritual perfection—and thus with his *Life of Anthony* helped popularize the burgeoning monastic movement within the church.

The austerity of the life of Anthony (251–356) served as a powerful inspiration to Christians in the ancient world. When Anthony was about twenty years old, he entered a church when the gospel story of the rich young man (Matt 19:16–22) was being read. Anthony was struck by the words of Jesus, "If you wish to be perfect, go, sell your possessions, and give the money to the poor, and you will have treasure in heaven; then come, follow me" (v. 21). Believing the gospel words were a command to him, Anthony sold his possessions and gave them away, reserving some money for the care of his sister, and moved into the Egyptian desert. He first lived in proximity to others on the border of the desert, but eventually moved farther into the desert where he lived in an abandoned fort for twenty years. Most desert dwellers cultivated gardens and had a craft, such as weaving baskets from reeds, that produced items that could be sold at markets in the local towns,[11] although when Anthony moved further into the desert, he relied, according to Athanasius, solely on what food was thrown over the wall for him. Also according to Athanasius, Satan tormented Anthony with terrifying visions and troubling thoughts. According to Athanasius's account,

> Nearly twenty years [Antony] spent in this manner pursuing the ascetic life by himself, not in venturing out and only occasionally being seen by anyone. After this, when many possessed the desire and will to emulate his asceticism, and some of his friends came and tore down and forcefully removed the fortress door, Antony came forth as though from some shrine, having been led into divine mysteries and inspired by God. This was the first time he appeared from the fortress for those who came out to him. And when they beheld him, they were amazed to see that his body had maintained its former condition, neither fat from lack of exercise, nor emaciated from fasting and combat with demons, but was just as they had known him prior to his withdrawal. The state of his soul was one of purity, for

it was not constricted by grief, nor relaxed by pleasure, nor affected by either laughter or dejection.[12]

Anthony reappeared in Alexandria twice, once to comfort Christians during a time of great persecution and another to support Athanasius during his struggles with the Arians.[13] By tradition, Anthony died at the age of one hundred five.

Anthony's way of life became a model of Christian discipleship for future generations. The overwhelming majority of Christians have not literally followed Anthony's example, but many Christians have recognized the essential role solitude plays in the spiritual life. The twentieth-century monk Thomas Merton wrote regarding "the desert fathers":

> What the Fathers sought most of all was their own true self, in Christ. And in order to do this, they had to reject completely the false, formal self, fabricated under social compulsion in "the world." They sought a way to God that was uncharted and freely chosen, not inherited from others who had mapped it out beforehand. They sought a God whom they alone could find, not one who was "given" in a set, stereotyped form by somebody else.[14]

Some Christians did literally emulate Anthony's example, taking to the desert, just as Jesus had done before his public ministry. Those who undertook this solitary existence (or the eremitical life) were the hermits. Women also lived as hermits; men were called *abbas*, meaning "fathers," and women were called *ammas*, meaning "mothers." Another form of monastic life that developed in the desert was communal in nature. Pachomius (ca. 290–ca. 347) developed this cenobite way of life in the Egyptian desert, but communities of cenobite monks and nuns were soon established throughout the Christian world.

St. Benedict (480–547) formalized the monastic tradition in the West. Benedict envisioned a life of prayer and work for the monks and nuns. This meant that the community would adhere to a schedule that allowed time for both manual labor and communal and private prayer. The day began at 2:00 a.m. and the monks retired for sleep at 7:00 p.m. The day itself revolved around a cycle of prayer known as the Divine Office, now called the Liturgy of the Hours. The Divine Office consisted of eight designated times for prayer, one at night and seven during the day (see Ps. 119:62, 164). In their private time, the monks and nuns practiced "divine reading" *(lectio divina)* in which they meditated on the spiritual mysteries contained in biblical texts. The manual labor included planting wheat, tending vineyards and bee hives, keeping flocks and herds, and baking bread. As Benedict warned, "Idleness is an enemy of the soul."[15]

Benedict's monastic blueprint became the standard for monasteries and convents in the West. Benedict himself established his chief monastery at Monte Cassino between Rome and Naples. Benedict envisioned the monastery or convent as a structured community governed by a set of regulations known as a Rule. The abbot or abbess presided over the community and enforced the Rule. The monks regarded each other as brothers; the nuns regarded each other as sisters. Because the monastery was in effect a new family, those entering monastic life took a new name before taking vows of poverty, chastity, and obedience. Benedict also placed a high value on stability. A monk or nun should always remain at the same monastery or convent. Finally, the monastery or convent was a self-sustaining community. The abbots or abbesses, or those whom they appointed to certain tasks, could deal with those outside the enclosure, but the monks and nuns themselves would have no need to leave the monastery or convent. Food, shelter, education, and medical care were all provided at the monastery or convent.

While Benedict was the pivotal figure in the history of monasticism in the West, the Cappadocian Fathers—Basil the Great, Gregory of Nazianzus, and Gregory of Nyssa—played significant roles in the development of monasticism in the East. Basil composed two monastic Rules that were influential in the East. Gregory of Nazianzus wrote poetry and powerful sermons regarding the Trinity and Christology. And Gregory of Nyssa became known as the "Father of Christian mysticism."[16]

While Gregory was indebted to earlier thinkers such as Origen, he also was a highly original thinker in his own right. Gregory developed the theme of the Christian life as an ascent. But like the ascent of Moses up Mt. Sinai, this ascent leads the person, not into greater light, but rather into darkness. As the theologian Charles Healey explained,

> Gregory follows Origen's lead and speaks of three stages in this ascent to God. However, there is this important difference between the two. Origen emphasizes a movement of increasing light; the soul moves from darkness to light and then on to greater light. For Gregory, however, the journey begins in light and moves towards lesser light and then into darkness. With Gregory, this apophatic way, the way of darkness, will take on great importance and significance for the first time.[17]

The theologian Andrew Louth described the view of the spiritual life that Gregory's theology generated:

> Gregory depicts vividly the bewilderment, despair and longing that possesses the soul that seeks God. In the dark we can form no finished conception of what is there: this experience is interpreted by Gregory in terms of an endless longing for God, continually satisfied yet always yearning for more, which the soul knows that embarks on the search for the unknowable God.[18]

Around the time of Gregory of Nyssa's death (395), another theologian who, like Gregory, wrote profoundly about the soul's longing for God became the bishop of Hippo in northern Africa. Augustine's *Confessions*, which he began soon after becoming a bishop, chronicled the events of his life leading up to his conversion in 386. The *Confessions* take the form of an extended prayer to God, and in the opening section Augustine says of God: "[You] have made us for yourself, and our heart is restless until it rests in you."[19] In his Confessions, Augustine tells the story of his own restlessness and the many choices, both moral and immoral, that he made in dealing with it. The result is both a deeply personal account of one individual's journey to Christianity and a general account of the weaknesses and possibilities of the human will. As the theologian Elizabeth Dreyer observed,

[Augustine's] careful attention to the human psyche resulted in a convincing portrayal of the complexity of human motivation. Doing the good was not the consequence of a simple, straightforward decision of the will. Augustine had experienced Paul's frustration at doing the evil he abhorred and failing to do the good he willed. Augustine's penetrating analysis of human psychology has been one of the hallmarks of his appeal through the centuries. One reads the *Confessions* as if it were a mirror, reflecting not only the ambiguous, struggling aspect of human freedom one recognizes in oneself, but also the liberating grace that ultimately saves us from eternal confusion.[20]

Augustine's account of his conflicted desires, intellectual pitfalls, and moral failings ends not in utter despair and misery, but in his conversion in a garden in Milan.

In his *Confessions* Augustine described in great detail the moment when he converted to Christianity.

For I felt that I was still the captive of my sins, and in my misery I kept crying, "How long shall I go on saying 'tomorrow, tomorrow'?" Why not now? Why not make an end of my ugly sins at this moment?

I was asking myself these questions, weeping all the while with the most bitter sorrow in my heart, when all at once I heard the sing-song of a child in a nearby house. Whether it was the voice of a boy or girl I cannot say, but again and again it repeated the refrain, "Take it and read, take it and read." At this I looked up thinking hard whether there was any kind of game in which children used to chat words like these, but I could not remember ever hearing them before. I stemmed my flood of tears and stood up, telling myself that this could only be a divine command to open my book of Scripture and read the first passage on which my eyes should fall...

I seized [the Bible] and opened it, and in silence I read the first passage on which my eyes fell: "Not in revelling and drunkenness, not in lust and wantonness, not in quarrels and rivalries. Rather arm yourself with the Lord Jesus Christ; spend no more thought on nature and nature's appetites." I had no wish to read more and no need to do so. For in an instant as I came to the end of the sentence, it was as though the light of confidence flooded into my heart and all darkness of doubt was dispelled.[21]

This passage from the *Confessions* would become the most famous conversion story in Christianity apart from St. Paul's. Drawing upon the story of Anthony who undertook his monastic way of life after hearing the gospel story of the rich young man, upon the association of light with knowledge found in Plato's philosophy, and upon the experience and words of Paul, Augustine crafted one of the most famous passages in the history of Christian spirituality.

Christian Spirituality in the Middle Ages

In the early Middle Ages a spirit of reform began to sweep through the Benedictine Order. The Benedictines suffered from what the historian R. W. Southern has described as a spiritual and economic malaise. Penitential activity on behalf of the monastery's benefactors came to occupy a disproportionate amount of time in the monks' day. In Southern's view, "the individual had been forgotten in the search for perfection in an external routine. This at least is what the monks themselves came increasingly to feel: they wanted a deeper personal religion and they were everywhere hindered by the heap of customary regulations that governed their lives."[22] In addition to this spiritual malaise, new economic realities impacted the life of the monasteries. Unlike earlier monasteries and convents that were endowed with larger tracts of land, monasteries and convents in the early Middle Ages were typically endowed with income from a number of smaller tracts of land. Southern reported,

A good example of the new type of endowment can be seen in the foundation of the priory at S. Mont in

Gascony. It was given by its founder the profits of forty-seven churches, one hamlet, seven manors, four parcels of land, one vineyard, six arable lots, one wood, one stretch of fishing rights, and various small rents and tolls. There were hundreds of foundations like this in the century from 1050 to 1150.[23]

Not only did the monks and nuns spend a good deal of time managing this assortment of properties, they often lived in small communities scattered throughout the countryside. The actual life of many monasteries and convents did not approach Benedict's model of stable communities living by a daily schedule of work and prayer.

The center of Benedictine reform was the monastery at Cluny in France, founded in 909. To eliminate local political and ecclesiastical interference in the life of the monastery, Cluny was placed under the direct control of the pope. Cluny and other monasteries, and convents affiliated with it, served as a training ground for many future reform-minded abbots and abbesses. The Cluniac monasteries and convents also inspired the creation of new religious orders. One of the most prominent of these was the Cistercian Order, founded by Robert of Molesmes at Citeaux (*Cistercium* in Latin) in 1098.[24] The Cistercians believed that the Cluniac reforms did not go far enough in terms of returning to a strict adherence to Benedict's Rule. The Trappist scholar Michael Casey wrote,

> A return to poverty, the desire to be 'poor with the poor Christ,' was a hallmark of the reform. This was expressed particularly with regard to the liturgy, which was radically simplified in its ritual; revenue, which was limited to the fruits of the monks' work; food; clothing; and style of living. Relations with the outside world were kept to a minimum.[25]

The Cistercians required all monks to perform manual labor, although the order included *conversi*, or lay brothers, who did the bulk of the physical labor. Unlike the Benedictines who wore a black habit, the Cistercian monks took a white habit (hence they are commonly called "white monks").[26]

The towering figure in early history of the Cistercian Order was Bernard of Clairvaux (1090–1153), a powerful preacher, a gifted spiritual writer, and a major power broker in church affairs during the twelfth century. He helped resolve disputed papal elections, relentlessly attacked the work of the theologian Peter Abelard, and preached in support of the Second Crusade. He also produced several classic works of Christian spiritual thought, including *On Loving God* and his sermons on the Song of Songs.

Emero Steigman, an authority on the work of Bernard, commented, "In the works of Bernard of Clairvaux (1090–1153) we meet a writer whose engagement in many subjects reveals one literary passion, love. Everything he concerns himself with either leads to love or is explained by love."[27] Bernard charted the progression of love in the Christian life in *On Loving God*. The theologian Bradley Holt summarized Bernard's thought in the following manner:

> In his teachings on the spiritual life, Bernard focuses most clearly on the relationship between the self and God. Borrowing a good deal from Augustine, Bernard, in his treatise "On Loving God," sets forth four degrees of this love. He sees the self first of all loving only itself, then loving the neighbor and God for its own sake. Third, the soul comes to love God for God's sake, normally the highest plane of love. But there is a fourth level, in which the soul loves itself for God's sake. This is found only fleetingly on earth but will be the constant state of the dead after the resurrection of the body.[28]

In his sermons on the Song of Songs, Bernard offered an allegorized interpretation of this romantic dialogue as the soul longing for unity with God. The power of desire for the beloved is the common denominator. But as Bernard reminds his readers, love is not understood by studying others who are in love, but by experiencing it for oneself. "Only the touch of the Holy Spirit teaches, and it is learned by experience alone. Let those who have experienced it enjoy it; let those who have not, burn with desire, not so much to know it as experience it."[29]

Another important monastic center in twelfth-century France was the Augustinian abbey of St. Victor in Paris. Hugh of St. Victor (d. 1141) and Richard of St. Victor (d. 1173) often employed a biblical image (e.g., Noah's ark, the patriarchs, the ark of the covenant) as the framework for their spiritual teachings. Richard's teaching regarding contemplation was especially influential in Christian history. The Dominican scholar Jordan Aumann commented,

> For Richard the goal of Christian perfection is contemplation, which presupposes a period of preparation through ascetical practices and the cultivation of virtue, starting with self-knowledge and prudence. Like Hugh, he admits of a contemplation which is purely natural and acquired, for he defines contemplation as "the free, more penetrating gaze of a mind, suspended with wonder concerning manifestations of wisdom"; and again as "a penetrating and free gaze of a soul extended everywhere in perceiving things."[30]

In the thirteenth century a new type of religious order developed, largely due to the personal charisma of one of Christianity's most beloved saints, Francis of Assisi (d. 1226). Like his contemporary Dominic of Guzman (d. 1221), Francis established a new mendicant order, meaning that they relied upon begging for all or some of their income. While the Benedictine monasteries and convents often stood on large tracts of lands and housed monks and nuns cloistered from the world, the mendicants lived in urban areas where they preached and lived the gospel message of poverty and simplicity. Francis's commitment to this way of life took shape gradually. Born the son of a wealthy textile merchant, the young Francis enjoyed the social life that came with his economic status. He also gloried in dreams of military adventure. At sixteen, however, he was taken prisoner and held captive for one year in Assisi's battle with the neighboring city of Perugia. At twenty-three he set out to join a military campaign led by one of the popular knights of his day. Then, according to the Franciscan scholar Regis Armstrong,

He had traveled no further than Spoleto when he was laid low by illness. During his recovery, Francis had a dream that made him wonder if he were meant for a military career. He dreamt of a hall filled with military weapons and heard someone ask him: "Is it better to serve the lord or the servant?" "The lord," he replied. "Then why," he heard, "do you serve the servant?" The questions haunted the young man and initiated an intense, restless search...[31]

Upon his return to Assisi, Francis spent a great deal of time in a dilapidated church named San Damiano. In prayer in the church one day, Francis heard the command "to rebuild the church." Taking this to be a literal command, Francis began repairing the church building. Selling some of his family's possessions to finance this renovation, Francis provoked the wrath of his father who at this point was exasperated by his son's way of life. In a last-ditch effort to convince Francis to renounce his lifestyle, Francis's father brought him before the bishop. In this famous scene from Francis's life, he renounces not his way of life, but his father. He undressed and handed his clothes to his father, and picked up a nearby smock and drew a cross on it with a piece of chalk. This is the origin of the brown habit worn by the Franciscans today.

In 1208 Francis embarked on a new adventure in his life. Responding to the gospel call to "take no gold, or silver, or copper in your belts, no bag for your journey, or two tunics, or sandals, or a staff (Matt 10:9–10)," he set out on a life of preaching and begging. His attracted followers, including Clare of Assisi, who will herself found the order known as the Poor Clares. Francis eventually appealed to Rome for approval of his Rule for a new order. His first Rule was a simple collection of scriptural verses, but Pope Innocent III approved it in 1209. A second, more formal Rule received approval in 1223. In the same year, in the city of Greccio, Francis originated the custom of building a manger to celebrate Christmas. In the following year, while on retreat on Mt. La Verna, Francis received the stigmata, the five wounds of Christ. He died in 1226.

The British theologian John Moorman argued "that Francis' spirituality was created out of four things: his total obedience to Christ, his prayer at all times, his desire to suffer with Christ, and his love for nature in all its forms."[32] While each of these character-istic is vital to a complete account of Francis' spirituality, the fourth is most distinctive of Franciscan spirituality. In the year before he died, Francis composed "The Canticle of Brother Sun," in which he praised the natural world as a showcase of God's beauty and majesty. "Praised be You, my Lord, with all your creatures, especially Sir Brother Sun, Who is the day and through whom You give us light. And he is beautiful and radiant with great splendor; and bears a like-ness of You, most High One."[33] Bonaventure, the leading theologian of the early Franciscan movement, wrote of Francis, "In beautiful things he saw Beauty itself and through his vestiges imprinted on creation he followed his Beloved everywhere, making all things a ladder by which he could climb up and embrace him who is utterly desirable."[34] Francis saw in the birds in the trees, the sun on the horizon, and the rabbits in the fields, a faint reflection of the wis-dom and love of the God who created the Earth and all that is in it.

In the fourteenth century, four important spiritual thinkers lived and wrote in England: Walter Hilton, Richard Rolle, an anonymous author, and Julian of Norwich. In *The Scale of Perfection*, Walter Hilton (d. 1396) described the stages of the spiritual life in terms of an ascent up a ladder. This image, taken from the biblical account of Jacob's vision at Bethel (Gen 28:12), had long been a favorite of Christian writers (e.g., John Climacus, Guigo II). The image of the ladder seems to possess an archetypal quality that allowed successive generations of Christians to see in it a powerful symbol of their journey to God. Hilton's fellow countryman Richard Rolle (d. 1349) did not use visual imagery as the primary means by which to describe the spiritual life. Rather, Hilton often compared the love of Christ to the pleasure of music. In her classic study of mysticism, the twentieth-century British scholar Evelyn Underhill commented,

> One contemplative at least, Richard Rolle of Hampole, "the father of English mysticism," was acutely aware of this music of the soul, discerning in it a correspondence with the measured harmonies of the spiritual uni-verse....The condition of joyous and awakened love to which the mystic passes when his purification is at an end

is to him, above all else, the state of Song. He does not "see" the spiritual world: he "hears" it. For him, as for St. Francis of Assisi, it is a "heavenly melody, intolerably sweet."[35]

Another important work that was probably composed in fourteenth-century England was anonymous: *The Cloud of Unknowing.* This work continued the apophatic tradition that stressed the unknowability of God. It also asserted the priority of love over knowledge in the spiritual life: "It is love alone that can reach God in this life, and not knowing."[36] Finally, the English mystic Julian of Norwich (d. ca. 1420) was an anchoress, a contemplative who typically lived in quarters attached to a church. In May 1373, Julian fell deathly ill at the age of thirty. During this illness, she received sixteen revelations or "showings" from God. Twice she committed these visions to writing: the first soon after they occurred, and a second time about twenty years later. Her *Revelations of Divine Love* is believed to be the first book written by a woman in English.[37] The topics of the visions varied, but one aspect of her work that strikes modern readers is her use of feminine language about Christ. "For in our mother, Christ, we profit and increase, and in mercy he reforms and restores us, and by virtue of his passion, death and resurrection joins us to our substance. This is how our mother, Christ, works in mercy in all his beloved children who are submissive and obedient to him."[38]

The fourteenth and fifteenth centuries were also a fertile time for spiritual thought on the Continent. The works of the German mystics (e.g., Meister Eckhart, d. ca. 1328) and the Flemish mystics (e.g., Jan van Ruysbroeck, d. 1381) tended to be more abstract and speculative in tone. The movement, known as the *Devotio Moderna* ("Modern Devotion") and which began in the Netherlands, stressed simplicity and practicality. From the *Devotio Moderna* came Thomas à Kempis's *Imitation of Christ,* one of the most widely read works of Christian devotional literature. Its tone is often anti-intellectual and other-worldly.[39]

I would rather feel compunction of heart for my sins than merely know the definition of compunction. If you know all the books of the Bible merely by rote and all the sayings of the philosophers by heart, what will it profit you without grace and charity? All that is in the world is vanity except to love God and to serve Him only. This is the most noble and the most excellent wisdom that can be in any creature: by despising the world to draw daily nearer and nearer to the kingdom of heaven.[40]

For a combination of worldly involvement and mystical speculation, no better example can be found than Catherine of Siena (d. 1380). Not only did she care for the sick at the local hospital, she also involved herself in the highest level of church politics, negotiating treaties and demanding that the Avignon popes return to Rome. In her spiritual writings, Catherine offered profound reflections on the wounded side and pierced heart of the crucified Christ.

Medieval spirituality included a deep devotion to Mary. As the theologian Elizabeth Johnson noted, "The rise of the cult of Mary, the Virgin Mother of God, is one of the most striking features of the landscape of medieval spirituality."[41] Earlier in Christian history, questions regarding Mary arose in two contexts: first, in the course of christological debates, and second, in reflections on the nature of the church. The second-century theologian Irenaeus located Mary in the larger sweep of the biblical narrative's account of humanity's fall in Adam to its restoration in Christ.

And just as it was through a virgin who disobeyed [namely, Eve] that mankind was stricken and fell and died, so too it was through the Virgin [Mary], who obeyed the word of God, that mankind, resuscitated by life, received life. For the Lord [Christ] came to seek back the lost sheep, and it was mankind that was lost; and therefore he did not become some other formation, but he likewise, of her that was descended from Adam [namely, Mary] preserved the likeness of formation; for Adam had necessarily to be restored in Christ, that mortality be absorbed in immortality. *And Eve [had necessarily to be restored] in Mary, that a virgin, by becoming the*

> *advocate of a virgin, should undo and destroy virginal disobe-*
> *dience by virginal obedience.*[42]

In the fifth century, Nestorius, the bishop of Constantinople, caused a stir when he taught that Mary could have only given birth to a human being, not a divine being. Therefore, according to Nestorius, Mary should be called *Christotokos* ("Christ-bearer"), but not *Theotokos* ("God-bearer"). The council of Ephesus (431) rejected this argument and decreed that Mary should properly be given the title "The Mother of God." In addition to her christological significance, Mary was frequently presented as a model of the church, embodying in her submission to the divine will the virtues that the church should possess. The bishops at Vatican II reaffirmed this idea, which was found in the writings of Ambrose, bishop of Milan: "As St. Ambrose taught, the Mother of God is a type of the Church in the order of faith, charity, and perfect union with Christ" (*Lumen gentium*, 63).

In the Middle Ages, Christians regarded Mary as a merciful intercessor to Christ, a loving, tender mother who wished the salvation of all her children. Elizabeth Johnson recounted the details of the popular legend of Theophilus that praised both Mary's maternal love and her hard-nosed negotiating skills.

> In this story, a man who wished to rise in worldly power bargained his soul to the devil. Riches and success accumulated, but Theophilus became stung with remorse. When he tried to repent, however, the devil would not return the contract which had sealed the renunciation of his soul. Theophilus turned then to the Blessed Virgin with a powerfully moving prayer for her help. In negotiations with the devil, she retrieved the contract, and Theophilus died in peace.[43]

In the medieval imagination, Mary would have known the difficulties of motherhood, the joys of celebrating at a wedding feast, and the heartache of losing a child. Full of grace, Mary was a model of compassion and tenderness, a merciful source of intercession to the Lord.

Christian Spirituality in the Protestant and Catholic Reformations

The leading figures in the Protestant Reformation, Martin Luther and John Calvin, attacked many of the features of medieval devotional life as unscriptural accretions that needed to be excised from the spiritual life of the church. Practices such as the collection of relics, the use of intercessory prayer to the saints and Mary, and the abstinence from meat on certain days were condemned by the Protestant Reformers. Luther believed that such practices either compromised the exclusive role of Christ as mediator between God and humanity, or represented an effort on the part of Christians to win the favor of God through works rather than faith. For Luther, the central message of the Gospel was the unmerited justification of sinners by Christ's death on the cross. Scripture proclaims that the gift of justification and the promise of eternal life is available to those who put their faith in Christ. Calvin agreed with Luther, but was more willing to speak of the Christian life as a process of sanctification, a growth in holiness. The theologian Lucien Richard explained that for Calvin, "Justification is based on what Christ has done for us; sanctification is based on what he does within us."[44] Justification occurs at a specific moment in time; but sanctification "is the continuing regenerative work of the Holy Spirit in us. Sanctification is a continual re-making of [humanity] by the Holy Spirit, a work which implies a gradual process leading to the ultimate end, holiness."[45]

Most of the significant developments in sixteenth-century Catholic spiritual theology took place in Spain. Two of the leading thinkers engaged in active reform of the Carmelite Order: Teresa of Avila (1515–82) and John of the Cross (1542–91). A third was Ignatius of Loyola (1491–1556), who founded an entirely new religious order, the Society of Jesus, or as they are more popularly known, the Jesuits.

Teresa of Avila and John of the Cross met in 1567 and mutually supported each other in their efforts at reforming the Carmelite Order. Earlier in 1562 Teresa had established her first reformed ("Discalced") Carmelite convent. Like Teresa, John established a reformed Carmelite monastery.[46] Some were hostile to John's reform efforts and had him imprisoned in Toledo, Spain, where he was treated harshly by his captors. It was during this imprisonment that John wrote some of his most moving spiritual poems. He was able to escape and soon composed some of his greatest prose works.

Teresa composed her spiritual masterpiece *The Interior Castle* in 1577. Jordan Aumann summarized the content of the work as follows:

> She pictures the soul as a castle composed of numerous suites or apartments *(moradas)*, in the center of which Christ is enthroned as King. As the soul progresses in the practice of prayer, it passes from one apartment to another until eventually, after passing through seven apartments, it reaches the innermost room. Outside the castle there is darkness and in the moat surrounding the castle there are loathsome creatures crawling in the mud. Once the soul resolves to follow the path of prayer and detaches itself from created things, it enters the castle and begins to follow the path of prayer, which leads first through three stages of active or ascetical prayer and then through four stages of passive or mystical prayer.[47]

The journey Teresa charted through the seven "mansions," or "dwelling places," corresponded to the purgative-illuminative-unitive scheme found in traditional works. In the first three dwelling places, the person cultivates the virtues and engages in mental prayer. In the fourth and fifth dwelling places, a shift in emphasis occurs. The active striving for God gives way to a more passive reception of the gift of God's presence, a quiet awareness of that presence within the soul. In the sixth and seventh dwelling places, the soul enters into a spiritual betrothal and marriage with God. The person may experience extraordinary spiritual phenomena, such as visions and locutions (a supernatural communication with the divine). Teresa was at a loss to find a suitable earthly comparison to describe the union of the soul with God. "What God communicates here to the soul in an instant is a secret so great and a favor so sublime—and the delight the soul experiences so extreme—that I don't know what to compare it to."[48] She strains to find an example:

it is like the union of two candle flames, or like the rain falling into the river and becoming one body of water, or like light entering a room from two different windows and filling the space.

Like Teresa, John of the Cross speaks of the flame of love and of spiritual marriage, but his most significant contribution to the history of Christian spirituality has been his description of the darkness into which the soul can plunge on its ascent to God. John of the Cross identifies two types of "dark nights" in the spiritual life: a "the dark night of sense" and "the dark night of the spirit." In the first type, persons suffer a "spiritual dryness" characterized by an inability to focus their thoughts or to experience satisfaction. Those experiencing the second type of darkness, according to the Carmelite Kevin Culligan, "believe that they no longer know God, that the God they related to so lovingly at earlier stages of their contemplative journey has vanished, and that, even if there is a God, that God could not possibly accept them because of the depravity they see in themselves."[49] Both of these painful periods of loss, uncertainty, and anguish signal the person's transition into a deeper stage in the spiritual life.

A third reform-minded Spaniard, Ignatius of Loyola, envisioned an order of well-educated, highly disciplined, deeply spiritual men who would go wherever in the world they were needed. This order became known as the Society of Jesus, or the Jesuits. The chief mechanism for imparting Ignatius's spiritual vision was a four-week sequence of meditations known as the *Spiritual Exercises*. The Jesuit theologian Harvey Egan outlined the four-week sequence as follows:

> The first week centers on the cosmic and historical unity of the mystery of evil. The exercitant must consider the cosmic origin of sin in the fall of the angels (n. 50), the beginning of sin in human history through the fall of Adam and Eve (no. 51), "the particular sin of any person who went to hell because of one mortal sin" (no. 52), the history of one's personal sins (nos. 55–61), and finally sin's ultimate consequence: hell (nos. 65–71)…
>
> Ignatius called the second week an exercise in the illuminative way (no. 10). The exercitant must focus

upon the biblical mysteries of the incarnation, Christ's birth, his early childhood, or "the life of our Lord Jesus Christ up to and including Palm Sunday" (no. 4)...

Ignatius gives detailed instructions during the second week for the choice of a way of life or the reformation of life. These instructions focus on the well-known Ignatian "Election," or choice, which many commentators consider the primary goal of the *Exercises*...

In their classical form, the exercises of the third and fourth weeks serve to stabilize, deepen, and confirm the Election of the second week. The third week centers on the Last Supper and the details of Jesus' passion, crucifixion, death and entombment...

The fourth week deals with the mysteries of the risen Christ. The exercitant asks to "feel intense joy and gladness for the great glory and joy of Christ our Lord" (no. 221).[50]

The resulting spiritual outlook intended by Ignatius was "contemplation in action." The life of prayer, which included meditation and the constant discernment of God's will, undergirded a life of action, a life in which we look to find God in all things, and to do all things for the greater glory of God.

The Council of Trent (1545–63) spawned a number of reform movements within the Catholic Church. In France the renewal efforts were undertaken with great vigor. Vincent de Paul (1580–1660) and Louise de Marillac (1591–1660) founded religious orders dedicated to helping the poor and sick. John Baptist de La Salle (1651–1719) established schools for the education of the poor. Following the lead of the Italian Philip Neri, Pierre de Bérulle (1575–1629) founded the French Oratory at Paris in 1611, a congregation dedicated to the spiritual renewal and educational formation of the diocesan clergy.[51] Bérulle wrote movingly about the glory of the incarnation, but he also held a pessimistic view of human nature. He described humanity as "the most vile and useless creature of all; indeed, as dust, mud and a mass of corruption."[52] The alternative to Bérulle, wrote the Salesian Jozef Strus, was the approach to spirituality fostered by St. Francis de Sales. Man is not just a mere "nothing"; rather, he is full of potentiality. Christian humanism had thought and acted in accordance with the following principle: human nature is not totally corrupt; it is only wounded because of original sin. In fact, it contains in itself a natural orientation towards God, seen as the supernatural end.[53]

Francis de Sales (1567–1622) also wrote spiritual works geared toward the common person. In the preface to his *Introduction to the Devout Life*, Francis identified his intended audience as "those who live in town, within families, or at the court, and by their state of life are obliged to live an ordinary life as to outward appearances."[54] These questions concerning the corruption of human nature and the religious value of secular activity would figure prominently in later movements of French thought known as Jansenism and Quietism.

Christian Spirituality in the Modern Age

While it is certainly true to say that the modern age presented a unique set of challenges to Christian thought and practice, it is also true that there is a continuity between the premodern and modern spiritual writers. Modern spiritual thinkers continued to struggle with the traditional questions of the relationship of mind and heart, theory and practice, and action and contemplation.

Rationalism dominated early modern thought, but soon movements such as Pietism and Romanticism reaffirmed the importance of feeling in the religious life. In Protestant thought, John Wesley (1703–91) sought to reawaken the church's spiritual vitality and enthusiasm through his forceful preaching and moving hymns. In Catholic thought, Alphonsus Liguori (1697–1787), founder of the Redemptorists, preached powerful sermons on the love of God. The Redemptorist Mark Miller noted, "He used his considerable musical and artistic talents to encourage a strong devotional life. He would not allow his preachers to use the flowery preaching style customary at the time, but demanded a simplicity and zeal that could both move the hearts and convince the minds of ordinary people."[55] The focus on the heart had its most direct expression in the popular devotion to the Sacred Heart. The image of Jesus with a radiating heart encircled with thorns topped by a crown became a staple of pre–Vatican II Catholic iconography.

In the twentieth century, Dorothy Day (1897–1980), a radical social thinker and convert to Catholicism, tackled the question how to relate theory and practice by establishing in New York City "houses of hospitality," soup kitchens and shelters for the homeless. In 1933 Day met Peter Maurin and together they began publishing *The Catholic Worker* newspaper. In 1936 Day began allowing those in need to sleep in her apartment. Soon afterward Day opened the first Catholic Worker house of hospitality in a donated building located on Mott Street in New York City. At the close of the twentieth century, according to the historian Chester Gillis, there were over one-hundred-thirty houses of hospitality, and *The Catholic Worker* newspaper enjoyed a circulation of over one-hundred-thousand copies worldwide.[56]

Dorothy Day grounded the Catholic Worker movement in the simple and direct gospel conviction that whatever we do for the least of our brothers and sisters we do for Christ (Matt 25:40). In her article for the Christmas edition of *The Catholic Worker* in 1945, Day wrote,

> It is no use saying that we are born two thousand years too late to give room to Christ. Nor will those who live at the end of the world have been born too late. Christ is always with us, always asking for room in our hearts.
>
> But now it is with the voice of our contemporaries that he speaks, with the eyes of store clerks, factory workers, and children that he gazes; with the hands of office workers, slum dwellers, and suburban housewives that he gives. It is with the feet of soldiers and tramps that he walks, and with the heart of anyone in need that he longs for shelter. And giving shelter or food to anyone who asks for it, or needs it, is giving it to Christ.[57]

Day repeatedly insisted that the poor, the homeless, and the addicted are not reminders of Christ, they *are* Christ. When we extend hospitality to them or any other human being, we are serving Christ in the midst of us.

The relationship of the contemplative and active life has been a constant concern in the Christian spiritual tradition. There is no better measure of the course of that debate in the twentieth century than the literary career of the Trappist monk Thomas Merton (1915–68). Merton gained wide popularity in 1948 with the publication of his autobiography, *The Seven Storey Mountain*, chronicling his years before entering the abbey at Gethsemani, Kentucky. Over the course of the next twenty years, Merton produced a remarkably large body of work. From the late 1950s until his death in 1968 Merton offered frequent commentary on the social issues of his day: the arms race, the civil-rights movement, and the Vietnam War. He also developed a deep interest in the Eastern religions. His death in Bangkok occurred during a rare trip outside the monastery to attend a conference on interreligious dialogue.

Merton's journey as a monk and spiritual writer mirrored the tremendous changes within American Catholicism in the twentieth century. However, as the theologian Lawrence Cunningham observed, Merton was firmed planted in an ancient tradition stretching back to the desert fathers and mothers.

> To understand Thomas Merton as a social critic is one valid approach to his life and work, but it is a very incomplete one if that social criticism is made to stand as an independent career understood apart from his own firm, yet evolving, monastic commitment. It may well have taken Merton years to understand fully how he could merge his contemplative life with a deep compassion for the world, and it may be equally true that he came down overly hard on the contemplative separation from the world in the first flush of his monastic life. Nonetheless, it is equally true that he tried various strategies to overcome the gap...[58]

Merton struggled with the role of contemplation in a world of action, and as he slowly arrived at his own answer, he imparted to his readers a constant stream of spiritual insights that were relevant to the times in which they lived. In doing so, he was continuing the tradition begun by Anthony centuries ago.

Discussion Questions

1. How would you define the term *spirituality?*
2. What is your evaluation of Anthony's decision to live in solitude in the desert?
3. Do you believe that sudden religious conversions can occur? Why? Why not?
4. In what practical ways could the "prayer and work" lifestyle of the Benedictine monks and nuns be incorporated into a modern person's busy life?
5. What does the beauty of the natural world teach us about God?
6. Do you believe that certain individuals have had mystical experiences of God?
7. Are the type of meditations introduced by Ignatius of Loyola in his *Spiritual Exercises* helpful ways of entering into the gospel stories?
8. Is working in a soup kitchen a spiritual work?
9. Why do the images of fire, music, and light appear so frequently in spiritual writings?
10. Which elements are indispensable to an authentic Christian spiritual life?

Suggested Readings

Two very readable historical surveys of Christian spirituality are Charles J. Healey, *Christian Spirituality* (New York; Alba House, 1999); and Richard Woods, *Christian Spirituality* (Allen, TX: Thomas More Publishing, 1996). Also helpful are Jordan Aumann, *Christian Spirituality in the Catholic Tradition* (San Francisco: Ignatius Press, 1985); Michael Cox, *Handbook of Christian Spirituality* (San Francisco: Harper and Row, 1985); and Bradley P. Holt, *Thirsty for God* (Minneapolis: Augsburg Fortress, 1993). See also Laura Swan, *The Forgotten Desert Mothers: Sayings, Lives, and Stories of Early Christian Women* (Mahwah, NJ: Paulist Press, 2001). For primary works, consult the Classics of Western Spirituality series published by Paulist Press. For a thematic study of Christian spirituality, see Lawrence S. Cunningham and Keith J. Egan, *Christian Spirituality* (Mahwah, NJ: Paulist Press, 1996). For excellent contemporary spiritual writing, see John S. Dunne, *The Reasons of the Heart* (Notre Dame, IN: University of Notre Dame Press, 1978).

Notes

1. Michael J. Buckley, "Seventeenth-Century French Spirituality: Three Figures," in Louis Dupre and Don E. Sailers, eds., *Christian Spirituality: Post-Reformation and Modern*, World Spirituality Series, vol. 18 (New York: Crossroad, 1989), 31.

2. Bart D. Ehrman, *The New Testament*, 3rd ed. (New York: Oxford University Press, 2004), 355.

3. I am using the translation of "The Martyrdom of Polycarp" in Maxwell Staniforth, trans., *Early Christian Writings* (New York: Penguin Books, 1968), 155–64.

4. Lawrence S. Cunningham, *The Catholic Heritage* (New York: Crossroad, 1983), 18.

5. "An Exhortation to Martyrdom" in Rowan Greer, trans., *Origen* (New York: Paulist Press, 1979), 68.

6. Michael Cox, *A Handbook of Christian Spirituality* (San Francisco: Harper and Row, 1985), 65.

7. Origen, Comm. Cant., 78. Here I am using the translation of Jean Danielou in *Origen* (New York: Sheed and Ward, 1955), 305. For comparison, see Greer, "Commentary on the Song of Songs," in *Origen*, 232.

8. This translation comes from Rowan Williams, "Athansius and the Arian Crisis," in G. R. Evans, ed., *The First Christian Theologians* (Malden, MA: Blackwell, 2004), 165.

9. Christoforos Savropoulos, "Partakers of Divine Nature," in Daniel B. Clendenin, ed., *Eastern Orthodox Theology* (Grand Rapids: Baker Books, 1995), 184.

10. Jaroslav Pelikan, *The Christian Tradition*, vol. 2 (Chicago: University of Chicago Press, 1974), 267.

11. See Thomas Merton, *The Wisdom of the Desert* (New York: New Directions Books, 1960), 16.

12. Athanasius, *The Life of Antony*, 14, Robert C. Gregg, trans. (New York: Paulist Press, 1980), 42.

13. Richard Woods, *Christian Spirituality* (Allen, TX: Thomas More Publishing, 1996), 92.

14. Merton, *The Wisdom of the Desert*, 5–6.

15. *The Rule of St. Benedict*, ch. 48, Anthony C. Meisel and M. L. del Mastro, trans. (Garden City, NY: Doubleday, 1975), 86.

16. Charles J. Healey, *Christian Spirituality* (New York: Alba House, 1999), 42.

17. Ibid., 43.

18. Andrew Louth, "The Cappadocians," in Cheslyn Jones, Geoffrey Wainwright, and Edward Yarnold, eds., *The Study of Spirituality* (New York: Oxford University Press, 1986), 167.

19. Augustine, *Confessions* I, 1, John Ryan trans. (Garden City, NY: Doubleday, 1960), 43.

20. Elizabeth Dreyer, *Manifestations of Grace* (Wilmington, DE: Michael Glazier, 1990), 76–77.

21. Augustine, *Confessions*, VIII, 12, R. S. Pine-Coffin, trans. (New York: Penguin Books, 1961), 177–78.

22. R. W. Southern, *Western Society and the Church in the Middle Ages* (New York: Penguin Books, 1970), 231.

23. Ibid., 233.

24. William R. Cook and Ronald B. Herzman, *The Medieval World View* (New York: Oxford University Press, 1983), 239.

25. Michael Casey, "Cistercian Spirituality," in Michael Downey, ed., *The New Dictionary of Catholic Spirituality* (Collegeville, MN: Liturgical Press, 1993), 175.

26. Kenneth Scott Latourette, *A History of Christianity* (New York: Harper and Brothers, 1953), 423.

27. Emero Stiegman, "On Loving God: An Analytical Commentary," in Bernard of Clairvaux, *On Loving God* (Kalamazoo, MI: Cistercian Publications, 1995), 45.

28. Bradley P. Holt, *Thirsty for God* (Minneapolis: Augsburg Fortress, 1993), 57.

29. Bernard of Clairvaux, *Sermons on the Song of Songs*, 1.11. This translation appears in Jean Leclercq, "Introduction," to G. R. Evans, trans., *Bernard of Clarivaux: Selected Works* (Mahwah, NJ: Paulist Press, 1987), 47.

30. Jordan Aumann, *Christian Spirituality in the Catholic Tradition* (San Francisco: Ignatius Press, 1985), 121.

31. Regis J. Armstrong, *St. Francis of Assisi: Writings for a Gospel Life* (New York: Crossroad,1994), 20.

32. John R. H. Moorman, "The Franciscans," in Jones, Wainwright, and Yarnold, eds., *The Study of Spirituality*, 303.

33. Francis of Assisi, "The Canticle of Brother Son," in Regis J. Armstrong and Ignatius C. Brady, trans., *Francis and Clare: The Complete Works* (New York: Paulist Press, 1982), 38.

34. Bonaventure, "The Life of St. Francis," 9.1, in Ewert Cousins, *Bonaventure*, trans., (Mahwah, NJ: Paulist Press, 1978), 263. I discovered this quotation in Ilia Delio, *Simply Bonaventure* (Hyde Park, NY: New City Press, 2001), 62.

35. Evelyn Underhill, *Mysticism* (New York: Doubleday, 1990), 77.

36. *The Cloud of Unknowing*, VIII, James Walsh, trans. (New York: Paulist Press, 1981), 139.

37. Ursula King, *Christian Mystics* (Mahwah, NJ: HiddenSpring, 2001), 135.

38. Juliana of Norwich, *Revelations of Divine Love*, 58, M. L. del Mastro, trans. (Garden City, NY: Image Books, 1977), 188.

39. Healey, *Christian Spirituality*, 209.

40. Thomas à Kempis, *The Imitation of Christ*, 1,1 (Garden City, NY: Image Books, 1955), 32.

41. Elizabeth A. Johnson, "Marian Devotion in the Western Church," in Jill Raitt, ed., *Christian Spirituality: High Middle Ages and Reformation* (New York: Crossroad, 1987), 392.

42. Irenaeus, "Proof of the Apostolic Preaching," 33. Quoted in Jaroslav Pelikan, *Mary Through the Centuries* (New Haven, CT: Yale University Press, 1996), 42–43. Italics his.

43. Johnson, "Marian Devotion in the Western Church," 403.

44. Lucien Joseph Richard, *The Spirituality of John Calvin* (Atlanta: John Knox Press, 1974), 106.

45. Ibid., 107.

46. Keith Egan, "Teresa of Avila, St.," and Michael J. Buckley, "John of the Cross, St.," in Richard P. McBrien, ed., *The HarperCollins Encyclopedia of Catholicism* (San Francisco: HarperCollins, 1995).

47. Aumann, *Christian Spirituality in the Catholic Tradition*, 191.

48. Teresa of Avila, *The Interior Castle*, VII, ch. 2, n. 3, Kiernan Kavanaugh and Otilio Rodriguez, trans. (New York: Paulist Press, 1979), 178.

49. Kevin Culligan, "The Dark Night and Depression," in Keith Egan, ed., Carmelite Prayer (Mahwah, NJ: Paulist Press, 2003), 125.

50. Harvey D. Egan, *Christian Mysticism* (New York: Pueblo Publishing Co., 1984), 37–42.

51. Healey, *Christian Spirituality*, 288.

52. Quoted in Aumann, *Christian Spirituality in the Catholic Tradition*, 221.

53. Jozef Strus, "Salesian Spirituality," in Emeterio De Cea, *Compendium of Spirituality*, vol. 2 (New York: Alba House, 1996), 199.

54. Francis de Sales, *Introduction to the Devout Life*, John K. Ryan, trans. (Garden City, NY: Image Books, 1966), 33.

55. Mark Miller, "Alphonsus Ligouri, St.," in Richard P. McBrien, ed., *The HarperCollins Encyclopedia of Catholicism*, 35.

56. Chester Gillis, *Roman Catholicism in America* (New York: Columbia University Press, 1999), 73–74.

57. Dorothy Day, "Room for Christ," in *The Catholic Worker*, December 1945. This is document #416 on the Catholic Worker website at http://www.catholicworker.org/dorothyday/reprint.cfm?TextID=416.

58. "Introduction," Lawrence Cunningham, ed., *Thomas Merton: Spiritual Master* (Mahwah, NJ: Paulist Press, 1992), 43–44.

14

ESCHATOLOGY

Christians in ancient Rome often painted anchors on the walls of the catacombs. By marking these burial places with the sign of the anchor, Christians were affirming their hope, that "sure and steadfast anchor of the soul" (Heb 6:19), for the future resurrection of those who have died in Christ. This hope prevented them from drifting into utter despair over the death of their loved ones. In this chapter we will focus our attention on the content of Christian hope. Known formally as eschatology, this branch of theology deals with "the end times." This includes discussions of both the end of human history and the end of our individual earthly lives. We will begin with the hopes for the future expressed in both the Old Testament and New Testament, and then survey the historical development of Christian eschatological thought to the present day.

Eschatology in the Old Testament

In the creation stories in the Old Testament we find some of the foundational theological claims that form the basis for the Christian hope regarding the future. In the first creation story (1:1—2:4a), the Lord creates by command: "Then God said, 'Let there be light'; and there was light" (Gen 1:3). Unlike the creation story that the Jews would have heard from their Babylonian captors, the first creation story in the Bible involved neither a cosmic battlefield in which the forces of chaos struggled with the forces of order, nor the creation of humans from the blood of a slain deity.[1] Instead, creation develops in an orderly sequence according to the will of the one Lord, and humans are created in the divine image (Gen 1:27). In the second creation story, we find the familiar account of Adam and Eve. Both are created from organic matter: the man from the soil and the

428

woman from the rib of the man. God places them in paradise where they have unhindered access to the tree of life. These classic literary images convey the sense that the original divine intention for humanity was incorruptibility and immortality. Through their misuse of freedom, the man and woman fall from this state of innocence. They become subject to disease and death. When they die, their bodies will return to the earth. By the end of the third chapter of Genesis, we have journeyed through two-thirds of the "paradise—paradise lost—paradise regained" scheme that underlies the whole biblical narrative.

Three themes in the creation stories would figure prominently in the development of eschatology in the Old Testament writings. First, the God who gave life to humans will later enter into covenants with them. Covenants bind both parties to fidelity, so not only must the humans obey the Lord, but the Lord must also remember the promises made to Abraham, Moses, and David. Biblical hope is grounded in the promises of God. Despite all evidence to the contrary, Abraham believed God's promise to him that he would have a son, and in his old age Abraham became the father of Isaac. Despite the power of the Egyptians, Moses was able to lead the people out of slavery. Despite the strength of a giant, the young shepherd boy David slays this enemy soldier and goes on to become the king of Israel.

Second, because humans were created in the image of God, they possess capacities such as freedom and love that reflect the nature of their Creator. However, with the exception of the later writings of the Old Testament that reflect contact with Greek thought, we do not find a clearly articulated sense of humans possessing an immortal soul. The bulk of the Old Testament writings, therefore, do not speak in any detail of the afterlife. The earliest understanding seems to have been that after death humans entered into Sheol—the nether world, or "the pit"—a somewhat undefined state of shadowy existence.

Third, life in the fallen world included not only disease and death, but also subjugation by foreign political powers and by religious persecution. The content of the hope to which the Israelites were called varied over time. In some writings it consisted of an individual living to a ripe old age. In other texts it anticipated the restoration of the royal line of David, the return to the land of Israel, or the rebuilding of the Temple. In the later writings of the Old Testament, there developed a hope for the future resurrection of the just. There was, in short, no single, unchanging eschatological hope that all Old Testament writers would have offered to their readers.

THE ESCHATOLOGY OF THE PROPHETS

The biblical hope in God's promises led naturally to a religious reading of history. This was most clearly evident in the prophetic writings in which historical events were seen as either blessings or punishments from God. Most prophets proclaimed both imminent doom and future hope. The first prophet who wrote, Amos, reversed the typical expectation of "the day of the Lord" (Amos 5:18–24). Instead of a future time when God would visit the people and carry out judgement on Israel's neighbors, the day of the Lord was for Amos a time when Israel's sins would be exposed by a just God. Isaiah compared Israel to a vineyard filled wild grapes that would be ripped up by its owner (Isa 5). Jeremiah used the analogy of a potter smacking the clay down to the wheel when it doesn't take the intended form (Jer 18). Jeremiah even called Nebuchadrezzar, the Babylonian leader who destroyed Jerusalem, a servant of God (Jer 25:9).

While the prophets often preached a message of imminent destruction, they did not believe that God would forever abandon Israel. Isaiah, for example, spoke of a future banquet on Mt. Zion (i.e., Jerusalem) in which all peoples of the world would gather and celebrate. At that time, God would "swallow up death forever" (Isa 25:8). Isaiah also predicted that a future ruler would come from the line of David. The Spirit of the Lord would rest upon this ruler, he would rule with justice, and his reign would be a time of peace (Isa 11). Isaiah grounded his hope in an earlier divine promise regarding the royal line of David: "Your house and your kingdom shall be made sure forever before me; your throne shall be established forever" (2 Sam 7:16). After the word reached Ezekiel in Babylon that Jerusalem had fallen, he offered prophecies of hope for those who despaired. Ezekiel had a vision of a valley filled with dry bones. At the Lord's commands, the scattered bones formed skeletons, then grew flesh, and returned to life (Ezek 37). Ezekiel's vision provided Israel with a powerful message of future restoration. Christians would see in this a foreshadowing of Christ's resurrection.

The prophets who preached during the final years of the Babylonian exile and the early years of the Jews' return to the promised land introduced elements into biblical thought that would impact later Christian eschatological beliefs. Second Isaiah (Isa 40–55) contains four "Servant Songs" that speak of a mysterious figure who suffers on behalf of the people (see Isa 52–53:12). Perhaps the Servant was intended as a personification of suffering Israel, but Christians would regard these passages as foreshadowings of Christ. The post-exilic prophet Zechariah also contributes much to Christian thought about the future. We find references to Satan (Zech 3:1–2) and to a future pair of Messiahs or anointed ones (Zech 4:14). Both the figure of Satan (see Job 1–2; 1 Chr 21:1) and the concept of a Messiah played a relatively minor role in the Old Testament, but both would play dominant roles in New Testament thought.

THE GREEK INFLUENCE ON OLD TESTAMENT THOUGHT

The two Books of the Maccabees and the Book of Daniel reflect the struggles of the Jews during the Greek domination of Israel. Judas, the leader of the Jewish revolt against the Greek ruler Antiochus Epiphanes, was known as Maccabee, meaning "the Hammer." This designation was extended to Judas's brothers who succeeded him after his death. Antiochus Epiphanes instituted a series of repressive measures against the Jews. He prohibited, under penalty of death, the observance of the Sabbath or the practice of circumcision. He erected an altar to Zeus in the Temple in Jerusalem around 167 BC and offered swine as a sacrifice there. By 164 BC, the Maccabees were able to regain control of the Temple. The Jewish feast of Hanukkah commemorates the rededication of the Temple after its defilement by Antiochus.

In an account of one of Judas's battles in 2 Maccabees, when the fighting has ended and Judas's troops are gathering up the bodies of their slain comrades, they discovered that the soldiers who were killed in battle were wearing amulets devoted to a foreign god.

Judas announced that the soldiers had died fighting a just cause, but that this sin of wearing these amulets must be atoned.

> He also took up a collection, man by man, to the amount of two thousand drachmas of silver, and sent it to Jerusalem to provide for a sin offering. In doing this he acted very well and honorably, taking account of the resurrection. For if he were not expecting that those who have fallen would rise again, it would have been superfluous and foolish to pray for the dead. But if he was looking to the splendid reward that is laid up for those who fall asleep in godliness, it was a holy and pious thought. Therefore he made atonement for the dead, so that they might be delivered from their sin. (2 Mac. 12:43–5)

This passage would figure prominently in later Christian debates regarding the existence of purgatory.

The Book of Daniel also offered hope to the Jews suffering persecution under Antiochus IV. Unlike the militaristic response of the Maccabees, the Book of Daniel offers an apocalyptic view of history in the form of a vision of four beasts. Before God will bring judgement upon the earth, these beasts, in the form of Kings, must rise up and rule. After the time allotted to the ten-horned, fourth beast, Daniel saw a figure "like a human being," or "like a Son of Man," appearing before God.

> To him was given dominion
>   and glory and kingship,
> that all peoples, nations, and
>   languages
>   should serve him.
> His dominion is an everlasting
>   dominion
>   that shall not pass away,
> and his kingship is one
>   that shall never be destroyed. (Dan 7:14)

This Son of Man carries out God's judgement at the appointed time. Apocalyptic writing sustains the hope that God will soon intervene in history and punish the wicked and reward the righteous. Apocalyptic literature also reaffirms the readers' confidence in the justice of God. God will raise the dead so that those who committed past injustices will be punished, and those who performed noble acts will be rewarded. In Daniel we find, therefore, the earliest explicit affirmation of the future resurrection of the dead: "Many of those who sleep in the dust of the earth shall awake, some to everlasting life, and some to shame and everlasting contempt" (Dan 12:2).

Eschatology in the New Testament

The prophetic and apocalyptic traditions of eschatological thought in the Old Testament carry over into the New Testament. For Christians, both converge at Jesus of Nazareth, who is the fulfillment of Old Testament prophecy, as well as the Son of Man who proclaims and inaugurates the kingdom of God. Just as is true of the Old Testament, the New Testament holds within its pages a diversity of eschatological perspectives. Our examination of the New Testament will focus on the Synoptics, John's Gospel, Paul's writings, and the Book of Revelation.

According to the late scripture scholar Norman Perrin, "[Mark] holds strongly the early Christian apocalyptic hope for the imminent coming of Jesus as Son of Man; moreover, [Mark] thinks of himself and his church as caught up in the events that mark the end of history."[2] In this apocalyptic drama, Jesus as Son of God (Mark 1:1) and Messiah begins the decisive overthrow of Satan's kingdom. (While Jesus is referred to both as Son of Man and Son of God in the New Testament, scholars debate exactly what the terms meant to the scripture writers, especially *Son of God*.) By healing the sick, exorcising demons, and calming the seas, Jesus exercises his authority as the Son of Man. He is also, however, the Suffering Servant of 2 Isaiah who must suffer and die in Jerusalem. In Mark 13 Jesus delivers a lengthy apocalyptic discourse about the signs that must precede the end. "When you hear of wars and rumors of wars, do not be alarmed; this must take place, but the end is still to come"

(Mark 13:7). Mark wrote somewhere around the year AD 70. The Jewish revolt against the Romans began in AD 66, and resulted in the destruction of the Temple in 70. "This shattering event," wrote Perrin, "would have brought the apocalyptic expectation to a fever pitch—such an event *must* be the beginning of the End—and Mark writes to support this view, to encourage his readers to wait and hope, and to instruct them that as Jesus himself had to go through his passion to his glory, so too they must be prepared for discipleship that involves suffering."[3]

Matthew tones down the apocalyptic fervor of Mark. We can detect this most easily by focusing on some of the parables that only appear in Matthew's Gospel. The parable of the wheat and the weeds (Matt 13:24–30) includes the typical image of judgement day as a time of separation, but the parable stresses that this separation will be a future event. In the parable of the ten bridesmaids (Matt 25:1–13), "the bridegroom was delayed" (v. 5), suggesting that the return of Christ would not occur as quickly as many thought it would. The scripture scholar Vincent Branick identified the theme of this parable as "vigilance despite delay."[4] A third parable unique to Matthew concerns the Last Judgement (Matt 25:31–46). At the end of time, the Son of Man will gather all the nations of the world and render a judgement. Like a shepherd separating sheep from goats, the Son of Man will separate the people into two groups: one will "inherit the kingdom prepared for you from the foundation of the world" (Matt 25:34), while the other will suffer "the eternal fire prepared for the devil and his angels" (Matt 25:41). The just ones receive eternal life because they fed the hungry, clothed the naked, cared for the sick, and visited the imprisoned. Those who are punished failed to do these things. This parable contains three important elements of Christian eschatology: judgement day, heaven, and hell.

Two passages found only in Luke's Gospel add to the eschatological teachings found in the Synoptic Gospels. In the parable of the rich man and the beggar Lazarus (Luke 16:19–31), Lazarus died "and was carried away by the angels to be with Abraham" (v. 22). The unnamed rich man—who would not give even a crumb to the beggar—died and was taken to a place of torment. In language reminiscent of Greek mythology, Luke describes an afterlife consisting of two areas separated by a great chasm so that those on one side may not cross over to the other. A second passage that is unique to Luke's Gospel appears in the crucifixion scene. Two criminals are crucified along with Jesus, one at each side. When one of the criminals mocks Jesus, the other rebukes him, stating that they both deserved their punishment, but that Jesus was being unjustly condemned. "Then he said, 'Jesus remember me when you come into your kingdom.' He replied, 'Truly I tell you, today you will be with me in paradise'" (Luke 23:42–43). Not only does this episode illustrate the compassionate love Christ had for the sinner, it also has been taken to mean that on that very day the criminal would be with Christ in heaven.

One of the distinctive features of the eschatology found in John's Gospel is "realized eschatology." This expression means that in Jesus, judgement came to the world. Judgement Day is not only a future event; it is a present moment in which an individual accepts or rejects Christ. "Very truly, I tell you, anyone who hears my word and believes him who sent me has eternal life, and does not come under judgment, but has passed from death to life" (John 5:24). John retains a future dimension to his eschatology, but more than any other gospel writer, he conveys the sense that the present moment is also a time of crisis and judgement.[5] Twentieth-century existentialist theologians such as Rudolf Bultmann would highlight this aspect of John's thought in their own theologies.

Paul's letters are filled with eschatological teachings, from his earliest correspondence in which he discusses the Lord's *parousia*, or second coming (1 Thes 4:13–18), to his later rhetorical heights in his Letter to the Romans: "For I am convinced that neither death, nor life, nor angels, nor rulers, nor things present, nor things to come, nor powers, nor height, nor depth, nor anything else in all creation, will be able to separate us from the love of God in Christ Jesus our Lord" (Rom 8:38–39). We will, however, focus exclusively on three passages from 1 Corinthians.

In the opening chapters of 1 Corinthians, Paul reaffirms his fundamental conviction that the crucifixion is the turning point of history. While the world may see the cross as a symbol of defeat, Christians see it as a demonstration of the power and wisdom of God (1 Cor 1:24). In this context, Paul quotes a saying based on Isaiah 64:4 that is one of the most beloved concerning the future hope of Christians: "[No] eye has seen, nor ear heard, nor the human heart conceived, what God has prepared for those who love him" (1 Cor 2:9).

In 1 Corinthians 13, we have another memorable passage, this one devoted to love. Speaking of our future destiny with God, Paul writes, "For now we see in a mirror, dimly, but then we will see face to face. Now I know only in part; then I will know fully, even as I have been fully known" (1 Cor 13:12; see also Rev 22:4). This heavenly state, which Paul describes as one in which the blessed will see God face to face and have complete knowledge of God, would later be known as "the beatific vision."

Paul addresses the question of the future resurrection of the dead in 1 Corinthians 15. Many in the Corinthian church apparently rejected the notion of the resurrection of the dead. Reading 1 Cor 15, one can surmise what objections they had to such a teaching. Aren't we body and soul, and doesn't the body return to the earth? If there is a future resurrection of the body, would a seventy-year-old person have the body of a seventy-year-old or a twenty-year-old? Paul's argument is fairly straightforward. If there is no resurrection of the dead, then Christ was not raised. If Christ has not been raised from the dead, then Christianity is a fraud (1 Cor 15:12–14). Paul insists instead that Christ's resurrection is a foreshadowing of the future resurrected state of those who have died in Christ. Using the agricultural metaphor of "the first fruits"—namely, the first crops to ripen and thus that signal the harvest is near—Paul speaks of Christ's resurrection as the "first fruits" of the future resurrected state of all believers. Paul agrees with his opponents that our physical bodies will not be resurrected, but insists that at the final judgement, the dead will be raised and will be given "spiritual bodies." "Listen, I will tell you a mystery! We will not all die, but we will all be changed, in a moment, in the twinkling of an eye, at the last trumpet. For the trumpet will sound, and the dead will be raised imperishable, and we will be changed" (1 Cor 15:51–52). Paul's concept of a single judgement day at the end of time for both the living and the dead stands in tension with the more common belief that at the end of each individual's death, the person enters into the afterlife.

The fantastic imagery of the Book of Revelation has garnered much attention in the history of Western thought. The four horsemen (Rev 6:1–8), the fall of Satan (Rev 12:7–9), and the battle of Armageddon (Rev 16:16) have inspired countless sermons, novels, and paintings. It has also produced its share of speculation over the meaning of the passages regarding the thousand-year reign of Christ (Rev 20:1–10) and "the second death" (Rev 20:6). As a work of Christian apocalyptic, Revelation offers comfort and assurance to Christians suffering religious persecution. It offers a vision of martyred Christians praising God in heaven (Rev 7:9–17) and a future age in which God will wipe every tear from our eyes, death will no longer exist, and there will be no wailing or pain (Rev 21:4). In terms of the entire biblical narrative, Revelation returns us to paradise where we once again enjoy unfettered access to the tree of life (Rev 22:14). This rich symbolism of the biblical narrative generates the Christian grand vision of time as a movement from paradise, to paradise lost, to paradise regained. The theological subdivisions (Christology, ecclesiology, eschatology, etc.) are simply chapters in a larger story that spans from creation to the end of time.

Eschatology in the Early Church

Second-century Christian writers were divided on the question of how to interpret the apocalyptic predictions found in the Book of Revelation. Some thinkers shared the apocalyptic expectation of Christ's return on the clouds of heaven and the beginning of his thousand-year reign. This belief is known as chiliasm or millenarianism. The theologian Josef Finkenzeller explained, "By chiliasm (Greek: *chilioi* = a thousand) or millenarianism (Latin: *mille* = a thousand) is meant the expectation of a thousand-year reign during which, even before the end of the world, Christ will rule together with the just who have already been raised from the dead."[6] The second-century apologist Justin Martyr wrote, "But I, and all other entirely orthodox Christians, know that there will be a resurrection of the flesh, and also a thousand years in a Jerusalem built up and adorned and enlarged, as the prophets Ezekiel and Isaiah, and all the rest, acknowledge."[7] Other theologians seemed to have little interest in end-time speculation and often understood passages about the nearness of Christ's return to be incentives to repent.[8]

One belief contained in the Book of Revelation was undisputed: the immediate acceptance of the martyrs into heaven. In John's vision of heaven in Rev 7, "there was a great multitude that no one could count, from every nation, from all tribes and peoples and languages, standing before the throne and before the Lamb, robed in white, with palm branches in their hands" (v. 9). The elder explains to John, "These are they who have come out of the great ordeal; they have washed their robes and made them white in the blood of the Lamb. / For this reason they are before the throne of God, / and worship him day and night within his temple, / and the one who is seated on the throne will shelter them" (Rev 7:14–15). The consensus in the early church was that the martyrs, those who had "washed their robes in the blood of the Lamb," were received into God's heavenly temple immediately upon their deaths. Clement of Rome believed that the apostle Peter "left us for his well-earned place in glory." Referring to Paul, Clement also wrote, "He taught righteousness to all the world; and after reaching the furthest limits of the West, and bearing his testimony before kings and rulers, he passed out of this world and was received into the holy places."[9] Because death does not break the bond of believers, the saints in heaven join with those on earth in offering praise to God. This concept of the unity of the church on earth with the saints in heaven would later be called "the communion of saints."

Irenaeus of Lyons (ca. 130 to ca. 200) offered a creative, original synthesis of anthropology, Christology, and eschatology that would prove highly influential in Eastern Christian thought. Instead of seeing the original state of humanity as one of perfection, Irenaeus regarded it as a state of immaturity. Adam and Eve were not disobedient sinners as much as curious children. Furthermore, Irenaeus saw two distinct claims being made in the biblical verse that states that humans were created in the image and likeness of God (Gen 1:26). According to the theologian John Hick, Irenaeus believed that "the image of God" represented our "nature as an intelligent creature capable of fellowship" with God, while "likeness of God" referred to our "final perfecting by the Holy Spirit."[10] Human history is the arena in which the spiritual transition from image to likeness occurs.

The appearance of Christ is both a recapitulation of what has gone before, and an anticipation of what is to come. As the patristics scholar Rowan Greer explained,

> [Christ] fulfills for the first time the promise of Adam's creation. The summing up is referred by Irenaeus both to the Incarnation (*AH* 3.16.6) and to Christ's second coming at the end of the age (*AH* 1.10.1). It seems clear that we should understand that what is in principle true in Christ is made true in fact at the end of the age. Or, to put it another way, human destiny, which is presently fulfilled in the Incarnate Lord, will be consummated in the age to come.[11]

In Eastern thought, the transfiguration (Mark 9:2–8) would come to occupy a prominent role in linking Christology with eschatology. In his dazzling white appearance, Christ prefigured the state of the resurrected bodies at the end of time.

The theologian Origen (ca. 185 to ca. 254) advanced the most controversial eschatological proposals in the early church. Origen's theology revolved around the Greek term *apokatastasis* that appears in Acts 3:21 and is usually translated "universal restoration." Origen envisioned a future age in which all creation would be restored to God. In his work *On First Principles*, Origen asserted that "the end is always like the beginning."[12] We can detect in Origen's thinking the basic Christian pattern of paradise—fall—restoration, but he included one more element in the mix. Origen believed that there had been a succession of ages before the one in which we now live, and held that there would be a future succession of ages after the present one. In Ecclesiastes we read, "Is there a thing of which it is said, 'See, this is new'? It has already been, in the *ages before us*" (Eccl 1:10, emphasis added; see Origen *OFP* III, V, 3). The letter to the Ephesians speaks of "the ages to come" (Eph 2:7; see Origen *OFP* II, III, 5). Origen concluded that a succession of ages followed the beginning and another succession will precede the end.

Based on his interpretation of scripture, Greek philosophy, and the various texts he would have studied over the course of his classical education, Origen forged a grand vision of the past, the present, and the future life of the souls inhabiting the universe. Origen speculated that at the beginning, all rational minds would have existed in a spiritual heavenly paradise where they would have unceasingly contemplated God. The minds, however, became distracted or inattentive; consequently, they fell. In the course of their fall, they "cooled," and took on various types of material bodies (*OFP* II, 8, 3). Origen sees an etymological connection between the words *soul* and *coldness*.[13] The various material forms that the souls acquired account for the existence of angels, demons, and humans. The only mind not to fall was the mind of Christ. If the end will in fact be like the beginning, then the journey is one in which the souls will return to the original place in the heavenly realm, individually purified and collectively unified.

Here we reach the most controversial element of Origen's scheme. Could even Satan be restored to God in the end? If so, what is the meaning of the biblical passages regarding the eternal punishment of hell? If the end is indeed like the beginning, then even Satan could be restored to God. What then of the punishment of hell? For Origen, all punishment is educational in nature. He commented that

> towards certain sinners God is longsuffering, not without reason, but because in regard to the immortality of the soul and the eternal world it will be to their advantage that they should not be helped quickly to salvation but should be brought to it more slowly after having experienced many ills. For physicians also, even though they may be able to heal a man quickly, yet act in a contrary way whenever they suspect the existence of a hidden poison in the body. They do this because they wish to heal the patient more surely, considering it better to let him remain in his fever and sickness for a long time in order that he may regain permanent health, rather than appear to restore him quickly to strength and afterwards to see him relapse and this quicker cure prove only temporary.[14]

The punishment of hell, therefore, is not everlasting in the sense of enduring for all time, but rather until the end of this age. In later ages, the possibility of repentance exists. God will not force the devil to return, but given enough ages to come, and the free will of souls, then perhaps all things will once again be subject to God. As Paul writes in 1 Corinthians: "When all things are subjected to him, then the Son himself will also be subjected to the one who put all things in subjection under him, so that God may be all in all" (1 Cor 15:28). Origen's supporters would insist that we could at least hold out hope for such an outcome.

While Origen's theology captivated the imagination of many of the early theologians, others openly attacked his work. Methodius of Olympius (d. 311) argued that Origen's view of the resurrection of the body was especially deficient. Methodius wanted to preserve a far greater continuity between our present earthly bodies and our future resurrected bodies. According to the patristics scholar J. N. D. Kelly, Methodius insisted that our resurrected bodies "will indeed have heightened qualities, for they will return to the impassability and glory which the human form possessed before the Fall; but they will be *materially* identical with our present earthly bodies."[15] While the state of the future resurrected body may seem a very abstract or speculative question to tackle, it was one of great pastoral significance. As the theologian Alister McGrath noted,

> The issue emerged as theologically significant during the persecution of Christians in Lyons around the years 175–77. Aware that Christians professed belief in the "resurrection of the body," their pagan oppressors burned the bodies of the Christians they had just martyred, and threw their ashes into the River Rhone. This, they believed, would prevent the resurrection of these martyrs, in that there was now no body to be raised. Christian theologians responded by arguing that God was able to restore all that the body had lost through this process of destruction.[16]

Methodius compared the resurrection of the dead to the sculptor who casts a gold statue only to have it senselessly defaced by someone who could not stand its beauty. The sculptor then melts the statue and recasts it, restoring it to its original form without any defect or flaw.[17]

The early church theologians also speculated about what eternal life with God would be like. The theologian Walter Burghardt wrote,

> Finally, for the fathers, what is life everlasting? Different writers stress different facets. For Origen, the blessedness of the saints is a gradual progress in understanding until, loving God so utterly as to outlaw sin forever, they have "only one occupation...the contemplation of God, so that, being formed in the knowledge of the Father, they may all become in the strict sense Son, just as now it is the Son alone who knows the Father." In Cyril of Jerusalem's grasp on the Creed, "eternal life," the purpose of Christian existence, means being forever with the Lord. For Basil, the risen enjoy one another and God as friends, contemplate God with rapturous awareness of His person and presence. For Gregory of Nazianzus, heaven is festival unending, joyous gazing on the Trinity, deification.[18]

Not all theologians shared Origen's optimism that all souls might enjoy this future heavenly state. For them, hell was an eternal punishment, a place "where their worm never dies, and the fire is never quenched" (Mark 9:48).

Augustine's *City of God*, which took him over ten years to write, is a masterful synthesis of Augustine's eschatology, theology of history, and political theory. Written ostensibly as a defense against the charge that the cessation of the state worship of the Roman gods caused the fall of the Roman Empire, *City of God* also presents a panoramic view of history from the time of Cain and Abel to the end of the world. For Augustine, humans live in either "the city of God" or "the city of man." Those who live in the city of God turn their love toward God while those who live in the city of man seek their own satisfaction as the highest good.

> What we see then, is that two societies have issued from two kinds of loves. Worldly society has flowered from a

selfish love which dared to despise even God, whereas the communion of saints is rooted in a love of God that is ready to trample on self. In a word, this latter relies on the Lord, whereas the other boasts that it can get along by itself. The city of man seeks the praise of men, whereas the glory of the other is to hear God in the witness of conscience.[19]

Augustine believed that the destiny of the city of God was "an eternal kingdom under God" while the city of man would suffer "eternal punishment along with the Devil."[20] In the meantime, Augustine saw life in this world as a struggle between the two cities. This, in part, underlies what has been called Augustine's "political realism." According to the theologian Eugene TeSelle, this "political realism" is "a refusal to hold illusions about the nature of political life, a willingness, on the one hand, to make use of the methods that are effective in the real world, but at the same time an exercise of restraint growing out of the sense of the limitations of the political process."[21]

Eschatology in Medieval Thought

Augustine's theological reading of history deeply influenced Joachim of Fiore (ca. 1135–1202). Joachim divided human history into three eras, each corresponding to one of the three persons of the Trinity. The theologian William Placher explained,

Joachim has sought the hidden meaning of history, writing works full of numerical symbols. He divided history into three great ages: the Age of the Father, ruled by law, in which people were to work and marry and the ideal was the Old Testament patriarch; the Age of the Son, ruled by grace, in which people were to learn and the ideal was the priest who teaches; and the Age of the Spirit, ruled by love, in which people were to praise God and the ideal is the monk filled with the love of God.[22]

Joachim included in this scheme a criticism of the institutional church. Joachim called for an end to the "ecclesiastical order, which struggles over the letter of the Gospel" and the beginning of "a new [form of] religion, which will be altogether free and spiritual."[23] A branch of the Franciscans known as the "Spirituals" were drawn to this teaching and saw in the life of Francis of Assisi the start of the age of the Spirit.

The rise of cities was one of factors that allowed the mendicant orders such as the Franciscans to flourish. With the concentration of the population in cities, monks could earn enough money begging to carry out their ministry. The rise of cities also impacted how Christians spoke of the afterlife. Alister McGrath observed, "The rise of the Italian city state and a new interest in urban architecture led to the image of the heavenly city gaining priority over the paradisiacal garden in the twelfth and thirteenth centuries. Great Renaissance cities such as Florence saw themselves as recapturing the glory of ancient Rome, and lent new credibility to conceiving heaven in urban terms."[24] The end of human history was pictured not as a return to the Garden of Eden, but as entrance into the heavenly Jerusalem.

The theologian Dermot Lane argues that thinkers in the medieval period increasingly posed questions of eschatology in individual rather than collective terms. This shift can be detected in the medieval interest in purgatory. Lane wrote,

> One such development in the late twelfth century is the emphasis given to purgatory as a separate place and state existing somewhere between heaven and hell. While it is true that a sense of purgation and the forgiveness of sins can be found in the biblical tradition (2 Mac 12:43–46; Mt. 12:32; 1 Cor 3:10–15) and in the early Christian tradition (e.g., through the practice of praying for the dead which was established by the third century), it was only in the twelfth century that the existence of purgatory as a place came into prominence. The Second Council of Lyons (1274) refers explicitly to purgatory, though it carefully avoids any discussion of the question of fire out of deference to the Eastern Church. Less than a hundred

years later purgatory was to become fixed in the western imagination through Dante's Divine Comedy.[25]

Theologians spoke less about the final, or last, judgement that awaits all humans and spoke more about what happens at the moment of each individual's death.

The concept of purgatory also raised fundamental questions about the relationship of body and soul. The Platonic tradition sharply distinguished between the body and soul. For the Platonists, death was seen as the separation of the soul from the body. In contrast to his teacher Plato, Aristotle offered a more unified view of body and soul in the human person. With the rediscovery of Aristotle's writings in the West during the Middle Ages, thinkers such as Thomas Aquinas began to rethink the relationship of body and soul. As then Cardinal Ratzinger explained, for Aquinas "both body and soul are realities only thanks to each other and as oriented towards each other. Though they are not identical, they are nevertheless one; and as one, they constitute the single human being...the soul can never completely leave behind its relationship with matter."[26]

Because he did not hold to the idea that soul would exist as a disembodied entity, it would seem that Aquinas would have argued that persons enter into the afterlife immediately upon their deaths. But, as the historian Jeffrey Burton pointed out, Aquinas "held to the dominant belief of his time that souls must wait for reembodiment until the general resurrection and the Last Judgment."[27] Aquinas and other like-minded thinkers struggled to reconcile their understanding of the human person as both body and soul with the scriptural claim that there will be a last judgement. How, then, should we understand this interim, or intermediate state, between an individual's death and the last judgement? As Burton noted,

> The problem of the interim continued to vex the theologians on into the fourteenth century. Either we have complete beatitude at the moment of death, or we do not have it before the Last Judgment. If we have to wait to the endtime, where and in what form are we waiting? But if we have it right away, do we have it without our

445

bodies? The dispute racked the church of the early four-teenth century, as theologians ransacked the fathers to support one or another position. Most of the earlier fathers had assumed that souls had to wait until the end-time for the beatific vision. But others took the view that the blessed see God right away at death, and this latter view had become dominant in the West during the scholastic period and was asserted again at the Council of Vienne in 1311. The East on the whole continued to accept the earlier views.[28]

Most theologians combined the belief in an individual judgement and a general, or final, judgement by arguing that at the death of each individual the soul enters into eternity where human distinc-tions of past, present, and future do not apply.

Aquinas's positive regard for the material world and the human body stemmed from his grand vision of creation as a move-ment from God *(exitus)* and eschatology as a return to God *(redi-tus)*. The nature of the human being longs for its ultimate happiness in God, and the moral and spiritual life of the Christian is a deepening of this innate attraction. The supreme good, the ultimate happiness, draws humans back to God. In this earthly life, each individual is a pilgrim, "one on the way,"[29] and at journey's end, the pilgrim receives a heavenly "homecoming."[30] In this per-spective, the natural and the supernatural have a continuity; the former being elevated into the latter.

Not all in Aquinas's day shared his fundamental optimism about the human condition. In the thirteenth century, the hymn *"Dies Irae"* ("Day of Wrath") appeared, a "chant synonymous with funeral liturgies until the reform of the funeral rite following Vatican II (1962–65)"; it's traditionally attributed to the Franciscan Thomas of Celano (d. 1260).[31] The hymn begins, "The day of wrath, the day when the world is reduced to ashes…"[32] The *"Dies Irae"* accents the terror that judgement day will bring, but also looks to the merciful Christ to save the sinner. The terror described by the *"Dies Irae"* became palpable when the Black Death swept throughout Europe in the fourteenth century. The wrath of God provoked by human sinfulness, and the mercy of Christ as the one

who gave his life as an offering for sin, would become two dominant themes in Luther's thought.

Eschatology in the Protestant
and Catholic Reformations

Martin Luther shared many of the eschatological expectations
of his medieval forebears. Firmly rooted in the Augustinian monk
was an emphasis on the sovereignty of God, the disordered nature
of the human will, and the centrality of faith to the Christian life.
Luther did not, however, accept the existence of purgatory. The
theologian William J. La Due summarized Luther's view in the following manner:

> The eschatology of Martin Luther (1483–1546) is
> absolutely opposed to anything resembling purgatory, but
> the basic orientation of his thought generally follows the
> medieval patterns. He describes death as the result of
> God's anger against humankind. It is seen as the punish-
> ment par excellence for human sinfulness. No one views
> death without agitation and fear. The gospel, however,
> gives Christians a new approach to death. We are urged to
> die willingly, and we are able to do so through the power
> of Christ's death, which transforms death into a kind of
> "slumber" into which believers move peacefully.[33]

The existence of purgatory is a prerequisite for the practice of selling indulgences, which Luther vehemently rejected. The twenty-
seventh thesis of the famous Ninety-Five Theses stated, "There is
no divine authority for preaching that the soul flies out of purgatory immediately the money clinks in the bottom of the chest."[34]

In response to Luther's charges, the bishops at Trent reaffirmed
the Catholic belief "that purgatory exists, and that the souls detained
there are helped by the prayers of the faithful and most of all by the
acceptable sacrifice of the altar; the holy council charges bishops to
ensure that sound teaching on purgatory, handed down by the holy

fathers and sacred councils, is to be believed and held by the christian faithful and everywhere preached and expounded."[35]

When discussing the papacy, Luther frequently spoke in highly charged eschatological language, often calling the pope the Antichrist. As the Lutheran scholar Paul Althaus explained,

> For Luther, eschatological events are taking place in the midst of the present. Because the anitchrist is already present, Luther expects and hopes that the end will come in the near future and desires it. The Middle Ages feared the Day of Wrath but Luther desires the coming of Jesus, because he will bring an end to the antichrist and bring about redemption.[36]

Reflecting on the state of humanity, Luther commented, "I am forced to firmly believe that Christ must soon return because their sins are so great that heaven can no longer tolerate them. They incite and resist judgment day so much that it must come upon them before too much time."[37]

The Protestant Reformers held a variety of views on the eschatological significance of the events swirling around them. In the city of Münster apocalyptic fervor reached its highest pitch. A succession of religious leaders there proclaimed the city "the new Jerusalem" of the Book of Revelation. Rival forces eventually attacked the city, killed most of its inhabitants, captured and tortured the remaining leaders, and displayed their bodies in an iron cage hung from the tower of St. Lambert's church.[38] John Calvin, by contrast, was far more restrained in his application of biblical eschatological language to his own time. The theologian David Fergusson observed,

> John Calvin, while more reserved in his use of apocalyptic language imagery—Revelation was the only book of the New Testament on which he did not write a commentary—had a strong sense of the union of the believer with the risen and ascended Lord, particularly in his doctrine of the Lord's supper. The assurance of salvation with Christ in heaven is here affirmed in a more immediate and particular way.[39]

Eschatology in the Modern Age

The leading thinkers in the early modern age saw little practical value in the traditional discussions of eschatology. As the theologian Alister McGrath observed, "The intensely rationalist atmosphere of the Enlightenment led to criticism of the Christian doctrine of the last things as ignorant superstition, devoid of any real basis in life."[40] The great Enlightenment thinker Immanuel Kant reinterpreted theological categories along moral lines. Christ, for example, became the supreme teacher of morality. As the theologian and cardinal Avery Dulles noted, "The eschatological teaching of Scripture, for Kant, was a purely symbolic portrayal of the ideal to be approached through the practice of pure rational religion. The Kingdom of God established itself invisibly within the souls of those who followed the precepts of pure reason."[41]

This Kantian approach was given a theological endorsement in the Protestant liberalism of Albrecht Ritschl (1822–89). Ritschl understood the Kingdom of God to be "the organization of humanity through action inspired by love."[42] The historian James Livingston noted,

> According to many interpreters, the Kingdom of God is the regulative principle of Ritschl's theology and reveals his concentration on the social and teleological character of Christianity. For Ritschl Christianity is not principally a good already gained for the individual but a social ideal yet to be realized. The Kingdom of God is the highest good of the Christian community, but only insofar as "it forms at the same time the ethical ideal, for whose attainment the members of the community bind themselves together through their definitive reciprocal action."[43]

Many of Ritschl's followers linked this understanding of the Kingdom of God as the ethical ideal of humanity with a belief in the inevitable progress of the human race. Human history seemed to be on a path toward victory over disease, strife, and ignorance.

A similar sense of the inevitability of historical progress can be detected in the work of G.W. F. Hegel (1770–1831). Hegel insisted that historical developments had an internal logic that could be discerned by the human mind. In this dialectical progress opposing ideas are reconciled and reach a higher unity or expression of thought. Some of Hegel's interpreters believed that Hegel had provided the framework in which we can best understand the incarnation—the unity of divine and human nature in a person. Others, such as Karl Marx, understood history to be headed to a communistic state in which social and economic distinctions would be overcome. The final realization of the deepest aspirations of humanity are for Marx found not in a heavenly state beyond this world bestowed by God, but in the earthly realm brought about by human struggle.

Biblical scholarship around the turn of the twentieth century demolished the foundation upon which liberal and Hegelian theologians had constructed their positions. Johannes Weiss (1863–1914) and Albert Schweitzer (1875–1965) insisted that Jesus' proclamation of the kingdom of God had little to do with either the establishment of "an ethical commonwealth" (Kant) or the progression of human history. According to Weiss and Schweitzer, Jesus preached the kingdom of God as a future reality, not a present one. God alone would bring about this kingdom; human effort played no role in the coming of the kingdom. Jesus called for a renunciation of the world, not a commitment to its improvement. The "kingdom of God" did not refer to individuals' inner surrender to God as the king of their lives. Rather, contended Weiss, "The Kingdom of God as Jesus thought of it is never something subjective, inward, or spiritual, but is always the objective Messianic Kingdom..."[44] Weiss and Schweitzer left twentieth-century theologians with the challenge of finding the relevance of the future-oriented, eschatological preaching of Jesus for a modern, scientific audience.

This question of the relevance of the eschatological preaching of Jesus for modern Christians far removed from the worldview of first century Jewish and Christian thought preoccupied the biblical theologian Rudolf Bultmann (1884–1976). Bultmann insisted that Christians should differentiate between the message of the New Testament and the mythological framework that the New Testament writers used to convey their message. The message endures; the framework probably doesn't. The apocalyptic worldview that envisioned the coming of the Son of Man on the clouds of heaven, great signs of tribulation in heaven and on earth, and judgement day, can be transposed into modern existentialist categories. The eschatological character of Jesus' preaching can now be understood as the moment of decision confronted by every person at every moment of his or her life. Bultmann wrote,

> According to the New Testament, *Jesus Christ is the eschatological event*, the action of God by which God has set an end to the old world. In the preaching of the Christian Church the eschatological event will ever again become present and does become present ever and again in faith. The old world has reached its end for the believer, he is "a new creature in Christ." For the old world has reached its end with the fact that he himself as "the old man" has reached his end and is now "a new man," a free man.[45]

In the preaching of the church, the eschatological offer is made available to every person of every generation. "Jesus Christ is the eschatological event not as an established fact of past time but as repeatedly present, as addressing you and me here and now in preaching."[46]

Whereas Bultmann reinterpreted biblical eschatological language in individualistic terms, Jürgen Moltmann (b. 1928) emphasized the social and political significance of eschatology. In his highly influential work *Theology of Hope*, which was first published in 1964, Moltmann argued for theological priority of eschatology. "A proper theology would therefore have to be constructed in light of its future goal. Eschatology should not be its end, but its beginning."[47] Moltmann is quick to note, however, that for Christian theology, speculation about the future is not simply a flight of imagination, but is based on the resurrection of Christ. "Hence the question whether all statements about the future are grounded in the person and history of Jesus Christ provides it with the touchstone by which to distinguish the spirit of eschatology from that of utopia."[48] This eschatological hope, therefore, does not draw our attention away from the world to some heavenly afterlife, but rather focuses our attention on the "possibilities of change" in the social, economic, and political realities of the world.[49]

Moltmann's work on eschatology inspired feminist theologians to envision a future era in which gender divisions would be overcome, and more importantly, create practices that anticipate the future full realization of equality. The theologian Letty Russell, for example, applies Paul's proleptic teachings to the cause of feminism. "Proleptic actions [are those that] anticipate the situation for which they work by living *as if* the situation, at least in part, has already arrived."[50] Russell continues,

> A woman who is an ordained minister also becomes a sign of the longed-for future of liberation and equality....Her presence in the pulpit or at the Holy table helps to symbolize the presence of the coming God who is beyond all distinctions of male and female. The singing of a hymn in which a mixture of female and male pronouns are used to speak of God and the human beings present may have the same proleptic effect. The changing of language has the power to change the way people think about and name the world, as well as being a way of demonstrating in fact that "you are all one in Christ Jesus" (Gal 3:28).[51]

Commenting on Russell's "proleptic eschatology," the theologian M. Shawn Copeland wrote, "Loyalty to [the authority of the Word of God] is measured by solidarity with the poor and marginalized, action for justice, and new spiritual and practical disciplines for holistic living. This is what Russell calls full partnership with one another and with God in Christ in the power of the Spirit."[52]

Many of the documents produced at Vatican II incorporate eschatological themes. Perhaps most notably, the Dogmatic Constitution on the Church *(Lumen gentium)* speaks of the church as a "pilgrim church":

> Already the final age of the world is with us (cf. 1 Cor. 10:11) and the renewal of the world is irrevocably under way; it is even now anticipated in a certain real way, for the Church on earth is endowed already with a sanctity that is real though imperfect. However, until there be realized new heavens and a new earth in which justice

dwells (cf. 2 Pet. 3;13) the pilgrim Church, in its sacraments and institutions, which belongs to this present age, carries the mark of this world which will pass, and she herself takes her place among the creatures which groan and travail yet and await the revelation of the sons of God (cf. Rom. 8:19–22).[53]

The church possesses an eschatological character; the Church "longs for the completed kingdom, with all her strength, hopes and desires to be united in glory with her king."[54] Unlike earlier theological manuals in which the kingdom of God was equated with the church, *Lumen gentium* preserved an eschatological tension between the present reality of the Kingdom in the life of the church and its future, full, and final realization.

In Dante's *Inferno*, the sign above the gate leading to hell reads, "ABANDON ALL HOPE, YOU WHO ENTER HERE."[55] The hope of Christians, a hope that must never be abandoned, is not rooted in reports of those who have been revived after being declared clinically dead, or a general optimism that everything works out in the end, but rather in the belief that Christ suffered, died, and was raised. In faith, we hope that we too will one day share in the eternal presence of God's love.

Discussion Questions

1. What role does hope play in the Christian life?
2. Do you believe that there will be a future bodily resurrection of the dead?
3. Do you believe that some who have died are already in heaven?
4. Can those who have died pray with us to God?
5. Does the Book of Revelation offer a literal description of the events surrounding the end of the world?
6. Is it possible for Satan to return to God at the end of time?
7. How would you describe heaven?
8. Do you believe in hell? Why? Why not?

9. Do you believe in purgatory? Should we pray for the dead? Why? Why not?
10. Can we by our actions bring about the kingdom of God on the earth?

Suggested Readings

For a very helpful overview, see William L. La Due, *The Trinity Guide to Eschatology* (New York: Continuum, 2004); and chapter XXXI of Richard P. McBrien, *Catholicism*, New Edition (San Francisco: HarperCollins, 1994). Also helpful is Zachary Hayes, *Visions of a Future* (Collegeville, MN: The Liturgical Press, 1992). A more technical work, but also very helpful is Hans Schwarz, *Eschatology* (Grand Rapids: Eerdmans, 2000). Alister E. McGrath, *A Brief History of Heaven* (Malden, MA: Blackwell, 2003) is a very readable work. See also Bernard McGinn, *Antichrist: Two Thousand Years of the Human Fascination with Evil* (San Francisco: HarperSanFrancisco, 1994).

Notes

1. Lawrence Boadt, *Reading the Old Testament* (Mahwah, NJ: Paulist Press, 1984), 116.
2. Norman Perrin, *The New Testament: An Introduction* (New York: Harcourt Brace Jovanovich, 1974), 144.
3. Ibid.
4. Vincent P. Branick, *Understanding the New Testament and Its Message* (Mahwah, NJ: Paulist Press, 1998), 131.
5. See Raymond E. Brown's discussion of the vertical and horizontal dimensions of John's eschatology in *The Gospel According to John I–XII*, Anchor Bible, vol. 29 (Garden City, NY: Doubleday, 1966), cxv–cxvi.
6. Josef Finkenzeller, "Chiliasm," in Wolfgang Beinert and Francis Schüssler Fiorenza, eds., *Handbook of Catholic Theology* (New York: Crossroad, 1995), 69.

7. Justin Martyr, "Dialogue with Trypho" LXXX, 5. Quoted in L. W. Barnard, "Justin Martyr's Eschatology," in *Vigiliae Christianae* 19 (1965): 93.

8. See Brian E. Daley, "Eschatology," in Everett Ferguson, ed., *Encyclopedia of Early Christianity* (New York: Garland Publishing, 1997), 383; and Rudolf Bultmann, "Man Between the Times According to the New Testament" in *Existence and Faith* (New York: World Publishing Co., 1960), 251.

9. Clement of Rome, "The First Epistle of Clement to the Corinthians," 5, in Maxwell Staniforth, trans., *Early Christian Writings* (New York: Penguin Books, 1968), 25.

10. John Hick, *Evil and the God of Love*, rev. ed. (San Francisco: Harper and Row, 1977), 211.

11. Rowan A. Greer, *Broken Lights and Mended Lives* (University Park, PA: The Pennsylvania State University Press, 1986), 38. The citation AH refers to Irenaeus' work *Against Heresies*.

12. Origen, *On First Principles* I, VI, 2, G. W. Butterworth, trans. (Glouster, MA: Peter Smith, 1973), 53.

13. See the "Introduction," in *Origen*, trans. and with an intro. by Rowan Greer, (New York: Paulist Press, 1979), 10–12.

14. Origen, *On First Principles* III, 1, 13, 181.

15. J. N. D. Kelly, *Early Christian Doctrines*, rev. ed. (San Francisco: Harper and Row, 1978), 476. Emphasis his.

16. Alister McGrath, *A Brief History of Heaven* (Malden, MA: Blackwell, 2003), 34.

17. Ibid., 34–35.

18. Walter J. Burghardt, "Eschaton and Resurrection: Patristic Insights," in Joseph Papin, ed., *The Eschaton: A Community of Love* (Villanova, PA: Villanova University Press, 1971), 209.

19. Augustine, *City of God* XIV, 28, translated by Gerald G. Walsh, Demetrius B. Zema, Grace Monahan, and Daniel J. Honan (Garden City, NY: Image Books, 1958), 321.

20. Ibid., XV, 1, 323.

21. Eugene TeSelle, *Augustine the Theologian* (Eugene, OR: Wipf and Stock Publishers, 1970), 272.

22. William C. Placher, *A History of Christian Theology* (Philadelphia: Westminster Press, 1983), 149–50.

23. Quoted in Jaroslav Pelikan, *The Christian Tradition*, vol. 3 (Chicago: University of Chicago Press, 1978), 302.

24. McGrath, *A Brief History of Heaven*, 19.

25. Dermot A. Lane, "Eschatology," in Joseph A. Komonchak, ed., *The New Dictionary of Theology* (Wilmington, DE: Michael Glazier, 1987), 334.

26. Joseph Cardinal Ratzinger, *Eschatology: Death and Eternal Life*, vol. 9 of Johann Auer and Joseph Ratzinger, *Dogmatic Theology*, Michael Waldstein, trans. (Washington, DC: The Catholic University of America Press, 1988), 178–79.

27. Jeffrey Burton Russell, *A History of Heaven* (Princeton, NJ: Princeton University Press, 1997), 136.

28. Ibid., 138.

29. Josef Pieper, *On Hope*, Mary Frances McCarthy, trans. (San Francisco: Ignatius Press, 1986), 11.

30. Joseph Cardinal Ratzinger, "The End of Time," in Tiemo Rainer and Claus Urban, eds., *The End of Time?* (Mahwah, NJ: Paulist Press, 2004), 21

31. "Dies irae," in Richard P. McBrien, ed., The *HarperCollins Encyclopedia of Catholicism* (San Francisco: HarperCollins, 1995), 417.

32. Quoted in Rosalind and Christopher Brooke, *Popular Religion in the Middle Ages* (London: Thames and Hudson, 1984), 152.

33. William J. La Due, *The Trinity Guide to Eschatology* (New York: Continuum, 2004), 18.

34. Martin Luther, "Ninety-Five Theses," in John Dillenberger, ed., *Martin Luther* (Chicago: Quadrangle Books, 1961), 493.

35. Council of Trent, Session 25, in Norman Tanner, ed., *Decrees of the Ecumenical Councils*, vol. 2 (London: Sheed and Ward; Washington, DC: Georgetown University Press, 199), 774.

36. Paul Althaus, *The Theology of Martin Luther* (Philadelphia: Fortress Press, 1966), 420.

37. Quoted in Hans Schwarz, *Eschatology* (Grand Rapids: Eerdmans, 2000), 311.

38. Carter Lindberg, The European Reformations (Cambridge, MA: Blackwell, 1996), 224.

39. David Fergusson, "Eschatology," in Colin Gunton, ed., *The Cambridge Companion to Christian Doctrine* (New York: Cambridge University Press, 1997), 232.

40. Alister McGrath, *Christian Theology* (Cambridge, MA: Blackwell, 1994), 469.

41. Avery Dulles, "The Church as Eschatological Community," in Papin, *The Eschaton*, 77.

42. Quoted in James C. Livingston, *Modern Christian Thought*, 2nd ed., vol. 1 (Upper Saddle River, NJ: Prentice Hall, 1997), 280.

43. Ibid. Italics his.

44. Quoted in Wendall Willis, "The Discovery of the Eschatological Kingdom: Johannes Weiss and Albert Schweitzer," in Wendall Willis, ed., *The Kingdom of God in 20th-Century Interpretation* (Peabody, MA: Hendrickson Publishers, 1987), 4n24. See also Richard H. Hiers, *Jesus and the Future* (Atlanta: John Knox Press, 1981), 2–4.

45. Rudolf Bultmann, *History and Eschatology* (New York: Harper and Brothers, 1957), 151; italics are Bultmann's.

46. Ibid., 151–52.

47. Jürgen Moltmann, *Theology of Hope* (San Francisco: HarperCollins, 1991), 16.

48. Ibid., 17. See also Richard Bauckham, "Moltmann's *Theology of Hope* Revisited," *Scottish Journal of Theology* 42 (1989): 199–214.

49. Moltmann, *Theology of Hope*, 25.

50. Letty Russell, *Human Liberation in a Feminist Perspective—A Theology* (Philadelphia: Westminster Press, 1974), 46.

51. Ibid., 46–47.

52. M. Shawn Copeland, "Journeying to the Household of God," in Margaret A. Farley and Serene Jones, eds., *Liberating Eschatology* (Louisville, KY: Westminster John Knox Press, 1999), 42.

53. *Lumen gentium* 48, in Austin P. Flannery, ed., *Documents of Vatican II* (Grand Rapids: Eerdmans, 1975), 408.

54. *Lumen gentium*, 5 in Flannery, *Documents*, 353. See also Dulles, "The Church as Eschatological Community" in Papin, *The Eschaton*, 81.

55. Dante, *Inferno*, Canto III translated by Robert Pinsky (New York: Farrar, Straus, and Giroux, 1994), 19.

15

PUTTING IT ALL TOGETHER

Our exploration of the major divisions within Catholic Christian theology has included discussions about the Bible, church history, revelation, God, Christ, the church, the sacraments, moral theology, spirituality, and eschatology. As we conclude our investigation, we need to look back over the topics that we have covered and look ahead to how we might continue our study of theology. In terms of looking back over the course, it might be helpful to take a moment and ask ourselves what exactly we believe with regard to the subjects we have covered. In terms of looking ahead, we need to consider the ongoing role of theology in the life of the church and our own personal faith journeys.

Looking Back: A Personal Inventory

In order to investigate a topic as broad as Christian theology, we needed to divide our study into manageable units. Focusing on one specific area of Christian thought or practice at a time seemed to be the most orderly way to survey the field. This systematic approach, though useful and perhaps even necessary in an academic setting, does have one chief disadvantage. In the course of learning what the great thinkers of the tradition have taught, we often devote more attention to understanding their positions than formulating our own.

One of the values of taking a course in theology is that it provides students with the opportunity to clarify their own positions on important matters relating to the Christian faith. While a theology course should impart the distilled wisdom of the great minds who struggled with the same questions that we ask today, it should also serve as an invitation to construct, clarify, or challenge our own thinking. We are aided in this endeavor by those around us, in class discussions, and in dorm room debates. However, after we have heard what everyone else has had to say, we still need to have some time to ourselves to think over the issues. This, of course, does not mean that we will resolve each and every question, or that our answers may not change over time. Nevertheless, there is a value to forcing ourselves to state as clearly as possible what we believe about God, Christ, and the other central questions of our faith. Taking a personal inventory of our beliefs, especially at the end of an introductory course in theology, might prove a useful exercise both academically and religiously. It may help us tie together many of the ideas discussed in the course as well as help us to articulate our own positions regarding Christian belief. Below are ten questions that might serve as a way of taking a personal inventory of one's Christian beliefs.

1. What effect should Christian faith make on how we live our lives?
2. What is the central message of the Gospel?
3. In what ways has God been revealed to us?
4. Who is God?
5. Who was Jesus Christ? What was his message?
6. What is the purpose of the church?
7. What do we mean when we say the Eucharist is "the Body of Christ"?
8. What is a sound moral code by which to live our lives?
9. How can we come to a greater awareness of the presence of God in our lives?
10. What happens to us after we die?

Answers to basic questions such as these form the very foundation on which even the most complex theological arguments are built. Returning to fundamental questions such as these often helps us construct our own positions as well as understand the positions of others.

Looking Ahead:
The Future Role of Theology

Taking a personal inventory of one's beliefs is one essential step in the theological thought process, but it is not the last. New situations develop in the life of the church and new questions arise in our own lives. How, then, do we continue the process of thinking about our faith over time? How can we be best equipped to contribute to the debates within the church? In essence, this returns us to where we began. In the opening chapter we discussed traditionalist, liberal, and radical theology and described how each conceived of the task of theology. For the traditionalist, theology involves the faithful *transmission* of Christian belief; for the liberal, theology involves critical *dialogue* with others; and for the radical, theology engages in *reconstruction* of the church's beliefs or practices.

As we also discussed in the first chapter, trying to decide questions on the task of theology also necessarily involves a reading of the current situation. David Tracy argued, "Each theologian addresses three distinct and related social realities: the wider society, the academy and the church. Some one of these publics will be the principal, yet rarely exclusive, addressee."[1] Depending on which audience the theologian is engaging, there needs to be some assessment made about the current situation in the church, the wider culture, or the academic world. Are the church's beliefs and practices consistent with the Gospel? Is the wider culture open, indifferent, or hostile to the Christian message? What weight should Christians give to the leading ideas espoused in the academic world?

The assessment of the current situation in the church, the wider culture, and the academic world vary considerably from person to person. For example, church members differ widely on what created the climate for the sexual abuse scandal that has rocked the Roman Catholic Church. In his review of three works dealing with the future of Roman Catholicism, Christopher J. Ruddy of St. John's University in Minnesota wrote,

> While most commentators agree that there really are two scandals—clerical sexual abuse itself and the subsequent episcopal dereliction—they differ on their diagnoses of

both the causes and the appropriate remedies. Some attribute the crisis in part to a centuries-old repressive sexual ethic, while others indict the church's ambiguous and permissive moral teaching of recent decades. Some hold that numerous bishops have failed because of their complicity in corrupt ecclesial structures, while others believe that these leaders lacked the courage to teach unpopular truths and to govern their own dioceses.[2]

In terms of the wider culture, some theologians known as postliberals insist that as western culture becomes increasingly secularized, the church of the future needs to become more "sectarian." The Lutheran theologian and ecumenist George Lindbeck wrote, "'Sectarian' does not necessarily imply a divisiveness internal to the Church, but rather points to the intensity and intimacy of the communal life of a minority sharply differentiated from the larger society."[3] A sectarian church could best survive if there should be "a fundamental de-Christianization of the Western culture, so that, in all strata of society, explicit profession of the faith would be socially odd...a world in which the majority of the people everywhere are indifferent or hostile, for either secular or religious reasons, to anything which could claim to be distinctively Christian."[4] Finally, what is the state of affairs in institutions of higher learning, especially Catholic college and universities? The English scholar Christopher Derrick commented, "Most colleges and universities today provide excellent education of the servile kind; but along with this, most of them provide also an indoctrination in scepticism, and this is something which paralyzes and imprisons the mind."[5] Others see the Catholic university as the place where faith can seek understanding, where truth in all its manifestations is pursued in light of the ultimate Truth.

The three approaches in theology—the traditionalist, the liberal, and the radical—emphasize different qualities that need to be developed in order to do theology well. For the traditionalist, fidelity best characterizes the life of the theologian. The theologian preserves and hands on the truths of the Gospel. For the liberal, openness to truth is the defining characteristic of a sharp theological mind. The liberal theologian embraces truth wherever truth is to be found. For the radical, the theologian needs to be bold.

Theology involves the unrelenting scrutiny of the accepted patterns of belief and practice, and requires us to make bold proposals where the situation warrants.

Rather than regarding fidelity, openness, and boldness as three separate characteristics unique to the traditionalists, liberals, and radicals, perhaps it would be more accurate to say that all three are needed in both our personal reflection and church debates. The wisdom that is required, of course, is knowing when to use each one, and to what degree. We need what the ancient and medieval thinkers called prudence. As described by the Thomist scholar Josef Pieper, "Prudence means the studied seriousness and, as it were, the filter of deliberation, and at the same time the brave boldness to make final decisions."[6] Thomas Aquinas once noted, "Prudence is praised, not only for arriving at the right diagnosis, but also for applying effective treatment."[7] If we can arrive at the right diagnosis and apply the effective treatment to the situations that develop in our lives, our church, and our world, then our study of theology has been well worth the effort.

Notes

1. David Tracy, *The Analogical Imagination* (New York: Crossroad, 1981), 5.

2. Christopher J. Ruddy, "Tomorrow's Catholics," *Christian Century*, January 25, 2003, 24.

3. George Lindbeck, "Ecumenism and the Future of Belief," in *The Church in a Postliberal Age*, James J. Buckley, ed. (Grand Rapids: Eerdmans, 2002), 100.

4. George Lindbeck, "The Sectarian Future of the Church," in Joseph P. Whelan, *The God Experience: Essays in Hope* (New York: Newman Press, 1971), 229.

5. Christopher Derrick, *Escape from Scepticism* (LaSalle, IL: Sherwood Sugden, and Co., 1977), 47.

6. Josef Pieper, *The Four Cardinal Virtues* (New York: Harcourt, Brace and World, 1965), 22.

7. Thomas Aquinas, *Summa Theologica* 2a–2ae. xlvii. I, ad 3 in Thomas Gilby, ed., *St. Thomas Aquinas: Theological Texts* (New York: Oxford University Press, 1955), 231.

TIME LINE

For a quick overview of church history, refer to this time line of key people and events. For exact dates, I referred to Richard P. McBrien, ed., *Encyclopedia of Catholicism* (San Francisco: Harper-Collins, 1995).

ca. 49 Council of Jerusalem. Church leaders rule that Gentile converts do not need to be circumcised.

64 Fire in Rome. Nero blames the Christians. By tradition, Peter and Paul are martyred during Nero's reign.

ca. 140 Marcion (ca. 85–ca. 160) preaches in Rome. Marcion's heretical theology pushes the church to define the canon.

ca. 165 Justin Martyr (b. ca. 100) dies. Included the concept of the *Logos* in his Christology.

202 Irenaeus (b. 140) dies. Bishop of Lyons who battled Gnosticism.

225 Tertullian (b. ca. 160) dies. North African theologian who composed foundational works on the Trinity and Christology.

ca. 236 Hippolytus of (b. ca. 170) Rome dies. *The Apostolic Tradition* provides an account of the sacraments of initiation in the early church.

ca. 250 The Emperor Decius orders all Roman citizens to offer sacrifice to the Roman gods or face execution.

ca. 254 Origen (b. ca. 185) dies. Brilliant, controversial thinker who taught in Alexandria.

258 Cyprian (b. ca. 200) dies. Important thinker on the nature of the church.

303–4 Diocletian issues strong edicts against Christians.

312	Constantine defeats Maxentius at the Battle of the Milvian Bridge.
313	Edict of Milan grants toleration to all religions in the Roman Empire.
325	First Council of Nicaea. Athanasius (ca. 296–373) battled Arius (ca. 250–336) over the divinity of Christ.
ca. 339	Eusebius of Caesarea (b. ca. 260) dies. Often called the father of church history.
356	Anthony (b. ca. 251) dies. Considered the father of monasticism.
381	First Council of Constantinople.
ca. 382	Pope Damasus commissions Jerome (ca. 347–ca. 420) to produce a Latin translation of the Bible.
late 300s	"The Cappadocian Fathers": Basil the Great (ca. 330–79), Gregory of Nazianzus (ca. 329–90), and Gregory of Nyssa (ca. 335–ca. 395). Their writings were influential in discussions of the Trinity, Christology, and spirituality.
410	Alaric sacks Rome.
430	Augustine of Hippo (b. 354) dies. Highly influential ancient theologian and author of the *Confessions* and *City of God*.
431	Council of Ephesus.
451	Council of Chalcedon.
461	Pope Leo the Great (b. fourth century?) dies. His *Tome* was influential in the deliberations at the Council of Chalcedon in 451. Negotiated with armies invading Rome led by Attila the Hun.
476	The last Roman Emperor in the West is deposed.
553	Second Council of Constantinople.
ca. 547	Benedict of Nursia (b. ca. 480) dies. He was the founder of the Benedictine Order and established a monastery at Monte Cassino.
604	Pope Gregory the Great (b. ca. 540) dies. Pope from 590–604, influential pastoral writer.
680–81	Third Council of Constantinople.
787	Second Council of Nicaea deals with the iconoclastic controversy.

800	Pope Leo III (b. ?–816) crowns Charlemagne (ca. 742–814) Emperor of the Holy Roman Empire on Christmas Day.
869–70	Fourth Council of Constantinople.
1054	Schism between Orthodox and the Roman Catholic Church.
1085	Gregory VII (b. ca. 1020) dies. Reformer pope who clashed with German emperor Henry IV.
1095	Pope Urban II (ca. 1035–1099) calls the First Crusade.
1109	Anselm of Canterbury (b. ca. 1033) dies. Wrote important works on faith and reason, and on soteriology.
1123	First Lateran Council.
1139	Second Lateran Council.
1179	Third Lateran Council.
1215	Fourth Lateran Council.
1226	Francis of Assisi (b. 1181/82) dies.
1245	First Council of Lyons.
1274	Thomas Aquinas (b. ca. 1225) dies. Author of the *Summa Theologiae*.
1274	Second Council of Lyons.
1311–12	Council of Vienne.
1378–1417	Rival popes in Avignon and Rome.
1414–18	Council of Constance.
1431–45	Council of Basel-Ferrara-Florence-Rome.
1512–17	Fifth Lateran Council.
1517	Martin Luther (1483–1546) posts the Ninety-Five Theses.
1534	English Parliament passes the Supremacy Act; Church of England established.
1540	The founding of the Society of Jesus by Ignatius of Loyola (1491–1556)
1545–63	The Council of Trent.
1564	John Calvin (b. 1509) dies, the author of the *Institutes of the Christian Religion*.
1582	Teresa of Avila (b. 1515) dies; Spanish mystic.
1642	Galileo Galilei (b. 1564) dies.

1650	René Descartes (b. 1596) dies. Considered the father of modern philosophy.
1662	Blaise Pascal (b. 1623) dies; author of the *Pensées*.
1727	Isaac Newton (b. 1642) dies.
1791	John Wesley (b. 1703) dies; founder of the Methodist church.
1803	Immanuel Kant (b. 1724) dies.
1815	John Carroll (b. 1736) dies; the first bishop of the United States.
1834	Friedrich Schleiermacher (b. 1768) dies. Considered the father of Liberal Protestant theology.
1855	Søren Kierkegaard (b. 1813) dies; theologian and father of modern existentialism.
1883	Karl Marx (b. 1818) dies.
1864	"Syllabus of Errors" issued by Pius IX (1792–1878).
1869–70	First Vatican Council.
1890	John Henry Newman (b. 1801) dies; influential convert and theologian.
1900	Friedrich Nietzsche (b. 1844) dies; influential philosopher and a critic of culture, morality, and the Judeo-Christian tradition.
1941	Rudolf Bultmann's essay "New Testament and Mythology" appears.
1962–65	Second Vatican Council.
1968	Thomas Merton (b. 1915) dies; influential Trappist monk and spiritual writer.
1978	John Paul II (1920–2005) becomes pope.
1980	Dorothy Day (b. 1897) dies; cofounder, with Peter Maurin, of the Catholic Worker movement.
1984	Karl Rahner (b. 1904) dies.
2005	John Paul II dies and is succeeded by Benedict XVI.

GLOSSARY

biblical theology: Deals with the proper interpretation and use of biblical writings in contemporary theology.

canon: List of accepted books of the Bible; may differ between religions and denominations.

Christology: Literally, "the study of Christ"; investigates the question of Jesus' identity.

ecclesiology: Literally, "the study of the church"; deals with questions of the nature and purpose of the church, including questions of church authority and the relationship between the church and the world.

eschatology: Literally, "the study of the 'last things'"; deals with the "end" either in a personal sense of afterlife or in the end of human history.

Gnosticism: Derived from the Greek word for "knowledge"; a movement in the early church that sharply distinguished between matter and spirit.

homoousios: Term used in the Nicene Creed meaning "of the same substance," or "one in being with."

Logos: Word of God; important concept in Christology. See John 1:1.

moral theology: Deals with the proper conduct for Christians in personal and social matters; synonymous with Christian ethics.

philosophical theology: Concerned with the overlapping areas of inquiry in both philosophy and theology (questions of ultimate reality, the relationship between time and eternity, etc.).

sacramental theology: Discusses the theory and practice of what Catholics hold to be the seven central celebrations in the life of the church.

sacraments of commitment: Designation for the sacraments of marriage and holy orders. Both sacraments together are also known as sacraments of vocation or sacraments at the service of communion (*Catechism*, Pt. 2, sec. 2, ch. 3).

sacraments of healing: Designation for the sacraments of reconciliation and of the anointing of the sick.

sacraments of initiation: Designation for the sacraments of baptism, confirmation, and Eucharist, usually received at different times in a Catholic's life. All three were received at once at the Easter Vigil in the ancient church, and in the current RCIA (Rite of Christian Initiation) program.

soteriology: Literally, "the study of salvation"; studies the work of Christ as the one who brings about salvation.

spiritual theology: Explores the various ways in which we come to a greater knowledge and love of God.

Synoptic Gospels: Term applied to the Gospels of Matthew, Mark, and Luke.

systematic theology: An orderly investigation of the entire body of Christian beliefs (e.g., Christology, ecclesiology, eschatology).

theological anthropology: Constructs a Christian understanding of the human person.

theology: Literally, "the study of God"; evaluates Christian beliefs and practices; when used in the most restricted sense, deals with questions related to God (God's nature, God's activity, the Trinity, etc.).

INDEX